W9-DJD-223

Research Methods in Human Development

Research Methods in Human Development

Second Edition

Kathleen W. Brown

Paul C. Cozby

Daniel W. Kee
California State University, Fullerton

Patricia E. Worden
California State University, San Marcos

Mayfield Publishing Company

Mountain View, California
London · Toronto

Copyright © 1999, 1989 by Mayfield Publishing Company

All rights reserved. No portion of this book may be reproduced in any form or by any means without written permission of the publisher.

Library of Congress Cataloging-in-Publication Data

Research methods in human development / Kathleen W. Brown . . . [et al.] – 2nd ed.
    p.   cm
  Rev. ed. of: Research methods in human development / Paul C. Cozby, Patricia E. Worden, Daniel W. Kee. 1989.
    Includes bibliographical references and index.
    ISBN 1-55934-875-5
    1. Social sciences–Methodology.   I. Brown, Kathleen W.
II. Cozby, Paul C.   Research methods in human development.
H61.R4657   1998
300′.72–DC21   98-16053
                                                          CIP

Manufactured in the United States of America

  3 4 5 6 7 8 9   BKM BKM   0 9 8 7 6 5 4

Mayfield Publishing Company
1280 Villa Street
Mountain View, California 94041

Sponsoring editor, Franklin C. Graham; production editors, Linda Ward and Lynn Rabin-Bauer; manuscript editor, Kay Mikel; text and cover designer, Susan Breitbard; art editor, Amy Folden; illustrator, Joan Carol; manufacturing manager, Randy Hurst. The text was set in 10/12 Berthold Baskerville by G & S Typesetters

Page 37, from *Psychological Abstracts,* Vol. 79, #19842, p. 2397. Reprinted with permission of the American Psychological Association, publisher of *Psychological Abstracts.* Copyright © 1995 by the American Psychological Association.

◆ Contents

CHAPTER 3   *Origins of Scientific Inquiry*   28

CHAPTER 14 *Understanding Research Results*   228

◆ *Preface*

Our goal in revising *Research Methods in Human Development* was to produce an undergraduate level textbook that introduces students to basic research techniques and methodology. The book is intended to teach students to evaluate research critically, assessing strengths and weaknesses of various research paradigms. In addition, the textbook provides a framework for students to conduct research as part of their scholastic or professional endeavors. The textbook is appropriate for students in a wide variety of disciplines in human development, including child development, education, family relations, psychology, gerontology, human services, counseling, social work, and sociology. We hope that our enthusiasm for research and for the importance of a solid research foundation is evident in our writing.

The second edition represents a major revision, incorporating suggestions offered by reviewers and previous users of the textbook. We have retained the best features of the first edition and updated research examples to maintain currency in the field. Coverage is expanded on research techniques such as observational research and survey research. To the summary and study questions at the end of each chapter we have added a listing of key terms. Key terms appear in bold type within the chapters, to help students recognize important terms, and are defined in the glossary. Also new to the second edition are "Research in Action" boxes that highlight major methodological concepts with detailed examples from published research. A new appendix is devoted to writing research reports using the guidelines provided by the American Psychological Association.

ORGANIZATION

The book is designed to allow flexibility to assign chapters in the order appropriate for your course objectives. Chapter 1 introduces the scientific method and its objectives. Different types of research are defined, including basic, applied, evaluation, developmental, and cultural research. Chapter 2 discusses ethical concerns. Chapter 3 explores how topics are selected for study and includes practical information on literature searches. Chapter 4 introduces scientific variables and distinguishes between independent and dependent variables. Chapter 5 distinguishes correlational and experimental research. Descriptive research methods are discussed in Chapters 6 and 7, with observational research, case studies, and archival research in Chapter 6 and survey research in Chapter 7. Chapter 8 presents the features that distinguish poorly designed and well-designed experiments. Chapter 9 addresses developmental designs and single-subject designs for special applications in human development research. Guidelines for conducting research are covered in Chapters 10 and 11, with Chapter 10 discussing practical aspects of conducting research such as obtaining participants and selecting variables. Chapter 11 discusses the assessment process and gives practical guidelines on working with special populations and selecting standardized tests appropriate for human development research. Chapters 12 and 13 describe the complexities of factorial designs and their interpretation. Chapters 14 and 15 cover the logic and basic procedures of statistical analysis, including both descriptive and inferential statistics. Chapter 16 examines issues of generalization. Appendixes on writing research reports, analyzing data, and statistical tables are included.

We gratefully accept any comments and suggestions from readers and instructors using our textbook. Electronic mail addresses are: <kbrown@fullerton.edu>, <cozby@fullerton.edu>, <dkee@fullerton.edu>, and <pworden@mailhouse1. csusm.edumail>. The mailing addresses are: Kathleen Brown, Paul C. Cozby, or Daniel W. Kee, Department of Psychology, P.O. Box 6846, California State University, Fullerton, CA 92634-6846; Patricia E. Worden, College of Arts & Sciences, California State University, San Marcos, CA 92096.

ACKNOWLEDGMENTS

A challenge as large as producing a textbook requires the contributions of many people. We thank Frank Graham at Mayfield Publishing Company for supporting the project. The staff at Mayfield have been invaluable; we are grateful to Linda Ward and Lynn Rabin-Bauer for production management, and to Kay Mikel for her diligent editing of the manuscript. We are grateful to the reviewers who provided valuable suggestions for the revision: F. Scott Christopher, Arizona State University; E. Margaret Evans, University of Toledo; Dr. Pamela Roberts, California State University, Long Beach; and Sally St. George, Lindsey Wilson College. In addition, we owe a debt of gratitude to Nancy Caudill, head of the Interlibrary Loan Unit at California State University, Fullerton, for bringing the resources of distant universities to us. We also thank our students who have offered helpful feedback on the first edition.

We particularly thank our friends and colleagues for their encouragement and motivation to work on the project. A special note of thanks to Peter Benson, Bruce Brown, Brisco Cozby, Matt Kee, Jeanne King, Helen Lopez, Judy Todd, and the "giant panders" at CSUF.

Kathleen W. Brown
Paul C. Cozby
Daniel W. Kee
Patricia E. Worden

CHAPTER 1   ◆

The Scientific View

As the term begins and you open your books for the first time, you may be asking: "Why am I taking this course? How will this course help me?" Our goal is to introduce you to the methodology of research in human development and to demonstrate the application of research to your academic and professional career. By the end of the term, you will have the tools you need to critically evaluate research, conduct your own studies, and write reports of your investigations.

Research methods for the study of human development include techniques appropriate for research with children of different ages as well as with adults, and research with individuals as well as with groups (for example, families and classrooms). In all cases, the goal is the same: to use the tools of the scientific method to understand the process of human development. These tools can help you clarify your knowledge of age-related changes and guide you to explore new areas of study. In this chapter we introduce the scientific method for studying human behavior and discuss how research is relevant to you as a student and as a future professional in human development and family studies.

USE OF RESEARCH METHODS

Having some knowledge of research methods can help you evaluate information you read in daily newspapers or in general interest magazines. The headlines may read: "Music lessons increase IQ," "School uniforms reduce gang violence," "Teach your child at home," "Flexible work schedules reduce stress for working parents," "Secondhand smoke causes hyperactivity." Are the views presented in these stories correct? Should you accept the conclusions because the research appears to be scientific? A background in research methods will help you to read the articles critically, looking for key elements that are characteristic of sound research. You will become an "informed consumer" of research, with the skills to decide whether the results of the study are valid.

Your understanding of research methods will undoubtedly be useful in your academic career when one of your instructors asks you to conduct an independent research project. You may also be asked to write a literature review or a term paper involving critical evaluation of published research. You will have a solid foundation in the basics of research and will be able to do the assignment by relying on the information in this textbook.

Human development and family relations professionals rely on research findings. For example, counselors need to know about the latest advances in family or play therapy techniques. A gerontologist may examine the most effective way to help elderly adults cope with loss of memory skills. A pediatric nurse working with chronically ill children may find ways to reduce children's fear of medical procedures. An elementary school teacher may want to investigate the current debate in reading instruction before designing a curriculum based entirely on phonics. Educators must keep up with research on the effectiveness of different teaching strategies for visual, auditory, and kinesthetic learners. People who work in the business sector rely on research to make decisions about how to improve employee productivity and morale. For example, employees with families benefit from flexible work schedules that allow them to spend time with their children and spouses for important family occasions, reducing the stress of balancing work and family. Knowledge of research methods and the ability to evaluate research reports are useful skills in many fields.

In addition, research knowledge will help you become a more informed citizen on issues of public policy and planning. For example, the emerging debate on national educational standards in the Goals 2000 program needs extensive input from parents, educators, and applied developmental researchers. Successful bilingual education requires an understanding of the special educational, social, and psychological needs of culturally diverse groups. Research is also important when developing and assessing the effectiveness of pilot programs designed to achieve certain goals—for example, to reduce teen pregnancy or to increase low-income elderly adults' access to health care. If successful, such programs may be implemented on a large scale. The fact that so many policy decisions and political positions are based on research makes knowledge of research methods particularly important for all of us as informed citizens who must ultimately evaluate the policies at the voting booth.

THE SCIENTIFIC APPROACH

Scientists seek to describe, predict, explain, and understand behavior. To achieve these goals they use the **scientific method.** The essence of the scientific method is the insistence that all assertions about human behavior be subjected to an empirical test. When the scientific method is used, reliable and valid information can be provided. Unfortunately, many people base their views of development solely on intuition and authority.

The Limitations of Intuition and Authority

Intuition Most of us know of a married couple who, after years of trying to conceive, adopts a child. Then, within a very short period of time, the woman becomes pregnant. This observation leads to a common belief that adoption increases the likelihood of pregnancy among couples who are having difficulty conceiving a child. Such a conclusion seems intuitively reasonable, and people usually have an explanation for this effect—for example, the adoption reduces a major source of marital stress, and the stress reduction in turn increases the chances of conception (see Gilovich, 1991).

When you rely on **intuition,** you accept unquestioningly what your own personal judgment tells you about the world. The intuitive approach takes many forms. Often, it involves finding an explanation for our own behavior or the behavior of others. For example, you might develop an explanation for why you keep having conflicts with a sibling, such as "sharing a car puts us in a conflict situation" or "she's jealous of my financial independence." Other times, intuition is used to explain intriguing events that you observe, as in the case of concluding that adoption increases the chances of conception among couples having difficulty conceiving a child.

A problem with intuition is that numerous cognitive and motivational biases affect our perceptions, so we may draw erroneous conclusions about cause and effect (cf. Fiske & Taylor, 1984; Gilovich, 1991; Nisbett & Ross, 1980; Nisbett & Wilson, 1977). Gilovich points out that there is, in fact, no relationship between adoption and subsequent pregnancy according to scientific research investigations. So why do we hold this belief? Most likely it is because of a cognitive bias called **illusory correlation,** which occurs when we focus on two events that stand out and occur together. When an adoption is closely followed by a pregnancy, our attention is drawn to the situation, and we are biased to conclude that there must be a causal connection. Such illusory correlations are also likely to occur when the events are consistent with our beliefs. Although this is a natural thing for us to do, it is not scientific. A scientific approach requires much more proof before drawing conclusions.

Authority   The philosopher Aristotle was concerned with the factors associated with persuasion or attitude change. In "Rhetoric," Aristotle describes the relationship between persuasion and credibility: "Persuasion is achieved by the speaker's personal character when the speech is so spoken as to make us think him credible. We believe good men more fully and readily than others" (1984, p. 2155). Thus, Aristotle would argue that we are more likely to be persuaded by a speaker who seems prestigious, trustworthy, and respectable than by one who lacks such qualities.

Many of us might accept Aristotle's arguments simply because he is considered to be a prestigious **authority,** and his writings remain important. Similarly, many people accept anything they learn from the news media, books, government officials, or religious figures because they believe that the statements of such authorities must be true. The problem, of course, is that the statements may not be true. The scientific approach rejects the notion that one can accept on faith the statements of any authority; again, more proof is needed before we can draw scientific conclusions.

Skepticism, Science, and the Empirical Approach

The scientific approach to knowledge recognizes that both intuition and authority are sources of ideas about behavior. However, scientists do not unquestioningly accept anyone's intuitions—including their own. Initial research may be guided by a scientist's intuitions, which then leads to systematic testing of these intuitive beliefs using scientific methods.

The scientific approach is empirical rather than intuitive. An **empirical approach** relies on direct observation and experimentation as a way of answering questions. There are two components to the empirical approach. First, an idea must be studied under conditions in which it may be either supported or refuted. Second, the research must be done in a way that can be observed, evaluated, and replicated by others.

Thus, the scientific method, in contrast to intuition or authority, does not rely on accepting ideas generated by someone else or ideas generated from one's own personal, unsystematic perceptions of the world. The scientific method embodies a number of rules for testing ideas through research—ways that observations are made and experiments are designed and conducted. These rules will be explored throughout this book.

GOALS OF SCIENCE

The primary **goals of science** are: (1) to describe behavior, (2) to predict behavior, and (3) to identify causes and explanations for behavior.

Description of Behavior

A basic goal of science is to describe events, providing a complete description of an activity or a situation. For example, a researcher interested in marital discord would use research methods to provide a complete picture of the family's communication and conflict management skills. In human development research, one common focus is on describing behavior that is systematically related to age. Thus, a researcher might consider how reactions to stressful events change between ages 4 and 8 years. Another researcher might study how reactions to traumatic, stressful events differ among children from culturally diverse homes. Many questions that interest researchers focus on how events are systematically related to one another. Does a family move affect children's emotional development? Do children recall events better if they draw a picture depicting the incident? Do girls perform better in science classes when enrollment includes both genders or when only girls participate? Do grandparents phone their grandchildren more when they live farther away from one another?

Prediction of Behavior

A second goal of science is to predict behavior. Can healthy family relationships be predicted from certain types of parent-child relationships? Can alcohol dependency be predicted from binge drinking behavior during the high school years? Can IQ be predicted if you know how much time a parent reads to a child? Once it has been observed with some regularity that two events are systematically related to one another, it becomes possible to make such predictions. Whether or not we have identified the causes for a relationship, we can still anticipate events and make predictions. For example, gang membership is a good predictor of adolescent delinquency and school dropout (Cairns, Cairns, & Neckerman, 1989). Research by Dishion, Patterson, Stoolmiller, and Skinner (1991) identified a cluster of variables in 10-year-olds that are related to subsequent antisocial behavior. Academic failure, peer rejection, and lack of parental monitoring consistently predict chronic antisocial behavior. Knowing that these behaviors are related to antisocial behavior enables us to design interventions. Thus, an effective intervention to reduce involvement with antisocial peers would target the child's aggressive behavior, the mother's and father's parenting skills, and the child's academic skills.

Causes and Explanations of Behavior

A third goal of science is to determine the causes of behavior. What are the factors that cause children who watch violence on television to display aggression? Why does aggression occur? A substantial body of research has shown that a child's aggressive behavior is related to the amount of violence the child watches on television (Liebert & Sprafkin, 1988), but the cause for that behavior is a more complex issue. Do children imitate what they see on television? Are children desensitized to violence? Or, does watching TV violence lead children to believe that aggression is a normal reaction to frustration?

Identifying causality is challenging because multiple forces interact to create behaviors. A child's aggression may relate to television watching, age, experiences with peers, sibling rivalry, biological factors such as hormone levels, and the parents' child-management styles. To change the child's aggressive behavior, the causes must be understood. Researchers often measure several behaviors using different measurement methods (e.g., observation and parent-report) in an attempt to understand why a particular behavior is occurring. This multitrait, multimethod approach is time-consuming, yet it is an effective way to investigate the cause for behavior.

As you can see, the activities of identifying the causes of behavior and advancing explanations are closely related. Because research consists of a series of analytical steps, causes identified in early phases of research may suggest explanations that later prove inadequate as new and additional causes are identified. Part of the excitement of conducting research is knowing that you are involved in the discovery of knowledge; with each new finding, additional opportunities for inquiry are created.

BASIC AND APPLIED RESEARCH

Human development and family studies research falls into two general categories that differ by the goal of the research. These two categories are basic and applied research.

Basic Research

Basic research is designed with the single goal of understanding fundamental behavioral processes. The purpose is to describe an aspect of human nature, with the immediate goal of acquiring knowledge. Basic research may address theoretical issues concerning cognition, learning, personality development, aging, education, or psychobiology. In all cases, the goal is very "basic"—describe the phenomenon of interest and increase the existing knowledge base. Here are some examples of journal articles that address basic research questions:

de Haan, M., & Nelson, C. A. (1997). Recognition of the mother's face by six-month-old infants: A neurobehavioral study. *Child Development, 68,* 187–210.

Jones, M. S., Yokoi, L., Johnson, D. J., Lum, S., Cafaro, T., & Kee, D. W. (1996). Effectiveness of elaborative strategy use: Knowledge access comparisons. *Journal of Experimental Child Psychology, 62,* 401–409.

McLoyd, V. C., & Wilson, L. (1992). Telling them like it is: The role of economic and environmental factors in single mothers' discussions with their children. *American Journal of Community Psychology, 20,* 419–444.

Strough, J., Berg, C. A., & Sansone, C. (1996). Goals for solving everyday problems across the life span: Age and gender differences in the salience of interpersonal concerns. *Developmental Psychology, 32,* 1106–1115.

Applied Research

Applied research adresses practical problems. The knowledge gained in applied research is often aimed at social change and may be intended to provide a solution to a problem or to improve a situation. Basic research can describe children's memory abilities; applied research would be interested in enhancing children's eyewitness memory. The following citations illustrate applied issues:

Campbell, A. J., Borrie, M. J., & Spears, G. F. (1989). Risk factors for falls in a community-based prospective study of people 70 years and older. *Journal of Gerontology: Medical Sciences, 44,* M112–117.

Hudley, C., & Graham, S. (1993). An attributional intervention to reduce peer-directed aggression among African American boys. *Child Development, 64,* 124–138.

Senturai, Y. D., Christoffel, K. K., & Donovan, M. (1996). Gun storage patterns in US homes with children: A pediatric practice-based survey. *Archives of Pediatrics and Adolescent Medicine, 150,* 265–269.

Whitehurst, G. J., Arnold, D. S., Epstein, J. N., Angell, A. L., Smith, M., & Fischel, J. E. (1994). A picture book reading intervention in day care and home for children from low-income families. *Developmental Psychology, 30,* 679–689.

Much applied research in human development is funded by contracts issued by sponsoring agencies such as state or local departments of education. The results of such research are often published in technical reports for the sponsor rather than in scientific journals. An example is the Children's Defense Fund (1994) report, *Wasting America's Future: The Children's Defense Fund Report on the Costs of Child Poverty.* The report (sponsored by the Prudential Foundation) presents information about poverty in America's children and estimates the costs, both human and financial, of the poverty crisis. Poverty is estimated to cost taxpayers as much as $177 billion per year, although it would take only $62 billion per year to end poverty by providing financial assistance and support to families in need. Here are some facts in the report (pp. xvi, xvii, xxi):

- Nearly one in every three American children will be poor for at least a year before turning 16.
- One in five American children is poor.
- The younger children are, the poorer they are. One in every four children under age 6 is poor, as are 27% of children under age 3.
- Low-income children are two times more likely to die from birth defects, three times more likely to die from all causes combined, four times more likely to die from fires, five times more likely to die from infectious diseases and parasites, and six times more likely to die from other diseases.
- More White than Black children are poor.
- Most poor families that turn to welfare for help move off the welfare rolls within two years.

Comparing Basic and Applied Research

Both basic and applied research are important, and neither can be considered superior to the other. In fact, they are commonly used together and are best conceptualized as interconnected (see Berk, Boruch, Chambers, Rossi, & Witte, 1986). Basic research investigations provide the fundamental building blocks. The immediate goal of basic research is to acquire knowledge. Applied researchers use this knowledge to solve a particular problem, examining the same issue in a natural setting, which provides important context for the earlier findings. This cycle is often repeated, as the results of the applied research may lead to more basic research. The interplay of basic and applied research is exemplified by **prevention science,** a new research discipline that studies the prevention of human dysfunction (Coie et al., 1993). Risk factors that are early indicators of dysfunction or mental illness can be identified through basic research. Protective factors that minimize the potential dysfunction can also be identified in basic research in family, school, and community settings. Then this basic knowledge can be applied in interventions to facilitate protective factors, such as teaching children social skills and enhancing parental competence. To illustrate, basic research by Wakschlag, Chase-Lansdale, and Brooks-Gunn (1996) indicates that multigenerational ties promote positive parenting skills in adolescent mothers living in poverty. This suggests that children, mothers, and grandmothers should be included in family interventions.

In recent years many in our society, including legislators who control the budgets of research-granting agencies of the government, have demanded that research be directly relevant to specific social issues. The problem with this attitude toward research is that we can never predict the ultimate applications of basic research. Psychologist B. F. Skinner, for example, conducted basic research in the 1930s on operant conditioning, which carefully described the effects of reinforcement on such behaviors as bar pressing by rats. Years later this research led to many practical applications in therapy and education. Research with no apparent practical value ultimately can be very useful. Because no one can predict the eventual impact of basic research, support for basic research is important both to advance science and to benefit society.

EVALUATION RESEARCH

A major area of applied research is called **evaluation research** (or program evaluation research). Evaluation research assesses the effectiveness of social programs or human service organizations, such as schools, hospitals, and government agencies, so the administrators can find out if the program is having its intended effect. Campbell (1969) argues persuasively that social policy programs can be viewed as experiments designed to achieve certain outcomes. Examples include the Head Start program for disadvantaged children and the DARE (Drug Abuse Resistance Education) program to reduce drug use in school-aged children. Here are some sample journal articles:

Aber, J. L., Brooks-Gunn, J., & Maynard, R. A. (1995). Effects of welfare reform on teenage parents and their children. *The Future of Children, 5* (2), 53–71.
Palumbo, D. J., & Ferguson, J. L. (1995). Evaluating Gang Resistance Education and Training (GREAT): Is the impact the same as that of Drug Abuse Resistance Education (DARE)? *Evaluation Review, 19,* 597–619.
Pentz, M. A., Dwyer, J. H., MacKinnon, D. P., Flay, B. R., Hansen, W. B., Wang, E. Y. I., & Johnson, C. A. (1989). A multicommunity trial for primary prevention of adolescent drug abuse: Effects of drug use prevalence. *Journal of the American Medical Association, 261,* 3259–3266.

Four general types of evaluations are depicted in Figure 1.1. The first is the *evaluation of need.* Needs assessment studies ask whether there are, in fact, problems that need to be addressed in a target population. For example, is there drug abuse by children and adolescents in the community? What services do the elderly lack? What is the pattern of high school dropout rates among various ethnic groups? After a need has been established, programs can be designed to address the need.

The second program evaluation question is *process evaluation,* which involves monitoring the day-to-day activities of the program. Is the program being implemented properly by the program staff? Are the planned activities being conducted? Is the program reaching the target population? This research is extremely important because we would not want to conclude that a program itself is ineffective if, in fact, implementation of the program is not working.

Figure 1.1
Four phases of
program evaluation

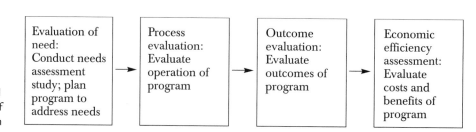

The third question concerns *outcome evaluation*. Are the intended outcomes of the program being realized? Is the goal—reduce drug use, provide medical services to the elderly, lower the high school dropout rate—being achieved? To determine this, the evaluation researcher must devise a way of measuring the outcome. For example, we could compare self-report measures of drug use for children who participated in the DARE program with the amount of drug use reported by children who did not participate in the drug awareness program.

The final program evaluation question is *economic efficiency assessment*. This research question is guided by a cost-benefit analysis. Is the program economically effective? Given that the stated outcome has been achieved, is the investment of time and money reasonable? If a program is not cost-efficient, the researcher may recommend modification of the program or investment in alternative programs. Programs such as Head Start require large capital expenditures, yet the long-term benefits are overwhelmingly positive, thereby justifying the cost. For example, Pentz et al. (1989) estimate a savings of more than $40,000 for each male adolescent who does not become a smoker. Savings of this magnitude illustrate the potential of prevention efforts and the need for program evaluation studies.

DEVELOPMENTAL RESEARCH

Developmental research focuses on the change and process of human development. Developmentalists may examine age-related changes in individual behavior, patterns of functioning and change in family relations, or aspects of behavior in particular sociocultural contexts. They may be interested in how chronic illness affects children of different ages, the age at which children know what *pollution* means, the long-term effects of welfare dependence, age differences in social skills, or factors that protect children, adolescents, and adults from the negative consequences of extreme poverty. Many developmentalists have adopted a life span perspective to examine major changes in human development from conception through adulthood. Life span research is typically multidisciplinary, relying on research methods and theories from different areas of study, such as biology, medicine, education, psychology, sociology, and anthropology (Baltes, 1987; Hinde, 1992).

In developmental research, the major variable is age. However, it is difficult to determine if the age-related changes occur due to maturational factors or environmental factors. Developmental researchers study the age variable by selecting individuals of different ages or studying the same individuals at different points in their lives. In this way, researchers can search for similarities and differences between people of similar chronological age. Such descriptions contribute to building theoretical models to explain human development.

CULTURAL RESEARCH

Cultural research focuses on aspects of development and social structure among people of different cultural backgrounds. Such comparisons allow researchers to search for "universals" in developmental processes—characteristics that are common to children and adults who differ in ancestry and geographic location. In addition, cultural studies inform us about differences between cultural groups, contributing to our understanding of the different ways people view the world, teach their children, maintain intergenerational family ties, make the transition to retirement, treat disadvantaged members of their society, and so on. By varying the background of participants, researchers can examine the role of contextual factors in development.

Knowledge of development in culturally diverse environments gives us important insight into larger patterns of human development and provides a viewpoint that differs from the middle-class Western way of life. Research conducted on individuals of a particular culture may not apply to other cultures or subcultures. Generalizability across cultural and ethnic groups is an important issue; we return to this topic in Chapter 16.

A good example of cultural research is a study examining cultural differences in Korean American and Anglo-American preschools (Farver, Kim, & Lee, 1995). Teachers provided different play environments for the children. Anglo-American teachers provided many opportunities for play and an active involvement in learning. The classrooms of Korean American teachers reflected traditional Korean values and educational goals, emphasizing academic skills, passive involvement in learning, and fewer opportunities for play. The children's behaviors reflected the cultural traditions evident in the classrooms. Korean American children were more cooperative and shared more, reflecting an emphasis on harmony and cooperation in their culture. Anglo-American children were more independent and more social but also were more aggressive, reflecting an emphasis on competition in Western culture.

SUMMARY

In this chapter we examined the scientific approach to researching human development. The advantage of the scientific approach over other ways of knowing about the world (e.g., authority and intuition) is that it provides an objective set of rules for gathering and evaluating information. The three major goals of scientific research are: (1) to describe behavior, (2) to predict behavior, and (3) to identify causes and explanations for behavior. Human development and family studies research falls into two categories, basic and applied research. Program evaluation is a special type of applied research. Developmental research examines the role of age-related changes on behavior. Cultural differences are an important source of variation in development, allowing researchers to examine the contribution of different environments to developmental outcomes.

KEY TERMS

applied research	developmental research	illusory correlation
authority	empirical approach	intuition
basic research	evaluation research	prevention science
cultural research	goals of science	scientific method

REVIEW QUESTIONS

1. Why is it important for anyone in human development and family relations to have knowledge of research methods?
2. How does the scientific approach differ from other ways of gaining knowledge about behavior?
3. Distinguish between description, prediction, and explanation as goals of scientific research.
4. Distinguish between basic and applied research.
5. Describe the four phases of evaluation research.
6. Provide examples of developmental research.
7. Provide examples of cultural research.

◆

CHAPTER 2

Ethical Concerns

In this chapter we explore in detail the nature of ethical problems that arise in research, especially with participants from particular populations. We must be aware that our experimental procedures might inadvertently produce negative effects on our participants or violate their individual rights. Considering ethical problems when planning, conducting, and evaluating research is important, especially when studying children. We begin with a brief historical vignette, which introduces the concept of **psychological risk.**

MILGRAM'S OBEDIENCE EXPERIMENTS

Stanley Milgram studied obedience to authority in a series of controversial experiments (1963, 1964, 1965). Milgram placed an ad in the local newspaper offering to pay $4.50 to volunteers for a "scientific study of memory and learning" conducted at Yale University. When the participants reported to the laboratory, they were met by a scientist dressed in a white lab coat and another participant in the study—a middle-aged man named "Mr. Wallace." The scientist explained that he was examining the effects of punishment on learning. One man would be a "teacher" who would administer the punishment, and the other would be the "learner." A rigged drawing always assigned Mr. Wallace as the learner and the volunteer participant as the teacher.

The scientist attached electrodes to Mr. Wallace and placed the "teacher" in front of an impressive-looking shock machine. The machine had a series of levers that supposedly would deliver shocks to Mr. Wallace. The first lever was labeled 15 volts, the second 30 volts, the third 45 volts, and so on up to 450 volts. The levers were also clearly labeled "Slight Shock," "Moderate Shock," on up to "Danger: Severe Shock," followed by red Xs above 400 volts.

Mr. Wallace, the learner, was instructed to learn a series of word pairs. Then he was given a test to see if he could identify which words went together. Every time he made a mistake, the teacher was instructed to deliver a shock as punishment. For each subsequent mistake, the learner was to receive a higher level of shock. Although the learner, Mr. Wallace, never received any shocks, the participants in the role of teacher did not know that. As you can well imagine, Mr. Wallace made mistake after mistake, creating many opportunities for the teacher to deliver the shocks as the scientist had instructed. When the teacher "shocked" Mr. Wallace with about 120 volts, Mr. Wallace began screaming in pain with each shock. Eventually Mr. Wallace yelled that he wanted out and declared that he had a heart condition; soon after, Mr. Wallace did not respond further.

Some of the teachers became concerned and expressed reluctance to continue with the experiment. The scientist encouraged the teacher to continue. At first, the scientist simply stated, "Please continue," then gradually escalated his verbal prod to "The experiment requires that you continue" and "You have no other choice; you must go on!"

Did the participants obey the authority of the scientist? Amazingly, many did, with approximately 65% delivering shocks all the way to the maximum 450 volts. Milgram's study received a great deal of publicity, and the results challenged many of our beliefs about our ability to resist authority. The implications of Milgram's study are important for understanding obedience in real-life situations, such as Nazi Germany and the recent genocidal wars in Africa.

But what about the ethics of the Milgram study? What aspects of the experimental procedure might we find objectionable? Even though no actual physical pain was experienced by either the confederate or the volunteer participants, the situation produced extraordinary tension in the participants. Some men were observed to sweat, tremble, and display nervous laughter—obvious signs of stress. Milgram was careful to debrief his subjects, reuniting the teacher with Mr. Wallace to explain that no one had actually been hurt. But what about the long-range effects of knowing that you had administered shocks to another human being despite their resounding protestations?

THE PRINCIPLE OF PSYCHOLOGICAL RISK

Milgram's study was influential in helping researchers recognize that experimental procedures have the potential of harming participants both physically and psychologically. The question of physical harm is comparatively easy to identify and prevent. Medical procedures may cause physical harm or injury; for example, administering some form of drug, such as alcohol or caffeine, or depriving people of sleep for an extended period of time can cause physical harm. Psychological harm is much less clear. The possibility of stress, anxiety, self-doubt, fear, or lowered self-esteem must be carefully evaluated in behavioral research. Is it ethical to subject people to a stressful situation? Is the experiment justified?

Stressful Research With Children

In studies with children, there probably has not been an equally extreme counterpart to Milgram's research. However, experimental situations have been devised that cause children a certain amount of stress. For example, Mary

Ainsworth's classic research on attachment involved briefly leaving a baby alone in an unfamiliar room (Ainsworth, Blehar, Waters, & Wall, 1978). The situation was designed to be mildly distressing to assess the infant's attachment to his or her mother. Note, however, that being left alone briefly is not an unusual situation for most infants.

A more contrived situation was devised by Mischel and his colleagues (Mischel & Ebbesen, 1970; Mischel, Ebbesen, & Zeiss, 1972) to study children's ability to delay gratification. Preschool children were left alone in a room for 15 minutes while the experimenter surreptitiously observed them. The children were given a choice; they could have a desirable treat (such as a marshmallow) if they could wait for 15 minutes, or they could have a less desirable snack (a pretzel) if they couldn't wait and signaled the experimenter to return. Mischel et al. (1972) reported various activities children engaged in to reduce the "distress of waiting," such as making up songs, hiding their heads in their arms, pounding the floor with their feet, and falling asleep. Similar observations of children's stressful behavior have been made in variations of the "forbidden toy" paradigm (Parke, 1977), in which children are prohibited from playing with an inviting toy or looking in a particular location and then questioned about their behavior when the researcher returns a few minutes later. As you can see, sometimes children have been placed in research situations that make them uncomfortable.

Simply being questioned by an adult can be stressful for a child. An investigator might be interested in the effects of repeated questioning on a child's responses. Will the child change his or her mind after repeated questioning by an adult? Or will the child maintain that the original response is correct? Repeated prodding by an adult "Are you sure?" "Is that your answer?" may be interpreted as an indicator of failure. The child exposed to such a scenario may feel stress and self-doubt, potentially harmful psychological effects. In defense of such procedures, one might argue that there is no long-term threat. Additionally, being questioned by an adult is a common occurrence for a child; therefore, the experimental procedure may be representative of the child's typical activities, as is the case with an infant being left alone in the Ainsworth strange situation research.

Other research paradigms have induced children to exhibit undesirable behaviors. The classic studies of children's imitation of aggressive models (Bandura, Ross, & Ross, 1961, 1963) are powerful demonstrations of the ability of children to learn behaviors they have seen. Bandura and his associates arranged to have young children watch an adult sit on a Bobo doll (an inflatable punching bag), punch it in the nose, hit it on the head with a mallet, and kick it about the room. Later, the children who saw the adult aggress on the Bobo doll exhibited nearly twice as much aggression as did participants who did not witness the aggressive adult. In many cases children imitated the unusual patterns of behavior the adult had demonstrated. Primary ethical concerns are that the children were induced to behave more aggressively than usual and, to make matters worse, the behavior was induced by adult role models. This raises concerns about the effects on the children who participated in these studies. Do they understand that aggression is not generally an acceptable behavior? How do they differentiate between when to imitate an adult and when it is not appropriate?

As you can see, investigators must be sensitive to the possible psychological harm caused by their experimental procedures. We must carefully evaluate experimental procedures to minimize the potential for distress. Employing procedures that resemble situations a child normally encounters may contribute to reduced risk.

Ethical principles and standards for research with human participants have been formulated by the American Psychological Association (APA, 1992) and the American Sociological Association (ASA). The **ethics codes** address conduct in teaching, research, therapy, and other professional roles. The Society for Research in Child Development (SRCD), a professional organization of child researchers, has developed ethical standards designed specifically for research activities with children. (See Box 2.1.) The principles are intended to protect children participating in research and to provide a framework for investigators to determine the potential benefits and risks of research for the child and society. Read over the guidelines. You will see that responsibilities of the researcher are carefully delineated in all arenas—interactions with child and adult participants (such as teachers and parents), confidentiality of research records, and reporting scientific findings (including fraud and misconduct).

THE PRINCIPLE OF INFORMED CONSENT AND DECEPTION

Behavioral research justifies exposing subjects to potentially risky situations by relying on the principle of **informed consent,** which requires that experimental participants be told about potential stressors prior to their participation. Armed with this knowledge, subjects can then make an informed decision about whether to expose themselves voluntarily to such risks for the sake of science. Were subjects fully informed in the Milgram studies? Would Milgram have been able to investigate obedience if subjects had been fully informed?

Informed Consent

Ideally, all research should provide research participants with full informed consent. This means that research participants are informed about the purposes of the study, the risks involved with the procedures, and their rights to refuse or terminate participation in the study. All information is provided prior to a participant's decision to become involved in the research.

Because children may not understand the research situation, parents are asked to give informed consent on their behalf. The information given to parents is typically more complete and technical than that given to children. For example, a researcher may elicit a 3-year-old's participation by inviting him or her to play a "game," but only if the parent is informed about the real purpose of the study in advance. The child must assent to participate and has the right to withdraw participation at any time.

There are other populations for which informed consent is a special problem. People of all ages with mental handicaps that preclude their full understanding need to be represented by someone who can evaluate what it means to participate in the research. Such advocates can be parents of developmentally delayed adults in institutions, institutional officials, or in the case of elderly adults with mental limitations, perhaps their spouse or their children.

BOX 2.1

Ethical Standards for Research With Children

Principle 1. Non-harmful procedures: The investigator should use no research operation that may harm the child physically or psychologically. The investigator is also obligated at all times to use the least stressful research operation whenever possible. Psychological harm in particular instances may be difficult to define; nevertheless its definition and means for reducing or eliminating it remain the responsibility of the investigator. When the investigator is in doubt about the possible harmful effects of the research operations, consultation should be sought from others. When harm seems inevitable, the investigator is obligated to find other means of obtaining the information or to abandon the research. Instances may, nevertheless, rise in which exposing the child to stressful conditions may be necessary if diagnostic or therapeutic benefits to the child are associated with the research. In such instances careful deliberation by an Institutional Review Board should be sought.

Principle 2. Informed consent: Before seeking consent or assent from the child, the investigator should inform the child of all features of the research that may affect his or her willingness to participate and should answer the child's questions in terms appropriate to the child's comprehension. The investigator should respect the child's freedom to choose to participate in the research or not by giving the child the opportunity to give or not give assent to participation as well as to choose to discontinue participation at any time. Assent means that the child shows some form of agreement to participate without necessarily comprehending the full significance of the research necessary to give informed consent. Investigators working with infants should take special effort to explain the research procedures to the parents and be especially sensitive to any indicators of discomfort in the infant. In spite of the paramount importance of obtaining consent, instances can arise in which consent or any kind of contact with the participant would make the research impossible to carry out. Non-intrusive field research is a common example. Conceivably, such research can be carried out ethically if it is conducted in public places, participants' anonymity is totally protected, and there are not foreseeable negative consequences to the participant. However, judgments on whether such research is ethical in particular circumstances should be made in consultation with an Institutional Review Board.

Principle 3. Parental consent: The informed consent of parents, legal guardians or those who act *in loco parentis* (e.g., teachers, superintendents of institutions) similarly should be obtained, preferably in writing. Informed consent requires that parents or other responsible adults be informed of all the features of the research that may affect their willingness to allow the child to participate. This information should include the profession and institution affiliation of the investigator. Not only should the right of the responsible adults to refuse consent be respected, but they should be informed that they may refuse to participate without incurring any penalty to them or to the child.

Principle 4. Additional consent: The informed consent of any persons, such as school teachers for example, whose interaction with the child is the subject of the study should also be obtained. As with the child and parents or guardians informed consent requires that the persons interacting with the child during the study be informed of all features of the research which may affect their willingness to participate. All questions posed by such persons should be answered and the persons should be free to choose to participate or not, and to discontinue participation at any time.

Principle 5. Incentives: Incentives to participate in a research project must be fair and must not unduly exceed the range of incentives that the child normally experiences. Whatever incentives are used, the investigator should always keep in mind that the greater the possible effects of the investigation on the child, the greater is the obligation to protect the child's welfare and freedom.

Principle 6. Deception: Although full disclosure of information during the procedure of obtaining consent is the ethical ideal, a particular study may necessitate withholding certain information or deception. Whenever withholding information or deception is judged to be essential to the conduct of the study, the investigator should satisfy research colleagues that such judgment is correct. If withholding information or deception is practiced, and there is reason to believe that the research participants will be negatively affected by it, adequate measures should be taken after the study to ensure the participant's understanding of the reasons for the deception. Investigators whose research is dependent upon deception should make an effort to employ deception methods that have no known negative effects on the child or the child's family.

Principle 7. Anonymity: To gain access to institutional records, the investigator should obtain permission from responsible authorities in charge of records. Anonymity of the information should be preserved and no information used other than that for which permission was obtained. It is the investigator's responsibility to ensure that responsible authorities do, in fact, have the confidence of the participant and that they bear some degree of responsibility for giving such permission.

Principle 8. Mutual responsibilities: From the beginning of each research investigation, there should be clear agreement between the investigator and the parents, guardians or those who act *in loco parentis,* and the child, when appropriate, that defines the responsibilities of each. The investigator has the obligation to honor all promises and commitments of the agreement.

Principle 9. Jeopardy: When, in the course of research, information comes to the investigator's attention that may jeopardize the child's well-being, the investigator has a responsibility to discuss the information with the parents or guardians and with those expert in the field in order that they may arrange the necessary assistance for the child.

(continued)

Principle 10. Unforeseen consequences: When research procedures result in undesirable consequences for the participant that were previously unforeseen, the investigator should immediately employ appropriate measures to correct these consequences, and should redesign the procedures if they are to be included in subsequent studies.

Principle 11. Confidentiality: The investigator should keep in confidence all information obtained about research participants. The participants' identity should be concealed in written and verbal reports of the results, as well as in informal discussion with students and colleagues. When a possibility exists that others may gain access to such information, this possibility, together with the plans for protecting confidentiality, should be explained to the participants as part of the procedure of obtaining informed consent.

Principle 12. Informing participants: Immediately after the data are collected, the investigator should clarify for the research participant any misconceptions that may have arisen. The investigator also recognizes a duty to report general findings to participants in terms appropriate to their understanding. Where scientific or humane values justify withholding information, every effort should be made so that withholding the information has no damaging consequences for the participant.

Principle 13. Reporting results: Because the investigator's words may carry unintended weight with parents and children, caution should be exercised in reporting results, making evaluative statements, or giving advice.

Principle 14. Implications of findings: Investigators should be mindful of the social, political and human implications of their research and

Deception

At times, full informed consent would compromise the researcher's goals. The Milgram experiment illustrates the use of **deception.** Participants agreed to take part in a study of memory and learning, but they actually took part in a study on obedience. They were not given an accurate account of the purpose of the study and the risks involved before they consented to take part in the experiment. Imagine what could have happened if subjects had known more details of the Milgram design.

First, suppose they were told that they would be expected to shock another person. What type of person would volunteer to deliver shocks? A biased sample would have been likely, with some individuals declining to participate. This would have limited the results of the study to the "type" of person who agreed to participate rather than describing behavior typical of most individuals.

Second, if subjects had known the shocks were *not* being delivered, clearly the meaning of the experiment would have been entirely different. With full disclosure, Milgram would not have been able to study the concept he was interested in. And third, if subjects had known the experiment was about obedience, not learning and memory, no doubt the participants' behavior would have differed.

should be especially careful in the presentation of findings from the research. This principle, however, in no way denies investigators the right to pursue any area of research or the right to observe proper standards of scientific reporting.

Principle 15. Scientific misconduct: Misconduct is defined as the fabrication or falsification of data, plagiarism, misrepresentation, or other practices that seriously deviate from those that are commonly accepted within the scientific community for proposing, conducting, analyzing, or reporting research. It does not include unintentional errors or honest differences in interpretation of data.

The Society shall provide vigorous leadership in the pursuit of scientific investigation which is based on the integrity of the investigator and the honesty of research and will not tolerate the presence of scientific misconduct among its members. It shall be the responsibility of the voting members of Governing Council to reach a decision about the possible expulsion of members found guilty of scientific misconduct.

Principle 16. Personal misconduct: Personal misconduct that results in a criminal conviction of a felony may be sufficient grounds for a member's expulsion from the Society. The relevance of the crime to the purposes of the Society should be considered by the Governing Council in reaching a decision about the matter. It shall be the responsibility of the voting members of the Governing Council to reach a decision about the possible expulsion of members found guilty of personal misconduct.

SOURCE: Society for Research in Child Development, 1996, pp. 377–339. © The Society for Research in Child Develoment, Inc. Reprinted with permission.

Few of us like to think of ourselves as blindly obedient, and the "teachers" may have gone out of their way to prove their independence.

The problem of deception is not limited to laboratory research. Procedures in which observers conceal their purposes, presence, or identity are also deceptive. What relationship should an ethnographer take with the people being studied? Rose (1987) lived and worked with a working-class African American community in Philadelphia for two years without disclosing his identity as an ethnographer, taking a job as an auto mechanic and renting an apartment in the community to facilitate his study.

When is deception acceptable? Never, if there is another way to elicit and study the behavior. If deception is a critical element of the research, however, the importance of the research is paramount in determining if deception is acceptable. Who decides if the research is sufficiently important? The researcher cannot make the judgment alone; research involving deception must be reviewed by an **Institutional Review Board** (IRB) consisting of scientists and laypersons. IRBs did not exist when Milgram's research was conducted. Do you think an IRB today would consider his findings sufficiently valuable to justify the extreme level of deception he employed? This question has inspired much debate on the subject of research ethics—with strong support on both sides of the argument.

There are good reasons to withhold information such as the hypothesis of the study or the condition an individual is participating in (see Sieber, 1992). Sometimes, deception is necessary for the success of the study. Milder forms of deception (which may be termed "incomplete information") occur more frequently than complete deception, as in the incidental recall paradigm in which participants are given a surprise memory test. Researchers commonly provide a general description of the topic of the study and assure participants that they can withdraw from the study without penalty at any time. Most people who volunteer for experiments do not expect full disclosure about the study prior to participation. They do, however, expect a thorough debriefing after they have completed the study.

DEBRIEFING

The traditional solution to the problem of deception is to debrief participants thoroughly after the experiment. **Debriefing** is necessary to fulfill our responsibility to the rights of subjects. Even when there is no stress and virtually no possibility of harm to subjects, debriefing is included as a standard part of experimental procedure. This educational feature of debriefing is important whether participants are young adult college students, older adults, or the elderly. In theory, debriefing is intended to remove any unwarranted negative effects of participation, especially when stress and deception are involved. Let's examine Milgram's research further.

Milgram went to great lengths to provide a thorough debriefing session. Participants who were obedient were told that their behavior was normal in that they had not acted differently from most other participants. They were made aware of the strong situational pressure that was exerted on them, and efforts were made to reduce any tension they may have felt. Participants were assured that no shocks were actually delivered, and there was a friendly reconciliation with the confederate, Mr. Wallace. Milgram also mailed a report of his research findings to his participants and at the same time asked about their reactions to the experiment. The responses showed that 84% were glad they had participated, and 74% said they had benefited from the experience. Only 1% said they were sorry they had participated. When interviewed by a psychiatrist a year later, no ill effects of participation could be detected. We can only conclude that debriefing had its intended effect. Other researchers who conducted further work on the ethics of Milgram's study have reached the same conclusion (Ring, Wallston, & Corey, 1970).

What about research with children? Successful debriefing of a child depends on the child's age and cognitive development, with age-appropriate explanations provided. For example, a second grader may fully understand a study intended to examine the effects of music on completing math problems, but the point of a more sophisticated study examining something less tangible, such as intrinsic and extrinsic motivation, may be more difficult to convey. In any case, it is the researcher's responsibility to communicate the information at a level commensurate with the child's level of understanding.

There are some situations in which children should not be debriefed. If deception has occurred, it may do more harm to explain that an adult has lied or played a trick on a young child. A child's self-esteem also should be considered when debriefing. As part of the experiment, suppose the child was told that he or

BOX 2.2   RESEARCH IN ACTION

Deception and Debriefing Issues

A study conducted at UCLA on boys (mean age = 10 years) diagnosed with attention-deficit hyperactivity disorder (ADHD) illustrates many of the ethical issues regarding deception and debriefing. Whalen, Henker, Hinshaw, Heller, and Huber-Dressler (1991) evaluated the boys' expectations about the effects of medication by varying what the boys were told about their daily pills. The study was conducted for two days. The boys were told they took a placebo one day and medication the other day, when, in fact, they took a placebo both days or medication both days. In this way the boys were misinformed half of the time.

The purpose of the study had been explained to the boys in advance, and they were told that sometimes the staff might give them fake pills. None of the boys objected to the possibility of deception. The authors acknowledge the important ethical issues involving disclosure about placebo use and misinformation about medication, especially when children are involved. However, the boys were in a carefully controlled environment (a summer camp program) and were monitored by staff for any unforeseen behavioral consequences. The deception was essential to the study; there was no other way to assess cognitive expectations associated with medication.

The children were misled by adults in a very deliberate manner—sealed envelopes marked with their name and the word "Confidential" were opened to reveal a card that said either "Placebo" or "Medication." According to ethical guidelines, should the researchers debrief the children? Whalen et al. decided *not* to debrief the children. Telling the children the truth about the deceptive manipulation may undermine the children's positive attitudes toward medication or medical personnel. Second, the deception was very temporary, occurring on only two occasions.

You might be curious about the outcome of the study. Overall, the results suggest some unintended cognitive effects associated with medicating ADHD boys. When informed they were on medication, the boys predicted better performance on math quizzes. The medication information was also related to higher evaluations of effort and ability on a computer game for boys who actually took placebos but were told they had been medicated. The boys were very convinced about the misinformation they had been given and reacted according to what they were told about their medication.

she had performed especially well on a test. Should the child then be left with the message that he or she didn't do so well after all? What if the child performed poorly on the test? In this case, the child would benefit from being told that he or she really did okay on the test. These questions should be carefully evaluated in deciding how to handle the debriefing. The SRCD ethical guidelines provide some assistance, but there is no absolute rule that applies to all cases. The judgment of the IRB should be considered when deciding what course of action to follow. Box 2.2 describes the ethical dilemmas faced by researchers investigating the effects of medication on hyperactive boys.

INSTITUTIONAL REVIEW OF RESEARCH

Every institution that receives funds from the U.S. Department of Health and Human Services (HHS) must have an Institutional Review Board. Each university campus typically has an IRB composed of a multidisciplinary group of faculty members including scientists and nonscientists. IRBs may also include student and community members, including legal specialists. The purpose of the IRB is to ensure that ethical guidelines are followed in every department on campus. Each piece of research must be evaluated in terms of whether there are any ethical problems with the procedure, whether alternative, more ethical procedures are available, and whether the importance of the study is such that the ethical problems are justified.

The Department of Health and Human Services has developed regulations (U.S. Department of Health and Human Services, 1981) that attempt to categorize research according to the amount of risk imposed on the subjects. These rules are designed to be minimal standards; some universities have developed more stringent guidelines.

Research in which there is no risk is exempt from review. Exempt research activities include nonexperimental work such as surveys, questionnaires, and educational tests in which the respondents are anonymous. Naturalistic observation in public places is also exempt if subject anonymity is not compromised. Archival research is exempt if the data are publicly available and the participants cannot be identified.

A second type of research activity is called **minimal risk.** Minimal risk means that the risk of harm to participants is no greater than risks encountered in daily life or in routine physical or psychological tests. When minimal risk research is being conducted, elaborate safeguards are less of a concern and approval by the IRB is routine. Some of the research activities considered to have minimal risk are: (1) recording routine physiological data from adult participants (e.g., weighing, tests of sensory acuity, electrocardiography, electroencephalography, diagnostic echography, and voice recordings; note that this would not include recordings that might involve invasion of privacy or invasive recordings such as X rays); (2) moderate exercise by healthy volunteers; and (3) research on individual or group behavior or characteristics of individuals, such as studies of perception, cognition, or test development in which the research investigator does not manipulate participants' behavior and the research will not involve stress to participants.

Any research procedure that places the subject at greater than minimal risk is subject to thorough review by the IRB. Complete informed consent and other safeguards may be required before approval is granted.

Determining whether research procedures fall into the category of minimal risk is not always simple. For example, a recent controversy has arisen in research assessing children's peer relations. A self-report procedure called sociometric nominations is used that involves giving children a list of names or photographs of the children in their classroom. Positive nominations are elicited by asking children to indicate three classmates they like the most; negative nominations are obtained by asking children to indicate three classmates they like the least. Concerns have been raised by ethical review boards, teachers, and parents that the negative peer nomination technique may be harmful to children, especially unpopular children. One ethical concern is that asking a child to make a negative statement might indicate approval for such statements. An additional concern is that unpopular children might experience even more negative treatment from their peers. Such issues prompt many IRBs to deny permission to do sociometric research (Iverson, Barton, & Iverson, 1997).

Is the potential risk associated with sociometric nominations within the range of "normal" experiences? To address these concerns, Iverson and colleagues interviewed children about their reactions to completing sociometric assessments. No evidence of harm to the children was found, with no reports of hurt feelings. Considering that children's normal behavior includes teasing and hurt feelings, it appears that sociometric methods do not pose any undue risk for children.

The rights and safety of human participants are well protected by the ethical codes of professional organizations such as the American Psychological Association and the Society for Research in Child Development, the HHS regulations, and the review of research by the IRB. Failure to conduct research in an ethical manner may lead to substantial legal and financial penalties for individuals and institutions, and it also diminishes the public's respect for science. For these reasons, researchers and review board members tend to be very cautious in terms of what is considered ethical.

OTHER ETHICAL ISSUES IN RESEARCH

Special Concerns Working With Children

Do people really understand what is being asked of them when they serve as experimental participants? For example, it is doubtful that children fully understand the concept of research or experimentation until at least early adolescence. For younger children, the closest situation in their experience is likely to be school, which means that children may mistake the experiment for a kind of test. This contributes to concern over getting the "right" answer and may alter the children's behavior in artificial ways.

As discussed earlier, it is not appropriate for minors to give consent on their own; parents must provide informed consent in advance. The minor then has the right to "assent" to participate (or "dissent," if they decline to participate). Even when a child's parents provide informed consent and the experimental procedure has begun, the child has the right to refuse to continue participation at any time, without coercion or threat. In our experience, very few children decline to take part in research studies. However, this practice presents several problems. We are not certain that young children actually understand the implications of the activity they are involved in, and therefore they may not have the ability to make informed decisions about choosing to participate.

Research by Abramovitch, Freedman, Thoden, and Nikolich (1991) investigated several ethical concerns regarding children's participation in research. Most children between the ages of 5 and 12 understood what the research involved and were able to tell the experimenter what was going to happen in the study, although the youngest children were less competent than the older children. Children understood that they could stop, but more than 40% of the youngest group did not know how to stop participating. Many children felt obligated to participate to avoid disappointing the experimenter or their parents. In addition, a large number of children did not believe that the testing would be confidential. This has clear implications for research on sensitive matters and legal situations when children may be asked to provide crucial testimony. Children may be unwilling to provide personal information about their family if they think their answers are not confidential.

To summarize, the study by Abramovitch and colleagues highlights the difficulties inherent in obtaining children's consent. Obtaining permission to assess a child does not mean that you have also obtained the child's full understanding. Although children have the right to refuse participation, many children do not feel that they can exercise this freedom.

Research Not Involving Informed Consent

Although most studies in the area of human development and family relations require some kind of informed consent of the participants, some research formats do not. For example, observation of naturally occurring behavior in public settings does not ordinarily require informing people they are being studied, provided that the observation is performed unobtrusively (see Principle 2, SRCD standards). That is, subjects are not aware they are being studied, are behaving in voluntary, natural ways, and are not going to be identified as research participants. Thus, you would be within ethical guidelines if you went to a local shopping mall and observed parent-child interactions without asking permission from each family—if anonymity and unobtrusiveness are ensured.

A more tricky situation involves research with participant observers, in which a researcher becomes part of a group to gather information about its normal activities. Suppose a researcher is interested in studying homeless families by posing as a homeless person, staying in a shelter to observe such families and the difficult world in which they live. Should this researcher inform fellow shelter guests that they are being studied? The answer is "yes," if practicably possible and if the study is not compromised by so doing. However, you can probably think of some reasons why giving such information may be harmful to the research. For example, shelter guests may feel more comfortable if they do not know they are being observed than if they are so informed. They may behave more naturally if they are not aware of the participant observer's objective.

In some circumstances, especially in observational research, informed consent is not required, and in other situations, obtaining informed consent may interfere with the observational process. The IRB will help the researcher resolve decisions about when and how informed consent is to be obtained.

Privacy and Confidentiality

Researchers must take care to protect the privacy of individuals. When studying human subjects, the researcher often obtains personal information about participants and their families. For example, a developmentalist studying family relationships may obtain information about family history, family income, parenting behaviors, marital satisfaction, and various aspects of each family's daily routine. This information may be vital to the research issues, but it is very personal to the participants. Ethical standards require that safeguards be taken to maintain **confidentiality** of the research records and that participants have the right to be informed about these safeguards. Data on individuals are typically maintained in locked areas with restricted access.

Privacy concerns are fundamental when researching a sensitive topic such as sexual behavior, divorce, religious beliefs, or medical history. Researchers sometimes need to ask people sensitive questions about their private lives, but participants are likely to be very concerned about who has access to this information. It is extremely important that responses to such questions be both anonymous and confidential. Without assurances of anonymity and confidentiality, few individuals may be willing to participate.

The investigators may need to carefully plan ways of coding questionnaires and interviews to maintain participant anonymity. One easy solution to keep participation anonymous is by having individuals not put their names on test instruments. When individuals are studied on multiple occasions, numbers can be randomly assigned to participants at the beginning of the study. Only these numbers appear on the participants' written records. And, of course, the master list linking names with code numbers is carefully protected. Consent forms should also be removed from test materials and filed in a secure location, along with the list of participants' names. Access to such information should be highly restricted to ensure privacy.

When reporting findings, anonymity is also needed. One solution is to report group data rather than individual data. Another solution, when reporting individual information such as a case study, is to conceal the identity of the participant and reveal only vital demographic characteristics such as gender or parental status. Revealing sensitive information about individuals without their permission is a serious ethical violation.

The Issue of Nontreated Controls

Clinical or applied researchers involved in treating a specific problem face another ethical issue. Suppose a therapist devises a special program for treatment of eating disorders in adolescent girls. A basic research design includes comparison of the behavior of an experimental group, which receives the new therapy program, with a control group, which does not receive the treatment. If the treatment is effective, the girls in the experimental group will have improved attitudes toward eating, and their eating behaviors will have changed, diminishing the incidence of anorexia or bulimia.

The ethical question involves the next step required of the researcher. What about the girls in the control group? Is their contribution limited to providing a description of untreated behavior for the project? The answer is "no." Ethical guidelines compel the researcher to offer the treatment to the participants in the **nontreated control** group. The investigator's obligations are not fulfilled until the girls in the control group have also completed the therapy program.

You may already have thought of a real issue here—when does the researcher know the treatment is actually effective? After one group of girls improves? After the first signs of improvement? And how much do they have to improve to determine that the program is effective? These are clearly judgment calls, and they become more difficult when researching especially compelling problems. Suppose you are testing a means of diminishing the violent self-abuse exhibited by certain autistic children or a new medical treatment for a devastating illness such as AIDS. In cases such as these, the researcher has the additional ethical dilemma of deciding when there is sufficient evidence to warrant the conclusion that the treatment really is effective. Is more research needed, or should the treatment be offered on a wide-scale basis? At that point the ethical responsibility to offer the treatment to the control group outweighs the importance of pursuing the study to its completion.

Alternative designs avoid the untreated control group dilemma. For example, intervention procedures can be used that add new members to the therapy group at various intervals, building in a replication of the study with new members. This approach is often used in single-subject designs, which are discussed in Chapter 9.

SUMMARY

In this chapter we reviewed the ethical principles relevant to research with human participants as well as the guidelines for institutional review. Primary concerns are minimizing physical and psychological risk and obtaining informed consent from participants. Prior consent must be obtained from the participants, their parents, or other advocates. Deception is acceptable under very limited circumstances and must be followed by a complete debriefing. Ethics codes guide the researcher in devising appropriate procedures for treatment of participants and respecting the confidentiality of their responses. Institutional Review Boards are instrumental in assisting researchers in adherence to ethical standards. Important ethical concerns arise when working with children, such as careful consideration of the child's rights to terminate participation. In all types of research—laboratory experiments, naturalistic observations, surveys, or interviews—the privacy and confidentiality of participants must be carefully guarded.

KEY TERMS

confidentiality	ethics code	minimal risk
debriefing	informed consent	nontreated controls
deception	Institutional Review Board	psychological risk

REVIEW QUESTIONS

1. Discuss the major ethical issues in developmental research: physical and psychological harm, deception, debriefing, and informed consent. How can researchers weigh the need to conduct research against the need for ethical procedures?

2. Give an example of research that may place participants in physical danger. Contrast your example with an example of research that places participants at psychological risk. How is the principle of informed consent used under such circumstances?

3. Think of a research topic that necessitates a certain degree of deception. Describe the debriefing process that should be used in that situation.

4. How would you go about obtaining informed consent in a study of children's attitudes toward television cartoon characters? Whose consent should you get? How should you get it?

5. Is informed consent necessary for an unobtrusive study of naturally occurring social behavior in a public shopping mall? Why, or why not?

6. What is the function of an Institutional Review Board?

7. What is the nontreated controls issue?

CHAPTER 3

Origins of Scientific Inquiry

As part of your course requirements you may be expected to conduct a research project. Where do you begin? First, you will need an idea to research. Where do scientists come up with their ideas? How do you find out about other people's ideas and past research? In this chapter we will provide a brief overview of the initial steps in your project.

SOURCES OF IDEAS

Scientific researchers study an enormous variety of questions about human development and family relations, ranging from detailed microanalyses of interactions to global descriptions of development across decades of the life span. Where do these questions come from? You may feel that you are not creative enough to come up with a good idea for research. You may also be surprised to know that the process does not necessarily begin with a trip to the university library—idea sources are all around us. We will look at four sources: common sense, observations of the world around us, theories, and past research.

Common Sense

One good source of ideas that can be tested by research is your own common sense about things we all believe to be true or things our grandparents may have told us. Does a "healthy body lead to a healthy mind"? Is a "picture worth a thousand words"? An entire line of research on the effects of physical punishment was inspired by the Victorian warning, "Spare the rod and spoil the child!" Converging evidence now suggests long-term negative consequences of physical punishment, including increased juvenile delinquency, poor academic performance, and low self-esteem (cf. Rothbaum & Weisz, 1994).

Testing a commonsense notion can be very informative because you may find that proverbs or adages such as these are not supported by research. The real world may be more complicated than our commonsense ideas suggest. The phrase "use it or lose it" has been tied to research in cognitive deficits that may accompany aging. In this case, it appears that the commonsense notion is correct. Adults with opportunities to practice problem-solving skills do not show the typical decline found in earlier studies (Schaie & Willis, 1986; Willis, 1990).

Observation of the World Around Us

Observations of personal and social events provide some of the best ideas for research. You may become intensely curious about something important in your life and begin to study that topic. In fact, this type of curiosity is what drives many students to engage in their first research project. You may have been wondering if "Joe Camel" really did entice children to smoke. Do children really lose 11% of their knowledge over the summer as stated in the *Phonics Game* advertisement?

Sometimes a serendipitous (lucky or fortuitous) event occurs that provides an opportunity for researchers to investigate topics that cannot be manipulated in an experimental situation, allowing for careful study of social events. Examples of serendipitous events include changes in the legal system, such as enactment of laws for child restraint seats and bicycle helmets, and reactions to natural disasters, such as hurricanes or earthquakes. Does a natural disaster increase children's fears? Clearly this can be investigated only after such an event occurs. Examples of such investigations include: (1) the consequences of prolonged exposure to political violence in Palestinian children (Garbarino & Kostelny, 1996); (2) the effects of the Los Angeles riots on aggression in children's story narratives (Farver & Frosch, 1996); and (3) the physical and psychological effects of war in Central American refugees (Locke, Southwick, McCloskey, & Fernandez-Esquer, 1996).

At times current events lead researchers to modify their original design. As luck would have it, researchers Bowman and Okada (1997) were in the midst of an investigation on attitudes toward justice before the arrest of O. J. Simpson on murder charges. Data already had been collected for one group of participants who evaluated the degree of justice in hypothetical scenarios several months before the arrest of O. J. Simpson. To examine the impact of the publicity surrounding the Simpson criminal trial, additional participants were surveyed on two more occasions, one month after the verdicts were rendered and one year after the verdicts. The additional information allowed the investigators to assess the immediate and long-term effects of the Simpson verdicts. Perceptions of justice changed dramatically immediately after the verdicts, suggesting a lack of faith in the criminal justice system. By one year later, however, the impact had faded, leading Bowman and Okada to conclude that extensive media coverage of high-profile events does not have a lasting impact.

There is almost always a current event issue related to human development in the news media. In recent years, people have been concerned about rating the content of television programming, the effects of a reduced hospital stay on mothers and newborns, the causes and prevention of Alzheimer's disease, the characteristics of a quality day care program, and so forth. All of these issues can be approached empirically—that is, with research designed to address specific questions. For example, the rising cost of living has made it increasingly difficult for young adults to establish their own residences (Aquilino, 1990). This leads to delayed departure from their parental home. An adult may also return to the home of a parent after a divorce or the loss of a job. Based on a national sample of nearly 5,000 parents, Aquilino reports that co-residence is predicted best by the adult child's marital status; unmarried adult children are most likely to live in their parents' home. In most cases, co-resident living was a result of the adult child's needs; few adult children lived in the parental home to care for their parents. A natural research question concerns the effects of these extended co-residence situations on family members. How does the living arrangement affect the parents? the young adults?

The world around us is a rich source of material for scientific investigation. When psychologist Robert Levine was teaching in Brazil several years ago, he noticed that Brazilian students were much more casual about both getting to class on time and leaving afterwards than were their counterparts in the United States. That observation led him to begin studying the pace of life in a variety of countries, as well as in numerous U.S. cities (Levine, 1990). This example illustrates how empirical research is sometimes motivated by observation of personal and social events, allowing scientific thinking to test the ideas through research.

Theories

Research is often conducted to test theories of behavior. **Theories** serve two important functions. First, theories organize and explain a variety of specific facts or descriptions of behavior. Such facts and descriptions are not very meaningful by themselves; theories are needed to impose a framework on them. This broad framework makes the world more comprehensible by providing a few abstract concepts around which we can organize and explain a variety of behaviors. As an example, the information processing approach to cognition organizes a variety of facts about memory and perception. Using the computer as an analogy, this approach explains phenomena such as individual differences in short-term memory, utilization of strategies to encode material, and selective attention. In education, a popular theory is Howard Gardner's multiple intelligences theory (Gardner, 1983), which proposes at least seven different types of intelligence. Teachers strive to address as many of these different intelligences as possible when developing curriculum materials. To teach a lesson on time, students may be asked to read the lesson (linguistic intelligence), calculate the number of minutes before and after the hour (logical-mathematical intelligence), draw the hands on a clock (spatial intelligence), demonstrate the positions of the clock with their arms (bodily-kinesthetic intelligence), and sing a song about telling time (musical intelligence).

You may also have noticed that many theories have their own distinctive terminology. Piaget's cognitive developmental theory uses the terms *equilibration, organization, accommodation,* and *assimilation.* Albert Bandura's social learning approach uses the terms *modeling* and *imitation* to explain development. The unique vocabulary of each theory is one of the ways a theory organizes information to help us understand development.

The second function of theories is to generate new knowledge by focusing our thinking so that we notice new aspects of behavior. Theories guide our observations of the world. The theory generates ideas about behavior, and the researcher conducts a study or series of studies to see if these ideas are correct. A theory is never *proven,* only *supported.* "Proof" is not possible due to the probabilistic foundations of statistical interpretation. The outcome of research (with a small "r") is not sufficient to disconfirm a major Theory (with a capital "T"). However, research findings can provide evidence to disconfirm a hypothesis associated with a theory.

When a theory is not supported, researchers are forced to modify the theory or develop a new, more comprehensive one. According to Bjorklund (1997), a new theoretical orientation for cognitive developmentalists is needed due to the diminished influence of Piaget and weaknesses in the information processing perspective (cf. Stanovich, 1990). With an increasing emphasis on the role of biology in development, developmental biology may be the "hot" new theory at the turn of the century. Erikson's stage theory of psychosocial development has been reexamined as well. One recent longitudinal study found Eriksonian stages to be influenced by cultural, historical, and social effects of the environment, an important addition to Erikson's theory (Whitbourne, Zuschlag, Elliot, & Waterman, 1992). Findings such as these can lead to new or revised theories, which in turn generate their own set of research questions.

Past Research

A fourth source of ideas is past research. Because the results of past research are published, the body of past literature on a topic can be used to refine and expand our knowledge. Knowing the background of a given issue can save us from "reinventing the wheel," in case someone has already found a definitive answer to our question. By examining the methods and results used by others, questions are raised that can be addressed in subsequent research by extending the findings to a different setting, a different age group, or a different methodology to replicate the results.

Earlier in the chapter we mentioned that research shows long-term negative consequences for children whose parents use physical punishment. However, most of the literature is restricted to middle-class, European American families, a common problem in child development research. A logical research question is: Does this relationship exist in other ethnic and cultural groups? The answer appears to be "no" according to a longitudinal study (Deater-Deckard, Dodge, Bates, & Pettit, 1996). More behavior problems were evident only for European American children exposed to physical punishment. These results add important information to existing knowledge by informing us that the effect of physical punishment on children's aggressive behavior is not universal, but culturally specific.

As you become familiar with the research literature on a topic, you may see inconsistencies in research results that need to be investigated, or you may want to study alternative explanations for the results. Also, what you know about one research area often can be successfully applied to another research area.

Let's look at a concrete example of a study that was designed to address methodological flaws in previous research. The study was concerned with a method for helping children who are diagnosed with autism. Childhood autism is characterized by a number of symptoms, including severe impairments in language and communication ability. Recently, parents and care providers have been encouraged by a technique called "facilitated communication," which apparently allows an autistic child to communicate with others by pressing keys on a keyboard showing letters and other symbols. A facilitator holds the child's hand to facilitate the child's ability to determine which key to press. With this technique, many autistic children begin communicating their thoughts and feelings and answer questions posed to them. Most people who see facilitated communication in action regard the technique as a miraculous breakthrough.

The conclusion that facilitated communication is effective is based on a comparison of the autistic child's ability to communicate with and without the facilitator. The difference is impressive to most observers. Recall, however, that scientists are by nature skeptical. They examine all evidence carefully and ask whether claims are justified. In the case of facilitated communication, Montee, Miltenberger, and Wittrock (1995) noted that the facilitator may be unintentionally guiding the child's fingers to type meaningful sentences. In other words, the facilitator, not the autistic individual, is controlling the communication. Montee et al. conducted a study to test this idea. In one condition, both the facilitator and the autistic child were shown a picture, and the child was asked to indicate what was shown in the picture by typing a response with the facilitator. This was done on a number of trials. In another condition, only the child saw the pictures. In a third condition, the child and facilitator were shown different pictures, but the facilitator was unaware of this fact. What do you think happened? As you may have guessed, the pictures were correctly identified only in the condition in which both the child and the facilitator saw the same pictures. The results by Montee et al. are an important extension of previous research and clearly change the interpretation of the effectiveness of facilitated communication.

HYPOTHESES

We have looked at four sources for obtaining ideas for research, ranging from formal scientific theories to ordinary observations. Did you think of some ideas for your own research? The next step is to formulate a hypothesis. A **hypothesis** makes a statement about something that may be true. Based on the idea that you want to investigate, it is often helpful to generate possible research questions in a "brainstorming" fashion. Think of some questions that relate to the topic described earlier of adult children living with their parents. Is it more common for males or females? Why do young adults return home—finances, health, child care? How long do they usually stay at home? Do young adults return more than once? Is self-esteem affected? Are the young adults in school or employed? With such questions in mind, the research study can be designed to collect data to address these hypotheses.

Hypotheses are often stated in more specific and formal terms. Usually, such formal hypotheses state that two or more variables are related to one another.

Thus, researchers might formulate hypotheses such as "grandmothers are more nurturant than grandfathers" or "male adolescents in Hispanic families experience more parental support than adolescents in European American families." Such hypotheses are formulated on the basis of past research findings and theoretical considerations. The researcher will then design a study to test the hypothesis. In the grandparents example, the researcher might invite grandparents and their grandchildren into a laboratory playroom and observe their interactions.

When the results of a study confirm a prediction, the hypothesis is supported, not proven. The observations may indicate that grandmothers are, in fact, more nurturant to their grandchildren. However, it is possible that grandfathers and grandmothers do not differ on the emotional concern they offer to their grandchildren, demonstrating similar levels of support, caring, and comforting. The researcher will then either reject the hypothesis or conduct further research using different methods to study the hypothesis.

LIBRARY RESEARCH

Before an investigator conducts a research project, a trip to the library is in order. As explained earlier, you need to determine what information already exists on the topic. Even if you only have a general idea about the area you are interested in, a **literature review** of existing studies can help clarify your concept and provide helpful hints on design issues. It is important to know how to use the library resources to find literature on a topic. In this section, we will discuss the fundamentals of conducting library research. For further information, check your library for printed materials; on-line tutorials are also available for most computerized databases. Some universities offer seminars and course work instructing students in the use of the library; these are valuable resources to take advantage of as early as possible in your academic career.

The Nature of Journals

Your library undoubtedly subscribes to an enormous number of professional journals. In these journals researchers publish the results of their investigations. After a research project has been completed, the study is written as a report, which then may be submitted to the editor of an appropriate scientific journal. The editor solicits reviews from other scientists in the same field. Based on these peer reviews, the editor decides whether the report is to be accepted for publication. Most good journals use a "blind" review process wherein the author is not identified, so that this knowledge cannot influence the reviewer's judgment. It is extremely unusual for a manuscript to be accepted for publication exactly as is. In fact, high-quality journals routinely reject the majority of manuscripts due to various methodological and conceptual flaws. For many journals a rejection rate exceeding 80% is common. Most of the manuscripts that are not rejected outright are returned to the author for revisions to clarify writing, to reanalyze the results, or to conduct additional research to support their theoretical explanations. (Even your profes-

BOX 3.1

Leading Journals in Human Development and Family Relations

Adolescence

Advances in Child Development and Behavior

Aging and Health Research

American Educational Research Journal

American Journal of Community Psychology

American Journal of Orthopsychiatry

American Journal of Sociology

Applied Cognitive Psychology

Child Development

Child Welfare

Clinical Gerontologist

Cognition

Cognitive Development

Contemporary Educational Psychology

Developmental Psychobiology

Developmental Psychology

Developmental Review

Educational Gerontology

Exceptional Children

Experimental Aging Research

Family and Child Mental Health Journal

Family Planning Perspectives

Family Process

Family Relations

Genetic Psychology Monographs

Gerontologist

Gerontology: International Journal of Experimental and Clinical Gerontology

Gifted Child Quarterly

Human Development

Infant Behavior and Development

Intelligence

International Journal of Aging and Human Development

Journal of Abnormal Child Psychology

Journal of Adult Development

Journal of Aging and Identity

sors may be asked to rewrite their manuscripts!) Papers that are accepted are typically published a year or more after the original submission, contributing to a publication lag between the time the research was conducted and the time the professional audience has access to the information. Because of this lag, scientists maintain active networks of colleagues to share early reports of noteworthy findings. National and regional conventions are also a source of preliminary research reports, which provide a preview of ongoing projects.

Journals on Human Development

Of the dozens of journals in the human development field, you should know about a few leading publications (see Box 3.1). *Child Development* is published by the Society for Research in Child Development, and it features both research reports and theoretical reviews of research with children and families. *Developmental Psy-*

Journal of Aging and Physical Activity	*Journal of Marriage and the Family*
Journal of Applied Behavior Analysis	*Journal of Mental Deficiency Research*
Journal of Applied Developmental Psychology	*Journal of Pediatric Psychology*
	Journal of Psycholinguistic Research
Journal of Autism and Developmental Disorders	*Journal of Women and Aging*
	Journals of Gerontology
Journal of Child Language	*Learning and Individual Differences*
Journal of Clinical Child Neuro-psychology	*Merrill-Palmer Quarterly*
	Monographs of the Society for Research in Child Development
Journal of Clinical Geropsychology	
Journal of Comparative Family Studies	*OMEGA: The International Journal of Death and Dying*
Journal of Contemporary Ethnography	*Pediatrics*
Journal of Cross-Cultural Psychology	*Psychology and Aging*
Journal of Divorce	*Psychology in the Schools*
Journal of Early Adolescence	*Reading Research Quarterly*
Journal of Educational Psychology	*Review of Educational Research*
Journal of Experimental Child Psychology	*Sex Roles*
	Social Casework
Journal of Experimental Education	*Social Psychology Quarterly*
Journal of Family Psychology	*Studies in Educational Evaluation*
Journal of Genetic Psychology	*The Gerontologist*
Journal of Learning Disabilities	*Young Children*

chology is published by the American Psychological Association, and it covers the entire life span and includes research with animals. The *Journal of Educational Psychology* concentrates on topics relevant to learning, whether in the formal educational setting or in other settings. The *Journals of Gerontology* present information on biological and medical aspects of aging. The *Journal of Family Psychology* focuses on changes in family processes.

Literature Searching

The number of journals in many areas is so large that it is almost impossible for anyone to read them all. Clearly, it would be difficult to read all of the journals even in a single area such as aging. Moreover, if you were seeking research on a specific topic, it would be impractical to look at every issue of every journal in which relevant research might be published (even if your library did have them all on the shelf!). Fortunately, there are systems for organizing and retrieving information based on brief summaries or abstracts of each article.

Psychological Abstracts

Psychological Abstracts contains "nonevaluative summaries of the world's literature in psychology and related disciplines." *Psych Abstracts* is published monthly by the American Psychological Association, and each volume contains thousands of abstracts of recently published articles. To find articles on a specific topic in which you are interested, you would consult the index at the end of each volume. If the abstract is relevant to your research topic, you can go to the periodical stacks and locate the complete article. The reference section of the library has abstracts for many disciplines. Check your library for these other valuable resources in human development and related fields:

> *Child Development Abstracts and Bibliography*
> *ERIC, Resources in Education*
> *Gerontology Abstracts*
> *Sociological Abstracts*
> *Family Studies Abstracts*
> *Criminal Justice Abstracts*

The following example illustrates how to use the printed version of *Psychological Abstracts,* although similar strategies can be effectively applied to other abstracts. First, locate the index that accompanies each volume. The index is organized by subject category. Some categories, such as "preschool-aged children," "retirement," and "cognitive development," are quite large; others, such as "runaway behavior" and "homesickness," are narrower and contain relatively few references. As a general rule, you can search most efficiently when you have narrowed the category; try to get your topic as specific as possible. The *Thesaurus of Psychological Index Terms* helps you choose the proper words to use in your search. For example, the term *eyewitnesses* is not used in *Psych Abstracts;* instead, proper search terms are *witnesses* and *legal testimony.*

Suppose you are interested in finding out about research on father absence. You locate the index for a volume of *Psych Abstracts;* for this example we chose Volume 79 (1992). There you find a category labeled "father child relations," as well as one on "father absence." In each category, the publications are listed under serials (articles in periodicals), chapters, and books. For father absence, there are seven articles, three chapters, and no books. Here are four of the serial listings:

> father absence due to work requirements, wives' perceived social support & children's coping & adjustment & academic performance, 8–11 yr olds & their 26–45 yr old mothers, 23058
>
> father vs mother absence & family income & background & demographics & parent & student behavior, GPA & test scores, high school students, 2 yr followup, 29242

race & father absence, sex role orientation & achievement & affiliation needs, middle class Black vs White 17–22 yr old females, 19842

sex of child, contributions to well being of child, absent fathers, 16271

Each listing describes the content of the study and gives an abstract number. You can narrow the abstract search down to the most relevant articles, then find the full abstract in the appropriate volume of abstracts (in this case, Volume 79). The abstracts are listed in numerical order. If you looked up article 19842, you would find this information:

> 19842. **Harris, Shanette M.; Gold, Steven R. & Henderson, Bruce B.** (U Tennessee, Knoxville) **Relationships between achievement and affiliation needs and sex-role orientation of college women whose fathers were absent from home.** *Perceptual & Motor Skills,* 1991 (Jun), Vol 72(3, Pt 2), 1307–1315.–Examined the influence of fathers' absence and race on the gender-roles orientation, achievement, and affiliation of middle class, college-aged women. 271 women (aged 17–22 yrs) were classified by race (Black or White) and the presence or absence of a father during adolescence and completed 4 questionnaires assessing achievement and affiliation, personal attributes, and demographic characteristics. The absence of a father did not seem to influence the gender-role orientation or achievement needs. However, Black Ss whose fathers were absent by death reported higher achievement needs than did other Ss, and Black Ss whose fathers left home during their development were rated higher on masculinity and androgyny.

After copying the information about this article, you could look up any other abstracts that seem relevant. To continue the search, you would then go to other volumes of *Psych Abstracts*. (Note the reference to "Ss" in the abstract. This is an abbreviation of the word *subjects* and is used in *Psychological Abstracts* to save space; the abbreviation is not used in the actual research article.)

The final step is to find the original articles in the journals. If your library has the journal, you can read it in the library, or make a photocopy, especially of the references. (These may help you find other articles on the same topic.) If the journal is not available in your library, many libraries have an interlibrary loan policy to obtain copies from another library. Ask your librarian for assistance in requesting the material.

Computer-Assisted Searches

A manual search through the volumes of *Psychological Abstracts* can be very time-consuming. In addition, you may find (as we did) that your university no longer subscribes to the paper version of *Psych Abstracts,* relying on computerized databases instead. A computer-assisted search is often a much more efficient way to find articles relevant to your topic of interest. The contents of *Psychological Abstracts,* as well as other bibliographic information sources such as ERIC, have been stored in computer databases. The *Psych Abstracts* database called PsycLIT is stored on a CD-ROM used with a microcomputer; Box 3.2 offers a brief guide to PsycLIT. Your library may provide access to other computer databases using either microcomputer terminals in the library or a connection to information retrieval services such as Lexis/Nexis and FirstSearch.

BOX 3.2

Using PsycLIT

In a search using PsycLIT, the first step is to specify the database to be used. On our library's computer, the choices are *PsycLIT Journal Articles from 1991 to current, PsycLIT Journal Articles from 1974–1990,* and *PsycLIT Chapters & Books 1/87 to current.* Function keys provide some information on searching: F1 provides help, F3 gives information about the PsycLIT database, F9 is the thesaurus of psychological terms.

One way to search is to enter a word or phrase to search at the FIND: prompt. The easiest way to do this is to type in specific terms or phrases to search. For example, let's do a search for references on computer-assisted instruction. Press the F2 key (FIND).

FIND: computer assisted instruction

When these three words are entered, the computer finds all abstracts that contain the word "computer" and all abstracts that contain the word "assisted" and all abstracts that contain the word "instruction." It then lists only those abstracts that contain all three words—in this case 847 abstracts. This is too many records to browse through, so we need to narrow the search. Let's narrow the search to one academic area, math. At the FIND: prompt, type Math. Now the computer is searching for Computer Assisted Instruction and Math. This search returns 20 records, a very workable number to browse through. The search history is:

No.	Records	Request
#1	6355	Computer
#2	1890	Assisted
#3	4201	Instruction
#4	847	Computer Assisted Instruction
#5	634	Math
#6	20	#4 and Math

Next, press the F4 key to show the actual abstracts. Here is one from our search:

TI DOCUMENT TITLE: Learning with computers in small groups: Cognitive and affective outcomes.

AU AUTHORS: Mevarech,-Zemira-R.; Silber,-Ora; Fine,-Devorah.

IN INSTITUTIONAL AFFILIATION OF FIRST AUTHOR: Bar-Ilan U, Ramat Gan, Israel

JN JOURNAL NAME: Journal-of-Educational-Computing-Research; 1991 Vol 7(2) 223–243

IS ISSN: 07356331

LA LANGUAGE: English

PY PUBLICATION YEAR: 1991

AB ABSTRACT: Examined the effects of cooperative and individual-istic computer-assisted instruction (CAI) programs on cognitive and affective variables in mathematics. Participants were 149 Israeli 6th-grade students. Pupils were stratified by previous achievement into triplets and then randomly assigned to 1 of 2 treatment conditions: using CAI in pairs or individually. Results show that students who used CAI for drill and practice in pairs performed better than students who used the same program individually. In addition, the indi-vidualistic and cooperative CAI methods equally affected students' mathematical self-concept, but the cooperative treatment alleviated math anxiety of low ability students more than did the individualistic treatment. (PsycLIT Database Copyright 1991 American Psychological Assn, all rights reserved)

KP KEY PHRASE: cooperative vs individualistic computer assisted mathematics instruction; achievement & mathematics self concept & anxiety; 6th graders; Israel

DE DESCRIPTORS: COMPUTER-ASSISTED INSTRUCTION; MATHEMATICS-ACHIEVEMENT; SELF-CONCEPT; MATHE-MATICS ANXIETY; ELEMENTARY-SCHOOL-STUDENTS; CHILDHOOD.

CC: 3530; 35

PO POPULATION: Human

AG COMPOSITE AGE GROUP: Child

UD UPDATE CODE: 9112

AN PSYCH ABS. VOL. AND ABS. NO. 78-34618

JC JOURNAL CODE: 3439

The search results can be reviewed on the computer monitor. If the computer is connected to a printer, one or more of the abstracts can be printed by pressing the F6 key. You can specify the fields you want to print; you can print just the citation or the full abstract. The search results can be downloaded to your diskette to use later in a word processing program. To download information, press F10 and follow the instructions. And don't forget to print your search history; if you need to do the search over, you will have a record of the terms you used.

The search described found the terms in any of the fields in the record. You may prefer to narrow the search to get articles that use the terms *computer assisted instruction* in the key phrase field. The way to do this is to specify:

FIND: computer assisted instruction in KP

You may also want to limit the search by age group. PsycLIT uses four age categories: CHILD (birth to 12 years), ADOLESCENT (13–17 years),

(continued)

ADULT (18 and over), and ELDERLY (65 and over). The CHILD category is very broad but can be narrowed by using terms such as *Neonates, Infants, Preschool Age Children, School Age Children, Elementary School Students,* and *High School Students.* To limit the search to children, at the FIND: prompt type CHILD in AG (for child in the age group field). The "and" is a logical operator that narrows the search to only those abstracts that match both conditions specified. Using "or" as a logical operator expands the search to include abstracts that match either condition specified.

Another way to limit the search is to locate articles in a particular language. To find articles in English, type LA=English at the FIND: prompt. If you search for "computer assisted instruction" and "math" and LA=English and AG=Child, you will find 13 abstracts.

The procedures for searching other library databases will be quite similar. The reference librarians in your library can provide you with guidance and information on the specific requirements of your school's computer system.

SOURCE: Reprinted with permission of the American Psychological Association, publisher of *Psychological Abstracts* and the PsychLIT Database. Copyright © by the American Psychological Association. All rights reserved.

The Internet

The Internet is also becoming increasingly useful as a means of locating information via computer. Many universities have Internet access available in the library or computer center. To access the Internet, you need a computer with a modem, an Internet service such as *America Online* or *Earth Link,* and lots of free time. A home page from the National Institute on Drug Abuse is shown in Figure 3.1. Pages are updated regularly, so the current home page for this site may display different content. The following sites are worth a look:

Children's Defense Fund
   http://www.tmn.com
   The Children's Defense Fund has links to news and reports about children and also has a list of publications available for purchase such as *The State of America's Children Yearbook 1997,* an annual analysis of the status of children in the United States.

Children's Literature Web Guide
   http://www.ucalgary.ca/~dkbrown/index.html
   Features links to Internet resources related to books for children and young adults. Includes links to movies and television programs based on children's books, children's publishers and booksellers on the Internet, and lists of recommended children's books.

The Gerontological Society of America
   http://www.geron.org
   Posts a column from their monthly journal on the web page. Includes information about the society, their publications, and conferences.

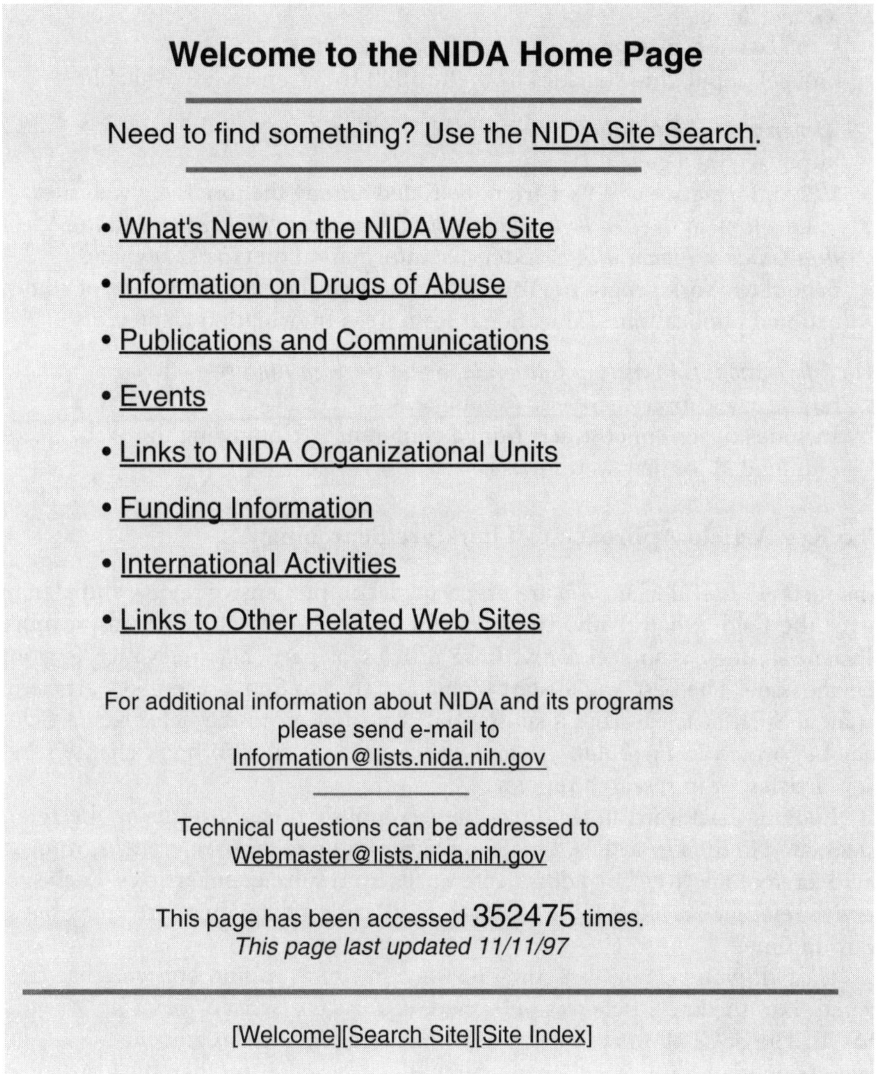

Welcome to the NIDA Home Page

Need to find something? Use the NIDA Site Search.

- What's New on the NIDA Web Site
- Information on Drugs of Abuse
- Publications and Communications
- Events
- Links to NIDA Organizational Units
- Funding Information
- International Activities
- Links to Other Related Web Sites

For additional information about NIDA and its programs
please send e-mail to
Information@lists.nida.nih.gov

Technical questions can be addressed to
Webmaster@lists.nida.nih.gov

This page has been accessed 352475 times.
This page last updated 11/11/97

[Welcome][Search Site][Site Index]

Figure 3.1
Internet home
page from NIDA
(http://www.nida.
nih.gov)

National Institute of Aging Exploratory Center on Demography of Aging Metapage
http://www.psc.lsa.umich.edu/meca/meta.html
Includes links to other sites related to aging such as research projects
at the University of California, Berkeley, Duke University, and the Rand
Corporation.

National Institute on Drug Abuse
http://www.nida.nih.gov
Extensive information on drug prevention programs is available on-line
and can be downloaded to your computer. NIDA sponsors many drug
prevention programs such as Project STAR, Project Family, and Adolescent
Transitions Program.

U.S. Census Bureau
http://www.census.gov
Official population statistics from the 1990 U.S. Census are available.

U.S. Department of Education
http://www.ed.gov/
Very informative and user-friendly. Rated among the top 5% of web sites. Take a look at the *Teacher's Guide to the Department of Education* and the *Student Guide to Financial Aid.* Extensive information on Goals 2000 and School-to-Work programs. You can also search the ERIC database of educational publications, Educational Resources Information Center.

Web Information: University of California, Santa Barbara Library
http://www.library.ucsb.edu/untangle/
Includes dozens of abstracts from a conference "Untangling the Web." Recommended for new web surfers.

The Key Article Approach to Literature Searching

Abstracts are useful when you are preparing a comprehensive review and plan to cover the field exhaustively. However, for specific research problems, a more efficient strategy is to seek only those articles of particular relevance to your specific issue. The best way to start such a search is to find a recent key article in an area. Such articles make a substantial contribution to the field. Key articles may be located in *Psych Abstracts* and are commonly cited in book chapters, review articles, or in research reports.

Looking backward in time can be accomplished easily by using the references cited in the key article. Once you locate some of those references, you can build a reference "tree" by adding references from subsequent articles. Each successive reference is likely to be an earlier publication date, therefore going backward in time.

How do you accomplish going forward in time? To find out what has happened since the key article was published, you use the *Social Science Citation Index* (SSCI). The SSCI allows you to search for subsequent articles that cite the key article. Begin your SSCI search in a volume that is more recent than the key article. In this way you can discover newer research that is related to the key article in some way, such as extensions of the research or criticisms of the key article. This will give you an extensive bibliography of articles relevant to your topic. As with *Psych Abstracts,* the SSCI may also be available on a computer, and a computer search of the SSCI database is much more efficient than a manual search.

ANATOMY OF A RESEARCH ARTICLE

Now that you have selected your research articles, what can you expect to find in them? Research articles describing empirical studies usually have five sections: (1) an abstract, such as the ones found in *Psychological Abstracts,* (2) an introduction section that explains the problem under investigation and the specific hypotheses being tested, (3) a method section that describes in detail the procedures used in the study, (4) a results section in which the findings are presented, and (5) a discussion section that interprets the results, proposes alternative explanations for the results, examines possible limitations of the study, and suggests directions for future research.

An overview of each section is presented here as a way to introduce you to the structure of an APA-style scientific report. Appendix A presents detailed information you will need to prepare a written report of your research, including suggestions for what to include in each section and how to prepare the manuscript. Stylistic and word processing guidelines are based on the fourth edition of the *Publication Manual of the American Psychological Association* (1994). APA style is used in many journals in psychology, mental health, family relations, and education. At the end of Appendix A you will find a sample APA-style paper with detailed annotations in the margins that point out important elements of APA style.

Abstract

The **abstract** is a summary of the research report and is usually no more than 100 to 120 words in length. The purpose of the abstract is to briefly introduce the article, allowing readers to decide if the article appears to be relevant to their own interests. The abstract contains basic information about each of the major sections of the article, the problem under investigation from the introduction, the method, the pattern of major results, and implications of the study. The abstract is meant to be self-contained; you should be able to understand the gist of the study without having to refer to the article itself. This is important because, as we have seen, abstracts are often published separately from their articles.

Introduction

In the **introduction** the researcher describes the problem under investigation. Past research and theories relevant to the problem are described. Specific expectations are usually stated as formal hypotheses. In other words, the investigator introduces the research in a logical format that shows how past research and theory are connected to the current research problem and the expected results.

Method

The **method section** is a straightforward report of what the researcher did. Subsections are used to organize the material in the method section. Both the order of the subsections and the number of subsections vary in published articles. Decisions about which subsections to include are guided by the complexity of the investigation. Sometimes the first subsection presents an *overview* of the design to prepare the reader for the material that follows. The next subsection describes the characteristics of the *participants*. Were they male, female, or were both sexes used? What was the average age? How many participants were there? Did these participants have any special characteristics? The next subsection details the *procedure* used in the study. Step-by-step details of the events are described, including careful descriptions of the situation participants were exposed to, the instructions they were given, the amount of time allotted for the task, and so on.

The details help the reader understand exactly how the study was conducted and allow other researchers to replicate the study. Other subsections may be needed to describe the *design, apparatus,* or testing *materials.*

Results

In the **results section** the author presents the findings, usually in three ways. First, there is a description in narrative form. For example, "Children who participated in the nutritional education program selected more fruit for lunch." Second, the results are described in statistical language, including numerical values and statistical symbols. Third, the material is often depicted in visual form using tables and graphs.

The statistical terminology of the results section may appear formidable. However, lack of knowledge about the calculations isn't really a deterrent to understanding the article or the logic behind the statistics. Statistics are only a tool the researcher uses in evaluating the outcomes of a study. Chapters 14 and 15 explain some of the mysteries of statistical language so you won't have to skip over it when reading articles!

Discussion

In the **discussion section** the researcher reviews the research from various perspectives. Do the results support the hypothesis that was stated earlier? If they do, the author should give some possible explanations for the results and discuss why one explanation is superior to another. This is often done by comparing the results to past research on the topic to show consistencies (or inconsistencies) in the field. If the hypothesis has not been supported, the author offers suggestions for this by critically evaluating the methodology, the hypothesis, or both. The discussion also includes suggestions for practical applications of the research findings and for future research in the area.

Read as many research articles as possible to become familiar with the communication style and the structure of the reports. As you read more research, you will become expert at finding the information you are looking for. For a first reading, start with the abstract, then skim the article to decide whether the information is useful for your project. Then, go back and read the article closely. Critically evaluate the content of the article, looking for potential problems in the study. Students often generate the best criticisms. Before too long, you may find yourself generating research ideas and planning your own studies.

SUMMARY

Researchers select variables to study from a variety of sources. Common sense and curiosity have led to a number of surprising research findings. Observation of the world around us is a valuable source of inspiration for empirical research. Theories guide research by organizing facts and generating knowledge. By examining past research, we can identify questions that need to be answered. Based on the idea you want to investigate, a hypothesis is formulated that makes a statement about how variables are related to one another.

Research in the area of human development and family relations can be located in a variety of ways. Consulting journals or journal abstracts provides access to published research. The Internet also provides current information on many topics. One of the most efficient ways to begin a literature review is to find a key article and search backward in time (using its references) and forward in time (using the *Social Science Citation Index*).

Journal articles describing empirical studies usually follow a prescribed format. An abstract briefly summarizes the study. The introduction explains the problem under investigation and the researcher's hypothesis. A method section describes the participants and the procedures used to test the hypothesis. A results section presents the findings, usually with statistical analyses. A discussion section explains and evaluates the findings, including the broader implications of the results.

KEY TERMS

abstract	introduction	*Psychological Abstracts*
discussion section	literature review	results section
hypothesis	method section	theory

REVIEW QUESTIONS

1. What are the two functions of a theory?
2. What is a hypothesis? Where does a researcher get ideas for a hypothesis?
3. Think of three commonsense sayings about behavior (e.g., Like father, like son; Opposites attract). For each one, develop a hypothesis that is suggested by the saying. How would you test the hypothesis (based on Gardner, 1988)?
4. Describe how past research is found when using *Psychological Abstracts*. How can you locate information using the "key article" method?
5. What information does the researcher communicate in each section of a research article?

CHAPTER 4

Studying Relationships Between Variables

In this chapter, we will explore some of the basic issues and concepts that are necessary for understanding the scientific study of behavior. We will begin by looking at the nature of variables, including different kinds of variables and general methods to measure behavior.

SCIENTIFIC VARIABLES

A **variable** is a general class or category of objects, events, situations, or characteristics of a person. Examples of variables that a developmentalist might study include age, gender, temperament, intelligence, creativity, hostility, anxiety, parental warmth, self-esteem, and task performance. Each of these variables represents a general category. Within the category, specific instances will vary. These specific values of the variable are called levels. A variable must have two or more levels or values (otherwise it wouldn't be a "variable"). For some variables, the values will have true numeric or quantitative properties. For example, if task performance is a score on a mathematics achievement test on which the values can range from a low of 0% correct to a high of 100% correct, these values have numeric properties. The values of other variables are not numeric; rather, they simply identify different categories. An example is gender; the values for gender are male and female. These are different categories, but they do not differ quantitatively. Another example would be the condition to which participants are assigned in a laboratory study of memory. Participants may be asked to learn two different types of words: familiar words and unfamiliar words. In this case the category is type of word and the levels are familiar and unfamiliar.

Variables can be classified into three general categories. **Situational variables** describe characteristics of a situation or environment: time of day when mathematics lessons are conducted, the spatial density of an elementary school classroom, or the credibility of a child providing testimony. **Subject** or **individual difference** variables are a special category of situational variables that describe the characteristics of individuals, including gender, intelligence, and personality traits such as shyness. **Response variables** are the responses or behaviors of individuals, such as reaction time, performance on a cognitive task, and anxiety.

Here is an example that illustrates situation, subject, and response variables. Black, Hutchinson, Dubowitz, Starr, and Berenson-Howard (1996) examined parental competence and child competence during feeding and play observations among low-income, African American infants and toddlers and their mothers. The situational variable is the type of setting, with levels of feeding time and play time. The subject variables are the characteristics the individuals bring to the research, in this case their age group, infants and toddlers. Note that ethnicity is not a variable in this study because there is only one value for that variable; all participants are African American. The measures of parental competence and child competence are the response variables, measuring the behaviors by direct observation, standardized developmental assessments such as the Bayley Scales of Infant Development (Bayley, 1969), and parental self-report questionnaires such as the Parenting Stress Index (Abidin, 1990).

OPERATIONAL DEFINITIONS

In actual research, the researcher has to decide on a method to study the variables of interest. A variable is an abstract concept that must be translated into concrete forms of observation or manipulation. Thus, a variable such as anxiety, cognitive task performance, parental warmth, social competence, or attention must be defined in terms of the specific method used to measure or manipulate it. Scientists refer to this as the **operational definition** of a variable—a definition of the variable in terms of the operations or techniques the researcher uses to measure or manipulate it.

Variables must be operationally defined so they can be studied empirically. However, there is no single method for operationally defining a particular variable. A variety of operational definitions may be available for a given variable. Even a simple variable such as being an identical or fraternal twin may be operationally defined in terms of a person's self-report; on the basis of similarity of physical characteristics such as height, weight, and general appearance; or on the basis of a complex blood test. Using sophisticated techniques, individuals who thought they were identical twins have discovered they were actually fraternal twins, and vice versa.

Operational definitions also facilitate communication of our ideas to others. For example, if someone wishes to tell you about aggression, you need to know what the person means. Aggression could be defined as (1) the number of aggressive words used, (2) the number of times a teenager fights with other students during school, (3) a score on a personality measure of aggression, (4) frequency of violent criminal offenses, or (5) parental report of a child's aggression.

The task of operationally defining a variable forces scientists to discuss abstract concepts in concrete terms. The process can result in the realization that the chosen variable is too vague to study. This does not necessarily indicate that the concept is meaningless but rather that systematic research is not possible until the concept can be operationally defined. Behavior geneticists made a recent breakthrough in the search for a genetic contribution to dyslexia due in large part to modification of the definition for dyslexia. Rather than defining dyslexia in the traditional way (a general difficulty with learning to read), Grigorenko et al. (1997) operationally defined dyslexia by focusing on two specific components of dyslexia—single-word reading and identification of speech sounds. Using the more detailed definition, Grigorenko et al. successfully isolated two genetic markers for dyslexia.

There is rarely a single infallible method for operationally defining a variable; a variety of methods may be available, each of which has advantages and disadvantages. Researchers must decide which one to use given the particular research problem, the goals of the research, and other considerations such as ethics and costs. Because no one method is perfect, complete understanding of any variable involves using a variety of operational definitions. Researchers hope that results from these multiple approaches will provide converging evidence about the relationships being investigated.

INDEPENDENT AND DEPENDENT VARIABLES

So far, we have discussed variables from a general vantage point. Next we will consider two distinct types of variables, **independent variables** and **dependent variables.** The independent variable is considered the manipulated variable and, thus, is the "cause" of behavior. The dependent behavior is the observed variable that measures the participant's response and, thus, is the "effect."

Let's examine a simple research design to illustrate the terms. Suppose a teacher is interested in examining the effects of cooperative learning on mathematics skills. A direct way to address the question is to compare the performance of students who work in dyads to that of students who work alone. The situational variable is the type of group, with levels of working in a dyad and working alone. The type of group is called a **manipulated variable** because the researcher (the teacher, in this case) actively chooses the variable and its values. This variable is also the independent variable because the participants (the students) have no role in determining the levels of the variable—the teacher selected the variable beforehand.

The students are now assigned to work in dyads or to work alone, and the teacher assesses their learning by giving all students a math test. The scores on the math test are the dependent variable because these scores depend on how the students in each type of group perform. Each student responds to the situation he or she was exposed to; thus the dependent variable is considered the "effect" of the independent variable. In this hypothetical study, let's assume the dyads obtained higher scores on the math test. This means that the size of the study group (1 versus 2 students) has an effect on the math scores, "causing" the math scores to change. Working alone "caused" lower test scores; working with a partner "caused" higher test scores.

Thus, we see that the independent or manipulated variable is determined by the researcher and is considered the "cause" of the behavior. In contrast, the de-

pendent variable is the response variable, which measures the participant's behavior. It is considered the "effect" because it is a consequence of exposure to the
independent variable.

Let's practice on a study described in Chapter 3. Montee et al. (1995) were
concerned about the effectiveness of facilitated communication with autistic individuals. They compared three situations: child and adult saw the same picture,
child and adult saw different pictures, only the child saw the picture. What is the
independent variable? You should now recognize the three situations as levels of
an independent variable: type of communication. What is the dependent variable? The dependent variable selected for analysis was the number of correct responses. With practice you will be able to differentiate between independent and
dependent variables with ease.

TYPES OF DEPENDENT MEASURES

There are many approaches an investigator can take to measure the behavior and
responses of participants. The dependent variable in most experiments is one of
three general types: self-report, behavioral, or physiological.

Self-Report Measures

Self-report measures rely on the participants to describe their own behavior,
knowledge, opinions, or beliefs. The self-report can be oral in the form of an
interview or a survey that takes place in a face-to-face interview or over the telephone. Self-report measures can also be written, using a paper-and-pencil measure. Computer technology now allows researchers to obtain self-report measures
on the Internet. Regardless of the technique used to collect the information, self-
report always involves the respondent completing questions asked by the experimenter. Because of their ease of use, self-reports are the most commonly used
method of measuring behavior.

Self-report measures can be used to ask people about their child-rearing practices, sexual behaviors, health habits, attitudes, personality, or memory. Indeed,
the exams that you take in your classes are self-reports of your learning of the facts
and concepts presented in the class. Multiple-choice questions, which have a limited number of fixed response alternatives, are good examples of **closed-ended
questions.** Essay questions such as "What is your opinion of the role of nature
and nurture in development?" represent **open-ended questions** because many
different responses are possible and you choose to respond the way you like.

Closed-ended questions are clearly easier to score, and the response alternatives are the same for everyone. Responses to open-ended questions are more difficult to categorize and code and are therefore more time-consuming and costly
to evaluate. (How long does it take your professor to return multiple-choice exams? essay exams?) Sometimes an open-ended response cannot be categorized at
all because the response doesn't make sense or the person couldn't think of an answer. Still, an open-ended question can yield valuable insights into what people

are thinking and how they view their world. Closed-ended questions are more likely to be used when relevant variables and their dimensions have been defined through previous research or theoretical considerations. We will return to this topic in Chapter 7 in connection with survey research.

Behavioral Measures

Behavioral measures use direct observation of behavior rather than self-reports. The participant's behavior is evident to the researcher via observational methods or performance on structured tasks. As with self-reports, measurements of an almost endless number of behaviors are possible, and behavior can be directly observed in many different ways. Deciding which aspects of behavior to measure depends on what is theoretically most relevant for the particular study.

Consider an example of an observational study of the social and physical environment in a neonatal intensive care unit (Gottfried, 1985). Observers recorded *frequency* measures of the number of times behaviors occurred, such as feeding, crying, and medical interventions. To determine the *rate* of these behaviors, the frequency was divided by units of time, yielding the number of medical interventions per hour and per day. *Duration* was determined by timing the length of target behaviors: How long was the medical intervention? How long did the crying last?

Other behavioral assessments include *preference* measures in which a participant indicates a choice, for example, among objects or playmates. Latency measures of *reaction time* record how quickly a response occurs after a stimulus or signal. Cognitive task performance is typically assessed using *accuracy* and *recall* measures such as number of correct selections, number of problems solved, or number of items recalled.

Sometimes the nature of the variable being studied requires either self-report or behavioral measurement. A measure of helping behavior is almost by definition a behavioral measure because the researcher needs to see the actual behavior. A measure of personality characteristics, such as self-esteem or confidence, will employ self-report. For many variables, however, both self-reports and behavioral measures could be appropriate. Thus, liking or attraction could be measured on a rating scale (On a scale of 1 to 7, how much do you like this computer game?) as well as by using a behavioral measure of the amount of time the child plays with the game. Using multiple measurement techniques increases the investigator's confidence in the outcome.

Physiological Measures

Physiological measures are recordings of physiological responses of the body. Several somatic functions are commonly used in research. The galvanic skin response (GSR) is a measure of general emotional arousal and anxiety; it measures the electrical conductance of the skin, which changes when sweating occurs. Another physiological measure is the electroencephalogram (EEG), which records the electrical activity of the brain. The EEG measures cortical arousal and can be used to investigate activity in different parts of the brain as learning occurs.

Other physiological measures include heart rate changes, blood pressure, skin temperature, and blood or urine analysis. These measures offer valuable alternatives to self-report and behavioral measures. (Also see Cacioppo and Tassinary [1990] for a discussion of the relationship between psychological processes and physiological signals.)

EVALUATING DEPENDENT MEASURES

Each of the specific techniques for measuring or observing people has unique qualities that make it appropriate for a specific project. Measuring variables is a fundamental part of every research investigation. The purpose of measurement is to assign numbers to behaviors or events so that the numbers are related to the characteristic being investigated. We need to know that our measurement approach provides functional measures of behaviors or events. Some general considerations include reliability, validity, and reactivity.

Reliability

Reliability refers to the consistency or stability of a measure. For example, a reliable physical measurement of length yields the same dimension each time it is used. If a ruler is reliable, how tall is a standard sheet of notebook paper? You should find it is 11 inches in height every time you measure it. If you weigh yourself on a reliable bathroom scale several times in a row one morning, you will get the same result each time. If the results vary, the measuring device lacks perfect reliability and contains some "measurement error." A standardized psychological measure of intelligence is unreliable if it yields different interpretations each time the same person is assessed. Note that for concepts like intelligence, precise scores need not be replicated for reliability to be established. An intelligence test is unreliable if it measures the same person as average one week, low the next week, and bright the next week. Put simply, a reliable measure does not fluctuate randomly.

Any measure can be thought of as comprising two components: (1) a **true score,** which is the person's actual score on the variable being measured, and (2) **measurement error.** Because measures are not precise enough to be perfect, some measurement error is unavoidable. An unreliable measure of intelligence contains measurement error, providing an inaccurate indication of an individual's true intelligence. In contrast, a reliable measure of intelligence – one that contains little measurement error – yields an identical (or nearly identical) intelligence score each time the same individual is measured.

The importance of reliability is obvious. When conducting research, the researcher often measures each person only once; thus it is very important that a reliable measure is used. A single administration of the measure should closely reflect the person's true score. Researchers cannot use unreliable measures to systematically study variables or the relationships among variables.

Reliability is increased when several questions are used to measure the variable of interest. For example, a single-item measure of marital satisfaction is less reliable than a measure that contains a number of items asking about satisfaction in different ways. Reliability is most likely to be achieved when researchers use careful measurement procedures. In some research areas, this might involve carefully training observers to record behavior; in other areas, it might mean paying close attention to the way questions are phrased.

There are several ways to assess the reliability of a measure, all of which are based on **correlation coefficients.** Correlation coefficients are discussed in detail in Chapter 15; for now you should know that a correlation coefficient is a number that tells us how strongly two variables are related. The size of the coefficient ranges from 0.00, indicating no relationship, to 1.00, the strongest possible relationship. When scores on two variables are very similar, the correlation coefficient describing the strength of the relationship will be high. To assess reliability of a measure, we need to obtain at least two scores on the measure from many individuals. A high correlation then implies that the scores reflect the true score; a low correlation implies that the scores are not consistent due to measurement error. Let's examine specific methods of assessing reliability.

Test-retest reliability measures the same individuals at two points in time, usually not more than a few weeks apart. A correlation coefficient is then computed. A high correlation (over .80 or so) tells us that each individual's score on the first measure is quite similar to that individual's score on the same measure taken later. Thus, with test-retest reliability, the measure shows consistency over time. Test-retest reliability is useful if the attribute being assessed is relatively stable, such as intelligence or personality attributes. If a child takes an intelligence test twice, we expect the two test scores to be similar. In contrast, low test-retest reliability would be expected for characteristics that change frequently, such as emotional state or fatigue.

When it is impractical to take measures at two points in time, or if the measure isn't expected to be consistent over time, **split-half reliability** is a useful index. Here, a correlation is computed between scores on the first half of a measure and scores on the second half. (Items can be divided in other ways; odd numbered items versus even numbered items or random division into two sets will also split the items into two halves.) We can do this because most psychological and educational measures are made up of a number of different items. Again, if the measure is reliable, a high correlation is expected; the persons taking the test would score similarly on each half of the test. If the split-half correlation is small, the total score contains little true score and is obscured by measurement error.

Studies in which an observer records the behaviors of participants present a special problem of reliability. How do you know that the data recorded by the observers are in fact reliable? **Interobserver reliability** or **interrater reliability** can be determined by comparing the ratings of the observers. When the behavior under observation is relatively simple (e.g., observing whether a child gets up out of his chair), interobserver reliability can be calculated using the percentage of times the raters are in agreement.

Observers often code complex behaviors, such as conflict in a conversation between parents and children. If one observer codes 12 instances of conflict and a second observer codes only 8, the difference between their observations represents measurement error, and the correlation will be low. Alternatively, when there is agreement between the observers, the correlation coefficient will be high, indicating consistency among the observers.

Validity

A measure should have **validity,** which refers to the extent to which a variable has been adequately measured or manipulated. Do scores on the measure reflect the characteristic the researcher is interested in? Consider a few examples to clarify the definition. Grade point average is often used to estimate intelligence, but does GPA really measure intelligence? Depression could be measured by the amount of time spent alone, but is that the only reason people spend time alone? Creativity could be defined in terms of speed of performance on a novel problem-solving task—is this valid? Does speed really reflect creativity? There are several types of validity, each with a different purpose. As you will see, they also differ on how easy they are to establish.

Face validity is typically examined first. On the surface—literally on the face of it—does it look like the measure assesses the concept it is supposed to measure? To establish face validity, a researcher relies on commonsense judgment of whether the dependent measure appears to be appropriate. For example, a multiple-choice test based on terms from this textbook appears to have face validity as a measure of your learning. It seems like a valid approach and is clearly one used by many instructors. In a study of friendships, you are likely to ask children questions about who they play with at school, who they play with at home, what activities they engage in together, and why they are friends. Face validity is not very sophisticated, but it is useful as a first approximation of validity. Most researchers prefer to use measures that have face validity.

Criterion validity is important when the purpose of the current measure is to distinguish between individuals on the basis of some behavioral criterion. Criterion validity often serves a predictive function, to estimate how individuals will behave on some future criterion for assessment based on a current measure of behavior. Thus, high school seniors with high scores on the Scholastic Assessment Test (SAT) this year are presumed to be more likely to succeed in college later. The criterion of college performance is not currently available but is related to the existing measure, the SAT score.

Criterion validity is important in educational research because investigators frequently are concerned with predicting academic performance. The predictive value of criterion validity is also useful for other selection devices, such as evaluation of applicants for a job, a training program, or a professional license in medicine or law. In all cases, criterion validity is established when scores on the exam correlate with later success.

As an example of criterion validity, consider the recent introduction of the Fagan Test of Infant Intelligence (FTII) into the commercial market (Fagan & Shepherd, 1987; Fagan & Detterman, 1992). The FTII is a screening tool intended to identify infants at risk for cognitive delay. The FTII assesses infant information processing speed and perceptual preferences to predict a future criterion of normal cognitive development. If the Fagan test has good criterion validity, it will accurately predict infants who later have cognitive impairment, thus informing physicians and parents about the need for early intervention. If the FTII does not have good criterion validity, the test results will make inaccurate predictions, failing to identify infants at risk and perhaps falsely identifying normally developing infants. Currently, the criterion validity of the FTII is questionable (Andersson, 1996; Benasich & Bejar, 1992), with correlations between the Fagan test scores and scores on a standardized intelligence test as low as .22.

Construct validity is defined as the extent to which the operational definition of a variable reflects the theoretical concept underlying a variable. The term *construct* is another word for *concept*. Remember that an operational definition takes an abstract concept that is not directly observable and defines it in more concrete terms. Construct validity addresses a philosophical issue using empirical data—does the operational definition the researcher employed actually assess the abstract notion being investigated? Is "altruism" really reflected by sharing behavior? Is "social competence" reflected by a child's level of play? Is "love" reflected by time spent holding hands? Construct validity is difficult to establish, yet it is vital for basic theoretical research.

There are two approaches to construct validity. **Convergent validity** is demonstrated when evidence gathered from a variety of studies, using a variety of settings, participants, and methodological approaches, yields theoretically similar conclusions. When several measures of altruism (e.g., a personality test, direct observation of sharing behavior, ratings of cooperation obtained from teachers) agree with each other, we are more confident about our definition of the construct. A second approach to construct validation is **discriminant validity.** The measures of altruism should *not* relate to measures that do not theoretically assess altruism (e.g., social desirability or intelligence), showing that our measure is not measuring the wrong construct.

The multitrait-multimethod matrix (Campbell & Fiske, 1959; Kerlinger, 1986) provides a creative approach to construct validation by including at least two different ways of measuring at least two different traits in the same study. This matrix provides concurrent evidence for convergent validity (with measures of the same trait correlating) and discriminant validity (with no correlation between measures of different traits).

As you can see, the construct validity of a measure is rarely established in a single study but rather is built up over a program of research investigating the theoretical construct. As further studies are conducted, the measure may be modified, or better measures of the construct may emerge. The process of validating a measure is time-consuming, leading researchers to use measures that have already been validated. What do you do when the concept you are interested in has not been investigated systematically and no construct validation study exists? Let's see how researchers at UCLA developed a measure of loneliness.

Loneliness is an important concept to research because it is associated with many social problems, including delinquent behavior, alcoholism, depression, and physical illness. However, the concept of loneliness is difficult to manipulate experimentally, necessitating a self-report measure. Russell, Peplau, and Ferguson (1978) developed a 20-item, self-report measure of loneliness, but they were not satisfied with some aspects of their scale. Improvements to the UCLA Loneliness Scale (Russell, Peplau, & Cutrona, 1980) were needed. First, they revised the wording of items on the scale to include an equal number of items worded in the positive direction ("I feel part of a group of friends") and the negative direction ("I feel isolated from others"). Second, they established convergent validity by showing that scores on the loneliness scale were similar to other measures of social activities. The loneliness scores correlated with measures such as the amount of time spent alone each day, the number of times eating dinner alone, and the number of close friends. Third, Russell, Peplau, and Cutrona showed that the loneliness scores did not correlate with unrelated concepts such as thoughtfulness, embarrassment, and creativity.

Finally, they evaluated the correlations between loneliness and similar concepts such as depression, self-esteem, anxiety, and social desirability. Scores on the UCLA Loneliness Scale were independent of these other concepts, establishing a final measure of discriminant validity. Thus, we see that the UCLA Loneliness Scale may indeed possess construct validity and should be a good measure of loneliness.

Reactivity

A measure is said to have **reactivity** if awareness of being measured changes the individual's behavior. If the dependent measure is reactive, we don't know how the person would behave under natural circumstances. We only know how the person behaves when they know their responses are being recorded. As you can see, reactivity is a potential problem that investigators need to address regardless of their measurement technique.

Self-report measures can be reactive if respondents attempt to "look good" to the researcher by giving socially desirable responses. One possible solution is to include distracter items that ask questions about neutral topics, thus drawing attention away from the target questions. A well-constructed self-report instrument guides the respondent into a pattern of honest responding to all items. We return to this issue in Chapter 7.

Observations of behavior can lead to reactivity unless the observer is concealed. The mere presence of the observer can affect behavior, particularly with children. You may be surprised to find that even physiological measures may be reactive; just having electrodes and other recording devices attached to your body may change your physiological responses. Extending the period of observation can minimize reactivity in both of these situations; allow a warm-up period before recording data. This gives the participants time to adapt to the presence of the observer or the apparatus, and the target behavior returns to its natural level.

Using **unobtrusive measures** is another way to reduce reactivity. A measure is unobtrusive or nonreactive when participants are unaware that their behavior is being studied. This may be accomplished with technological aids, such as one-way mirrors or video cameras. Observation of behavior in public places can be unobtrusive. For example, Greenfield (1995) observed children in a science museum to determine which type of exhibit boys and girls preferred. Public records are also unobtrusive as such measures have usually been collected as part of normal record-keeping. Thus, various public health statistics; birth, marriage, and divorce records; census data; crime statistics; and so forth can be sources of nonreactive data.

Webb, Campbell, Schwartz, Sechrest, and Grove (1981) have drawn attention to a number of nonreactive measures. Many such measures involve clever ways of indirectly recording a variable. For example, an unobtrusive measure of the popularity of museum exhibits is the frequency with which tiles around each exhibit must be replaced—this technique showed that the most popular display at the Chicago Museum of Science and Industry was the chick hatching exhibit. Popularity of radio stations can be determined by asking mechanics to check the radio settings of cars in for service. A preference for male offspring can be determined by examining birth records in families; the last born is more likely to be male. A clever nonreactive measure of television viewing patterns relies on a city's water pressure records. In theory, water pressure should be high when people are watching a program because viewers cannot be using water at the same time they are watching television. During commercial breaks or when the program ends, water pressure should go down as viewers get a drink of water, take a shower, or wash the dishes.

Sir Francis Galton, a pioneer in experimental psychology, believed that anything and everything was measurable, including the boringness of lectures. A nonreactive measure was essential—if the lecturer knew about Galton's observation, the lecture style could clearly change. Galton counted the number of fidgets displayed by members of the audience as an indication of "boringness" (Galton, 1909). Even Galton, however, cautions that "these observations should be confined to persons of middle age. Children are rarely still, while elderly philosophers will sometimes remain rigid for minutes altogether" (p. 278).

SCALES OF MEASUREMENT

We conclude the chapter with a discussion of scales of measurement. Whenever a variable is studied, there is an operational definition of the variable. The operational definition is the specific method used to manipulate or measure the variable. There must be at least two values or levels of the variable. The levels can be conceptualized as a scale that uses one of four kinds of measurement: nominal, ordinal, interval, and ratio scales. The measurement scale is important (1) for interpreting the meaning of a particular score and (2) for selecting the appropriate statistical analysis.

Nominal scales use mutually exclusive categories or groups that differ from each other. Nominal variables are qualitative because they have no numerical or quantitative properties. The levels of nominal variables simply represent the "name" for each group. An obvious example is the variable of sex or gender. A person is labeled as either male or female. Another example is the classification of adults into categories of marital status (e.g., single, married, divorced, widowed). Numerical values can be assigned to these categories, but the data remain nominal. If you let "1" represent single, "2" represent married, "3" represent divorced, and so on, this does not imply that divorced individuals have three times as much "marital status" as people who are single. The numbers serve an identification purpose but cannot be used for arithmetic comparisons.

Ordinal scales allow us to rank order the levels of the variable being studied and therefore involve quantitative comparisons. One example of an ordinal scale is provided by the movie rating system used in the television section of our local newspapers. Movies are given one, two, three, or four stars, with more stars denoting a higher-quality film. (Viewer beware of a movie with no stars!) The number of stars provides a meaningful numerical measure of movie quality such that a value of 3 represents more movie quality than a value of 1 or 2.

With the movie ranking system we can distinguish high-quality movies from low-quality movies. However, we do not know how far apart the ranks are. Is a four-star movie twice as good as a two-star feature? The same thing is true about competitions in high school, such as an academic decathlon or a music festival. Knowing which school finished first, second, or third does not tell you how far apart the scores were. It is possible that the top two schools finished very close together, with a third school trailing behind substantially. The point is, based only on the rank order, you have no information about the size of the intervals between the categories. Thus, you cannot perform mathematical calculations on ordinal data; you are limited to comparisons of "greater than" and "less than" with quantitative ordinal data.

The **interval scale** goes one step further than ordinal measures. In addition to placing numbers in order, the differences between the numbers on an interval scale are equal in size. For example, the difference between 60 and 70 on the scale is the same size interval as the difference between 30 and 40. Because the intervals are equal, you can do basic mathematical calculations on interval data. The limiting feature of an interval scale is that it has no true zero, which restricts interpretation somewhat. Let's look at a few examples.

A household thermometer measures temperature on an interval scale. The difference in temperature between 40° and 50° is the same as the difference between 70° and 80°. However, there is no absolute zero on the Fahrenheit or Celsius scale that indicates the absence of temperature. The zero on an interval scale is only an arbitrary reference point. This means that we cannot form ratios of the numbers on interval scales. That is, we cannot say that one number on the scale represents twice as much (or three times as much, and so forth) temperature as another number. You cannot say, for example, that 60° is twice as warm as 30°.

A measure of happiness may qualify as an interval scale. The difference between scores of 20 and 30 on such a scale may be psychologically the same as the difference between scores of 40 and 50. However, we cannot say that the person who scores 40 is twice as happy as the person who scores 20, because there is no absolute zero to indicate the absence of happiness. Without a true zero, researchers must be careful when interpreting their data.

In the behavioral sciences, it may be difficult to know whether an ordinal or an interval scale is being used. However, it is often useful to assume that the variable is being measured on an interval scale, because interval scales allow for more sophisticated statistical treatments than do ordinal scales. Of course, if the measure is a rank ordering (for example, a teacher's ranking of students on the basis of popularity), an ordinal scale is clearly being used.

Ratio scales have all the properties of an interval scale, with the addition of an absolute zero point. Examples include many physical measurements, such as time, distance, and height. When measuring time, a zero point means that no time has elapsed. Because of the true zero, ratios can be calculated by dividing one score by another. A person who completes a task in 6 minutes is "twice as fast" as a person who finishes in 12 minutes.

Many variables in developmental, family, and educational research—such as intelligence, parental involvement, and prosocial behavior—rely on less precise measurement. Thus, you are more likely to read about nominal, ordinal, and interval scales than ratio scales. Suppose you are interested in creativity. If your goal is to identify creative children in a class, nominal data is sufficient (creative versus not creative). If your goal is to identify the three most creative children, an ordinal scale tells you that Tyler is more creative than Jamie, who in turn is more creative than Keisha. However, if you want to know how much creativity Tyler, Jamie, and Keisha have, an interval measure of creativity is appropriate. A ratio scale would only be needed if your goal was to identify one child as twice as creative as another child.

SUMMARY

A variable is a general class or category of events, situations, responses, or characteristics of individuals. For each variable, specific instances will vary. Every variable has two or more values or levels. For example, gender has two values; income has many values. Researchers must operationally define variables to study them. The operational definition of a variable specifies the operation used to measure or manipulate a concept. Both independent and dependent variables need operational definitions. In experiments, the independent variable is considered to be the manipulated variable and the "cause" of behavior. The dependent variable is the observed variable that measures the participant's response. Independent variables have effects on dependent variables.

Self-report measures are participants' responses to questions that are posed either on a questionnaire or by an interviewer. Behavioral measures are direct measures of behavior and include measures of frequency, rate, duration, preference, and reaction time. Physiological measures allow researchers to examine responses of the body, including measures such as the GSR, EEG, and body temperature.

Measures of behavior must be reliable. Reliability refers to the consistency or stability of a measure. Reliability is assessed in a variety of ways: test-retest, split-half, and interobserver and interrater reliability. Measures should also have validity. Validity is the extent to which a variable has been adequately measured or manipulated. Face validity refers to whether the measure appears to be a good indicator of the variable being measured. Criterion validity is the extent to which a measure relates to some behavioral criterion, which is quite important when a test is used to predict future behavior. Construct validity is the extent to which a measure of a variable relates to other variables that are theoretically expected to be related.

A measure is reactive if awareness of being measured changes a person's behavior. Reactivity can be reduced by allowing time for participants to adapt to the measuring device and by using unobtrusive measures in which participants are unaware of being measured.

Variables are measured on four kinds of measurement scales. Nominal scales have no quantitative properties; they simply assign names to different categories or groups. Ordinal scales rank order the levels of the variable along a numeric continuum, but there is no information about the size of the intervals between the numbers on the scale. With interval scales, the intervals between the numbers are equal in size. With ratio scales, an absolute zero point is added to the properties of the interval scale. The type of scale used in a study is important for interpreting scores and for determining the appropriate statistical analysis.

KEY TERMS

behavioral measure
closed-ended question
construct validity
convergent validity
correlation coefficient
criterion validity
dependent variable
discriminant validity
face validity
independent variable
individual difference
  variable

interobserver reliability
interrater reliability
interval scale
manipulated variable
measurement error
nominal scale
open-ended question
operational definition
ordinal scale
physiological measure
ratio scale
reactivity

reliability
response variable
self-report measure
situational variable
split-half reliability
subject variable
test-retest reliability
true score
unobtrusive measure
validity
variable

REVIEW QUESTIONS

1. What is a variable? List at least two different variables that are characteristics of (a) situations, (b) individuals, and (c) responses. Specify the levels of each variable.

2. What is an operational definition of a variable? Try to think of two operational definitions for each variable you listed in question 1.

3. What is the difference between an independent variable and a dependent variable?

4. Identify the independent and dependent variables in the following research examples:
   a. Adults watch a movie either alone or with others and then rate the violent content of the movie.
   b. Some elementary school teachers were told that a child's parents were college graduates, and other teachers were told that the child's parents had not finished high school. Teachers then rated the child's academic potential.
   c. Working mothers and mothers who do not work outside the home reported how much time they spend with their children on school nights.

5. What is a self-report measure?

6. When would a researcher use an open-ended or a closed-ended question?

7. Define behavioral measures.

8. How can you assess test anxiety with a self-report measure? with a behavioral measure? with a physiological measure?

9. What is meant by the reliability of a measure?

10. What is meant by validity of a measure? Distinguish between face validity and construct validity.

11. What is a reactive measure?

12. For each variable listed below, identify whether a nominal, ordinal, interval, or ratio scale is used.
    a. Numbers on the jerseys of athletes on your basketball team
    b. Intelligence test scores
    c. Your speeds on a 50-yard dash
    d. The number of hours you spent studying each day last week
    e. The most popular names for girls: (1) Jennifer, (2) Michelle, (3) Heather, and (4) Kimberly
    f. Ratings of marital conflict on a scale of 1 = hardly at all to 7 = all the time

CHAPTER 5

Correlational and Experimental Methods

As noted in Chapter 1, scientists conduct research investigations to describe, explain, and predict behavior. Most often, research focuses on the relationship between variables. In this chapter we explore such relationships and the general methods for studying them.

TYPES OF RELATIONSHIPS

A common reason for doing research is to establish relationships between variables. A relationship exists between variables when the two variables change together systematically. Do the values of one variable change when the variables of the other variable change? As age increases, does the amount of cooperative play increase? Does viewing television violence result in greater aggressiveness? Does community involvement result in greater life satisfaction among the elderly?

For the purpose of describing relationships, we start by discussing relationships in which both variables have true numeric properties. Recall that variables measured on interval or ratio scales have numeric properties; nominal and ordinal data do not. When both variables have values along a numeric scale, many different "shapes" can describe their relationship. These relationships are best illustrated by line graphs that show the way changes in one variable are accompanied by changes in a second variable. Four common relationships are found in research: the positive linear relationship, the negative linear relationship, the curvilinear relationship, and finally, no relationship between the variables. Figure 5.1 shows these four types of relationships.

On each graph in Figure 5.1 there is a horizontal axis and a vertical axis. Values of the first variable are placed on the horizontal axis, labeled from low to high. Values of the second variable are placed on the vertical axis, which is also labeled from low to high. As you may remember from algebra, each point on the graph represents a combination of two scores, one from each variable. Which variable should you place on the horizontal axis? The relationships we are discussing here involve two dependent variables, and the line on the graph will be the same

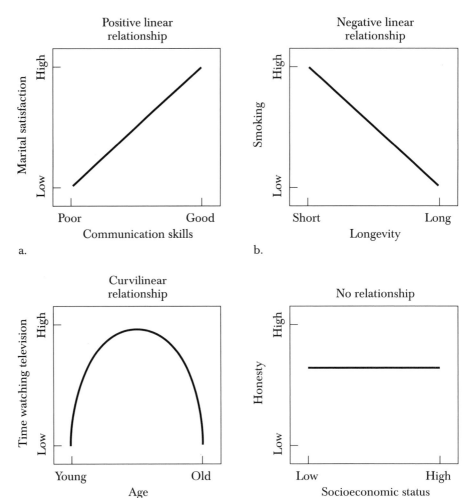

Figure 5.1
Four common
types of relation-
ships found in re-
search: (a) a positive
linear relationship,
(b) a negative linear
relationship, (c) a
curvilinear relation-
ship, and (d) no
relationship

regardless of which variable is placed on the horizontal axis. Theoretically it may make sense for one to be placed on the horizontal axis (e.g., age and time variables are usually placed on the horizontal axis), but the interpretation is not affected.

Positive Linear Relationship

In a **positive linear relationship,** increases in the value of one variable are associated with increases in the value of the second variable. This means that low scores on one variable correspond to low scores on the other variable. As seen in Figure 5.1a, a positive relationship is depicted graphically by a line that slants upward to the right. The graph shows the relationship between communication skills and marital satisfaction. When communication skills are poor, marital satisfaction is typically low. What happens with improved communication skills? Based on your own experience, you probably know that better communication skills are associated with higher marital satisfaction. Height and weight are classic examples of a positive relationship—as a child grows taller, the child also increases in weight. Try to think of other possible positive relationships. Do you think there is a positive relationship between health and life satisfaction? between maternal education and children's cognitive development?

Negative Linear Relationship

Variables can also be negatively related. In a **negative linear relationship,** increases in the value of one variable are associated with decreases in the value of the other variable. As seen in Figure 5.1b, a negative, or inverse, relationship is depicted graphically by a line that slants down to the right. The graph illustrates the relationship between longevity and smoking. On average, shorter life spans are associated with higher frequency of smoking. The reverse is true for longer life spans; adults who live longer tend to be nonsmokers.

In the negative relationship, the two variables are systematically related, just as in a positive relationship, but the direction of the relationship is reversed. Try to think of other possible negative relationships. How does your recall for an event (such as last week's lecture in this class) change over time—how much do you remember this week? How much will you remember next week? next year?

Curvilinear Relationship

In a **curvilinear relationship,** increases in the values of one variable are accompanied by both increases and decreases in the values of the other variable. In other words, there is a positive relationship when you examine part of the relationship, and a negative relationship for the other part. Figure 5.1c shows a curvilinear relationship between time spent watching television and age (Anderson, Lorch, Field, Collins, & Nathan, 1986). This particular relationship is called an *inverted-U relationship.* The inverted-U includes a positive relationship followed by a negative relationship. Hours per week watching TV increases with age (the positive relationship), reaches a peak in middle childhood, then gradually declines in adulthood as age continues to increase.

The curvilinear relationship can also take a U-shape. In this case, at first the relationship is negative, with increases in one variable related to decreases in the second variable. Then, after some point a positive relationship emerges. A fun example here is the relationship between excitement over an impending family event (such as a wedding or a new baby) and time elapsed. When plans are first made for the event, little time has elapsed, the event is far in the future, and excitement levels are high. Then, as the number of weeks increases and the event gradually gets nearer, excitement diminishes amidst all the decisions to be made. Excitement reaches a definite low. (In wedding planning this is the "let's elope" phase!) After this, excitement starts to increase again as the weeks go by until the long-awaited event finally arrives and excitement returns to its initial high level.

No Relationship

When there is no relationship between the two variables, the graph is simply a flat line. Unrelated variables vary independently of one another, so that values of one variable are not associated with any particular changes in the other one. Figure 5.1d illustrates the relationship between honesty and socioeconomic status. As we look at individuals with increasing socioeconomic status, we do not find any specific increase in their honesty. You are just as likely to find an honest person struggling to make ends meet as an honest person with substantial financial resources. Dishonesty is an equal opportunity variable—it is not related to your income level.

These graphs illustrate several kinds of shapes; almost any shape can describe the relationship between two variables. Other relationships are described by more complicated shapes than those in Figure 5.1. Remember that these are general patterns. Even if a positive linear relationship exists, that does not necessarily mean that everyone who scores high on one variable will also score high on the second variable. Individual deviations from the general pattern are possible.

Correlation Coefficient

In addition to knowing the general type of relationship between two variables, it is also necessary to know the strength of the relationship. That is, we need to know the size of the correlation between the variables. Sometimes two variables are strongly related to each other, and there is very little deviation from the general pattern. At other times the two variables are not highly correlated. In Chapter 4 we introduced the correlation coefficient as a way to assess reliability of dependent measures. The Pearson correlation coefficient, represented by the letter r, tells us how strongly two variables are related. The value of a correlation ranges between -1.00 and $+1.00$.

Two properties of the Pearson r are important for interpretation: (1) the size of the correlation and (2) the sign of the correlation. The *size* of the coefficient indicates the strength of the relationship. A correlation of zero means that the variables are not related at all and would be graphically depicted as the flat line in Figure 5.1d. As the magnitude of the correlation increases toward -1.00 or $+1.00$, the relationship is stronger. A correlation of $+.81$ is stronger than a correlation of $+.57$. The *sign* of the correlation indicates the direction of the relationship, positive or negative. A positive correlation indicates a positive linear relationship, as shown in Figure 5.1a. A negative correlation indicates a negative linear relationship, as shown in Figure 5.1b. We will return to this topic in Chapter 15.

STUDYING RELATIONSHIPS

There are two general approaches to the study of relationships among variables: the correlational method and the experimental method. When the **correlational method** is used, the researcher observes the behavior of interest as it occurs naturally, without manipulating independent variables. This may be done by asking people to describe their behavior, by directly observing behavior, or even by examining various public records such as census data. For example, Stevenson and his colleagues (Chen & Stevenson, 1995; Stevenson, Lee, Chen, & Lummis, 1990; Stigler, Lee, & Stevenson, 1987) used a correlational approach to investigate the academic environment of schools in Japan, Taiwan, and the United States.

Many variables were assessed as they naturally occurred: children's mathematics achievement, number of classroom hours spent on instruction in mathematics and language arts, time spent in off-task activities, and time spent listening to the teacher.

In contrast, the **experimental method** involves manipulation of variables. The researcher directly manipulates one or more variables by establishing the conditions for studying behavior; the behavior is then observed under the different conditions. For example, Crook and West (1990) used an experiment to assess memory for names in adults. Crook and West devised an "everyday" memory situation, learning the names for faces of people introduced to the participants on videotape. Adults ages 18 to 90 years viewed either 4, 6, or 14 sets of names and faces to learn. The researcher measured the number of correct name–face pairs. Overall, performance declines were most evident in the large sets of names. With adults ages 70 to 90 years, even a small set of 4 names was difficult to remember. The study is important because it shows that it is normal for adults (especially older adults) to be challenged by the everyday task of learning names of people they are introduced to—so it's no wonder your professors have trouble learning your names!

THE CORRELATIONAL METHOD

In a correlational study of the relationship between two variables, the researcher would operationally define the two variables and measure people on those variables. Of course, there are many different ways of operationally defining either of these variables. Thus, in a study of the relationship between viewing television violence and aggression, a researcher might (1) have teachers rate the children on their aggressiveness at school and (2) ask children to list their favorite television programs. Using a scoring system that indexes violence in various television programs, the amount of violent programming that each child watches can be determined. At this point each child has scores on two variables, one for the teacher rating and one for the television violence rating. The researcher wants to know if there is a relationship between the two variables: Are the children who prefer violent programs more aggressive?

Suppose such a study is conducted and it is found that there is a positive relationship between preference for television violence and aggressiveness. You might be tempted at this point to conclude that watching violent television causes aggressiveness. However, two problems arise when interpreting results obtained using the correlational method: (1) the direction of cause and effect and (2) the third variable problem.

Direction of Cause and Effect

The first problem that arises when interpreting correlational results is determining which variable caused the other. A correlation indicates that the variables are related, but it is not clear which variable is the "cause" and which variable is the "effect." Can we safely conclude that watching televised violence caused the aggressive behavior, or is it possible that aggressive people like to watch violent

BOX 5.1   RESEARCH IN ACTION

A Correlational Study

Unemployment is a source of stress in families, and single African American mothers are at particular risk for unemployment. This concern led McLoyd, Jayaratne, Ceballo, and Borquez (1994) to investigate the impact of family economic stressors on adolescent socioemotional functioning. McLoyd et al. interviewed single African American mothers and their seventh- and eighth-grade children. Many variables were assessed, including self-report measures of (1) economic variables (e.g., employment history, financial strain), (2) maternal depression and parenting behaviors, and (3) the adolescents' emotional functioning (e.g., depression, general anxiety, and self-esteem). This is a correlational design because all of the variables were observed as they naturally occurred, without manipulation or intervention by the researchers.

A positive correlation ($r = +.56$, $p < .001$) was found between frequency of aversive maternal punishment and the mother's negative perceptions of her role. This means that mothers who reported more aversive discipline (e.g., yelling or hitting the child or threatening to send the child to live with someone else) also reported more negative feelings about being mothers, such as wishing they had fewer responsibilities and fewer demands on their time. Because the study is correlational, we cannot determine which comes first—negative punishment techniques or negative self-perceptions. Does maternal dissatisfaction cause a greater reliance on punitive disciplinary practices? Or does the use of punitive disciplinary practices cause maternal dissatisfaction?

As it turns out, McLoyd et al. determined that both maternal negative perceptions and aversive punishment are byproducts of a third variable, maternal depression. Maternal depression is a result of financial strain and unemployment. McLoyd et al. can address the issue of causality by using more sophisticated statistical tools. We return to this topic in Chapter 15 when we discuss structural models.

programs? There are plausible reasons for either pattern of cause and effect. When the correlational approach is used, it is impossible to determine that television violence causes aggression. This is an important limitation, leading to the familiar adage "correlation does not imply causation." Regardless of the magnitude of a particular correlation coefficient, direction of causality cannot be determined when two variables are measured at the same point in time.

The Third Variable Problem

The second problem with the correlational method is the **third variable problem**—the possibility that some other third or extraneous variable could be responsible for the observed relationship. Box 5.1 highlights this problem in assigning causality. In a correlational study, it is possible that the two variables the researcher measured are not directly related at all.

Television violence causes aggression

    TV violence ⟶ Aggression

Aggression causes preference for violent television

    Aggression ⟶ TV violence

Amount of parental supervision causes both violent television viewing
and aggressiveness

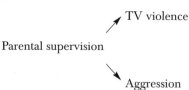

                        TV violence

Parental supervision

                      Aggression

Figure 5.2
Possible reasons for a
relationship between
television violence
viewing and aggres-
sion in a correla-
tional study

In a study on television violence and aggression, an observed relationship between the variables might be due to extraneous variables that the researcher did
not even measure. One possible extraneous variable is the amount of parental supervision. As seen in Figure 5.2, it is possible that children with little parental supervision watch more violent television and are more aggressive. Lack of parental
supervision could lead to all sorts of undesirable behaviors, including watching
violent television and aggression. A second possible extraneous variable is role
modeling by the parents. Aggressive children who watch violent television may
have aggressive parents who watch violent television. In this case, the children
learned both behaviors from their parents, and the parents serve as the "cause."
Biological causes must also be considered; there may be hormonal differences
that contribute to the preference for violence and to the aggression.

There are many alternative explanations for the link between children's
aggression and their preferences for television violence. When a researcher measures only two variables, it is not possible to rule out these competing explanations. Direction of cause and effect and the third variable problem represent
serious limitations of the correlational method. Often they are not considered in
media summaries of research results with headlines such as "Children whose
mothers drink to excess get injured more" implying causality (Children Whose
Mothers, 1992). The informed consumer should view such reports with skepti-
cism, carefully considering alternative explanations. Does alcoholism really *cause*
children to have more broken bones, contusions, and concussions? What is a
more likely cause of the increased number of injuries?

THE EXPERIMENTAL METHOD

The second approach to the study of relationships between variables is called the
experimental method. In contrast to the correlational method, the experimental
method involves manipulation of the variables. Using the experimental method,

a researcher interested in the effects of television violence on aggression might assign one group of children to a violent program condition in which they watched a predetermined show such as a segment of *Mighty Morphin Power Rangers*. Another group of children assigned to a nonviolent program condition would watch television for the same amount of time, but the content would differ, for example, an episode of *Touched by an Angel*. The researcher would then measure the amount of aggressive behavior during a free play episode to determine whether watching television violence did in fact affect their aggressive behavior.

With the experimental method, it is easier to infer that one variable caused the other because of (1) control of the experimental situation and (2) random assignment of participants to experimental groups.

Experimental Control

The experimental method makes it easier to infer the direction of cause and effect because the researcher determines the sequence of events and the experimental situation. This is called **experimental control.** Careful control is exercised to make sure that all participants are treated equally in all respects except their exposure to the independent variable. All participants are measured on the same outcome variable. Then, if the two groups differ on the dependent measure, the researcher concludes that the experimental manipulation caused the difference in the behavior.

In our hypothetical study of children's aggression, children in the violent and nonviolent program condition must watch TV for the same amount of time, at the same time of day, in groups of the same size. This controls for the possible extraneous variables of fatigue or group dynamics contributing to the observed aggression. The children in each group will be approximately the same age, with gender evenly distributed. To control for previous familiarity, all children should be previously acquainted with each other or all must be unacquainted with each other. All observations of the children's aggression should take place in the same playroom or playground so there are no differences in play equipment that may influence the results. Then, when there is a difference between the groups in aggression, one can be sure that the difference is the result of the type of television program rather than some other variable that was not held constant.

Randomization

Sometimes it is difficult to keep a variable constant. The most obvious such variable is any characteristic of the participants. In our study of television violence, the children in the two groups may differ on an extraneous variable, such as previous viewing history or parenting style. This difference could obscure the actual relationship between TV violence and aggression. How can the researcher eliminate the influence of such extraneous variables?

Any variable that cannot be held constant is controlled by making sure that the effects of the variable are random. Through **randomization,** the influence of any extraneous variable does not differ in the experimental conditions. In this way, children who routinely watch *Teenage Mutant Ninja Turtles* would be randomly divided among the two groups. **Random assignment** ensures that the extraneous variable is just as likely to affect one experimental group as it is to affect the other group. To eliminate the influence of individual characteristics, the participants are assigned to the two groups in a random fashion. As a result, individual characteristics such as intelligence, socioeconomic status, parenting style, and religious beliefs are equivalent in both groups.

Not all individual characteristics are likely to affect the relationship between TV violence and aggression. However, the researcher does not have a "crystal ball" and does not know in advance which variables will actually be important. That is why randomization is so valuable—it evenly distributes a host of individual features that the researcher might not even think about measuring or holding constant. This ability to randomly assign people to groups is an important difference between the experimental and correlational methods.

Direct control and randomization reduce the influence of any extraneous variables. Thus, the experimental method allows a relatively unambiguous interpretation of the results. Any difference between groups on the observed variable can be confidently attributed to the influence of the manipulated variable.

DISADVANTAGES OF THE EXPERIMENTAL METHOD

Thus far, the advantages of the experimental method have been stressed. However, there are disadvantages to experiments and many good reasons for using methods other than experiments. These reasons include (1) artificiality of experiments, (2) ethical considerations, (3) description of behavior, and (4) prediction of behavior. When researchers choose a methodology to study a problem, they must weigh the advantages and disadvantages in the context of the overall goals of the research.

Artificiality of Experiments

Most experiments take place in the carefully controlled confines of a laboratory. The "laboratory" may be a starkly furnished room at the university, a cubicle with high tech computerized equipment, or a playroom for children complete with one-way observation windows. In all cases, the researchers have predetermined the set-up of the physical environment, and outside influences, such as unexpected visitors, ringing telephones, and distracting surroundings, can be controlled to reduce extraneous influences on the participants. This may be especially important with young children, who are very curious and easily distracted by peripheral events. Box 5.2 describes one successful experimental study with very young children.

However, the high degree of control and the laboratory setting create an artificial atmosphere that may limit either the questions that can be addressed or the generality of the results. The problem of artificiality prompted a prominent developmentalist, Urie Bronfenbrenner (1977), to criticize the experimental method as "the science of the strange behavior of children in strange situations with strange adults for the briefest possible periods of time" (p. 513). Bronfenbrenner

BOX 5.2   RESEARCH IN ACTION

An Experimental Study

Evelyn Thoman, a psychologist at the University of Connecticut, has been studying sleeping and breathing problems in premature infants for more than a decade. She designed a "breathing bear" that is placed in the isolette as a companion for infants born too soon. The soft, plush blue bear is connected to a pump outside the crib that allows the bear to "breathe" in rhythm with the infant's own breathing. In her first study (Thoman & Graham, 1986) she randomly assigned premature infants to three experimental conditions: a breathing bear, a nonbreathing bear, and a no-bear group. No differences were found between the nonbreathing bear and the no-bear groups, so the no-bear group was dropped from further study. Thoman has repeatedly found positive benefits of the breathing bear.

In a recent investigation, Thoman, Hammond, Affleck, and DeSilva (1995) found differences between breathing bear and nonbreathing bear babies after only two weeks. Breathing bear infants (35 weeks chronological age) were less wakeful, spent more time in quiet sleep, startled less often in their sleep, and cried less than nonbreathing bear babies. They were also more likely to smile during sleep than nonbreathing bear infants. The results suggest that the breathing bear facilitates the regulation of sleep and wake states, an important developmental milestone for neonates. Using the experimental approach, Thoman et al. identified a valuable clinical tool for intervening with premature infants. In addition, the breathing bear may be useful for infants at risk for sudden infant death syndrome, a little-understood disorder associated with an interruption in breathing.

is a contextual theorist who asserts that natural environments such as family, friends, and school should be investigated because they are the major influence on development. Only by examining behavior in natural settings will research findings have **ecological validity,** meaning that researchers have accurately represented behavior as it would naturally occur.

A **field experiment** is an alternative that counters the problem of artificiality. In a field experiment, the independent variable is manipulated in natural settings, such as a school, hospital, or home. As in any experiment, the researcher attempts to control all extraneous variables via either randomization or experimental control. The advantage of the field experiment is that the independent variable is investigated in a natural context. The disadvantage is that the researcher loses the ability to directly control many aspects of the situation. The laboratory experiment permits researchers to more easily keep extraneous variables constant, thereby eliminating their influence on the outcome of the experiment. Of course, it is precisely this control that leads to the artificiality of the laboratory investigation.

The importance of context is illustrated by Crockenberg and Litman's (1991) investigation of the impact of maternal employment on young children. Em-

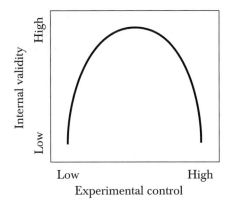

Figure 5.3
The relationship between control and internal validity

ployed and nonemployed mothers of 2-year-olds were observed in two settings, at home during mealtime and in the laboratory during a clean-up task. Negative effects of maternal employment emerged only in the laboratory. Employed mothers who were dissatisfied with their work role used more power assertive techniques, such as criticizing, threatening, or punishing, to get their children to comply with their requests to put away toys. In contrast, in the home setting the employed mothers used less power assertion than nonemployed mothers. Despite the lack of control in the home, important information was gained by using the field setting. If the researchers had restricted their study to the more controlled lab setting, they would have misrepresented the impact of maternal employment on young children.

Control and internal validity are related in a curvilinear fashion, so you do not want too much or too little control. This relationship is shown in Figure 5.3. With low control, there is low internal validity in the experiment—too many possible extraneous variables may confound the experiment. The laboratory situation, with high control, also may be criticized for low internal validity due to the artificial setting. Optimal internal validity then is usually attained with a middle-of-the-road approach to control—not too much, and not too little.

Ethical Considerations

A second reason many of the most important variables in human development and family relations are studied using the correlational method is that it would be unethical to use the experimental method. For example, it is impractical to manipulate child-rearing practices with the experimental method. Even if it were possible to assign parents randomly to two child-rearing conditions, such as using withdrawal of love versus physical types of punishment, the manipulation would be unethical. Instead of manipulating variables such as child-rearing techniques, researchers usually study them as they occur in natural settings. Many important research areas present similar problems: for example, studies of the effects of abuse in a family unit, divorce and its consequences, and the impact of maternal employment on children. These problems need to be studied, and generally the only techniques possible are descriptive methods.

Many variables cannot be manipulated at all, yet they are of paramount concern for developmentalists. These variables are subject variables, which are characteristics of persons, such as marital status, birth order, intelligence, gender, or personality. When subject variables are studied, the variables are measured (not manipulated). Subject variables are easy to recognize: If you cannot randomly assign a characteristic to a person, it is undoubtedly a subject variable. Consider a simple experiment that assesses gender differences in compliance—can you randomly assign children to be in the "boy" group or the "girl" group? Obviously, you must form groups on the basis of the preexisting characteristic; thus the variable is measured in the participant. Personality attributes present the same difficulty because you cannot randomly assign people to be shy, self-confident, or creative. To study a personality characteristic such as shyness, first you need to measure the variable, and then form groups based on the values you obtain.

To illustrate, consider a study examining the educational aspirations of African American early adolescents (Ford & Harris, 1996). The fifth and sixth graders were assigned to (1) gifted, (2) potentially gifted, and (3) regular education classrooms. Group membership was based on the school district's criteria for identifying children as gifted or potentially gifted. Because the experimenter did not manipulate this variable and could not randomly assign adolescents to these groups, the classroom membership constitutes a subject variable. Overall, Black adolescents in each group reported a high regard for school achievement and working hard. However, the gifted Black students were more achievement-oriented and perceived stronger parental support for achievement. In addition, the regular education students reported more negative peer pressures and were the least optimistic about their future.

Description of Behavior

A major goal of science is to provide an accurate description of events. The issues that experiments address are not really relevant to the primary goal of description. A classic example of descriptive research in child development comes from the work of Jean Piaget, who carefully observed the behavior of his own children as they matured and described in detail the changes in their ways of thinking about and responding to their environment (Piaget, 1952). Piaget's descriptions and his interpretations of his observations resulted in an important theory of cognitive development that greatly increased our understanding of this topic.

Cross-cultural research is often descriptive. MacPhee, Fritz, and Miller-Heyl (1996) examined cultural influences on child-rearing practices by comparing American Indian, Hispanic, and Anglo-American caregivers of preschool-aged children. Parents and guardians described their social networks to identify friends and relatives that they relied on for resources and support. The descriptions indicate that American Indian parents interact frequently with a large network of extended kin and siblings, Hispanic parents rely on immediate kin, and Anglo-American parents rely more on friends than the other groups. These results highlight the value of descriptive study and the importance of considering cultural ideologies.

Prediction of Behavior

In many real-life situations, a major concern is to make a successful prediction about a person's future behavior—for example, success in school, ability to learn a new job, and probable interest in various major fields of study in college. Questions about prediction cannot be answered with an experimental approach. The correlational method is appropriate when predicting behavior.

When researchers develop measures designed to predict future behavior, they must conduct research to demonstrate that the measure does, in fact, relate to the behavior in question. You may recognize this as another aspect of the construct validity of a measure. In such circumstances, it is possible to design measures that increase the accuracy of predicting future behavior. School counselors can give tests to decide whether students should be in "enriched" classroom programs; employers can test job applicants to help determine whether they should be hired; and college students can take tests that help them decide on a major. These types of measures can lead to better decisions for many people.

SUMMARY

There are four general types of relationships between variables. In a positive relationship, increases in the value of one variable are accompanied by increases in the value of the other variable. In a negative relationship, increases in the value of one variable are accompanied by decreases in the value of the other variable. In a curvilinear relationship, increases in one variable are accompanied by both increases and decreases in the other variable. When there is no relationship, increases in one variable are not accompanied by any systematic changes in the other variable.

The correlation coefficient describes the relationship between two variables. The size of the correlation indicates the strength of the relationship, with values closer to $+1.00$ or -1.00 indicating strong relationships. Values close to 0.00 indicate no relationship. The sign of the correlation indicates the direction of the relationship, positive or negative.

There are two general ways of studying relationships between variables. Correlational research is descriptive and nonmanipulated, involving observation or measurement of variables as they naturally occur. Two problems with the correlational method are (1) determining the direction of cause and effect and (2) the possibility that extraneous third variables influenced the results.

Experimental research involves manipulation of variables, control of the experimental situation, and random assignment of participants. Using the experimental method, it is easier to infer that one variable caused the other. A major drawback of experimental studies is their artificiality. However, experiments can be conducted in field settings. The experimental method cannot be used to address many important questions because it would be unethical or impractical to manipulate variables. Experimental methods are also not appropriate for description and prediction of behavior. There is no single best method for studying behavior. Sometimes an experiment is the best approach; however, often a descriptive approach is preferable.

KEY TERMS

correlational method
curvilinear relationship
ecological validity
experimental control
experimental method

field experiment
negative linear
 relationship
positive linear
 relationship

random assignment
randomization
third variable problem

REVIEW QUESTIONS

1. Describe the four general types of relationships between variables. Draw graphs depicting these relationships.
2. What type of relationship would you expect between the following variables:
   a. parental supervision and childhood injury
   b. accuracy of recall and stress
   c. musical ability and athletic ability
   d. educational degree and income
   e. birth complications and prenatal doctor visits
3. Knowing that weak correlations are close to zero, which one is stronger, $-.65$ or $+.42$? Why?
4. What is the difference between the correlational method and the experimental method?
5. What is meant by the problem of direction of cause and effect and the third variable problem?
6. How do direct experimental control and randomization influence the possible effects of extraneous variables?
7. What are some problems with the experimental method?
8. Distinguish between laboratory and field experiments.
9. What are some reasons for using the correlational method to study relationships between variables?
10. You observe that classmates who take morning classes get better grades than classmates who take evening classes.
    a. What are two possible explanations for this correlational observation?
    b. How can you investigate this relationship using a correlational approach?
    c. How can you investigate this relationship using an experimental approach?

CHAPTER 6　◆

Descriptive Methods

Description is the first goal of scientific inquiry. In this chapter and the next one we explore research methods that describe behavior. Such descriptive techniques may involve directly observing behavior, asking people to describe their behavior, or examining existing records of behavior, such as census data or hospital records. In this chapter we consider observational research, including field observation and systematic observation, case studies, and archival research. Chapter 7 considers survey research.

WHY CONDUCT DESCRIPTIVE STUDIES?

The distinction between descriptive and experimental methods was made in Chapter 5. In contrast to the experimental method, descriptive methods do not manipulate any of the variables of interest. Using a correlational approach, descriptive methods may be useful when ethical and practical considerations make the use of any other method impossible. Behaviors are observed as they occur naturally. Descriptive methods may be used to (1) describe behavior, (2) explore a phenomenon, and (3) test hypotheses about behavior.

First, descriptive methods may be used to provide an accurate description of events. Description is a major goal of scientific inquiry. Because behavior is so varied and occurs in so many settings, social scientists have developed many ways of achieving this goal. Observation, case studies, and surveys provide descriptions of behavior. Such descriptions allow us to understand more fully the behaviors in question.

Second, descriptive studies may be used simply to explore a phenomenon. Sometimes researchers begin with nothing more than an intense curiosity about some phenomenon. They may observe and interview people with the aim of finding out what people think, what variables are important, and what questions should be asked in future research.

Third, descriptive methods may be used in correlational studies designed to test hypotheses about the relationships between variables. However, because correlational methods are used, causal conclusions cannot be made about the reasons for the relationships examined.

For example, if you are interested in the general topic of women who return to college after many years as homemakers, you may begin by exploring the phenomenon. You might talk to a number of women about their experiences, telephone the directors of women's centers at several colleges, and ask professors to tell you their impressions of returning women students. You may also explore data available from college admissions officers on the age distribution of women students over the past 10 or 20 years. As a result of this exploration you should be able to accurately describe demographic and personal characteristics of women who return to college. Eventually, you would develop some specific ideas about these students, and you could conduct further research to test these ideas systematically (see Ballmer & Cozby, 1981).

QUALITATIVE AND QUANTITATIVE DATA

Descriptive methods can be broadly classified as primarily quantitative or qualitative. To understand the distinction, imagine that you are interested in describing the ways that the lives of teenagers are affected by working. To collect **quantitative data,** you might develop a questionnaire for a sample of teenagers to complete. You could ask precisely defined questions about the number of hours they work, the type of work they do, their levels of stress, their school grades, and their use of drugs. After assigning numerical values to the responses, you could subject the data to a quantitative, statistical analysis. A quantitative description of the results would focus on such things as the percentage of teenagers who work and the way this percentage varies by age. The results from a quantitative analysis are usually reported using tables, figures, and statistics.

Suppose, instead, that you took a qualitative approach to describing behavior. You might conduct a series of "focus groups" in which you gather together groups of 8 to 12 teenagers and engage them in a discussion about their perceptions and experiences with the world of work. You would allow the teenagers to tell you about the topic using their own words and cognitive frameworks. To record the focus group discussions, you might use an audiotape or videotape recorder and later have a transcript prepared. Or you might have observers take detailed notes during the discussions. **Qualitative data** would focus on the themes that emerge from the discussion and the manner in which the teenagers conceptualized the issues. Such qualitative results are typically presented in everyday language that reads more like a story, without reliance on numbers and statistics to present the behavioral descriptions. The number of social researchers who rely on qualitative methods has increased considerably in the past decade. A recent series of publications addresses qualitative methodology in the fields of anthropology (Bernard, 1994), family research (Gilgun, Daly, & Handel, 1992), aging (Gubrium & Sankar, 1993), and social work (Riessman, 1993).

Other methods, combining both qualitative and quantitative data, could also be used to study teenage employment. The choice of using qualitative or quantitative methods depends on the research purpose and the questions the investiga-

BOX 6.1   RESEARCH IN ACTION

Quantitative and Qualitative Approaches Combined

A national evaluation of Spanish-English preschool curriculum models (Chesterfield, 1986) demonstrates both quantitative and qualitative approaches to measurement. Head Start programs in California, New York, Texas, and Wisconsin implemented bilingual programs designed to increase the English language skills of preschool-aged children. Using a pretest-posttest design, children's knowledge of English was assessed before and after the program was implemented. This quantitative measure indicated an increase in the children's knowledge of English.

To supplement this measure, a participant observer at each of the four sites gathered ethnographic data on a subset of children. Extensive field notes were made at three time periods corresponding to the beginning, middle, and end of the school year. The qualitative data from the field notes demonstrated changes in the children's use of language. At the beginning of the school year, English was rarely used in the children's interactions, with a gradual increase in daily usage evident over the course of the school year. This information was not captured by the standardized quantitative tests of language, but it provided valuable insight into the effectiveness of the bilingual curriculum.

tor wants to address. For example, if the research question requires precise description, a numerical quantitative approach is appropriate. In contrast, qualitative studies are appropriate when the research focuses on the context in which an event occurs or the process of how an event occurs in a social setting. Such information is difficult to quantify with numbers and lends itself more naturally to a verbal, descriptive approach.

Keep in mind the distinction between quantitative and qualitative approaches to describing behavior as you read about specific descriptive research methods. Both approaches are valuable and provide us with different ways of understanding, as can be seen in the example in Box 6.1. It is also possible to conceptualize quantitative and qualitative methodologies as a continuum rather than a dichotomy (Hammersley, 1992; Maxwell, Bashook, & Sandlow, 1986). In this way, both approaches can be integrated into the same study to "triangulate" data, yielding converging results from two distinct modes of investigation.

FIELD OBSERVATION

Observations in Natural Settings

Field observation is sometimes called **naturalistic observation** because it usually takes place in the natural setting where the participants normally conduct their activities. The researcher makes in-depth observations of a particular natural setting (the field), using a variety of techniques to collect information. The field report includes these observations and the researcher's interpretations of the findings. This research approach has roots in anthropology and zoology (the study of human and animal behavior, respectively) and is currently widely used in the social sciences to study many phenomena in all types of social and organizational settings.

Corsaro's (1985) study of peer interaction in a preschool is a good example of a naturalistic observation study. Corsaro spent a year in a university preschool to observe children's play activities. The children accepted him as part of the school setting, engaged in normal play routines in his presence, and even included "Big Bill" in many activities. Using interviews, concealed observations, and recordings of the children's play, Corsaro compiled extensive data that identified many important aspects of the peer culture. For example, children rarely played alone, preferring the company of a classmate. Children who were already playing together typically resisted entry from others into their play, defending their territory. Out of this inevitable conflict, children learn important social skills, highlighting the importance of friendship.

Naturalistic observation is undertaken when a researcher wants to describe and understand how people in a social or cultural setting live, work, and experience the setting. If you want to know about bars as a social setting, for example, you will need to visit one or more bars over an extended period of time, talk to people, observe interactions, and become accepted as a "regular" (Cavan, 1966). If you want to know how people persuade or influence others, you can get a job as a car salesperson or take an encyclopedia sales training course (Cialdini, 1988). If you are interested in how people become part of some social group (e.g., marijuana users, prostitutes, a particular religious cult), you can arrange to meet members of such groups to interview them about their experiences (Becker, 1963, on marijuana users). Those who have studied what it is really like to be a patient in a mental hospital had themselves admitted as patients (Rosenhan, 1973). Of course, you might not want to do any of these things; however, if these questions interest you, the written reports of these researchers make for fascinating reading.

Ethnography

Ethnography is a specific type of field observation that has been especially popular in anthropology and sociology. An ethnographer spends an extended period of time immersed in the natural setting of a social group, with six months to two years being fairly typical (Fetterman, 1989). From the vantage point of a participant observer, the ethnographer lives and works in the community. Using naturalistic observation and interviews, the ethnographer's goal is to understand the group or culture from their own cultural worldview. For example, Dan Rose (1987) documented life in a Philadelphia neighborhood of African American working-class and welfare families, Jacobs (1974) described the lifestyle in a retirement community, and Thrasher and Mowbray (1995) conducted an ethnographic study of homeless women with children. Lancy is an anthropologist who conducted an ethnographic study of childhood development in a nontechnological African society in West Africa. In *Playing on the Mother Ground,* Lancy (1996) describes how children learn without benefit of formal schooling. Parents influence their children by example, not direct teaching. Children are expected to "play on the mother ground" near adults, observe adults, and learn through make-believe play, games, dances, and storytelling.

Features of Field Observation

The first feature of **field observation** is that it demands an immersion in the situation. The field researcher attempts to observe and describe everything—the physical features of the setting itself, the patterns of social interactions, typical behaviors of people in the setting, and so forth. Second, this immersion continues over an extended period of time, using a variety of procedures. Third, the goal of field observation is to provide a complete and accurate picture of the dynamics of the setting as a whole, rather than to test hypotheses formed prior to the study. Because a priori hypotheses are not tested, **observational research** is often exploratory in nature, with the purpose of theory building rather than theory testing. Based on the data obtained from the field observations, tentative hypotheses and theories may be generated that explain how the particular social system works.

To achieve this goal, the researcher uses a variety of techniques to gather information, including observing people and events, interviewing people about their lives, using key "informants" to provide information, and examining documents produced in the setting (e.g., newspapers, newsletters, or memos). The data and the subsequent analysis tend to rely on qualitative approaches that are nonnumerical and nonmathematical.

Issues in Field Observation

Two related issues facing the researcher are: (1) whether to be a participant or nonparticipant in the social setting and (2) whether to conceal the research purpose from the other people in the social setting. Do you become an active participant in the group, or do you observe from the outside? Do you conceal your purposes or even your presence, or do you openly let people know what you are doing? These decisions may have ramifications for the validity of your study, so it is important to consider the alternatives before observation begins.

Participation A nonparticipant observer is an outsider who does not become an active part of the setting, viewing the setting from an external, or "etic," viewpoint. In contrast, a **participant observer** assumes an active, insider role to gain the "emic," or insider's, perspective. A participant observer is involved in the setting, actively interacting with participants, and may actually become "one of them."

Because participant observation allows the researcher to observe the setting from the inside, he or she may be able to experience events in the same way as natural participants. Friendships and other experiences of the participant observer may yield valuable qualitative data that could not be obtained otherwise. However, the richness of this data may be compromised by a potential problem. The observer may lose the objectivity necessary to conduct scientific observation.

This may be particularly problematic when the researcher already belongs to the group being studied (e.g., a researcher who belongs to Parents Without Partners and who undertakes a study of that group). Remember that naturalistic observation requires accurate description and objective interpretation. If a researcher has some prior reason to either criticize people in the setting or give a glowing report of a particular group, the observations are apt to be biased and the conclusions will lack validity.

The nonparticipant observer does not face the problem of potential bias because he or she maintains physical and psychological distance. Although this may contribute to increased objectivity of the observations, the trade-off is that access to events in the social setting is limited. The decision to be a nonparticipant or a participant is not really a choice between one or the other—it is more like a continuum along which the researcher decides how much participation is appropriate to achieve the goals of the study. Clearly there is a middle ground between observing from the outside and being fully immersed as a member of the community that is being studied. For example, a nonparticipant observer may not become a member of the group but may over time become accepted as a friend or simply part of the ongoing activities of the group.

Concealment   Should the researcher remain concealed or be open about the research purposes? Concealed observation may be preferable because the presence of the observer may influence and alter the behavior of those being observed. Imagine how a nonconcealed observer might alter the behavior of high school students in many situations at a school. Concealed observation is less reactive than nonconcealed observation because people are not aware that their behaviors are being observed and recorded. However, nonconcealed observation may be preferable from an ethical viewpoint. Consider the invasion of privacy when researchers (Henle & Hubbell, 1938) hid under beds in dormitory rooms to discover what college students talk about! Also, people often quickly become used to the observer and behave naturally in the observer's presence. Two well-known examples of nonconcealed observation are provided by television. In the PBS documentary series *An American Family* and in MTV's *Real World,* people living together were filmed over an extended period of time. Many viewers of these series are surprised to see how quickly people forget about the cameras and spontaneously reveal many private aspects of their lives. Clark (1983) conducted ethnographic case studies of ten Black families by spending more than 48 hours in each home and following family members on errands to the store, school, and work. This allowed him to observe interpersonal styles, family activities, and casual conversation to supplement his semistructured interviews and questionnaires. Thus, concealed observation may not be necessary to obtain natural behavior.

The decision about whether to conceal one's purpose or presence depends on both ethical concerns and the nature of the particular group or setting being studied. As with participation in the setting, concealment is not an "either-or" decision. Sometimes, a participant observer is nonconcealed to certain members of the group, who give the researcher permission to be part of the group as a concealed observer. Often a concealed observer decides to say nothing directly about his or her purposes but will completely disclose the goals of the research if asked by anyone. Nonparticipant observers are also not concealed when they gain permission to "hang out" in a setting or use interview techniques to gather information (e.g., in Becker's [1963] study of marijuana users, some of the people who were interviewed first introduced Becker to their network of friends who were also marijuana users). In actuality, then, there are degrees of participation and concealment. Researchers who use naturalistic observation to study behavior must carefully determine what their role in the setting will be.

Steps in Conducting Field Observation

In this section we briefly summarize the steps a researcher follows in conducting field observation. For more extensive discussion, refer to Lofland and Lofland (1995), Maxwell (1996), Patton (1990), R. S. Weiss (1994), and Werner and Schoepfle (1987a, 1987b). After evaluating the goals of the study and determining that participant observation is appropriate, there are five basic steps to field observation: (1) selecting a group or environment to study, (2) deciding what to study, (3) gaining entry into the group, (4) observing and recording the data, and (5) analyzing the data.

Selecting a group to study is a very important decision for the field researcher. The researcher expects to invest a great deal of time and effort in the field setting, and an unfortunate choice of setting may lead to wasted time and resources. The research issues guide selection of a group to study. For example, suppose you are interested in children in poverty. To select a community, you need to narrow down the research question a bit. Are you more interested in children in an urban setting or a rural setting? Considering factors such as ethnicity, income, occupation, parental education, and perhaps religious involvement, you would make sure your target community represents a "typical" community. A final decision may rely on the researcher's judgment—and with a bit of good luck the choice will produce favorable results.

Deciding what to study involves limiting the scope of the observations to behaviors that are relevant to the central issues of the study. A researcher employing naturalistic observation may want to study everything about a setting. However, this is generally not possible, simply because a setting and the questions one might ask about it are so complex. For example, rather than trying to study everything that happens in a classroom, a researcher may focus only on how teachers and students interact.

Another approach to deciding what to study is to select general categories of behavior ahead of time, then modify the behaviors to be more specific as the study progresses. The advantage of this flexibility is that the researcher can adjust to the situation as new information is gained. The field worker may even change techniques in the middle of a study to capture behaviors or processes that were not conceptualized in advance.

Gaining entry into the group or environment that is the focus of the field observation may require the cooperation of a member of the group. This community member may assist the researcher in establishing a plausible reason for his or her presence in the community, and generally facilitates access to the group. An

---

| BOX 6.2 |

Advice for the Fieldworker

♦ Always be suspicious of data collection that goes according to plan.

♦ Research subjects have also been known to be people.

♦ The evaluator's scientific observation is some person's real-life experience. Respect for the latter must precede respect for the former.

♦ A fieldworker should be able to sweep the floor, carry out the garbage, carry in the laundry, cook for large groups, go without food and sleep, read and write by candlelight, see in the dark, see in the light, cooperate without offending, suppress sarcastic remarks, smile to express both pain and hurt, experience both pain and hurt, spend time alone, respond to orders, take sides, stay neutral, take risks, avoid harm, be confused, seem confused, care terribly, become attached to nothing. . . . The nine-to-five set need not apply.

♦ Always carry extra batteries and getaway money.

SOURCE: From *Qualitative Evaluation Methods,* Patton, 1980, p. 119. © 1980 by Sage Publications, Inc. Reprinted by permission of publisher.

---

introduction by a community member may lead to acceptance by others in the group, although it may take a while to establish rapport with the other group members. The observer needs to adopt a role that will allow access to the interactions of the group members without compromising the integrity of the group. See Box 6.2 for additional tips for participant observers. To maximize the opportunities for observation, the researcher should be in the center of action in the group or community. The issues of concealment and participation are clearly relevant to gaining entry into a group, because the observer does not want to cause others to change their behavior. For example, Rose (1987) took a job as an auto mechanic in the community, rented an apartment next door to the auto shop, and lived in the neighborhood for two years without revealing his identity as an ethnographer. In his study of the Kpelle-speaking people in West Africa, Lancy (1996) was "encouraged and expected to work, play, and get drunk with the townspeople" (p. 3).

Observing and recording data is the main objective of the field observer, often relying on simple paper and pencil. Field notes in the form of written notes or dictations on audiotape are the primary data gathering technique used by field observers. The purpose of field notes is to record all relevant information about the observation. This includes detailed information about the participants and the content of the interaction as well as descriptors about the location, time, and place of the interaction. Field observers must have good powers of observation, particularly if their presence is concealed. Concealed observers cannot make notes on a clipboard in full view of the group but must rely on their memory. Later, out of view of the group, they can unobtrusively jot down brief field notes or dictate a brief summary of the observation. Simultaneous recording of field notes may create the most accurate record of the event. However, it is not always possible to make notes while the action is taking place. Also, simultaneous recording may lead to reactivity if people change their behavior because the researcher is visibly making notes about their activity.

Gathering data typically continues for an extended period of time. In addition to observations of group interactions, interviews are useful for gathering data. A key informant who is knowledgeable about historical background information as well as current features of the culture may be a valuable source of detailed information. Lancy's Kpelle informants included his translator, the town's chief, a leatherworker-sage, and a musician-hunter. Interviews may also be conducted with other group members. These tend to be informal interviews that do not use a standardized set of questions. An effective interviewing technique resembles Piaget's clinical method, adjusting subsequent questions based on the informant's responses, gently probing to promote maximum disclosure. For additional information, refer to Fetterman's (1989) treatment of techniques for gathering data.

Accurate record-keeping is essential for field observation. The field observer makes as many brief notes as possible throughout the day, carefully recording as much information about the observation as possible. Promptly at the end of each day, audiotapes are transcribed. Field notes are expanded based on the observer's memory of the events. Field observers frequently use a coding system to keep track of the occurrence of particular target behaviors. The sheer volume of information being gathered is difficult to organize manually, making a word processor and a computerized database vital tools for the field observer. Computer programs devised specifically for coding the textual data of field observations are also very helpful. Weitzman and Miles (1995) compiled an excellent sourcebook of qualitative data analytic programs (see also Fielding & Lee [1991] and Miles & Huberman [1994]). Popular programs include *The Ethnograph* (Seidel & Clark 1984) and *NUD·IST* (Nonnumerical Unstructured Data Indexing, Searching, and Theorizing).

Analyzing the data and reporting the results are the final steps in conducting field observation. Data analysis may begin in the early stages of a field study. This provides the opportunity to alter the data collection strategies if unanticipated behaviors occur. Some field researchers may prefer to wait until after the observations are complete to ensure objective collection of the observations. The qualitative data does not lend itself to numerical, mathematical analysis. The vast amount of data collected in a field observation must be reduced in some way. A typical strategy for analysis is to categorize and classify behaviors. One way to do this is to look for similarities and dissimilarities in the events. Do common themes or behavior patterns occur repeatedly? What are the normative behavior patterns? Do any clusters of behavior contrast with these general norms? After identifying common themes, the researcher looks for specific examples that illustrate the themes, perhaps providing supporting evidence in the form of quotes from participants. The computer programs mentioned earlier may be helpful to identify common behavior patterns, but the interpretation is still left up to the field researcher.

Finally, the field observer attempts to formulate hypotheses and theoretical explanations for the social processes that were observed. This is the primary goal of the analysis. The final product of a field observation is typically presented in the form of a scholarly book that describes the history of the group and the socialization patterns that were observed. Although naturalistic observation research is a difficult and challenging scientific procedure, it can yield invaluable knowledge when done well.

Methodological Issues

External validity is a problem for field observation studies. External validity is the extent to which the results can be generalized to other populations and settings. Are the results obtained in a certain cultural context applicable to other contexts? Would the same pattern of results be obtained with different ages? In field observation, generalizability may be limited in several ways. First, the observations themselves may be biased. The observations and measurements made by a researcher immersed in a social setting may be unintentionally biased by the observer's personal experiences. It is certainly possible that a different observer in the same setting might gather different observations and insights. This does not make the results less meaningful, but their generalizability may be limited.

A second problem for generalizability is the comprehensive nature of the data itself. By definition, the field observer collects extensive, in-depth descriptions of a particular social setting. To achieve this goal, a great deal of rich, complex data is gathered that describes the members of the group and their social interactions. Unfortunately, there is no guarantee that the characteristics of this group and their interpersonal dynamics are in fact representative of other social groups. The field researcher may develop an insightful understanding of one particular group, but the outcome may not apply to other groups in other settings.

A third problem for external validity is the potential that the data gathered by the field researcher are not representative of that particular group. The informants used by the researcher may not be typical members of the social setting. Individuals who choose to speak out and share personal histories and openly discuss the activities of the group with the researcher may differ in important ways from other group members. As a result, the field data would be biased by these extreme views. The results of the study would not be an accurate description of this group and would definitely not be generalizable. We return to the complexities of external validity more fully in Chapter 16.

Ethical concerns for the field observer include consent and confidentiality. Recall from Chapter 2 that naturalistic observations in public places, such as in a shopping mall or a library, are ethical when participants remain anonymous. In this case, consent is not needed. But what about an ethnographer who conceals his or her identity, infiltrates a group, and conceals the purpose of the study? Does this amount to spying on them, collecting data without their consent? The Institutional Review Board (IRB) considers possible risks to the participants and decides if the research is sufficiently important to allow the potential invasion of privacy. The IRB also ensures that confidentiality is protected. This issue is of particular concern when private and intimate behaviors are observed, such as drug and alcohol use, sexual activity, and antisocial behavior. Additional ethical concerns are highlighted in Box 6.3. The field observer should also consider his or her personal ethics. Dan Rose's (1987) study of a Black neighborhood in Philadelphia was con-

BOX 6.3   RESEARCH IN ACTION

Bullies on the Playground

Aggressive children are at risk for developing maladaptive behaviors that may lead to increased antisocial behavior, yet there is very little research on aggressive children's playground behavior. Everyday conflicts that occur with bullies on the playground cannot be simulated in a laboratory setting because it would be unethical to introduce such potential stress. Yet conducting naturalistic observations on the playground is difficult. Reactivity is a major concern. If the observer is close enough to watch the child and record an aggressive interaction, the child may limit his or her activities. But, if the observer remains a bit distant, verbal interchanges will not be detected.

A technique developed by Craig and Pepler (1995) may solve these problems by using remote audiovisual observations. A wireless microphone placed on the target child records verbal interchanges, allowing a videocamera with a zoom lens to stay farther away from the target children. In this way, children are free to move around the playground, decreasing the threat of reactivity.

However, there are important ethical considerations. The videocamera is more distant from the target children; therefore, it is possible that children who did not consent to the study may enter the same playground area. If this occurs, should the filming stop? Can the film be edited to remove a non-consenting child from the film? Perhaps a proactive stance is appropriate—keep the nonconsenting children off the playground. But that creates another problem. What if these children are friends of the target child? The external validity may be compromised if the naturalistic observation isn't all that natural after all. The same issues apply to teachers and staff. They also must be informed about the study, and they also have the right to refuse.

A second ethical issue is the children's safety. When dealing with aggressive children, safety from extreme aggression or weapons is a concern. At what point do the researchers have a duty to warn about harmful or dangerous behavior? Is it ethical to videotape the entire episode and then inform the supervising adults? The answer is "no"; the researcher's obligation is to protect the child from physical or psychological harm.

Remote audiovisual recordings are a creative way to observe children. Although there are serious ethical concerns and some limitations, this technology allows researchers to take a "peek behind the fence" and learn about children's everyday behavior.

ducted covertly, against his personal and professional judgment. Rose reports the experience as being very negative, contributing to the 15-year delay in writing his ethnographic book.

Another source of ethical concern for a participant observer relates to the confidentiality of what is observed. What course of action should observers take if illegal activities are observed? Are they ethically bound to report the incident to the proper authorities? Can they be forced to reveal potentially harmful information under the force of a subpoena? The case of James Scarce addresses these topics. James Scarce was a graduate student studying radical social movements who had information about illegal activities conducted by animal rights activists. A federal grand jury very much wanted his information, but Mr. Scarce declined to cooperate. The American Sociological Association was so concerned about this ethical issue that they wrote an amicus brief (friend of the court) supporting rights of social researchers to protect the identity of their sources (Levine, 1993). Mr. Scarce spent five months behind bars and was eventually released without revealing his sources (Scarce Released from Jail, 1993).

SYSTEMATIC OBSERVATION

Systematic observation refers to the careful observation of one or more specific behaviors in a particular setting. This research approach is much less global than naturalistic observation research. The researcher is interested in only a few carefully defined variables. The purpose of systematic observation is to test pre-existing hypotheses about the relationships between behaviors. Systematic observations are structured, without the procedural flexibility that characterizes field observation. In contrast to field observation, immersion is not needed in the relatively short time frame of a systematic observation. The data are quantitative, often in the form of frequency counts, not field notes.

For example, Bakeman and Brownlee (1980; also see Bakeman & Gottman, 1986) were interested in the social behavior of young children. Three-year-olds were videotaped in a room in a "free play" situation. Each child was taped for 100 minutes; observers viewed the videotapes and coded each child's behavior every 15 seconds, using this coding system adapted from Parten's (1932) classic play categories:

Unoccupied: Child is not doing anything in particular or is simply watching other children.

Solitary play: Child plays alone with toys but is not interested in or affected by the activities of other children.

Together: Child is with other children but is not occupied with any particular activity.

Parallel play: Child plays beside other children with similar toys but does not play with the others.

Group play: Child plays with other children, including sharing toys or participating in organized play activities as part of a group of children.

Bakeman and Brownlee were particularly interested in the sequence or order in which the children engaged in the different behaviors. They found, for example, that the children rarely went from being unoccupied to engaging in parallel play. However, children frequently went from parallel to group play, indicating that parallel play is a transition state in which children decide whether to go ahead and interact in a group situation.

Coding Systems

Numerous behaviors can be studied using systematic observation. The researcher must first decide which behaviors are of interest, choose a setting in which these target behaviors can be observed, and most important, develop a **coding system** (such as the one just described) to measure the behaviors. Sometimes the researcher develops the coding system to fit the needs of the particular study. Coding systems should be as simple as possible, with clear operational definitions that allow observers to easily categorize behaviors. This is especially important when observers are coding "live" behaviors rather than viewing videotapes that can be reviewed or even coded on a frame-by-frame basis. Boyatzis, Matillo, and Nesbitt (1995) coded only one behavior—aggression—in an observational study investigating the effects of violent television programming on elementary school children. With only one easily identifiable behavior to code, interobserver agreement reached 99%.

Checklists can be used in systematic observation. Using a list of behaviors, the observer simply checks off the occurrence of each behavior. Developing a good checklist does take some experience. Once the systematic observation has started, the checklist cannot be changed, so the researcher may want to start with some casual, pilot observations to facilitate development of the checklist. The list cannot be too long. Another approach is to develop a "rule" for each behavior. How do you know when a child is off-task? Off-task may be defined by observing visual attention—the child is off-task when her eyes wander away from her paperwork. Or off-task may be defined based on the child's physical position—the child is off-task when she gets out of her seat during a written assignment. Inconsistent results will be obtained if observers interpret the categories of behavior differently; precise measurement depends on clear operational definitions.

An example of a simple coding system comes from a study of the social behavior of mild to moderately malnourished Kenyan school-aged children (Espinosa, Sigman, Neumann, Bwibo, & McDonald, 1992). Observers coded three categories of behavior on the playground: (1) activity level, (2) affect, and (3) social behavior. Activity level was recorded as low, medium, high, or very high. Affect was coded in two categories: positive or anxious affect. (Negative affect, such as anger or sadness, was not used as a category because it rarely occurred.) Social behaviors consisted of positive peer involvement, leadership, no peer interaction, and aggression. Better-nourished children were more active, were more happy, and showed more leadership behavior. In contrast, poorly nourished children were less active and more anxious. Although the study was conducted in Kenya, Espinosa et al. point out that it is unlikely that the results are culturally specific. Children in all countries are affected by undernutrition, supporting the need to provide adequate nutrition for school-aged children.

Sometimes researchers can use coding systems that have been developed by others. For example, the Home Observation for Measurement of the Environment (HOME) inventory (Caldwell & Bradley, 1984) is a widely used instrument that uses a checklist to determine the quality and quantity of social, emotional, and cognitive experiences in the home environment. The infant version of the HOME inventory includes 45 statements that are scored "yes" or "no" by a researcher who visits the home. Another example is the Family Interaction Coding System (FICS) (see Patterson & Moore, 1979). The FICS consists of 29 categories of interaction grouped in aversive (hostility), prosocial (helping), and general activities. Most of the research using the FICS has centered on how children's aversive behaviors are learned and maintained in a family. A major advantage of using an existing coding system is that a body of research already exists in which the system has proved useful, and training materials are usually available.

Time and Event Sampling

After the researcher works out a coding system of what behaviors to observe, the second methodological issue facing the researcher is when to make the observations. For many research questions, samples of behavior continuously taken over a long period of time will provide more accurate and useful data than single, short observations. However, this is not always possible and may not address the researcher's questions. Alternatives are time sampling and event sampling.

Using **time sampling,** the observer chooses particular time intervals to make the observations. The time intervals could be separated by seconds, minutes, hours, days, weeks, or months, depending on what schedule of observation makes sense for the target behaviors. Rapidly changing behaviors require more frequent sampling; behaviors that are more stable are sampled on fewer occasions. For example, measurement of infrequent behavior, such as children's aggression during free play, requires frequent sampling. When a behavior occurs fairly often, time sampling that observes only part of the time is likely to capture typical behavior. Recall in the study of bilingual preschool curriculum (Chesterfield, 1986) that language use was observed at only three time intervals during the school year.

Consider a study on television viewing in homes (Anderson et al., 1986). The researchers wanted to know how members of families actually watch TV. Data collected during a single evening could be distorted by short-term trends, such as time of day, a particular show, or the variations in family activities that influence TV viewing. A better method of addressing the question would be to observe TV viewing over a longer period. This is exactly what the researchers did. Video recordings were made of almost 5,000 hours of TV. Because coding this much data would be excessively time-consuming, Anderson et al. used time sampling to analyze only a segment of TV viewing every 55 minutes. Among other things, they found that no one is watching the TV 15% of the time and that TV viewing increases up to age 10 and then begins to decrease.

When the behavior being assessed is less frequent, **event sampling** may be more appropriate. Time sampling may limit opportunities to observe a behavior, leading to missed instances of the behavior. Time sampling may also observe only part of a behavior, especially when using an alternating on-off schedule of observation. To increase the likelihood that the particular event will actually be observed, event sampling allows the observer to record each event that meets the operational definition. For example, consider an observational study of the neonatal intensive care unit (Gottfried, 1985). The observers focused on events that involved interaction between the infants and medical staff. The "event" began when the staff member placed his or her hands inside the isolette and ended when the hands were removed from the isolette. This excludes time spent writing information on charts or adjusting medical equipment outside the isolette yet captures all the events that the infant experienced. The schedule is random, determined by the actual occurrence of a medical or caretaking intervention.

Methodological Issues

Reliability of the observations is the first issue. Recall from Chapter 4 that reliability refers to the degree to which a measure is stable or consistent. The method used to determine reliability when doing systematic observation is called interrater or interobserver reliability. This is an index of how closely two observers agree when independently coding the same events. Usually, such reliability is expressed as a percentage of the time that two or more observers coded the same behavior in the same way. Very high levels of agreement are reported in virtually all published research using systematic observation (generally 80% agreement or higher). Reliability is also reported using a statistic called kappa (Cohen, 1960). Kappa adjusts for chance agreements among the observers, providing a more conservative estimate of reliability.

To make sure the observations are precise and accurate, raters must be trained on the coding categories. When observations are made from "live" behavior, the observer does not get a second chance to replay the behavior. If an event is missed, the integrity of the data is compromised. Training involves practice judging prototypical and atypical events, with training continuing until an acceptable level of accuracy has been reached.

An observer's personal bias may also lead to inaccurate observations. Personal expectations may inadvertently contribute to an observer underreporting or overreporting certain events. For example, in an observational study of developmentally delayed and normally developing children, expectations about typical behavior may bias the observations. A developmentally delayed child who throws a toy may be coded as demonstrating regressive behavior; a normally developing child who throws a toy may be coded as engaging in solitary play. A solution is to keep the observers "blind" to the identity of the people being observed. In this example, the observer would not be told which child was developmentally delayed and which child was normally developing. It is also important to keep the observers "blind" to the hypotheses of the study.

The second issue in systematic observation is *reactivity*—the possibility that the presence of the observer will affect people's behaviors (see Chapter 4). If reactivity occurs, the events being observed are not natural behaviors and do not represent what typically occurs in the setting. This poses a threat to internal validity because this unnatural behavior is not what the researcher intended to measure. As we noted previously, reactivity can be reduced by unobtrusive methods such as concealed observation. The use of one-way mirrors, hidden videotape recorders, and microphones all can conceal the presence of an observer. Alternatively, reactivity can be reduced by extending the period of observation to allow enough time for people to become used to the presence of the observer and any recording equipment. Even for young children, the novelty soon wears off, and they act naturally.

Equipment is the third methodological issue in systematic observation. You can directly observe behavior and code it at the same time—for example, observing and recording the behavior of children in a classroom or couples interacting on campus. However, it is becoming more common to use videotape equipment to make such observations. Videotape recorders have the advantage of providing a permanent record of the behavior observed that can be coded at a later time. Observations can be coded using paper, pencil, and a clipboard, perhaps using a stopwatch to record the duration of events. Alternatively, you can use a computer recording device that is not much larger than a calculator. Keys on the device are pressed to code the behaviors observed as well as to keep track of their duration. These event recorders add to the expense of the research, and initial training of observers may take longer. However, research that requires observing several types of behavior and recording duration of behavior is facilitated by using these computer devices. Also, data analysis may be easier because the data can be automatically transferred from the device to the computer on which the analyses will be performed.

ADVANTAGES AND DISADVANTAGES OF OBSERVATIONAL METHODS

In general, observational research provides data that is more "real" than that of experimental methods because the participants are observed in their natural setting, thus enhancing the study's ecological validity (Bronfenbrenner, 1977). Minimal expense is incurred with observational research—all you really need is paper, pencil, a clipboard, and a stopwatch. Disadvantages are that observational research can be very time-consuming, involving hours of waiting for events and behaviors to occur. Imagine how uncomfortable it must have been for the observers under the beds in the college dorm study described earlier (Henle & Hubbell, 1938). In addition, the vast amounts of data collected in some observational studies can be challenging to analyze.

The decision to use either field observation or systematic observation depends somewhat on your vantage point. If you have qualitative research questions, field observation is the best choice. If you have quantitative research questions, systematic observation is appropriate.

Which approach is more valid? Participant observers who are trusted members of the group may have access to inside information, leading to subtle insights about the social setting that otherwise would be missed. But this richness may be compromised by the problems discussed earlier. The ethnographer who joins the social setting may inadvertently change the natural processes of the group. Personal bias may alter the observations. Also, recall that a concealed participant observer may have to rely on his or her memory because the observer cannot record behavior when it occurs. This creates questions about the accuracy of the data.

Relying on self-reports also may contribute to inaccurate data. Self-report of informants may be invalid; what someone says about their behavior may not be the same as what they actually do in a particular situation. Actual observation of the behavior may be necessary. Yet relying only on observation overlooks an understanding of the person's perspective. The bottom line is that a researcher may need both systematic observation and field observation to provide an accurate description of a social setting.

CASE STUDIES

A **case study** provides an in-depth description and analysis of an individual. This individual is usually a person, but it may also be a setting, such as a school, neighborhood, or business. Although often associated with the field of clinical psychology, the case study method is useful for child psychologists, anthropologists, sociologists, and criminologists. For example, the case study may be a description of a child by a school psychologist or a historical account of an event such as a model school that failed. Case studies use data obtained from written records, library research, interviews with persons familiar with the case, and possibly naturalistic observation. However, "direct" observation of the case is not required for a case study (cf. Yin, 1994).

Depending on the purpose of the investigation, the case study may present the individual's history, current symptoms, characteristic behaviors, reactions to situations, or responses to treatment. Typically, a case study is done when an individual possesses a particularly rare, unusual, or noteworthy condition. One famous case study in clinical psychology involved "Sybil," a woman with a rare multiple personality disorder (Schreiber, 1973). Over the course of therapy, it was discovered that Sybil had experienced severe beatings and other traumas during childhood. One explanation for the disorder, then, was that Sybil unconsciously created other personalities who would suffer the pain instead of her. A case study in language development was provided by "Genie," a child who was kept isolated in her room, tied to a chair, and never spoken to until she was discovered at the age of 14 (Curtiss, 1977). Genie lacked any language skills. Her case provided linguists and psychologists with the opportunity to attempt to teach her language skills and discover which skills could be learned. Apparently, Genie was able to acquire some rudimentary language skills, such as forming childlike sentences, but she never developed full language skills.

Case studies provide a richly detailed account of an individual, which contributes to the insights gained from the case. But at the same time, this uniqueness limits the generalizability of the findings. Theoretical explanations for Sybil's multiple personality disorder may not apply to other individuals who have a different family history. A second potential problem with case studies is that much of the information is gathered via interview, relying on the retrospective memory of informants. Memory for prior events is not necessarily accurate. A good case study researcher needs to verify as much of this information as possible, using unbiased written records or triangulating with confirming interviews from other informants where possible.

Case studies are valuable in informing us of conditions that are rare or unusual and thus not easily studied in any other way. M. Weiss (1994) used a case study approach to study six appearance-impaired children in Israel. Insights gained through the case study may also lead to the development of hypotheses that can be tested using other methods. However, like field research, case studies are very difficult to do, and they present unique challenges to the researcher in terms of providing explanations for the events that are described.

ARCHIVAL RESEARCH

Archival research involves using previously compiled information to answer research questions. The researcher doesn't actually collect the original data. Instead, he or she analyzes existing data such as census data, statistics that are part of the public record (e.g., number of divorce petitions filed, immigration records), reports of anthropologists, the content of information in the mass media (e.g., advertising, letters to the editor), or information contained in computer databases. In most cases, archival data were not originally collected as part of a research project. Box 6.4 describes one kind of archival research project. Judd, Smith, and Kidder (1991) distinguish between three types of archival research data: statistical records, survey archives, and written records.

Statistical Records

Statistical records are collected by many public and private organizations. The U.S. Census Bureau maintains the most extensive set of statistical records available to researchers for analysis. There are also numerous, less obvious ones, such as public health statistics and test score records kept by testing organizations such as the Educational Testing Service. Gilger (1991) assessed spousal similarity by examining test scores from standardized achievement tests taken in elementary school and high school. Jewett, Hibbard, and Weeks (1992) examined archival insurance data to predict health care utilization in a Medicare population. You may want to visit the government documents section of your university library to explore some of the existing statistical records available for analysis.

The official statistics of the U.S. Census Bureau are available on the Internet (http://census.gov), so anyone with a computer can readily access this information. The census web site is easy to use and allows you to download tables of statistical information to your printer. The census information extends well beyond a simple head count of residents. Browsing the site we found the statistics for Deer Lodge County in western Montana. The county includes 4,068 households, with approximately one-fourth including a person 65 years or older. About 12% of the elderly citizens live below the poverty level. There are 230 institutionalized persons who, upon further research in an atlas, apparently reside in a prison. Most residents go to work before 7:30 A.M. No homes are heated with solar energy, and as in many other parts of the United States, single mothers living in poverty ($n = 127$) are much more common than single fathers living in poverty ($n = 22$). You may think of some creative ways to use the census data for a research project. A new census will be conducted in 2000, but it will be a few years before that information is posted on the Internet.

BOX 6.4   RESEARCH IN ACTION

Archival Research

Written records may also be used for historical reconstruction of an event. Recently, Congress passed the Family Support Act (FSA), the first welfare reform package in more than two decades. The most controversial aspect of the Family Support Act is the "workfare" mandate, which stipulates that recipients of Aid to Families with Dependent Children (AFDC) be trained for jobs. To receive welfare, AFDC mothers of children over 3 years of age must receive job training and actively seek employment. Workfare was a topic of debate in politics long before the FSA. President Nixon and President Carter proposed welfare reform involving workfare, but these programs were defeated (Mead, 1992). What sociological or political forces led to the passage of the FSA?

To reconstruct the historical passage of the Family Support Act, Oliker (1994) conducted extensive archival research of written records from 1986 to 1988 that document passage of the FSA. These included four types of documents:

Legislative documents, such as congressional reports, hearings, and debates

Newspaper and magazine coverage

Written accounts by policy researchers and legislative personnel

Workfare evaluation reports

The archival researcher concluded that the Family Support Act was passed as a direct result of the influence of the Manpower Demonstration Research Corporation (MDRC), the private agency that prepared the workfare evaluation reports. MDRC published technical reports on workfare experiments and prepared press releases and distributed summaries of the findings to congressional staff members. They also gave briefings and lectures on their research. MDRC was viewed as a very credible source, and their work on welfare reform was never questioned. This acceptance of their work is a bit surprising because the data were not available for public or peer review. In addition, careful scrutiny of the MDRC reports reveals some misrepresentation of the welfare to work interventions. Oliker concluded that the Family Support Act achieved bipartisan support as a result of the consensus of opinion that was strategically forged by social science researchers.

Researchers Belmont and Marolla (1973) used statistical records when they examined the intelligence test scores of nearly all military inductees in the Netherlands born between 1944 and 1947. They discovered an interesting pattern in the data: Intelligence was systematically related to both birth order and family size. Specifically, intelligence was higher in families with fewer children and also higher for early-born than later-born children. Later, Zajonc (1976; Zajonc & Mullally,

1997) developed a confluence hypothesis to explain these data, a mathematical model based on the amount of intellectual stimulation received by children of differing family size and birth order. Zajonc was also able to replicate the original findings by studying a database consisting of test scores obtained in the United States.

Various public records can also be used as sources of archival data. For example, Gwaltney-Gibbs (1986) used marriage license applications in one Oregon county in 1970 and 1980 to study changing patterns of premarital cohabitation. She found that only 13% of the couples used the same address on the application in 1970 but that 53% gave the same address in 1980. She was also able to relate cohabitation to other variables such as age and race. The findings were interpreted as support for the notion that premarital cohabitation has become a new step in patterns of courtship leading to marriage. Another example of the use of public records is research by Anderson and Anderson (1984) that demonstrated a relationship between temperature and violent crime statistics in two U.S. cities. Data on both variables are readily available from agencies that keep those statistics.

Survey Archives

Survey archives consist of data from surveys that are stored on computers and available to researchers who wish to analyze them. Major polling organizations make many of their surveys available. Also, many universities are part of the Interuniversity Consortium for Political and Social Research (ICPSR), which makes survey archive data available. One very useful data set is the General Social Survey, a series of surveys funded by the National Science Foundation and intended as a resource for social scientists (Russell & Megaard, 1988). Each survey includes more than 200 questions covering a range of topics such as attitudes, life satisfaction, health, religion, education, age, gender, and race. This and other survey archives may be available through the computer system on your campus. Survey archives are extremely important because most researchers do not have the financial resources to conduct surveys of representative national samples; the archives allow researchers to access such samples to test their ideas. For example, Weissert (1986) was able to predict the institutionalization of elderly persons using demographic data (age, race, gender) from the National Health Interview Survey and the National Nursing Home Survey.

Although most survey archives consist of data obtained from adults, there are several major surveys of children. The National Survey of Children is a 1981 sample of elementary through high school students that has been used to study a variety of questions including the effects of divorce on behavior problems of children (see Peterson & Zill, 1986). Perhaps the most ambitious survey is the National Longitudinal Survey of Labor Market Experience of Youth, known as the NLSY. The NLSY is a very large (more than 12,000 persons) nationally representative sample of American youth who were aged 14 to 22 in the first year of the study. The NLSY includes information on the children and their parents. Longitudinal assessments track the educational and occupational attainment of the NLSY as well as their patterns of marriage and family formation. The NLSY provided the ammunition used by Richard Herrnstein and Charles Murray (1994) in their controversial book about intelligence and race, *The Bell Curve*.

Written Records

Written records consist of a variety of documents, such as diaries and letters, that have been preserved by historical societies; ethnographies of other cultures written by anthropologists; public documents, such as speeches by politicians; and mass communications, including books, magazine articles, movies, and newspapers. An example of the creative use of written records is Hill-Lubin's (1991) study of the grandmother in Black literature. Hill-Lubin examined the autobiographies of three eminent African Americans, Frederick Douglass (*Narrative of Frederick Douglass: An American Slave Written by Himself,* 1845/1968), Langston Hughes (*The Big Sea,* 1940), and Maya Angelou (*I Know Why the Caged Bird Sings,* 1969). Based on these autobiographies and other written records, Hill-Lubin suggested that the grandmother contributes importantly to African American families by preserving family history and encouraging positive values and ideals in the family.

Content Analysis of Documents

Content analysis is the systematic analysis of existing documents such as the ones described in this section (see Holsti, 1969; Viney, 1983). Like systematic observation, content analysis requires researchers to devise coding systems that raters can use to quantify the information in the documents. Sometimes the coding is quite simple and straightforward; for example, it is easy to code whether the addresses of the bride and groom on marriage license applications are the same or different. More often, the researcher must define the categories to code the information.

Potts, Runyan, Zerger, and Marchetti (1996) used content analysis to study safety behaviors in 52 TV programs watched frequently by children. Raters coded the location of each safety event, demographic characteristics of the safety models, the context of the event, and the outcome of the safety behavior. The content analysis revealed that most safety behaviors were shown in commercial advertisements, not during the TV programs. Male adult characters engaged in the most safety behaviors, yet the outcomes of the behaviors were rarely shown. Potts et al. point to the disparity in children's TV programming—lots of violence and risky behavior is learned by observing TV, yet few safety behaviors are modeled for children to learn. Content analysis has also been used to examine male and female roles in children's literature (Crabb & Bielawski, 1994) and in elementary school textbooks (Touba, 1987). The Touba study is intriguing because it was conducted after the 1978 political revolution in Iran and evaluated the government's position on gender equality. The content analysis showed that males and females were still portrayed in traditional sex roles, thus supporting traditional attitudes about women's roles despite their quest for equality.

The use of archival data allows researchers to study interesting questions, some of which could not be studied in any other way. Archives provide nonreactive measures of behavior because individuals are not directly observed; data is collected from already existing records. There is good external validity because the data often represent the behavior of thousands of individuals. However, there are at least three major problems with the use of archival data. First, the desired records may be difficult to obtain. They may be placed in long-forgotten storage places, or they may have been destroyed. Second, we can never be completely sure of the accuracy of the information collected by someone else. Others may not be as careful and consistent as you would be when gathering information. Third, there may be lots of information about groups, but little data on individuals. Archival data are a valuable supplement to more traditional data collection methods, but you may find that you need to collect your own data to answer your research questions.

SUMMARY

Descriptive methods are useful to describe behavior, explore a phenomenon, or test hypotheses about behavior. Descriptive methods rely on quantitative, numerical data as well as qualitative, nonnumerical data such as verbal reports. Field observation or naturalistic observation is the observation of activities in a natural setting over an extended period of time. Ethnographers typically live and work in the field setting to provide a comprehensive view of a social or cultural group. Information is gathered in a variety of ways, including observations and interviews. Field observations are often exploratory and do not involve testing preexisting hypotheses. Rather, field observations describe qualitative aspects of the social setting or group being studied.

Systematic observation is the careful observation of one or more specific behaviors in a particular setting. Coding systems or checklists may be used to record target behaviors, either by observing continuously or by using time sampling or event sampling. Using time sampling, the observer chooses particular time intervals to observe behavior. Using event sampling, the observer records each instance of a particular behavior. The quantitative data that is gathered can be used to evaluate specific hypotheses about these behaviors.

The researcher must consider the advantages and disadvantages of being either a participant or nonparticipant observer and whether or not to conceal the observation. Reliability, validity, and generalizability of the study depend in part on these decisions. In practice, the researcher may combine features of field observation and systematic observation to increase the meaningfulness of a study and to more accurately portray a particular social setting.

A case study is a detailed description of a single "case," which may be an individual or a specific event. Case studies are especially useful for studying rare, unusual events. Archival research uses existing information such as statistical records collected by public and private organizations, survey archives of data stored on computers, and various written records. Content analysis procedures are used to systematically code the information in written documents.

KEY TERMS

archival research
case study
coding system
content analysis
ethical concerns
ethnography
event sampling

external validity
field observation
naturalistic observation
observational research
participant observer
qualitative data
quantitative data

statistical records
survey archives
systematic observation
time sampling
written records

REVIEW QUESTIONS

1. What is field observation? How does a researcher collect data when conducting field observation research?
2. Distinguish between qualitative and quantitative data. Why is the data in naturalistic observation research primarily qualitative?
3. What is ethnography? Why do researchers conduct ethnographic research?
4. Distinguish between participant and nonparticipant observation. Distinguish between concealed and nonconcealed observation. What are some of the ethical concerns associated with these issues?
5. Describe the steps involved in conducting field observation research.
6. What is systematic observation? Why are data from systematic observation primarily quantitative?
7. What is a coding system? Distinguish between event sampling and time sampling.
8. What is a case study? When are case studies used?
9. What is archival research? What are the major sources of archival data?
10. What is content analysis?

CHAPTER 7 ◆

Survey Research

Surveys use self-report measurement techniques to question people about themselves—their attitudes, feelings, behaviors, and demographics (age, income, race, marital status, and so on). Of the various methods used by researchers, you are probably most familiar with surveys. As a student, you may be asked by your school to be part of a survey. A social services agency may survey elderly citizens in your area to determine which services are most needed by that population. A sample of teachers may be asked to evaluate training programs sponsored by the school district. Individuals might receive phone calls from marketing research firms asking about consumer preferences. Often, such surveys are used to help make important policy or marketing decisions.

Survey research design may employ careful sampling techniques to obtain an accurate description of an entire **population;** for example, the Gallup organization conducts surveys to find out what people are thinking about issues such as abortion or nuclear power or to obtain data on preferences for political candidates. When scientific sampling techniques are used, the survey results can be interpreted as an accurate representation of the entire population. Such accuracy can be achieved by sampling an extremely small percentage of a very large population, such as an entire state or even the nation. Surveys on a much smaller scale are going on all the time. A researcher may survey a sample of high school students to investigate who they talk to about personal problems; in this case, the researcher would probably obtain the sample in an unsystematic fashion (e.g., by going to a local high school and distributing questionnaires to students in a few classes). The researcher's concern in this case is not to describe high school students in the United States but to find out who high school students talk to, whether there are gender differences, or whether the students talk to different people about different types of problems. Sampling is discussed in more detail later in this section.

Most people think of surveys as a way of taking a "snapshot" of current attitudes and behaviors. However, the survey method is also an important way for researchers to study relationships among variables and ways attitudes and behaviors change over time. For example, Steinberg and Dornbusch (1991) examined the relationship between the number of hours high school students work and variables such as grade point average, drug and alcohol use, and psychosomatic distress. The sample consisted of 3,989 students in grades 10 to 12 at nine high schools in California and Wisconsin. The researchers found that "long work hours during the school year are associated with lower investment and performance in school, greater psychological and somatic distress, drug and alcohol use, delinquency, and autonomy from parents" (p. 304). Figure 7.1 shows a typical finding: There were frequently some positive aspects of working fewer than ten hours per week (as opposed to not being employed); however, increasingly negative effects were associated with longer work hours.

We turn now to some of the major considerations in survey research: using a questionnaire or an interview, sampling techniques, and constructing a survey instrument.

QUESTIONNAIRE VERSUS INTERVIEW

Survey research may use either questionnaires or interviews to ask people questions about themselves. With questionnaires, questions and statements are presented in written format, and the participants (or respondents, the term typically used to describe individuals in survey research) write their answers. Interviews involve a one-on-one verbal interaction between an interviewer and a respondent, either face-to-face or over the phone. The interviewer asks a series of questions orally and records the replies.

One advantage of using the questionnaire approach is that it generally costs less than interviews because questionnaires can be administered in groups or mailed to people. Further, questionnaires allow anonymity of the respondents, which may be particularly valuable when potentially sensitive topics are investigated. However, a disadvantage of questionnaires is that respondents must be able to read and to understand the questions. Also, many people are not motivated to sit by themselves and complete the questionnaire. This may be one reason the return rate for mail surveys is typically very low, with repeated mailings needed to increase the rate to the 60 to 70% range (Nederhof, 1985).

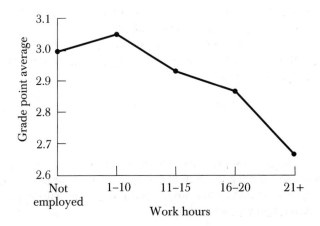

Figure 7.1
Relationship between hours of work and grade point average
SOURCE: Steinberg, L., & Dornbusch, S. M. (1991). Negative correlates of part-time employment during adolescence: Replication and elaboration. *Developmental Psychology, 27,* 304–313. Copyright © 1991 by the American Psychological Association. Reprinted by permission.

With interviews, there is more opportunity for the interviewer and the respondent to establish rapport, thus engaging the respondent more fully in the situation. The respondent may find it interesting to talk to the interviewer and can ask for clarification of questions that are not fully understood. Personal contact with the respondent also allows for the use of visual aids, such as graphic representations of the questions and the options for each answer. Telephone interviews are less expensive than face-to-face interviews, and new computerized telephone survey techniques lower the cost of telephone surveys even further by reducing labor and data analysis costs. With a computer-assisted telephone interview (CATI) system, the interviewer's questions are prompted on the computer screen, and the data are entered directly into the computer for analysis. The U.S. government recently switched to computer-assisted technology for the Current Population Survey, departing from the written format that had been used since 1967 (Bureau of Labor Statistics, 1992). Some surveys are even conducted on the Internet.

Conducting an interview is as much art as it is science, particularly when open-ended responses are used. Subtle aspects of the interviewer's behavior may influence the respondent's cooperation and honesty. Some general hints for conducting an interview are listed here. With sufficient training and practice, these suggestions are easy for an interviewer to master.

1. Be prepared to answer FAQs (frequently asked questions) concerning the purpose of the survey, why the respondent was selected, and what will happen to the responses.
2. Ask general questions first, followed by specific probes to clarify a particular reply. Follow-up questions help the interviewer get more in-depth information than is initially volunteered.
3. Allow sufficient time for the individual to respond.
4. Maintain good eye contact.
5. Keep the interview materials discreetly shielded from the respondent's view.
6. Write down the respondent's replies verbatim even if the interview is being recorded; this indicates interest in the replies and protects against loss of data due to mechanical failure. But don't write too much—that would slow down the conversation.
7. Do not talk rapidly or mumble, do not provide personal opinions, and do not answer for or argue with the respondent.
8. A neat and well-groomed appearance is appropriate. Do not overdress for the occasion; rapport is easier to establish if your wardrobe is similar to that of the participants.

SAMPLING

It is not practical to give a survey to everyone in the population—unless you have the resources of the federal government conducting the Census—so you are probably going to give your survey to a small group of people. However, you may be interested in generalizing to a larger group.

Most research projects involve **sampling** participants from a population of interest. The population is composed of all the individuals of interest to the researcher. One population of interest to a pollster might be all retired citizens in the United States. This implies that the pollster's population of interest does not include people who are still working, visitors from other countries, or people who were never employed. With enough time and money, a pollster could conceivably contact everyone in the population who is retired. Fortunately, the pollster can avoid this massive undertaking by selecting a sample from the population of interest. With proper sampling, the pollster can use information obtained from the sample to determine key characteristics of the population as a whole. Sampling is therefore very important in the generalization of research results.

There are two basic types of sampling techniques: nonprobability sampling and probability sampling. In **nonprobability sampling** we don't know the probability of any particular member of the population being chosen. Individuals in the population have unequal chances of being selected for the survey. In contrast, with **probability sampling** each member of the population has a specifiable probability of being chosen. Individuals in the population have an equal chance of being sampled for the survey. Probability sampling is necessary to accurately generalize results from a sample to the population from which that sample was drawn.

Nonprobability Sampling

Nonprobability sampling techniques are quite arbitrary. A population may be defined but little effort expended to ensure that the sample accurately represents the population. However, among other things, nonprobability samples are cheap and convenient. Two types of nonprobability sampling are haphazard sampling and quota sampling.

Haphazard sampling is a common form of nonprobability sampling. Haphazard, or "convenience," sampling could be called a "take-them-where-you-find-them" method of obtaining respondents. For example, a television reporter might poll people who happen to walk past a particular street corner at a particular time of day and are willing to say a few words to the camera. The population of interest might be "people who live in this city," but the results of this poll could not be generalized to this population. It would not be possible to specify the probability of a city resident being chosen as a participant in this poll. The probability would be high for some people (those who live or work near the street corner) and low for others. The haphazard sampling technique would exclude everyone who, for any reason, wasn't present at that location at that particular time. Thus, any generalization of the results to the entire city probably would be inaccurate.

Quota sampling is another form of nonprobability sampling. A researcher who uses this technique chooses a sample that reflects the numerical composition of various subgroups in the population. For instance, suppose your city has the following composition: 60% White, 20% African American, 10% Latino, 8% Asian American, and 2% Native American. A quota sampling technique that uses nationality and ethnic subgroups would produce a sample that numerically reflects these percentages. Thus, a sample of 100 people from your city would have

60 Whites, 20 African Americans, 10 Latinos, 8 Asian Americans, and 2 Native Americans. Similarly, subgroups might be based on age, gender, socioeconomic class, college majors, and so on. Although quota sampling is a bit more elegant than haphazard sampling, the problem remains that no restrictions are placed on how individuals in the various subgroups are chosen. The sample does reflect the numerical composition of the whole population of interest, but respondents within each subgroup are selected in a haphazard manner. Thus, quota sampling has the same problems of generalization as haphazard sampling.

Using Haphazard Sampling in Basic Research   Much of the research in the social sciences uses nonprobability sampling techniques to obtain participants for surveys or experiments. The advantage of these techniques is that the investigator can obtain research participants without spending a great deal of money or time selecting a specific sample group. It is common practice to select respondents from children enrolled in university day care facilities or students in introductory psychology who volunteer for experiments. These samples are based on convenience rather than the ability to generalize to a random sample.

If generalization is a potential problem, why do researchers use these techniques? The most important reason is that the research is being conducted to study relationships between variables rather than to accurately describe a population. Nonprobability samples are inexpensive and convenient. Researchers can then spend their precious resources conducting their experiments rather than obtaining representative samples using probability sampling techniques. Also, it may be difficult to find a sample of the general population willing to come into the lab for an experiment. If a relationship between the variables being studied is found, one can ask whether the same relationship would be observed with some other population. In some research areas, there isn't a compelling reason to believe or to suspect that the relationship would not be found among other groups. For example, a new test of infant intelligence, the Fagan Test of Infant Intelligence (Fagan & Detterman, 1992) relies on measures of visual processing that should be universal. Early studies of the Fagan test (Benasich & Bejar, 1992; DiLalla et al., 1990) were conducted on nonrandom samples of infants in the United States and later extended to random samples of Norwegian infants (Andersson, 1996). When there is a reason to hypothesize that other groups (e.g., younger or older children, the elderly, or various ethnic groups) would behave differently, researchers typically conduct research to test these hypotheses. Such concerns about generalizability are discussed further in Chapter 16.

Probability Sampling

With **simple random sampling,** every member of the population has an equal probability of being selected for the sample. If the population has 1,000 members, each individual has one chance out of a thousand of being selected. Suppose you want to sample students who attend your school. A list of all students would be needed; from that list, students would be chosen at random to form the sample. Note that this procedure doesn't introduce any biases about who is chosen. In contrast, a haphazard procedure in which you sampled from students walking by a certain location in the quad at 9 A.M. would involve all sorts of biases. For example, that procedure eliminates students who don't frequent this location, and it may also eliminate afternoon and evening students.

When conducting telephone interviews, researchers commonly have a computer randomly generate a list of telephone numbers with the dialing prefixes used in the city or area being studied. This will produce a random sample of the population because most people today have telephones. Some companies will even provide researchers with a list of telephone numbers in which the phone numbers of businesses and numbers that phone companies do not use have been removed.

Stratified random sampling is a somewhat more complicated procedure. This is analogous to quota sampling in that the population is divided into subgroups (or strata). Random sampling techniques are then used to select sample members from each stratum. Any number of dimensions could be used to divide the population, but the dimension (or dimensions) chosen should be relevant to the problem under study. For instance, a survey of attitudes toward welfare reform might stratify on the basis of age, gender, race, and amount of education because these factors are related to people's attitudes about social programs.

Stratified random sampling has the advantage of a built-in assurance that the sample will accurately reflect the numerical composition of the various subgroups. This kind of accuracy is particularly important when some subgroups comprise very small percentages of the population. For instance, if African Americans comprise 5% of a city of 100,000, a simple random sample of 100 people might not include any African Americans. But a stratified random sample would include 5 African Americans chosen randomly from the population. In practice, when it is important to represent a small group within a population, researchers will "oversample" that group to ensure that a representative sample of the group is surveyed. Thus, if you need to compare attitudes of African Americans and Whites on your campus, you might need to sample a large percentage of African American students and only a small percentage of the White students to obtain a reasonable number of respondents in each group. Oversampling is standard in behavioral toxicology studies because it is critical to sample enough people who were exposed to high levels of the toxic substance (Jacobson & Jacobson, 1996). Inadequate sampling procedures contribute to conflicting results from different studies.

Cluster sampling is a technique that can be used to sample a very large population, such as all cable TV subscribers in the United States. This method involves sampling from groups (or clusters) that already exist, such as geographic areas (e.g., city blocks) or organizations (e.g., business firms or schools). To randomly sample people receiving cable television, you would need an exhaustive list of all individuals in the United States who subscribe to cable TV. This is not practical. Instead, the researcher can use multistage cluster sampling. First, obtain a complete list of cable television providers in your city. Second, randomly select a subset of these companies that each serve a "cluster" of households. Third, obtain a complete listing of households from these cable TV providers. Now you have a list of households to sample from, perhaps using a stratified random approach.

You could also employ cluster sampling using geographical areas as the clusters. Rather than random sampling from a list of individuals, the researcher samples from a list of geographical areas. For instance, a city can be described as a list of city blocks. Each city block is considered to be a "cluster." The researcher then takes a random sample of the city blocks and creates a list of cable TV subscribers who live on those blocks. The final sample of cable TV subscribers is then selected randomly from this list. Multistage cluster sampling involves several cycles of listing potential participants and sampling from each successive list until the final representative sample is identified.

CRITICALLY EVALUATING SURVEY SAMPLES

The **response rate** in a survey is the percentage of people in the sample who actually completed the survey. If you mail 1,000 questionnaires to a random sample of families in your community and 500 are completed and returned to you, the response rate is 50%. Response rate is important because it indicates how much bias there might be in the final sample of respondents. Nonrespondents may differ from respondents in any number of ways, including age, income, marital status, and education. The lower the response rate, the greater the likelihood that such biases may distort the findings and, in turn, limit the ability to generalize the findings to the population of interest. A response rate of about 50% is generally considered *adequate* for survey research, 60% is considered a *good* return rate, and 70% is *very good* (Babbie, 1995). Typical return rates, however, are only about 30%.

In general, mail surveys have lower response rates than telephone surveys. With both methods, however, steps can be taken to maximize response rates. With mail surveys, an explanatory postcard or letter can be sent a week or so prior to mailing the survey. Follow-up reminders and even second mailings of the questionnaires are often effective in increasing response rates. With telephone surveys, respondents who aren't home can be called again, and people who can't be interviewed today can be scheduled for a call at a more convenient time.

The **sample size** in a survey may provide a clue about the generalizability of the results. How many people should be included in a survey? There are no precise answers to this question. The sample size required for a survey depends in part on the size of the target population, the type of sampling, and the frequency of occurrence of the variables of interest. Small samples may not be representative and can lead to sampling error. A larger sample is more likely to accurately represent the population. Even modest increases in a small sample size (e.g., from 100 to 150) are important, because proportionally you have increased the sample by half. Increasing the sample size from 1,000 to 1,050 will not have the same impact.

Sampling bias can occur if sampling procedures consistently overlook certain categories of people in the population. For example, telephone interviews omit people who do not have telephones and may oversample people who spend more time at home than others. When research is intended to tell us precisely what a population is like (e.g., state or national opinion polls), careful sampling procedures must be used. This requires defining the population, sampling indi-

BOX 7.1   RESEARCH IN ACTION

The U.S. Census in the Year 2000

The U.S. Constitution requires a strict head count of the nation's residents every 10 years. Statisticians and politicians are currently debating the accuracy of the old way of counting people. Some argue that using door-to-door or mail-in surveys leads to an inaccurate and expensive census count. The 1990 Census missed almost 10 million people, most of whom were minorities (Azar, 1997). The Census Bureau wants to use statistical sampling for the 2000 Census, but Congress is not supportive, remaining a bit skeptical about the validity of using sampling techniques to estimate the population. The accuracy of the Census is important. Census figures determine funding for some government programs; the number of seats in the House of Representatives is determined by the Census count. In addition, researchers rely on Census data for a wealth of information about family demographics.

The Census Bureau is currently trying to inform Congress about the validity of a statistical sampling approach. The proposed plan for the 2000 Census would improve the accuracy of the count and reduce the cost. The plan includes survey mailings, telephone calls, and door-to-door polling as in previous years. Statistical sampling would be used to limit door-to-door polling to 90% of the households in each geographic area known as a census tract. Of the remaining nonrespondents, one in ten would be interviewed, and the results from those interviews would be used to estimate the characteristics of the other nonrespondent households.

In a few years we will find out if the statisticians in the Census Bureau were able to convince Congress about the validity of the scientific principles we describe in this chapter.

viduals from the population in some random fashion, and maximizing the response rate so no biases will be introduced into the sample. Box 7.1 highlights the importance of accurate sampling for the U.S. Census. To learn what elderly people think about the social services available to them, a careful sample of the elderly population is needed. Obtaining the sample by going only to nursing homes would bias the results because these individuals are not representative of all elderly people in the population.

In the study of high school students cited previously (Steinberg & Dornbusch, 1991), the population of interest was teenagers in the United States; however, the sample included only high school students in California and Wisconsin. Although this sample obviously excludes many potential respondents in other areas of the United States, it is superior to those used in previous studies of teenage employment. In the Steinberg and Dornbusch study, the researchers were not interested in accurately describing the number of hours that teenagers in the United States work; they were more interested in whether the number of hours that teenagers work is related to variables such as grade point average and alcohol use.

When evaluating survey data, it is important to examine how the responses were obtained and what population was investigated. Major polling organizations typically take great care to obtain representative samples. Many other surveys, such as surveys on marital satisfaction or dating practices published in a magazine, have limited generalizability because the results are based on people who read the particular magazine and are sufficiently motivated to complete and mail in the questionnaire. When Dear Abby asks readers to write in to tell her whether they have ever cheated on their spouse, the results may be interesting but would not give a very accurate estimate of the true extent of extramarital activity in our society.

CONSTRUCTING QUESTIONS

A great deal of thought must be given to writing questions and statements for a survey. A poorly constructed survey instrument leads to unreliable data. The survey must be carefully constructed so the feelings, thoughts, and behaviors you are interested in are measured accurately. If not, you will have problems with face validity and, ultimately, with construct validity. This section describes some of the most important factors a researcher must consider.

Defining Research Questions

The first thing a researcher must do is define the research questions. Before constructing questions for a survey, the researcher explicitly determines the research questions: What is it that he or she wants to know? In well-designed surveys, the survey questions correspond directly to research questions. Too often, surveys get out of hand when researchers begin to ask any question that comes to mind about a topic without considering exactly what useful information will be gained by doing so. Before you begin writing survey questions, write your hypothesis.

Using Closed-Ended Versus Open-Ended Questions

Questions may be either closed- or open-ended. With closed-ended questions, a limited number of response alternatives are given, and the respondent is forced to choose from these options. With open-ended questions, respondents are free to answer in any way they like. An example of a closed-ended question would be: "Which of the following problems is the greatest one facing our children today?" The respondent would then choose from a list of options such as drugs, neighborhood violence, moral values, obtaining a quality education, or disintegration of the family. An open-ended question on the same topic might ask, "What is the greatest problem facing our children today?" The open-ended question permits the respondent to generate the answer and may produce some very interesting responses.

Using closed-ended questions is a more structured approach. Closed-ended responses are easier to code, and the response alternatives are the same for everyone. However, the closed-ended options also can be a disadvantage. The respondent may find it difficult to answer a question if the options are not mutually exclusive or if there are not enough alternatives. For example, 5- or 7-point scales ranging from "agree to disagree" or "positive to negative" may be preferable to simple "yes versus no" or "agree versus disagree" alternatives. It is also important to consider including an option for "I don't know" or "Other" responses.

Open-ended questions require time to categorize and code the responses and are therefore more costly. Coding the responses is much like coding the raw data in field notes. If a qualitative approach is used, the text of open-ended survey responses is searched for common themes in the respondents' attitudes, feelings, and behaviors. If a quantitative approach is used, the coding procedures are similar to those described in Chapter 6 for the analysis of systematic observation data. Open-ended questions are particularly useful during exploratory phases to help the researcher find out what options people choose that can later be incorporated into closed-ended questions.

The choice of open-ended or closed-ended question format may ultimately affect the results of the survey. Research by Schuman and Scott (1987) evaluated telephone interviews asking respondents to identify an important event or change that happened in the nation or the world in the last five decades. When an open-ended format was used, less than 2% of the respondents mentioned the invention of the computer. When a closed-ended format that presented four options was used, the response rate increased to approximately 30%. This clearly illustrates the influence of the phrasing of a question, leading Schuman and Scott to caution researchers about conclusions based on survey data.

Wording Questions

Once the questions have been written, it is important to edit them and pilot test them on others. Vague or ambiguous questions can easily introduce error into the survey. Questions with complex grammatical structure or difficult vocabulary may confuse the respondents. Avoid jargon and technical terms when writing survey items. Keep items short to avoid ambiguity. Bordens and Abbott (1991) even suggest avoiding words with more than six or seven letters!

Beware of "double-barreled" questions that ask two things at once; a question such as "Should senior citizens be given more money for recreation centers and food assistance programs?" is difficult to answer because it taps two potentially different attitudes. As a general guideline, the word "and" as well as "or" in a questionnaire item is a red flag for a double-barreled question. Check these items carefully and divide them into separate questions.

Avoid items phrased with negative wording because they are more difficult to understand. Recall how confusing exam questions are when the instructor asks, "Which of the following are not true?" It would be much easier to rephrase the question in the affirmative, "Which of the following is false?" The same concept applies to surveys. "The school district should not offer psychological counseling for students" is easily confused because the negative may be overlooked. Present the item in the affirmative, or emphasize the word *not,* perhaps with capital letters or bold type.

Even subtle changes in the wording of questions can introduce bias. The classic work of Loftus and Palmer (1974) on eyewitness testimony indicates that people gave higher estimates of speeding vehicles when asked "About how fast were the cars going when they smashed into each other?" compared to "About how fast were the cars going when they hit each other?" Avoid questions that "lead" people to answer in a certain way or that might be misinterpreted. For example, the questions "Do you favor eliminating the wasteful excess in the public school budget" and "Do you favor reducing the public school budget?" are likely to elicit different answers simply because of the way the questions are phrased. Emotionally laden terms lead to biased responding. Young children are particularly susceptible to the wording of questions and can easily be misled by the phrasing of a question (Ceci & Bruck, 1993). Even adults can be misled, with the elderly at particular risk (Loftus, Levidow, & Duensing, 1992).

It is a good idea to "pretest" the survey items by giving the questions to a small group of people and have them "think aloud" while answering them. Ask these individuals to tell you how they interpret each question and how they respond to the response alternatives. This procedure can provide valuable insights that you can use when editing the questions. For additional material on how to write survey questions, refer to Converse and Presser (1986).

Ordering Questions

It is always a good idea to carefully consider the sequence in which you will ask your questions. In general, it is best to ask the most interesting and important questions first to capture the attention of your respondents. Roberson and Sundstrom (1990) obtained the highest return rates in an employee attitude survey when important questions were presented first and demographic questions (age, gender, educational level, and so on) were asked last. Not everyone agrees with this viewpoint, however. It is possible that answering a few easy questions at the beginning will help respondents relax and become more comfortable with the process of answering questions about their personal attitudes and behaviors.

Another concern is that items located toward the beginning of the survey may alter responses to later items. Such "carryover" effects can be minimized by placing general questions before specific questions addressing the same topic. For the same reason, questions on sensitive topics should appear later in the questionnaire. Avoid these questions unless the information is essential to your survey.

RATING SCALES

Rating scales are the most commonly used approach to measure behavior. They are generally easy to administer and easy to score and may even be administered by a computer. Rating scales use a variety of different formats, including (1) numerical scales, (2) graphic rating scales, (3) comparative rating scales, (4) the semantic differential scale, and (5) Likert scales. The exact method of obtaining a self-report measure will depend to a large degree on the topic being investigated.

Perhaps the best way to gain an understanding of self-report scales is simply to look at a few examples.

Numerical Scales

Numerical scales are a group of rating scales that rely on a sequence of numbers for the response categories. These numbers may be stated for the participant's use, or they may be implied. A dichotomous response such as "yes–no" implies that numerical values of 1 and 0 can be assigned to the answers. For example, you might ask someone to respond to the following 5-point scale:

> Elementary school teachers should be required to pass a comprehensive examination every five years to retain their teaching credential.

| Strongly agree | Agree | Undecided | Disagree | Strongly disagree |

This type of rating scale is called a step scale and can use words, numbers, phrases, or even drawings for each step on the scale. Young children may not be able to comprehend many items and scales devised for adults. Simple drawings are often used in step scales for young children because they cannot understand verbal and numerical labels. A national survey of reading in first- through sixth-grade children used a pictorial rating scale of Garfield cartoon characters (McKenna, Kear, & Ellsworth, 1995). Another pictorial scale that is used frequently for self-report measures in children is a scale of smiling and frowning faces like this one:

Point to the face that shows how you feel about the toy.

Other rating scales do not label all the response alternatives but only the end or anchor points. Thus, a participant could be asked to indicate liking for someone on the following scale, which has seven possible responses:

How much do you like this person?

Dislike very much   Like very much

Graphic Rating Scales

A **graphic rating scale** is a second type of scale. A graphic rating scale requires the survey respondent to place a check mark along a continuous line that is anchored at each end with bipolar descriptive terms such as "favorable" and "unfavorable." The line may be presented horizontally or vertically like a thermometer.

The respondent makes a check mark to indicate his or her rating. To score the responses, the length of the line is measured with a ruler. The process can be simplified by using a 100-mm line; scores would then range from 0 to 100. For example, students might be asked to evaluate a movie using the following graphic rating scales:

How would you rate the movie you just saw?

Not very enjoyable _____ Very enjoyable

Not very violent _____ Very violent

Not very realistic _____ Very realistic

Comparative Rating Scales

A **comparative rating scale** provides a standard of comparison for the respondent so that all ratings are made against some standard comparison. For example, many graduate school applications require a reference from one of your college professors. Commonly asked questions include evaluating the applicant on characteristics such as academic ability, professional commitment, emotional maturity, and potential for professional success. The questions usually take the form of:

In comparison with other undergraduate students at your university, please rate the applicant's potential for success:

Lower 50%	Upper 50%	Upper 25%	Upper 10%	Upper 5%	No Basis for Judgment

Semantic Differential Scales

The **semantic differential scale** is a measure of the meaning of concepts that was developed by Osgood and his associates (Osgood, Suci, & Tannenbaum, 1957). Respondents rate any concept or person on a series of bipolar adjectives with 7-point scales anchored at either end by adjectives such as good–bad, or strong–weak. The semantic differential asks the respondent to choose between the two opposite terms. An example is the following rating of the concept "smoking." Notice that the positive and negative adjectives are randomly arranged on both sides of the response list.

SMOKING

Good	___	: ___	: ___	: ___	: ___	: ___	: ___	: Bad
Foolish	___	: ___	: ___	: ___	: ___	: ___	: ___	: Wise
Strong	___	: ___	: ___	: ___	: ___	: ___	: ___	: Weak
Beautiful	___	: ___	: ___	: ___	: ___	: ___	: ___	: Ugly
Active	___	: ___	: ___	: ___	: ___	: ___	: ___	: Passive

Research on the semantic differential shows that virtually anything can be measured using this technique. Respondents' ratings of specific things (marijuana, foreign cars), places (library, hospital), people (the president, one's mother), ideas (communism, abortion), or behaviors (going to church, riding a bus) can be measured. The concepts are rated along three basic dimensions: (1) evaluation (e.g., good–bad, wise–foolish, beautiful–ugly, kind–cruel), (2) activity (e.g., active–passive, slow–fast, excitable–calm), and (3) potency (e.g., weak–strong, large–small, hard–soft).

Likert Scales

With a **Likert scale** (Likert, 1932) the participant responds to a set of statements on a topic. Typical Likert scales use five categories on a scale that varies from "strongly agree" to "strongly disagree." The statements are arranged in random order, and respondents choose the response alternative that most closely represents their own feelings about the statement. For example, suppose we wanted to assess attitudes toward the new restrictions on teenagers' driving privileges that have been passed recently in some states (so far, Florida, Michigan, Georgia, and North Carolina). To do this, we first need to generate a set of items about driving; then ask a sample of teenagers to agree or disagree with each statement. (Of course, you will get different results if you sample adults!) Part of the questionnaire might be as follows:

Indicate how much you agree or disagree with the following statements, using these alternatives:

SA = Strongly Agree

A = Agree

U = Undecided

D = Disagree

SD = Strongly Disagree

1. Teenage drivers are more likely to crash than other drivers.	SA	A	U	D	SD
2. Restrictions on teenage drivers limit their constitutional rights.	SA	A	U	D	SD
3. Teenage drivers are more careful when they are alone in the car than when they have friends in the car.	SA	A	U	D	SD
4. Restrictions on teenage drivers are a form of discrimination.	SA	A	U	D	SD
5. Restrictions on teenage drivers will save lives.	SA	A	U	D	SD
6. Teenage drivers are more accident prone at night.	SA	A	U	D	SD

POTENTIAL PROBLEMS WITH SURVEYS

Three potential sources of bias can arise when questionnaires and interviews are used: interviewer bias, response sets, and retrospective memory.

Interviewer bias refers to all the biases that can arise from the fact that the interviewer is a unique human being interacting with another human. Thus, one potential problem is that the interviewer could subtly bias the respondent's answers by inadvertently showing approval or disapproval of certain answers. This is particularly important when working with children, who are easily influenced by adults. Or, if there are several interviewers, each could possess different characteristics (e.g., level of physical attractiveness, age, race, sex) that might influence the way respondents answer. Another problem is that interviewers may have expectations that could lead them to "see what they are looking for" in the respondents' answers. Such expectations could bias their interpretations of responses or lead them to probe further for an answer from certain respondents but not others—for example, when questioning Whites but not people from other groups, or when testing boys but not girls. Careful screening and training of interviewers helps to limit such biases, but they remain a possibility in interview research.

A **response set** is a tendency to respond to all questions from a particular perspective rather than to provide answers that are directly related to the questions. What this means is that the respondent is not providing an honest, truthful answer but is answering according to some "pattern" or personal bias. The use of a response set may be intentional, but it is just as likely to be unintentional, particularly with children.

The most common response set is called **social desirability,** or "faking good." The social desirability response set leads the individual to answer in the most socially acceptable way. A socially acceptable answer is the way that "most people" are perceived to respond or the way that would reflect most favorably on the person. Social desirability can be a problem in many research areas, but it is probably most acute when the question concerns a sensitive topic such as violent or aggressive behavior, substance abuse, prejudice, or sexual practices. Children are just as likely as adults to respond in a socially desirable way. For example, it is very difficult to obtain truthful answers about transgressions such as stealing, lying, or cheating at school. Interviews may be especially prone to problems of social desirability because of the personal nature of the situation. For sensitive topics, it may be wise to use anonymous questionnaires or telephone interviews rather than personal interviews.

It should not be assumed, however, that people consistently misrepresent themselves. Jourard (1969) suggested that people are most likely to lie when they don't trust the researcher. If the researcher openly and honestly communicates the purposes and uses of the research, promises to provide feedback about the results, and assures anonymity, then the participants can be expected to give reasonably honest responses.

Another response set is the tendency of some participants to consistently agree or disagree with questions ("yea-saying" or "nay-saying"). Imagine the frustration of interviewing a young child who answers "no" to every question in the interview! The solution to this is relatively straightforward: Ask several questions on the same topic, and pose the responses in both positive and negative directions. For the respondent to be consistent and truthful, he or she will have to answer "yes" to one question and "no" to the second question. For example, in a study of family communication patterns, the researcher might ask people how much they agree with the following statements: "The members of my family spend a lot of time together" and "My family members don't usually eat dinner together." If the respondent agrees with both statements, the researcher is alerted to the possibility that a response set is being used.

However, this method of posing both positive and negative questions does not work well with children. Benson and Hocevar (1985) have studied the difficulty children have with negative items on such questionnaires. As pointed out by Marsh (1986), the double-negative logic required for such items may be cognitively more difficult for children than positive items. That is, "My family members don't usually eat dinner together" requires the answer "false" to indicate that the family usually eats together. Young children (and poorer readers) may not employ this logic appropriately and may give the opposite answer from what they intend.

A third type of response set may occur with closed-ended questions. Recall that closed-ended questions present options to select from. Providing a list of items, even a short list of only two or three items, can challenge attention and short-term memory for many individuals—young children, the elderly, or any individual with memory deficits. As a result, people with limited memory skills may consistently choose the first item in the series. A possible explanation is that they focus exclusively on the first thing you said and do not attend to the rest of the list. Can you think of a good reason why they might choose the last option in the series? For the researcher, the problem is that the responses do not reflect actual attitudes or experiences, and the integrity of the data is jeopardized.

By now you've probably thought of some additional methods of "creative responding" that may occur with children. We already discussed the possibility of saying "yes" to every question, but children may also say "yes" to alternate answers, pick round numbers or favorite numbers, or consistently choose the item presented on the right (or left). If the survey measure is carefully designed, such

EUREKA!/Munro Ferguson

Copyright © 1989 Munro Ferguson. Newspaper distribution, Universal Press Syndicate.

response sets will result in essentially chance-level scores, and the researcher can detect the child's guessing behavior. If the measure is poorly designed (e.g., the correct answers systematically alternate), the scores of subjects who exhibit certain response sets (e.g., answer alternation) will be highly misleading.

Retrospective Memory

One final issue in self-report measures is **retrospective memory.** When researchers must ask participants to recall something about past behaviors, how accurate are such retrospective memories?

Most people have great difficulty remembering anything from before they were 2 or 3 years old (see Bauer [1996] for an alternate view). This *childhood amnesia* was investigated by Pillemer, Picariello, and Pruett (1994), who asked children to recall an emergency school evacuation to a fire alarm at their preschool. Two weeks after the alarm, all children showed some memory for the event. However, seven years later, only the children who were over 4 years old at the time of the fire alarm showed long-term memory of the event. Studies of adults' childhood memories (Sheingold & Tenney, 1982; Usher & Neisser, 1993) report that people who were less than 2 years old when a younger sibling was born have practically no recall for the event; however, people who were 4 years old had good memory for details such as whether they visited their mother in the hospital and what presents the baby received.

The birth of a sibling is an especially noteworthy event in life. Other studies suggest a gradual fading away of much information for several years, coupled with a surprising resistance to forgetting of certain salient events and facts (Bahrick, Bahrick, & Wittlinger, 1975; Squire, 1989). For example, we soon forget those Ds we got in high school (Bahrick, Hall, & Berger, 1996), but our memory for Spanish that was learned in school appears relatively intact for decades (Bahrick, 1984). What influences which facts will be retained and which will be forgotten is one of the more interesting mysteries in memory research today. Most disturbing from the point of view of research methods is the general tendency to modify retrospective memories to enhance social desirability. Thus, memories of earlier behavior become more socially desirable without any real awareness that memories have changed. For these reasons, survey researchers should always be a bit skeptical about data that rely heavily on retrospective memories.

Ethical Concerns

Although it is difficult to predict what people may be offended by, researchers must carefully consider possible negative reactions to survey content. Parents may be offended by the inclusion of survey items that address sensitive topics such as sex, drugs, or religion. In 1991, opposition led to cancellation of a national survey of teenagers, the American Teenage Study (Senate Action, 1991). The survey was funded by the National Institute of Child Health and Human Development and had the potential of contributing to the prevention of sexually transmitted disease. However, opponents successfully argued that teens should not be asked questions about sexual practices, and the survey was not conducted.

Panel Study

Surveys most frequently study people at one point in time. On many occasions, however, researchers wish to make comparisons over time. A **panel study** examines changes over time: How do people change as they grow older? How do children of divorce make the transition to adulthood? Does interest in political issues change in presidential election years? One way to study changes over time is to conduct a panel study in which the same people are surveyed at two or more points in time. In a "two wave" panel study, people are surveyed at two points in time; in a "three wave" panel study, there are three surveys, and so on. Panel studies are particularly useful when the research question addresses the relationship between one variable at "time one" and another variable at some later "time two." For example, Harris and Marmer (1996) analyzed data from three waves of the National Survey of Children in 1976, 1981, and 1987 to examine the role of father involvement in poor and nonpoor families. They report that fathers in poor and welfare families are less involved with adolescents, especially if poverty is constant. Panel studies have been used for topics as diverse as attitudes toward eating and body weight in college and 10 years later (Heatherton, Mahamedi, Striepe, Field, & Keel, 1997), marital happiness in Black and White newlyweds (Timmer, Veroff, & Hatchett, 1996), and the effects of welfare on self-esteem in older men and women (Krause, 1996).

Panel studies can be quite difficult and expensive; it isn't easy to track the same people over a long period of time. Another way to make a comparison over time is to conduct a similar survey with a different sample at a later point in time. This allows the researcher to test hypotheses concerning how behavior may change over time. For example, Weiderman and Sensibaugh (1995) analyzed the acceptance of legalized abortion among males and females across two decades. The General Social Survey (GSS) is administered to different individuals each year. Using GSS data from 1972 to 1991, Weiderman and Sensibaugh determined that men's acceptance of legalized abortion had not changed over time, and for women there was a slight decrease in abortion acceptance.

SUMMARY

In survey research, self-report measures are used to question people. Questionnaire techniques are generally cheaper than interviews. However, many people are not interested in completing questionnaires by themselves. With interviews, people are more motivated to respond to the interviewer's questions. In addition, respondents have personal contact with the interviewer and can clarify questions that are not fully understood.

Most research projects sample a group of participants that represent a larger group of people. With proper sampling, the survey results can be generalized to the population. Nonprobability sampling is quite informal. One type of nonprobability sampling is haphazard sampling, in which no specific effort is made to select participants according to specific characteristics. Quota sampling involves selecting a sample that reflects the numerical composition of various subgroups in the population. Probability sampling is more involved, and it requires more systematic information about the population's characteristics. With simple random sampling, for example, every member of the population has an equal probability of being selected for the research sample. A somewhat more complicated procedure is called stratified random sampling, which involves dividing the population into subgroups (or strata) and selecting proportions of participants in the sample that correspond to proportions in the strata. Cluster sampling uses geographical areas as the basis for sampling and is commonly used in survey research.

When evaluating survey data, it is important to examine how the responses were obtained and what population was investigated. Sampling bias may limit generalizability due to a low response rate, a small sample size, or nonrepresentative selection of respondents.

Survey questions must be carefully chosen so the responses are valid. Questions may be either open-ended or closed-ended. Double-barreled and leading questions should be avoided. Both children and adults can be misled by the phrasing of a question. Rating scales, including numerical scales, graphic rating scales, semantic differential scales, and Likert scales, are also used to obtain self-reports of behavior.

Survey researchers try to eliminate interviewer bias that may inadvertently alter the respondent's answers. Response sets such as social desirability and consistent agreement or disagreement with questions can be minimized with careful item construction. Questions about past events or behaviors may not be answered correctly because retrospective memories of prior events are not necessarily accurate. It is difficult to verify the accuracy of self-report measures, and questions about events in the past are particularly problematic.

A panel study is a research design that offers a way to find out how behaviors and attitudes change over time. In a panel study, a group of people responds to a survey at two or more points in time, providing the researcher with a way to compare their responses.

KEY TERMS

cluster sampling	numerical scales	sampling
comparative rating scale	panel study	sampling bias
graphic rating scale	population	semantic differential scale
haphazard sampling	probability sampling	simple random sampling
interviewer bias	quota sampling	social desirability
Likert scale	response rate	stratified random sampling
nonprobability sampling	response set	survey research
	retrospective memory	
	sample size	

REVIEW QUESTIONS

1. What is a survey? Describe some research questions you might address with a survey.

2. What are the advantages and disadvantages of using questionnaires versus interviews in a survey?
3. Distinguish between probability and nonprobability sampling.
4. Distinguish between haphazard and quota sampling.
5. Distinguish between simple random, stratified random, and cluster sampling.
6. What is sampling bias?
7. What are some factors to take into consideration when constructing questions for surveys?
8. What is a semantic differential scale? What is a Likert scale?
9. Define interviewer bias.
10. Discuss types of response sets and possible solutions to the problem of response sets.
11. What are the issues and problems associated with retrospective information?
12. When would you use a panel study design?

CHAPTER 8

Designing Experiments

In the experimental method, extraneous variables are controlled. Suppose you want to test the hypothesis that crowding impairs cognitive performance. To do this, you might put one group of people in a crowded room and another group in an uncrowded room. The participants in each of the groups would then complete the same cognitive tasks. Now suppose that the people in the crowded group do not perform as well on the cognitive tests as those in the uncrowded condition. Can the difference in test scores be attributed to the difference in crowding? Yes, if there is no other difference between the groups. But what if the room in which the crowded group was placed had no windows and the room with the uncrowded group did have windows—for example, they were two different rooms in a high school? In that case, it would be impossible to know whether the poor scores of the participants in the crowded group were due to the crowding or to the lack of windows. The presence versus absence of a window is confounded with the manipulation of crowding: crowded versus uncrowded group, respectively.

In this chapter, we discuss the fundamental procedures of experimental design. Recall from Chapter 5 that the experimental method has the advantage of allowing a relatively unambiguous interpretation of results. The researcher manipulates the independent variable to create groups that differ in the levels of the independent variable (e.g., crowded versus uncrowded classroom). The groups of participants are then compared in terms of their scores on the dependent variable (e.g., test score on cognitive task). All other variables are kept constant, either through direct experimental control or through randomization. If the scores of the groups are different, the researcher can conclude that the independent variable caused the results because the only difference between the groups is the manipulated variable.

CONFOUNDING AND INTERNAL VALIDITY

Although the task of designing an experiment is logically elegant and seems simple, you should be aware of potential pitfalls. In the hypothetical crowding experiment just described, the variables of crowding and window presence are confounded. **Confounding** occurs when the researcher fails to control or randomize some extraneous variable and something other than the independent variable differs in some systematic way. The window variable was not held constant, and now the researcher is faced with an alternative explanation for the results—the presence or absence of windows may affect the test performance. Remember that the goal of the study was to evaluate the effects of the crowding independent variable; this cannot be done if crowding and the presence of windows are both varying. The interpretation is confused, and the researcher cannot rule out the possibility that any difference in the dependent variable of test performance is a result of the window variable.

One way to solve the problem is to hold the window variable constant by using two rooms with windows or two rooms without windows. It does not matter which type of room is selected as long as the same type of room is used for all participants. In this way the effect of windows (or no windows) is held constant and cannot have a differential effect on the dependent variable. Notice that it does not matter if performance is higher without windows (perhaps due to less distraction), because all participants have this advantage. In this way the researcher can make a direct comparison of performance in the two levels of the independent variable, crowding versus no crowding.

Good experimental design involves eliminating confounding, thus reducing the possibility of alternative explanations for the results. When the variation in the dependent variable can be confidently attributed to the manipulation of the independent variable, the experiment has **internal validity.** An internally valid experiment is conceptually equivalent to having no confounds, thereby eliminating competing explanations for the results through careful control. To achieve internal validity, the researcher must design and conduct the experiment so that only the independent variable can be the cause of the results.

The internal validity of a study should not be confused with external validity, which refers to the generalizability of a study. As discussed in Chapter 6, external validity is the extent to which the results can be generalized to other cultural contexts, different settings, populations, and age groups. We return to the issue of external validity in Chapter 16.

EXAMINING DESIGNS FOR THREATS TO VALIDITY

When you design an experiment or read about someone else's research, it is important to consider internal validity. Using the terminology of Campbell and Stanley (1966; see also Cook & Campbell, 1979) we will now describe seven different kinds of confounds that pose threats to internal validity. After reviewing these sources of confounding, we will look at several different experimental designs that illustrate potential confounds along with techniques for controlling confounds. Box 8.1 describes some of the pitfalls of poor experimental design.

History

History refers to any event that takes place in the participant's environment between the first and second measurements but is not part of the manipulation.

BOX 8.1   RESEARCH IN ACTION

Confounding

A first-grade teacher was concerned that his class of 16 boys and 16 girls was already becoming judgmental against other children based on their physical attractiveness. He decided to test out the theory by individually telling each of his students a story about a girl who was caught stealing a candy bar by her grandmother. For half of the boys and half of the girls, he said the little girl who stole the candy bar was pretty and showed them a picture of a very attractive girl with ribbons in her hair, wearing a fancy party dress. The teacher told the other half of the boys and girls that the girl was not very pretty and showed them a picture of an unattractive little girl with short hair who was wearing baggy jeans and a dirty t-shirt. Next he asked the children to decide how the little girl would feel, based on a 5-point rating scale of smiling and frowning faces.

Can you figure out what's wrong with this design? How can this design problem be solved?

The teacher has confounded several things about the girl. This manipulation is intended to vary the attractiveness of the girl, but it also varies her clothing and her hair style at the same time. The physically attractive girl has long hair, has ribbons in her hair, and wears a fancy dress. The physically unattractive girl has short hair and wears baggy jeans and a t-shirt.

To solve this confounding problem, both the attractive and unattractive girls should wear the same wardrobe and have the same hair style. This would reduce the number of variables and increase the teacher's confidence that appearance is causing the judgments. In addition, the teacher has provided the labels for attractive and unattractive. Perhaps the children like the girl with the baggy jeans better. This will also threaten the validity of the design because the teacher cannot be sure the response on the rating scale is due to the attractiveness manipulation. Overall, this is a very poor design.

A **history confound** occurs outside the experimental situation, but it may inadvertently threaten internal validity by changing participants' responses. This is a potential confound because the change in the dependent variable is due to an outside event, not the independent variable as was intended. Historical events include current events, such as a natural disaster, war, or the release of a new movie, as well as mundane events, such as a family holiday or a substitute teacher in the classroom.

Suppose you are conducting a study on teaching techniques and start the project by randomly assigning fourth graders to a cooperative learning program that consists of four weekly lessons on dinosaurs. A control group does the same dinosaur lessons alone. Your intention is to evaluate the children's knowledge of dinosaurs after 4 weeks and compare the test scores of children in the cooperative group with those of children who worked alone. In the midst of your study, the movie *Jurassic Park* hits the big screen, imparting a great deal of educational information about dinosaurs. At this point you do not know if the fourth graders' knowledge has been influenced by the movie or by the instructional methods.

If the data were collected over a shorter period of time, there would be no problem with a history confound. Experiments that occur in one session are unlikely to have a history confound. History is most problematic when the experiment extends over a period of time, thereby giving "history" the opportunity to influence the data in some unintended fashion.

Maturation

People are continually changing, and those changes can affect the results of an experiment. Any changes that occur systematically over time are called **maturation effects.** Maturation effects include developmental changes related to aging. Children become more cognitively advanced, more analytical, and more experienced with age. Any time-related factor might result in a change from the first measurement to the last measurement in an experiment. If this happens, you might mistakenly attribute the change to the treatment rather than to maturation.

Suppose that the results on the cooperative learning experiment discussed earlier suggest that children learn more when they work together. The next school year you decide to use cooperative learning for all math lessons in fourth grade. By the end of the school year, most students have improved their math skills, but you may not be able to separate effects due to cognitive maturation from effects due to cooperative learning.

Testing

The **testing confound** may occur when participants are tested more than once. Simply taking a pretest may influence the person's behavior. For example, most students improve from the first exam in a course to the second exam because they are more familiar with the testing procedure and the instructor's expectations. The same thing applies to retesting in an experimental situation—just taking the pretest may lead to higher scores. Some of this improvement is due to increased familiarity with the situation, but some improvement may also come from knowledge gained from the pretest. In other contexts, taking a pretest may familiarize people with the issues being investigated, inadvertently causing the participants to think about the issues more, thereby changing their responses. Again, the experiment would lack internal validity.

Instrumentation

If the difference between pretest and posttest scores is due to changes in the measuring instrument, you have an **instrumentation confound** or **instrument decay.** The term is borrowed from the physical sciences and originally referred to deterioration of mechanical apparatus over time, such as a scale that wears out and loses sensitivity with age. In studies that use pagers to signal participants to record behavior, "dead" pager batteries would also represent instrument decay. In the social sciences, instrument decay applies when human observers are used to measure behavior. Over time an observer may gain skill, become fatigued, or unconsciously change the standards on which observations are based, becoming more or less lenient when rating behavior. Any of these changes may contribute to an instrumentation confound.

The reliability of observations can be verified by calculating interobserver reliability, as discussed in Chapter 4. The purpose of recalculating interobserver reliability several times during an observational study is to detect possible instrument decay. Unintentional changes in instrumentation threaten internal validity by providing a rival explanation for the differences in behavior across the observation periods.

Instrumentation can also be a problem for participants. A popular method to collect information about the activities of children and adolescents is the Experience Sampling Method (Csikszentmihalyi & Larson, 1987; Larson, 1989). Pagers are used to beep participants at various time intervals. When paged, they are supposed to record their moods, current activity, or perhaps their companions at the time (cf. Larson, Richards, Moneta, Holmbeck, & Duckett, 1996; Swarr & Richards, 1996). At the beginning of the experience sampling procedure, people may be highly motivated to respond to all pages and conscientiously record all the requested data, but after a week or two of paging, they may be tired of the task and sometimes forget to record their activities. Such instrument decay would weaken internal validity.

Statistical Regression

Internal validity may be threatened by **statistical regression** whenever participants are selected because they score extremely high or low on some characteristic. When they are retested, their scores tend to change in the direction of the mean, which is why this confound is also called *regression toward the mean*. Extremely high scores are likely to become lower, and extremely low scores are likely to become higher. The confound occurs because the change in scores may be erroneously attributed to the effects of the independent variable.

For example, you may want to examine the effects of an intervention program aimed at reducing depression in the elderly. First, you would select adults who have extremely high scores on a depression inventory pretest. Then, you would conduct the antidepression program. Finally, you would retest the participants to see if their depression scores had changed. Unfortunately, their scores are probably going to decrease on the second assessment regardless of the effectiveness of the antidepression program, giving the false illusion that the intervention program is effective. Regression occurs because of measurement error in each score. Recall from Chapter 4 that each score consists of a true score, which reflects the actual score, and measurement error. Ordinarily, repeated assessments of a dependent variable include measurement error in a random fashion, at times inflating and at times deflating the true score. But in the case of an extreme score, the only possible change is toward the middle. The end result is that an initially extreme score will be less extreme when the measure is readministered.

A subtle form of regression occurs when we try to explain events in the real world as well. Sports columnists often refer to the hex that awaits an athlete who appears on the cover of *Sports Illustrated*. The performances of a number of athletes have dropped considerably after they were the subjects of *Sports Illustrated* cover stories. Although these cover stories might cause the poorer performance (perhaps the notoriety results in nervousness and reduced concentration), statistical regression is also a likely explanation. An athlete is selected for the cover of the magazine because he or she is performing at an exceptionally high level; the principle of statistical regression states that very high performance is likely to deteriorate. We would know this for sure if *Sports Illustrated* also did cover stories on athletes who were in a slump and this became a good omen for them!

The point is that the sample of behavior that led to the athlete's selection for the cover story on the magazine is not representative of normal behavior but actually represents atypical behavior. Before too long, behavior will return to its norm. The same phenomenon may lead people to "superstitious behavior." For example, if a normally healthy person becomes ill but gets well after trying a new herbal treatment, the person is likely to attribute his or her recovery to the treatment. If a student is struggling with a course in school but improves his or her test scores after taking a long walk immediately before the next test, the student is likely to continue to take a walk before every exam. In fact, the improvements in behavior may be just an artifact of regression to the mean.

Mortality

A study may be affected by **mortality** when subjects drop out of the experiment. Another term for mortality is *attrition*. This is a particular concern for a study that lasts over a long period of time. People may drop out for reasons unrelated to the experimental manipulations, such as illness, moving away, or simply declining to continue the study. Losing some participants in a random fashion does not affect internal validity; the problem arises if the rate of attrition differs across experimental conditions. If this occurs, the independent variable manipulated in the study may be influencing the loss of participants. Even if the groups were equivalent when the study began, differential mortality can make the groups nonequivalent and confound interpretation.

To illustrate the impact of mortality, suppose we are interested in studying the effect of a 10-week-long program designed to improve attitudes toward participation in extracurricular activities in high school. Increased school participation leads to lower dropout rates, so there are good reasons for getting students involved in high school activities. Ninth graders are randomly assigned to the intervention program or to a control group. The experimental group attends orientation activities presented by ten high school clubs, whereas the control group does not. How might mortality affect the outcome? Teenagers who initially lacked interest in school activities are likely to leave the program, failing to attend meetings. At the end of 10 weeks, when the outcome of the program is assessed, only the most interested students remain in the study. A comparison of the experimental group and the control group would show more positive attitudes in the experimental group, even if the program had no effect.

Selection Differences

The **selection differences** problem usually occurs when participants in a study are assigned to experimental groups from naturally existing groups, precluding the possibility of random assignment. By definition, random assignment would make the groups equivalent; using preexisting groups creates nonequivalent groups. The experimenter does not have any control over which people are in each group when using existing groups, leading to a potential bias. This biased selection introduces the rival explanation that the effects of the study are due to the nonequivalent groups rather than to the independent variable.

As an example, let's reconsider the crowding experiment introduced at the beginning of the chapter. Recall that the investigator was testing the hypothesis that crowding impairs cognitive performance. After a bit of detective work, the investigator found that one professor teaches the same class twice in the same room. Fortunately, in one section the class is overenrolled and the room is very crowded, whereas in the second section the class has few students and the room is not crowded. On the surface this seems like a perfect solution—the same instructor covers the same lecture material for students at the same school.

Do you see the confound yet? If students made their own choices when enrolling in the class, some chose to enroll in the crowded class and elected to remain enrolled despite the crowding. This makes the crowded group inherently different from the group of students who remained enrolled in the uncrowded class. You may have spotted other differences as well, such as different times of day and the unavoidable fact that one lecture precedes the other. If these other variables have an impact on the dependent measure of cognitive performance, the experiment lacks internal validity and the investigator cannot unequivocally determine that the crowding variable affects cognitive performance.

DIAGRAMMING EXPERIMENTAL DESIGNS

When conceptualizing your own experimental design or when evaluating a design used by another researcher, one way to represent the design is with a simple diagram. Donald Campbell and Julian Stanley (1966) made extensive contributions to the field of research methodology, and their naming conventions and notation system are accepted as the standard. Using only four symbols (O, X, R, and a dashed line), basic experimental designs can be graphically represented. With this notation system and a few simple guidelines, you can easily identify potential confounds and quickly compare different designs.

First, you need symbols to represent the variables. The independent variable is the experimental manipulation—the presumed "cause" for the behavior—and is represented by the symbol X (as in *ex*-perimental). In a simple experiment, one group is exposed to the experimental treatment and a control group is not exposed to the experimental treatment. The absence of an X indicates no treatment.

The dependent variable is the observed variable, the variable that measures the participant's behavior. The symbol for the dependent variable is O (as in *ob*-served variable). The O refers to any way of measuring the participants' behavior, whether it is a behavioral, self-report, or physiological dependent measure. The dependent variable can be measured at more than one point in the study.

Next, arrange the symbols to represent the order of events in the study. The symbols for the independent variable and the dependent variable are arranged in temporal sequence, from left to right in the diagram. This means that the first symbol stands for the first thing that happened in the experiment—was it the experimental intervention X or was it an O to assess the participant's behavior? Logically, either one can come first: You can begin a study with the independent variable X, or you can begin a study by measuring the dependent variable O. An initial O is called a *pretest* and provides baseline information to the researcher. An O that follows the experimental treatment is called a *posttest*.

What if the design has more than one group of participants? Each experimental group or condition appears as a separate row of Os and Xs. Each row represents the chronology of events for each group. Events that happen at the same time to different groups appear in the same vertical column.

When there is more than one experimental group, one more design feature is added to the diagram. How were participants assigned to the different groups? If they were assigned randomly, the symbol R (as in *random* assignment) is written at the beginning of each row of Os and Xs. As discussed in Chapter 5, when subjects are randomly assigned, possible extraneous variables such as individual differences in socioeconomic status and personality characteristics are randomly distributed, thereby creating *equivalent* groups. Conversely, if random assignment is not used, the groups are *nonequivalent;* this is represented by a dashed line ————— between the rows of Os and Xs. Notice that in one study you would not use both an R and a dashed line; the groups are either equivalent (as the result of randomization) or nonequivalent (as the result of using preexisting groups without randomization).

That's all there is to it—four symbols and four decisions about the study. To summarize:

X represents the independent variable or experimental manipulation

O represents the dependent or observed variable

R represents random assignment of participants to experimental conditions

————— represents nonequivalent groups (no random assignment)

1. How many groups were in the study? This tells you how many rows of Os and Xs you need.
2. When did the researcher measure the participant's behavior? Before or after the independent variable? This tells you how to arrange the Os and Xs in each row.
3. How were people assigned to the groups? This tells you whether to use an R at the beginning of each row of symbols or a dashed line between the rows of symbols.
4. Keep Os and Xs on the same line for one group, and start a new line for each separate group of participants. Align symbols vertically to represent simultaneous events.

In the remainder of the chapter we discuss six experimental designs that range from poor to good. Poor experimental designs illustrate the internal validity problems that arise when there is a failure to control for extraneous, confounding variables. True experiments are well-designed studies that avoid most internal validity problems. Quasi-experimental designs are used when true experiments are not possible, but they also have limitations. As we move up the hierarchy from poor to good designs, you will see the advantages and disadvantages in each experimental design.

POORLY DESIGNED EXPERIMENTS: PRE-EXPERIMENTAL DESIGNS

One-Shot Case Study

Suppose you want to test the hypothesis that first-time parents who participate in a parent enrichment seminar are less anxious and report less stress about the transition to their new roles. The independent variable (X) is the enrichment program; the dependent variable (O) is parental stress. Now suppose that you found such a program—a seminar that meets once each week for 6 weeks in your community hospital—and gained permission to administer a parental stress scale at the end of the last meeting. The components of the design are:

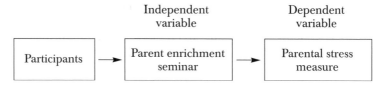

In the design, formally called a **one-shot case study** by Campbell and Stanley (1966), a single group of participants is studied only once, after an experimental manipulation of some kind. Participants are first exposed to the independent variable, and then behavior is measured. The design would be diagrammed as:

$$X \quad O$$

Suppose that the overall average parental stress score of the participants is 3 on a 1- to 7-point scale (1 corresponds to minimal stress). How can you interpret the results? Unfortunately, this finding is not interpretable. You don't know how much stress parents reported before the seminar began, making it difficult to determine if their stress actually decreased after the intervention. In addition, you don't know whether new parents who do not participate in the seminar are more stressed than the ones you tested. Parents who did not participate might be equally stressed or show even less stress than the participants.

How can you improve on the one-shot case study? The design lacks a crucial element: a control or comparison group. A well-designed experiment must include some sort of comparison condition to enable you to interpret your results. The one-shot case study has serious deficiencies in the context of designing an experiment to measure precisely the effect of an independent variable on a dependent variable. However, case studies are valuable in descriptive research contexts. For example, a researcher who becomes a participant observer in a new parent enrichment seminar can provide a rich account of the dynamics of the seminar experience, why people participate, and the possible effects of participation. Such approaches to scientific inquiry were described in Chapters 6 and 7. One way to provide a comparison is to measure parental stress before the intervention (a pretest) and again afterward (a posttest). This would add an O to the diagram and allow the investigator to compute an index of change from the pretest to the posttest. A second way to obtain a comparison is to administer the parental stress scale to a second group of parents who did not participate in the seminar program. Let's look at each of these design improvements.

One-Group Pretest-Posttest Design

Using a **one-group pretest-posttest design,** you would administer the measure of parental stress both before and after parents participated in the seminar. You would hope to find that the average score on the stress measure was lower the second time. The design would be diagrammed as:

O   X   O

The components of the design now include:

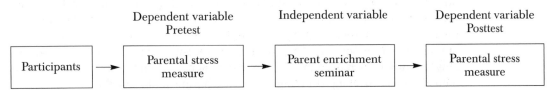

This clearly improves on the one-shot case study because now you have information about the parents' stress level prior to the seminar (the added O before the X). However, if you did find a decrease in stress, you would not be able to assume that the result was due to the parent enrichment program. This design fails to take into account several competing alternative explanations and is threatened by confounds of history, maturation, testing, instrument decay, and statistical regression.

For example, a *history* confound might occur if relatives came to stay with the new parents, providing valuable support and assistance in the care of the newborn. *Maturation* confounds the results because people change over time. New parents gain experience quickly; with each new day of parenthood, they become more capable of responding to the demands of parenting. *Testing* may confound the results because simply taking the pretest may influence the parents. The parental stress questionnaire might be enough to stimulate parents to change their perceptions about the transition to parenthood. *Instrument decay* occurs if parents attend carefully to each item on the initial questionnaire, providing an accurate assessment of their stress, but are less conscientious about responding accurately by the time the posttest is administered. *Statistical regression* would be a problem if parents were selected for the parent enrichment seminar because they scored especially high on the parental stress measure. By using only one group of parents, the researcher does not know if decreased stress is due to these potential confounds or due to the enrichment seminar.

Nonequivalent Control Group Design

The **nonequivalent control group design** improves on the one-shot case study by adding a control group for comparison. This is clearly an improvement, but the design is still pre-experimental because the two groups are not equivalent. The control group and the experimental group are formed without using random assignment, relying on naturally existing groups. The diagram for the design requires two lines, and a dashed line is added for the nonequivalent groups. Remembering to keep symbols aligned vertically when events occur at the same point in time, the design is:

$$\begin{array}{cc} X & O \\ \hline O \end{array}$$

If the nonequivalent control group design is used to study stress in new parents, the parents in the first group are given the parental stress measure after completing the enrichment seminar; the parents in the second group do not attend the seminars, but they do complete the parental stress measure. The investigator does not have any control over which parents are in each group. Thus, it is likely that parents in the seminar group chose to participate in the enrichment program, and the parents in the second group are simply parents who for whatever reason did not sign up for the seminar. For example, the second group of parents may be parents who are college students or may have been recruited from parents who attended a meeting at a local school. The design now looks like this:

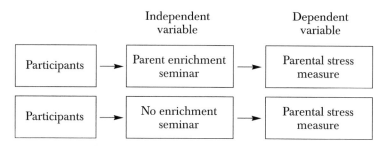

Because the groups are not equivalent, selection differences present a potential confound. Perhaps parents who choose to participate have especially difficult infants, creating a great deal of stress and anxiety for the parents. Alternatively, you might think of reasons parents who have especially quiet infants might participate. For example, because their infant is easier to care for, they may be more confident that a program can help them in their transition to parenthood. In either case, the preexisting differences make it difficult to interpret any results obtained in the experiment.

It is important to note that the problem of selection differences arises in this design even when the researcher apparently has successfully manipulated the independent variable using two similar groups. For example, a researcher might have all new parents in one hospital participate in the parent enrichment seminar, whereas new parents from a second hospital serve as a control group. The problem here, of course, is that the parents from the two hospitals may have differed in stress levels *prior* to the parental enrichment seminar. The design discussed in the next section addresses this issue.

QUASI-EXPERIMENTAL DESIGNS

A good way to determine if two groups of participants differ initially is to use a pretest. When a pretest is added to the nonequivalent control group design, we have a **nonequivalent control group pretest-posttest design.** This design is one of the most useful **quasi-experimental designs** described by Campbell (cf. Campbell, 1968, 1969; Cook & Campbell, 1979; Campbell & Stanley, 1966). This is not a true experimental design because assignment to groups is not random; the two groups may not be equivalent. This is represented by the dashed line in the diagram. However, we have the advantage of knowing the pretest scores. This design can be diagrammed as follows:

$$\begin{array}{ccc} O & X & O \\ \hline O & & O \end{array}$$

In the parental stress study, now we can see whether the parents in each group report similar stress levels *before* the enrichment seminar. Even if the groups are not equivalent, we can look at changes in scores from the pretest (the first O for each group) to the posttest (the second O for each group). If the independent variable (the parent seminars) has an effect, the experimental group will show a greater change in the dependent measure (the stress rating) than the control group (see Kenny, 1979). The components of the design now include:

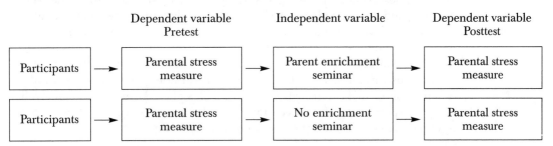

Such a quasi-experimental design could be useful in a variety of settings. For example, attitudes and behaviors of pediatric nurses in a neonatal intensive care unit of a hospital could be assessed before and after a new training program was administered. A control hospital of similar size could be chosen in which staff would be measured on the same variables without the new program. Even though

BOX 8.2   RESEARCH IN ACTION

Quasi-Experimental Research

Joy, Kimball, and Zabrack (1986) used a nonequivalent control group pretest-posttest design to study the effect of television on children's aggressive behavior. A Canadian town that did not have television reception until 1974 was the focus of the study (this town was dubbed "Notel"). The researchers measured children's physical and verbal aggression both before and after the introduction of television in Notel. At the same time, they measured aggression in two similar towns, one that received only a single Canadian station ("Unitel") and one that received both Canadian and U.S. networks ("Multitel"). Thus, it was possible to compare the change in aggression in Notel with that in the control communities of Unitel and Multitel. The results of the study showed that there was a greater increase in aggression in Notel than in either Unitel or Multitel, indicating the powerful influence of television programming on children's behavior.

the pretests may reveal initial differences between the two hospitals, change scores should indicate whether the program was effective. Similarly, this design could be used to assess the impact of an independent variable manipulation among residents of two different nursing homes or among students in two different schools. A nonequivalent control group pretest-posttest design was used in the research project described in Box 8.2.

WELL-DESIGNED EXPERIMENTS

Now that you understand the way an experiment is designed and some problems to avoid, let's look at a well-designed experiment, a "true" experimental design. The simplest possible experimental design has two variables—the independent variable and the dependent variable. In the simple design, the independent variable has two levels: an experimental group and a control group. Researchers make every effort to ensure that the only difference between the two groups is the manipulated variable. Remember, the experimental method involves control over extraneous variables, either by keeping such variables constant or by using randomization to make sure extraneous variables affect both groups equally. The simple experimental design can take one of two forms: a posttest only control group design or a pretest-posttest control group design.

Posttest Only Control Group Design

A researcher who uses the **posttest only control group design** (1) obtains two equivalent groups of participants, (2) introduces the independent variable, and (3) assesses the effect of the independent variable by using a posttest to measure the dependent variable. The design is diagrammed as:

> R   X   O
> R   O

The first step is to obtain two equivalent groups of participants. This is done by randomly assigning participants to the two groups, or by having the same individuals participate in both conditions. The R in the diagram means that participants were randomly assigned to the two groups from the same pool of potential participants. In the parental stress study, the researcher could recruit all first-time parents at one hospital and randomly assign parents to either the treatment group that attends the parent enrichment seminar or a control group that does not attend the seminar.

Next, the researcher must choose two levels of the independent variable, such as an experimental group that receives a treatment and a control group that does not. The parental stress study uses this approach. Another approach would be to use two different amounts of the independent variable—to compare the effects of a 6-week program to those of a 10-week program, for example. Both approaches provide a basis for comparison of the two groups. A researcher might study the effect of reward on motivation by rewarding one group of children after they played a game and by giving no reward to children in the control group. Alternatively, one group could receive more rewards than the other. The experimental design now incorporates these elements:

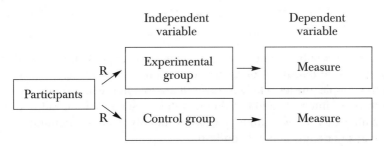

Finally, the effect of the independent variable is measured. The same measurement procedure is used for both groups, so that comparison of the two groups is possible. All participants in the study must be measured on the same dependent variable (or variables). For example, in the parental stress study, parents in the seminar group and parents in the control group must all complete the parental stress measure. Because the groups were equivalent to begin with, factors such as history or maturation should affect each group equally. In this way, any difference between the groups on the posttest measures of the dependent variable can be attributed to the independent variable. The result is an experimental design that has internal validity.

Pretest-Posttest Control Group Design

The **pretest-posttest control group design** improves on the posttest only control group design by adding a pretest (add one O to each line in the diagram) before introducing the independent variable. In all other respects the designs are similar. The researcher (1) obtains two equivalent groups of participants, (2) uses a pretest to assess the dependent variable at the beginning of the experiment, (3) introduces the independent variable, and (4) assesses the effect of the independent variable by using a posttest to measure the dependent variable. The design is diagrammed as:

$$R \quad O \quad X \quad O$$
$$R \quad O \quad\quad O$$

The pretest-posttest control group design makes it possible to ascertain that the groups were, in fact, equivalent at the beginning of the experiment. However, this precaution is usually not necessary if participants have been randomly assigned to the two groups. With a sufficiently large sample of participants, random assignment will produce groups that are virtually identical in all respects. The experimental design now contains these elements:

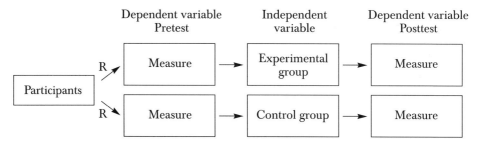

You are probably wondering how many participants are needed in each group to be sure that random assignment has made the groups equivalent. The larger the sample, the less likely the groups are to differ in any systematic way that might threaten internal validity. Although there are no clear-cut rules for specifying a "sufficiently large" sample, you will probably need a minimum of 10 to 20 participants per experimental condition.

DIAGRAMMING DESIGNS REVISITED

Now that you understand the basic elements of good experimental designs, here are a few more hints on diagramming designs. You can logically derive the pattern of Os and Xs for each design by thinking about the three questions posed earlier in the chapter. Let's review them here.

First, *how many groups were in the study?* How do you know if there is more than one group of subjects? Each time there is a comparison group, the term *control group* is included in the name of the design. If the name of the design includes *control group,* you will need two lines of Os and Xs, one for each group of participants. Otherwise you only need one line of Os and Xs.

Second, *when did the researcher measure the participant's behavior? Before or after the independent variable?* How do you know when the design needs an O before the experimental intervention X? Each time there is a pretest, the term *pretest* is in the name of the design. So if the design name includes *pretest,* put an O before

TABLE 8.1   Summary of Designs

Design Type	Problems
Pre-Experimental Designs	
One-shot case study X O	No comparison group
One-group pretest-posttest design O X O	History Maturation Testing Instrument decay Statistical regression Mortality

Nonequivalent control group design
    X   O
─ ─ ─
         O
	Selection differences
	Mortality

Quasi-Experimental Designs	

Nonequivalent control group
pretest-posttest design
   O   X   O
─ ─ ─ ─ ─
   O   O
	Selection differences are possible
	but change scores allow assessment
	of effect of independent variable

True Experimental Designs	

Posttest only control group design
   R   X   O
   R   O
	Possibly mortality

Pretest-posttest control group design
   R   O   X   O
   R   O   O
	Possibly mortality but can assess
	with pretest information
	Sensitizing subjects to hypothesis is
	a real problem

the X. Now consider the posttest—all designs do not include the name *posttest*, but good experimental design dictates that an investigator will always measure the effect of the independent variable after going to all the bother of setting up an intervention of some kind. This means that *every* X is followed by an O.

Finally, *how were people assigned to the groups?* How do you know if the groups were randomly assigned or nonequivalent? As it turns out, Campbell and Stanley (1966) were very logical here as well—if the term *nonequivalent* appears in the name of the design, the groups are not randomly assigned and you will need a dashed line. In the absence of the term *nonequivalent*, the groups are random; use an R in front of each line of Os and Xs. This question only arises when there is more than one group in the study.

Try your hand at diagramming designs. Table 8.1 reviews the design types we've presented and lists the principal problems of each design. Cover up the diagrams shown in the table and generate your own sketches for each design. You should be able to see the increasing complexity of each design. With the addition of pretests and control groups, poor experimental designs plagued with internal validity problems become true experimental designs that effectively reduce problems from potential confounds. With a good experimental design, an investigator can confidently attribute the observed variation in the dependent variable to manipulation of the independent variable rather than to some extraneous variable that interferes with the interpretation. Only then does the experiment have internal validity, allowing a cause-and-effect conclusion. This is the goal of good experimental design.

SUMMARY

Good experimental design requires control of extraneous variables so that only the independent variable can be responsible for participants' responses on the dependent measure. A confound exists when an extraneous variable co-varies along with the independent variable. Internal validity exists only when the investigator can confidently attribute the variation in the dependent measure to manipulation of the independent variable. When any rival explanation exists, internal validity is weakened. In contrast to internal validity, external validity is the extent to which the results of an experiment can be generalized to other types of participants, other settings, and other ways of operationally defining the variables.

The seven threats to internal validity are (1) history, (2) maturation, (3) testing, (4) instrument decay, (5) statistical regression, (6) mortality, and (7) selection differences. Poor experimental designs such as the one-shot case study and the one-group pretest-posttest design do not control for these confounds. Quasi-experimental designs are useful when true experiments are not possible; they allow assessment of naturally formed groups. The nonequivalent control group pretest-posttest design is a quasi-experimental design that improves on pre-experimental designs by adding a control group as well as a pretest.

True experiments are well-designed experiments that avoid most internal validity problems. Through experimental control and randomization, the experimenter makes every effort to eliminate confounds, ensuring that the only difference between the groups is the manipulated variable. Such true experiments may use either posttest only control group designs or pretest-posttest control group designs.

Designs can be diagrammed using four symbols. X represents the independent variable, O represents the dependent variable, R stands for random assignment, and a dashed line means the groups are not equivalent. The various designs are summarized in Table 8.1. As we move up the hierarchy from poor to good designs, you can see the advantages and disadvantages in each experimental design by looking at the diagram for each design. You should familiarize yourself with the designs, the diagrams, and the threats to internal validity.

KEY TERMS

confounding
history confound

instrument decay
instrumentation confound

internal validity
maturation effect
mortality
nonequivalent control group design
nonequivalent control group pretest-
  posttest design
one-group pretest-posttest design

one-shot case study
posttest only control group design
pretest-posttest control group design
quasi-experimental design
selection differences
statistical regression
testing confound

REVIEW QUESTIONS

1. What is meant by confounding?

2. What is meant by the internal validity of an experiment?

3. Describe the threats to internal validity discussed in the text: history, maturation, testing, instrumentation, statistical regression, mortality, and selection differences.

4. Why does having a control group eliminate the problems associated with the one-group pretest-posttest design? Sketch the design with Os and Xs to support your explanation.

5. How do true experimental designs eliminate the problem of selection differences?

6. Distinguish between the posttest only control group design and the pretest-posttest control group design. What are the advantages and disadvantages of each? Sketch each design with Os and Xs.

7. Using the system of Os and Xs, are the following designs possible? Explain your answer. For valid designs only, can you name the design?

   (a) R   O   X
        R   X

   (b) X   O

        X

   (c) O   X   O
        O   O

8. Recognizing that the first year of teaching elementary school can be very stressful, the administrators in Silver Lake School District adopted a support program for first-year teachers. However, due to budget limitations the program was only offered to elementary school teachers. The support program took place after school each Friday for 4 months. By the end of the school year, more teachers in the control group resigned their teaching positions. What type of design is this? What can you conclude about the effectiveness of the support program?

9. Design an experiment to test the hypothesis that pets are beneficial to the health of older adults. Operationally define both the independent and

dependent variables. Your experiment should have two groups. Defend your answer.

10. Boyatzis et al. (1995) randomly assigned children in an after-school program to a control group or a *Power Rangers* group, with an equal number of boys and girls in each condition. On the first day of the study, observers watched the children play in the classroom and recorded the number of aggressive acts in a 2-minute interval for each child in the control group. On the second day of the study, children in the *Power Rangers* group watched an episode of *Power Rangers*. Observers then recorded the aggressive acts for these children, observing each child in the *Power Rangers* group during free play for 2 minutes. The results indicated that children who watched *Power Rangers* displayed significantly more aggression; for every physically or verbally aggressive act by children in the control group, *Power Rangers* participants committed seven aggressive acts. These results were especially pronounced for boys in the *Power Rangers* group, who were the most aggressive overall.

a. Name and sketch the design.

b. Why did the researchers randomly assign children to the control group or the *Power Rangers* group?

c. What is the confound in the study? Suggest a solution for the design that would remove the confound.

d. Boyatzis et al. concluded that viewing *Power Rangers* causes aggressive behavior in children after watching only one episode. Is the conclusion warranted? Explain your answer.

CHAPTER 9

Developmental and Single-Subject Designs

One research question of interest to developmental scientists is how individuals change with chronological age. A researcher might test a theory concerning changes in ability to reason as children grow older, the age at which self-awareness develops in young children, or the global values people have as they move from adolescence through old age. In all cases, the major variable is age. Strictly speaking, age is not a true experimental variable because we cannot manipulate it directly. Developmental researchers study the age variable by selecting subjects at different ages or studying the same individuals at different points in their lives. Two general methods are used to study individuals of different ages: the cross-sectional method and the longitudinal method. Using the **cross-sectional method,** persons of different ages are studied at only one point in time. The **longitudinal method** involves observing the same subjects at two or more times as they grow older. To illustrate, consider two approaches to studying the transition to retirement. A cross-sectional design might compare the average time spent in leisure activities of three samples of adults ages 55, 60, and 65. A longitudinal design would study a sample of adults when they were 55 years old, and then measure them again at ages 60 and 65. These designs, plus a hybrid approach, the sequential design, are shown in Figure 9.1.

One obvious difference between cross-sectional and longitudinal approaches to measuring change over time is speed. The participants in the cross-sectional design can all be observed in a single day, but the longitudinal design may take 15 years to complete. Thus, time is a distinguishing feature of these designs; cross-sectional designs are faster and therefore less expensive than longitudinal designs. For these important reasons, cross-sectional studies are much more common than longitudinal studies.

CROSS-SECTIONAL RESEARCH

Suppose an educational researcher wants to determine the optimal age for introducing critical thinking instruction in the math and science curriculum. Critical thinking and problem-solving skills are important foundations for intellectual development—but how early can these skills be taught? A cross-sectional design is the most efficient way to address this issue. Children of different ages are studied at only one point in time. For example, the researcher can implement a critical skills program in three different classrooms (e.g., fifth grade, seventh grade, and ninth grade). After the program is completed, all children are assessed on the same dependent measure of decision-making skills. (An excellent instructional program designed to increase children's problem-solving skills is *The Adventures of Jasper Woodbury* [Cognition and Technology Group at Vanderbilt, 1997].)

As discussed above, two major advantages of the cross-sectional method are timeliness and economy. The cross-sectional method is very time-efficient; the researcher does not have to wait while the children progress through elementary school and junior high school. Time-efficiency translates to a financial savings; cross-sectional research is generally less costly because the data are obtained in a short time frame.

Although timeliness and economy are important considerations, cross-sectional designs also have some significant disadvantages. The most important disadvantage is that cross-sectional research informs us only about developmental differences, not developmental change. By comparing different children in each grade level, conclusions are limited to descriptions of typical age differences between the groups of children. Because a group of older children performs better than a different group of younger children, we are able to infer that critical thinking skills improve with age, but we haven't observed this improvement directly. Developmental change and intra-individual differences can only be detected when the same individuals are observed more than once.

Comparisons of different individuals are problematic because the groups or cohorts of individuals may not be equivalent. A **cohort** is a group of individuals that share a common characteristic. In developmental research, the term *cohort*

Cross-sectional design

	Year of birth (cohort)	Time 1: 2000
Group 1:	1945	55 years old
Group 2:	1940	60 years old
Group 3:	1935	65 years old

Longitudinal design

	Year of birth (cohort)	Time 1: 2000	Time 2: 2005	Time 3: 2010
Group 1:	1945	55 years old →	60 years old →	65 years old

Sequential design

	Year of birth (cohort)	Time 1: 2000	Time 2: 2005	Time 3: 2010
Group 1:	1945	55 years old →	60 years old →	65 years old
Group 2:	1935	65 years old →	70 years old →	75 years old

Figure 9.1 Cross-sectional, longitudinal, and sequential designs

usually refers to groups that are defined on the basis of biological age. People born in the same year (or range of years) are members of the same cohort. If you were born in 1976, you are a member of the 1976 cohort and are similar in many important respects to other individuals born in the same year. Major historical events happened to all members of the 1976 cohort at the same point in their lives—you experienced the *Challenger* disaster of 1986 when you were the same age, and you were influenced by the same demographic trends in divorce rates, family size, child poverty, and maternal employment. Differences among cohorts reflect different economic and political conditions, different cultural climates, different educational systems, and different child-rearing practices.

In addition to biological age, cohorts may be based on societal age, historical experiences, or other defining conditions. For example, a societally defined cohort may include people entering the workforce or beginning a second marriage; a history-based cohort may consist of the initial staff of a new university or hospital. Consider the different cohorts you represent: You may be in the cohort of Generation-X, the cohort of graduating seniors, or the cohort of working students.

In a cross-sectional study, a difference among groups of different ages may reflect developmental age changes; however, the differences may result from cohort effects (Schaie, 1986). Cohort differences (other than biological age) present a larger problem when comparing groups with wide age differences because of social and historical change. Comparisons of children who differ only by a few years are unlikely to have problems with cohort effects. Imagine a cross-sectional study of knowledge of authors. Most children in elementary school are familiar with *Goosebumps* and Judy Blume books, so you would not expect cohort differences when comparing 7-year-olds and 10-year-olds. However, increasing the age difference creates the potential for cohort effects. Stanovich, West, and Harrison (1995) report that young adults are familiar with authors such as Alice Walker, Stephen King, and Danielle Steele, yet older adults (mean age 79.9 years) are more familiar with James Michener, Leon Uris, and Bob Woodward as authors.

Suppose we want to compare intelligence of 20-year-olds with that of 80-year-olds. Our research question is whether intelligence changes with age. If we find that the 80-year-old cohort scores lower on our IQ test than the 20-year-olds, we may conclude that intelligence does indeed decline with age. However, a surprising number of differences between the two age groups may have nothing to do with age per se (e.g., the biological differences in body chemistry and function associated with aging). Box 9.1 lists some possible cohort differences between these two hypothetical groups. Note that many of the cohort differences, such as level of education and standard of living, seem to favor the younger cohort. However, some of the variables do not yield easy predictions. For example, there have been major dietary changes over this century. Which cohort do you think has had the most nutritious diet? The younger cohort has grown up with television and computers. Do you think this favors the younger or the older cohort when measuring intelligence?

The key point is that the cross-sectional method confounds age and cohort (see Chapter 8 for a discussion of confounding and internal validity). Cohort differences can obscure the developmental changes being examined because it is not certain which variable is responsible for any observed group differences—age

BOX 9.1

Hypothetical Cohort Differences Between 80-Year-Olds and 20-Year-Olds

Birth Order
More later-born individuals in older cohort because of larger average family size; it has been proposed that intelligence is negatively related to birth order position and family size.

Communications
Younger cohort has experienced information explosion because of global communications capability; the world of influence was smaller when older cohort was growing up.

Diet
Younger cohort has grown up with more synthetic food.

Education
Older cohort may not have as much formal education as younger cohort. Different trends in pedagogy existed throughout the decades; style of education may differ for each cohort.

Gender
Because of differential life spans of men and women, more females in older cohort.

Life Experiences
Older cohort has experienced Great Depression, major wars; younger cohort has experienced relative global political and economic stability and the end of the Cold War.

Standard of Living
Younger cohort has probably experienced higher average standard of living.

Technology
Younger cohort has grown up in technologically advanced environment.

Television
Younger cohort grew up with television.

Urbanization
Older cohort grew up in more agrarian society.

Values and Mores
Younger cohort has experienced erosion of family and traditional family values.

Women's Roles
Older cohort had fewer acceptable roles to which women could aspire.

or cohort. The 80-year-olds may score lower on a measure of intelligence because they have less education on average than 20-year-olds, not because of a decline in intelligence. The only way to determine conclusively whether we lose intellectual ability as we age is to conduct a longitudinal study.

LONGITUDINAL RESEARCH

In longitudinal designs, the same group of people is observed at different points in time as they grow older. Perhaps the most famous longitudinal study is the Terman Life Cycle Study, which was begun by Stanford psychologist Lewis Terman in 1921. Terman studied 1,528 California school children who had intelligence test scores of at least 135. The participants, who called themselves "Termites," were initially measured on numerous aspects of their cognitive and social development in 1921 and 1922. Terman and his colleagues continued studying the Termites during their childhood and adolescence and throughout their adult lives (cf. Terman, 1925; Terman & Oden, 1947, 1959). Terman's successors at Stanford plan to track the Termites until each one dies. The study has provided a rich description of the lives of highly intelligent individuals and disconfirmed many negative stereotypes of high intelligence. The Termites were very well adjusted both socially and emotionally, for example. The data have now been archived for use by other researchers. Friedman et al. (1993) used the Terman archives to show that the personality dimension of "conscientiousness" predicted survival across the life span; theirs was the first study to show a relationship between personality and longevity.

Most longitudinal studies do not take on the proportions of the Terman study in which individuals were studied over a lifetime, but any study that attempts to compare the same individuals at different ages is using the longitudinal method. Examples include (1) a 1-year study of the effects of retirement on mental health (Richardson & Kilty, 1995), (2) an 8-year study of the positive effects of day care in Sweden (Broberg, Wessels, Lamb, & Hwang, 1997), and (3) a 15-year study of antisocial behavior in New Zealand (Henry, Caspi, Moffitt, & Silva, 1996).

The primary advantage of the longitudinal design is that the researcher can observe actual changes occurring in the participants. Developmental change can only be detected when the same individuals are tracked over time. Longitudinal studies are used to study stability and change in behavior by assessing individual development at repeated times of measurement. Cohort effects are not a problem in longitudinal research because we are always studying the same cohort. However, longitudinal studies do have some problems. Disadvantages of the longitudinal method include: (1) cost, (2) time, (3) attrition, (4) confounding of age and time of measurement, (5) practice effects, (6) loss of funding, (7) generational change, and (8) measurement change.

The main disadvantage of the longitudinal method is that it is expensive and time-consuming. The Terman study has already spanned seven decades—imagine the cost associated with tracking a large group of people over 70 years! It can be very difficult to obtain funding to support such a long-term project. In addition, as the research project progresses, some participants will inevitably be lost; some will die, and some people will choose to discontinue participation in the study. Such selective dropout, attrition, or mortality can lead to the incorrect conclusion that the remaining participants' performance is improving as they get older. Suppose more intelligent people live longer, perhaps because they engage in less risky behavior such as smoking and drinking. Measures of IQ in a longitudinal design taken as participants age might show an increase in IQ over time because the lower-IQ individuals are no longer in the sample. The attrition may create an unrepresentative sample, potentially biasing the data gathered in later stages of the study in a positive direction.

Another problem is that longitudinal studies confound age and time of measurement. Recall from Chapter 8 that a history confound is some event that occurs outside the experimental situation between the time 1 and time 2 assessments. This presents a confound because the researcher cannot be sure whether the differences detected at time 2 are the result of a true age-related change or some historical event. Suppose you were conducting a longitudinal study of attitudes toward government spending. You sample a group of 50-year-old adults in 1997, 2002, and 2007. Although support for space travel was very high in your first assessment, it declined dramatically in 2002 and remained low in 2007. Is this an age-related change; that is, do we become less supportive of government spending as we age? Or is the high level of support in 1997 related to the *Pathfinder* landing on Mars, with extensive media coverage of this monumental event? If so, a historical event has influenced the measurement of your dependent variable, making it very difficult to determine what the developmental trajectory of support for government spending really is.

Practice effects can also occur in longitudinal studies as a result of multiple assessments with the same measures. Repeated administrations of the same survey of attitudes or the same intelligence test can easily lead to improved scores across time, and it is difficult to determine if the improvement is due to practice or to a true developmental change.

The sheer amount of time it takes to perform a longitudinal study presents several additional disadvantages. First, the research team may lose its funding in the middle of the project. Second, by the time the results are available, the original research questions may seem trivial or no longer appropriate due to cross-generational changes. Third, the development of a new measurement technique (e.g., a new revision of a standardized test) can make the early results obsolete or at least difficult to compare to the later measurements. In the midst of a relatively short 2-year study of young adolescent girls' eating problems, the new EAT-26 was developed (Attie & Brooks-Gunn, 1989), prompting researchers Swarr and Richards (1996) to change their measure of eating problems in the midst of their longitudinal study. Although the second instrument is reliable and valid, the interpretation of the study is compromised by the new assessment tool.

Comparisons of Cross-Sectional and Longitudinal Methods

Cross-sectional research is appropriate to assess any issue about age differences. The spectrum of topics amenable to cross-sectional research is large. What behaviors are typical of bullies in elementary school and junior high school? Does poverty affect the social and emotional development of young children in the same way it affects adolescents? Do young parents rely on more physical discipline than older parents? What activities are typical for adults in their 50s, 60s, and 70s? For all these examples, the researcher can select several groups of people who differ in age and measure them at the same point in time. When interpreting the results, however, cohort effects limit conclusions to descriptions of average or typical differences between the age groups.

Longitudinal research is appropriate to assess stability and continuity of a behavior over time. But to determine the long-term impact of an experience (e.g., Head Start, child abuse, death of a parent, disadvantaged home environment), repeated assessments of an individual are required. Long-term assessments of Head Start have established many positive outcomes, including increased school completion rates and diminished teen pregnancy and juvenile delinquency (Barnett, 1995; Yoshikawa, 1995). If a researcher wants to study how the home environment of children at age 5 is related to school achievement at age 13, a longitudinal study provides the best data. The alternative in this case would be to study 13-year-olds and ask them or their parents about the earlier home environment. But this *retrospective* approach has its own problems, including the difficulty of retrieving accurate memories of events in the distant past (see the discussion of retrospective memory in Chapter 6).

To summarize, cross-sectional designs are fast and inexpensive, but they are limited by the confound of age and cohort to descriptions of developmental differences. Longitudinal designs assess developmental change, but they can be time-consuming and costly and confound age and time of measurement. With an increasing emphasis on a life span perspective in developmental science, longitudinal methodology is increasing in popularity, but the cross-sectional approach remains more common.

SEQUENTIAL DESIGNS

An alternative method is a **sequential design** that combines longitudinal and cross-sectional approaches in one study. The first phase of a sequential design begins with the cross-sectional method. These individuals are then studied using the longitudinal method, with each individual tested at least one more time. One example is illustrated in Figure 9.1. At the outset of the study, two different groups of adults are tested when they are 55 and 65 years old. This is a cross-sectional comparison. Then, after a 5-year interval, the adults are retested; at this point they are 60 and 70 years old. This second comparison is also cross-sectional. Five years later, the adults are tested again, when they are 65 and 75 years old. This provides the researcher with three cross-sectional comparisons to evaluate developmental differences, one at each time of measurement. In addition, two longitudinal sequences are available to assess developmental change. Sequential designs offer a less expensive, time-efficient alternative to longitudinal approaches. A complete longitudinal study from ages 55 to 75 would take 20 years of data gathering, compared to only 10 years for a sequential approach. Also, the researcher has a built-in replication across cohorts by comparing the assessment for 65-year-olds in the first longitudinal sequence to the 65-year-olds in the second longitudinal sequence. The inclusion of two different cohorts provides extended generalizability and provides a great deal more information than a standard longitudinal design.

Schaie (1996) proposes an extension of the sequential design to "the most efficient design" by adding cross-sectional comparisons of the same age range. Beginning with a cross-sectional study, the participants are retested after a period of years, providing longitudinal data on these cohorts. At the time of this second assessment, a new cross-sectional sample is recruited who are the same age as members of the first sample. The process is repeated every 5 or 10 years, continually retesting the longitudinal waves and adding new cross-sectional groups. Schaie used this approach in his life span study of intelligence. A first sample was recruited in 1956 with adults between the ages of 21 and 70. A second sample added in 1963 ranged between ages 21 and 74; a third sample added in 1970 was ages 21 to 84; a total of seven samples have been recruited to date. Figure 9.2 shows the different samples and times of measurement in the Seattle Longitudinal Study. As you can see, each sample is retested every 7 years. At each time of measurement, another sample is recruited, adding participants until the sample now consists of more than 5,000 adults; some have been followed for 35 years.

Schaie's work exemplifies the important distinction between cross-sectional and longitudinal approaches. Cross-sectional comparisons of intelligence typically show declines in IQ beginning in the 30s for some cognitive functions. However, longitudinal comparisons present a more optimistic view, with many mental abilities continuing to increase until the mid-50s. Different conclusions emerge because of the design problems we discussed earlier. Cross-sectional studies create a bias against older adults because of cohort differences in intelligence that are not age-related (e.g., different educational opportunities; see Box 9.1). Longitudinal studies are biased in favor of older adults because of selective dropout of low-IQ individuals, thus inflating the IQ of the older adults. Longitudinal studies may also benefit from repeated practice with an intelligence test, thereby minimizing the decline in IQ with age.

Using a sequential design, Schaie is able to separate effects due to confounds of age, time of measurement, and cohort by treating them as independent variables in his analyses. Although not all theorists concur with Schaie's conclusions (cf. Williams & Klug, 1996), his work has been extremely influential, contribut-

Tested in 1956	Tested in 1963	Tested in 1970	Tested in 1977	Tested in 1984	Tested in 1991
Sample 1	Sample 1	Sample 1	Sample 1	Sample 1	Sample 1
	Sample 2	Sample 2	Sample 2	Sample 2	Sample 2
		Sample 3	Sample 3	Sample 3	Sample 3
			Sample 4	Sample 4	Sample 4
				Sample 5	Sample 5
					Sample 6

Figure 9.2   Sequential design of Schaie's Seattle Longitudinal Study

BOX 9.2   RESEARCH IN ACTION

Children of the Depression

The work of Glen H. Elder, Jr., illustrates the use of a sequential approach to study families in the Great Depression. Elder's work compares the impact of the Depression on children of different ages. Elder (1974, 1979; Elder, Liker, & Cross, 1984; Elder, Nguyen, & Caspi, 1985) used archival data from longitudinal studies of two cohorts of children born in the San Francisco Bay area in the 1920s. The first cohort was drawn from the Oakland Growth Study of children born in 1920–1921. The second cohort was drawn from the Berkeley Guidance Study of children born in 1928–1929. Each cohort was tested intensively as children and then followed intermittently through adulthood. Some general patterns emerged in the Depression-era families. Sudden income loss changed family roles, shifting responsibilities to mothers and older children. Girls assumed household responsibilities; women entered the workforce. A father's loss of earnings reduced his power in the family and contributed to increased marital conflict.

The experience of the Depression differed for each cohort. The Oakland group were children during the prosperous '20s and entered the Depression after a relatively secure early childhood. They did not experience the joblessness of the Depression era because they were old enough to join the military during the mobilization for World War II. Although only eight years younger, the Berkeley cohort experienced a very different life course; they were young children during the Depression, were adolescents during the war years, and suffered more hardship from the Depression because of the war. The young Berkeley males suffered the most from the family stresses associated with the Depression.

By comparing the impact of a major economic event on two different birth cohorts, Elder's work provides extraordinary insight into the impact of sociohistorical events on individual development and intergenerational relations. Although economic deprivation altered family relationships in each cohort, the effects varied because each cohort was in a different stage of life.

ing to theoretical debates about declines in intellectual functioning across adulthood. The sequential approach is useful for many situations in which the cross-sectional approach or the longitudinal approach alone would not address the researcher's questions. For example, a sequential approach was used to study the effects of poverty (Bolger, Patterson, & Thompson, 1995) precisely because most research in this area is limited by its cross-sectional nature. Even longitudinal studies of persistent poverty (e.g., Duncan, Brooks-Gunn, & Klebanov, 1994; McLeod & Shanahan, 1993) tend to assess children's functioning at only one point in time. By using a sequential design following three cohorts of Black and White students for 3 years, Bolger et al. (1995) inform us about the effects of enduring economic hardship. Sociologist Glen Elder, Jr., uses a sequential approach in his work described in Box 9.2.

SINGLE-SUBJECT DESIGNS

Another approach to the manipulation of variables over time frequently takes place within the context of research on reinforcement. This research tradition can be traced to the work of B. F. Skinner (1953) on reinforcement schedules, and it is often seen in applied and clinical settings when behavior modification techniques are used. However, the techniques and logic of **single-subject experiments** can be readily applied to other research areas.

Single-subject experiments (or $n = 1$ designs) study only one subject—but the subject can be one person, one classroom, or one city. The goal of single-subject experiments is to establish a functional relationship between the independent variable and the dependent variable such that changes in the dependent variable correspond to presentations of the independent variable. In a single-subject design, the subject's behavior is measured over time during a **baseline** control period. The manipulation is then introduced during a **treatment period,** and the subject's behavior continues to be observed. The treatments are usually some type of reinforcement, such as a smile, praise (e.g., Good job!), or a tangible reward such as stars, stickers, or coupons to exchange for privileges. A change in the subject's behavior from baseline to treatment periods is evidence for the effectiveness of the manipulation. The problem, however, is that there could be many reasons for the change other than the experimental treatment. For example, some other event may have coincided with the introduction of the treatment. The single-subject designs described in the following sections address this problem.

Reversal Designs

The basic issue in single-subject experiments is how to determine that the manipulation of the independent variable has an effect. One method is to demonstrate the reversibility of the manipulation. A simple **reversal design** takes the following form:

A (baseline period) → B (treatment period) → A (baseline period)

The design, called an **ABA design,** requires that behavior (dependent variable) be observed first during the baseline control (A) period. Next, the independent variable is introduced in the treatment (B) period, and behavior is observed again. Then, the treatment is removed in a second baseline (A) period, and behavior is observed once more. (Sometimes this is called a *withdrawal design,* in recognition of the fact that the treatment is removed or withdrawn.) There are repeated measures of the behavior during each phase: before the intervention, during the intervention, and after the intervention is withdrawn. For example, the effect of a reinforcement procedure on an adolescent's studying behavior can be assessed with an ABA design. The number of minutes spent studying can be observed each day during the first baseline (A) control period. Then a reinforcement treatment (B) would be introduced in which the adolescent earns the right to watch a certain amount of television for every half hour of schoolwork. Later, this treatment would be discontinued during the second baseline (A) period. Hypothetical data from such an experiment are shown in Figure 9.3. The fact that

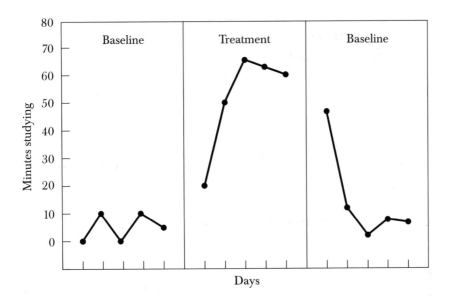

Figure 9.3
Hypothetical data
from ABA reversal
design

study time increased when the treatment was introduced, and reversed when the treatment was withdrawn, is evidence for the effectiveness of the treatment.

The ABA design can be greatly improved by extending it to an ABAB design, in which the experimental treatment is introduced a second time, or even an ABABAB design, which allows the effect of the treatment to be tested a third time. This is done to address two problems with the ABA reversal design. First, a single reversal is not extremely powerful evidence for the effectiveness of the treatment. The observed reversal might have been due to a random fluctuation in the adolescent's behavior. Or perhaps the treatment happened to coincide with some other event, such as a major test in one of the student's classes during the treatment phase. The upcoming test might actually have motivated the student to study more, so the increased study time is not necessarily related to the treatment. These possibilities are much less likely if the treatment has been shown to have an effect two or more times; random or coincidental events are unlikely to be responsible for both reversals in an ABAB design. The second presentation of B is a built-in replication of the pattern of results seen with the first presentation of B.

The second problem with the ABA design is ethical. As Barlow and Hersen (1984) point out, it doesn't seem right to end the design with the withdrawal of a treatment that may be beneficial for the participant. Using an ABAB design provides the opportunity to observe a second reversal when the treatment is introduced again. This sequence ends with the treatment rather than with the withdrawal of the treatment.

Multiple Baseline Designs

It may have occurred to you that a reversal of some behaviors may be impossible or unethical. For example, it would be unethical to reverse treatment that reduces dangerous or illegal behavior, such as drug abuse, eating disorders, or

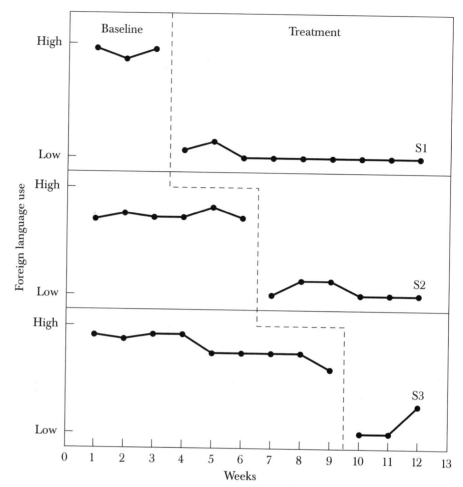

Figure 9.4
Hypothetical multiple
baseline experiment

self-injurious behaviors. An alternative approach is the **multiple baseline design,** in which multiple measures over time can be made before and after the manipulation. In a multiple baseline design, the effectiveness of the treatment is demonstrated when a behavior changes only after the manipulation is introduced. Such a change must be observed under multiple circumstances to rule out the possibility that other events are responsible for the change in behavior.

There are several variations of the multiple baseline design (Barlow & Hersen, 1984). In the multiple baseline *across subjects,* the behavior of several subjects is measured over time. For each subject the manipulation is introduced at a different point in time. Figure 9.4 shows data from a hypothetical experiment conducted by a school psychologist to determine if teacher praise is an effective intervention for increasing the use of English in a multicultural classroom. The experiment uses three students, S1, S2, and S3. Note that introduction of the manipulation was followed by a change in behavior for each subject. However, because this change occurred across individuals and because the manipulation was introduced at a different time for each student, we can rule out explanations based on chance, historical events, and so on. This type of approach has been used to combat fear of dental procedures in autistic children (Luscre & Center, 1996). Using anti-anxiety treatment, Luscre and Center were able to help three boys (ages 6 and 9 years) tolerate the procedures involved in a dental exam.

In a multiple baseline *across behaviors,* several different behaviors of a single subject are measured over time. At different times, the same manipulation is applied to each of the behaviors. For example, a reward system could be instituted to increase the socializing, grooming, and language behaviors of a hospitalized Alzheimer's patient. The reward system would be applied to each of these behaviors at different times. Demonstrating that each behavior increased when the reward system was applied would be evidence for the effectiveness of the manipulation. This approach was used to improve the morning routine of a 12-year-old boy with developmental disabilities getting ready for school, a challenge for most parents and children (Adams & Drabman, 1995). The intervention targeted a variety of behaviors over 44 school days, increased the child's on-time behavior, reduced the time required to get ready for school, and decreased negative parent-child interactions.

The third variation is multiple baseline *across situations,* in which the same behavior is measured in different settings. The eating behaviors of an anorexic teen can be observed both at home and at school. The manipulation is introduced at a different time in each setting, with the expectation that a change in the behavior in each situation will occur only after the manipulation.

Problems With Single-Subject Designs

One obvious objection to single-subject designs is the small sample. When relying on only one participant, external generalizability may be hard to establish, even when reversals and multiple baselines are employed. Replications with other subjects might extend the findings somewhat, yet even that would be a small sample by social science standards. However, many researchers who use single-subject designs are not interested in generalizing; the primary purpose of single-subject designs is to alter the behavior of a particular individual who presents a problem behavior.

A second issue relates to the interpretation of results from a single-subject experiment. Traditional statistical methods are rarely used to analyze data from single-subject designs. A typical approach relies on visual inspection of patterns in graphs of the data. If the treatment has a reliable effect on the behavior (diminishing undesirable behavior or increasing desirable behavior), the connection should be evident without a formal statistical analysis. Reliance on such subjective criteria can be problematic because of the potential for lack of agreement on the effectiveness of a treatment. For information on more objective methods of statistical evaluation, refer to Kratochwill and Levin (1992).

Despite this tradition of single-subject data presentation, however, the trend increasingly has been to study larger samples using the procedures of single-subject designs and to present the average scores of groups during baseline and treatment periods. Summarizing the data from a number of subjects by using group means can sometimes give a misleading picture of individual responses to the manipulation. For example, the manipulation may be effective in changing the behavior of some subjects but not others. An emphasis on the individual subject quickly reveals that the manipulation was not effective for some subjects, and steps can then be taken to discover why the manipulation wasn't effective for these individuals.

A final limitation is that not all variables can be studied with the reversal and multiple baseline procedures used in single-subject experiments. Specifically, these procedures are useful only when the behavior is reversible or when one can expect a relatively dramatic shift in behavior after the manipulation. Nevertheless, single-subject studies represent an important, if specialized, method of research.

Applications for Education and Counseling

Single-subject designs are popular in applied educational, counseling, and clinical settings for assessment and modification of behavior. A counselor treating a client wants to see if the treatment is effective for that particular person. If a student is excessively shy, the goal of treatment is to decrease shyness in that one student. In the classroom, a teacher working with a highly distractible child wants to find an effective treatment for that individual. The single-subject design presents a good alternative for situations such as these when a researcher is interested in the cause of one individual's behavior. For example, single-subject approaches have been used successfully to eliminate out-of-seat behavior of a 14-year-old boy (Ramasamy, Taylor, & Ziegler, 1996) and to reduce a 4-year-old girl's excessive dependence on a preschool teacher (McNamee-McGrory & Cipani, 1995).

Single-subject designs are also effective when treating a group, such as a classroom or a community. A teacher may institute a token economy for the entire class to increase the number of books children read. The school community may implement a program of differential reinforcement to increase parental involvement in school activities. One example is a study by Johnson, Stoner, and Green (1996) that tested the effectiveness of three interventions to reduce undesired behaviors and increase desired behaviors in the classroom. Using three different seventh-grade classes, the multiple baseline design found that active teaching of the classroom rules was the most effective method.

The key to successful implementation of a behavior modification program is to identify a reinforcer that is rewarding for that particular individual. Children and adults respond differentially for various categories of rewards—tangible and intangible. Contrary to popular myth, money is not a universal reward! The use of reinforcers for appropriate behavior provides a good alternative for controlling behavior in the classroom without relying on aversive techniques such as punishment or time-out.

SUMMARY

In developmental research, three kinds of designs can be used, cross-sectional, longitudinal, and sequential. In the cross-sectional design, participants of different ages are studied at a single point in time. This method is time-efficient and economical, yet the results may be limited by cohort effects. Groups with substantially similar characteristics are called cohorts, and they are most commonly defined on the basis of biological age. Researchers wishing to study biological age differences must be aware of possible cohort differences between groups, which have nothing to do with age per se. These cohort differences are a possible source of experimental confounding in cross-sectional research.

Longitudinal studies test the same participants at two or more points in time, thus avoiding cohort differences. The primary advantage of the longitudinal method is that the researcher can observe developmental changes in the participants by tracking the same individuals over time. Disadvantages of longitudinal research include expense, attrition, and other problems associated with the amount of time needed to complete a longitudinal study.

Sequential designs combine cross-sectional and longitudinal approaches in one study. The sequential approach is appropriate for many life span issues in human development.

Single-subject experiments are a special class of research designs that typically involve only one participant. The goal of single-subject experiments is to demonstrate a reliable connection between the independent variable and the dependent variable. The basic design involves systematically presenting and withdrawing the independent variable and observing changes in the dependent variable. A reversal design (also known as the ABA design) involves a control condition, followed by an experimental treatment, then another control condition. The ABAB design extends this design by adding another treatment to ensure that behavioral changes are associated with the independent variable and not with other coincidental factors.

A multiple baseline design is used when reversal of the target behavior is not possible or is unethical. Multiple baseline designs are used to compare the same behavior across different individuals, different behaviors of one person, and the behavior of one person in different situations. Single-subject experimental designs are useful in educational, counseling, and clinical settings to evaluate the effectiveness of interventions that rely on behavior modification.

KEY TERMS

ABA design	longitudinal method	sequential design
baseline	multiple baseline	single-subject
cohort	design	experiment
cross-sectional method	reversal design	treatment period

REVIEW QUESTIONS

1. Distinguish between cross-sectional and longitudinal designs.
2. What is a cohort effect?
3. Why do cross-sectional designs describe developmental *differences* but not developmental *change?*

4. What types of questions are best addressed by cross-sectional designs? longitudinal designs?

5. Explain how attrition of participants in a longitudinal study can produce systematic bias in the results as the study progresses.

6. Using two age groups, design a cross-sectional study and a longitudinal study to evaluate the effect of divorce on children's academic performance. Operationally define the dependent variable and the independent variable.

7. What is a sequential design? Design a sequential study on the topic in question 6.

8. Why do researchers use single-subject experiments?

9. What is a reversal design? Why is an ABAB design superior to an ABA design?

10. What is meant by baseline in a single-subject design?

11. What is a multiple baseline design? Why is it used? Distinguish between multiple baseline designs across subjects, across behaviors, and across situations.

CHAPTER 10 ◆

Conducting Research

The previous chapters have laid the foundation for planning a research investigation. After the investigator selects an idea for research, many practical decisions must be made before participants are contacted and data collection begins. In this chapter we examine some of the general principles researchers use when planning the details of their studies. Careful planning is essential to the success of a research project.

ETHICAL CONSIDERATIONS

Ethics should be considered during all phases of your research, including the planning phase. Review the ethical guidelines for working with children and adults before you conduct your study. It is extremely important to prevent psychological or physical harm to the participants. According to ethical guidelines, you may not even test participants until your project has ethical approval from your Institutional Review Board.

You also have an ethical responsibility to treat participants with courtesy and respect. Participants have allocated time from their schedules to assist you. In turn, you should take care to allot sufficient time to provide complete explanations for any questions participants may have. Although it is tempting to be more "efficient" by testing participants rapidly, it is unwise to rush through the initial greeting, the experimental procedures, or the debriefing at the end of the session.

In Chapter 2 we discussed other important ethical guidelines. Researchers must also be extremely careful about potential invasion of privacy and are responsible for protecting participant anonymity. Keep these issues in mind when designing your study to ensure that you conduct an ethical investigation.

OBTAINING PARTICIPANTS AND SAMPLING

A major practical problem facing the researcher is where to find subjects. How are you going to get all the participants you need? Once you locate them, how will you select the ones to include in your study? The method used to select participants has implications for generalization of the research results.

Recall from Chapter 7 that most research projects involve sampling research participants from a population of interest. The population is composed of all the individuals of interest to the researcher. Samples may be drawn from the population using probability sampling or nonprobability sampling techniques. When it is important to accurately describe the population, as in scientific polls, you must use probability sampling. Much research, however, is more interested in testing hypotheses about behavior. Here the focus of the study is on examining the relationships between the variables being studied and testing predictions derived from theories of behavior. In such cases, the participants may be found in the most convenient way possible using a nonprobability haphazard, or "accidental," sampling method. You may ask students in introductory psychology classes to participate, you may knock on doors in a residential area to find families for your study, or you may choose a class to test children because you know the teacher. Nothing is wrong with such methods as long as you recognize that they affect the generalizability of your results. The issue of generalizing results is discussed in Chapter 16. Despite the problems of generalizing results based on convenient haphazard samples, replication evidence supports the view that we *can* generalize findings to other populations and situations.

Sources of Research Participants

Depending on your research interests, you may find yourself looking outside the college campus for participants for your study. College students, faculty, staff, and their families represent a restricted population that may not be appropriate for your study. Locating a potential pool of participants outside the campus community can challenge the researcher's ingenuity and patience. Convincing someone of the importance of your project is not always an easy task.

Infants can be found by contacting hospitals, obstetricians, or pediatricians. Other sources include classes for prospective parents and newspaper birth announcements. Toddlers can be found at day care centers and churches. Elementary school children are almost as easy to find as college sophomores. They are conveniently rounded up for several hours a day in schools, and they usually stay in the same classrooms most of the day. Moreover, elementary schools are often cooperative in providing useful demographic information on their student population. Older school children (junior and senior high school students) are more difficult to schedule for research studies because they typically move from class to class throughout the school day, and they often take part in a variety of extracurricular activities. Older adolescents become progressively harder to locate; some of them drop out of the school system, enter the workforce, or otherwise become unreachable.

Adults are especially difficult to recruit outside of college, but they can be recruited from church groups, clubs, political associations, conventions, class reunions, singles bars, and so on. Newspaper solicitations are not recommended as a fruitful avenue for obtaining a representative sample of adults—although you may get some very interesting phone calls! Older adults are a little easier to locate, especially if they are retired. You may find them in retirement communities,

BOX 10.1   RESEARCH IN ACTION

Designing an Intervention Program in a Diverse Community

The benefits associated with sensitivity to cultural differences are well illustrated by the excellent work of Dumka, Roosa, Michaels, and Suh (1995) in their development of a prevention program for child mental health problems. The parenting intervention program was aimed at low-income, ethnically diverse families. Families in the target area were predominantly low income and educationally disadvantaged, with 25% African American and 70% Mexican or Mexican American. Although the program targeted inappropriate parenting as a contributor to child mental health, the program was named "Raising the Successful Children Program" to emphasize the positive aspects of authoritative parenting rather than deficits associated with authoritarian practices.

Recognizing that any intervention can only be effective if the target group participates in the program, Dumka et al. involved members of the community in focus groups to design the program and incorporated their needs in the program. As a result of their practical suggestions, transportation, child care, and meals were offered to increase participation in the program. The researchers also relied on community members to recruit families. Families were paid for their participation in an initial interview conducted in their homes. These initial home visits were scheduled when the male adult would be home to respect the cultural value placed on his authority in the home.

Community aides maintained contact with the participating families through weekly home visits or phone calls to enhance rapport and increase attendance at the program meetings. The approach was very successful, with recruitment and retention substantially higher than in other prevention programs in low-income populations. If you are interested in designing an intervention program, the Dumka et al. article is highly recommended reading.

nutrition centers, and senior citizens clubs. Nearly one third of universities in the United States now have continuing education courses for older adults; see if your school has a program of courses and workshops designed for older learners.

Recruiting members of ethnic groups may be facilitated through community contacts. For example, Brody, Stoneman, and Flor (1996) investigated the role of religion in the academic and socioemotional competence of African American youth in the rural South. Families were recruited by an African American staff member who contacted community members such as pastors and teachers. Prospective families were then contacted by these community members. Only after a family expressed interest in the study did an African American staff member approach the family directly. This type of approach contributes to the success of a study by removing barriers to cultural understanding and strengthening rapport between the participants and the research staff. Box 10.1 presents another example of a culturally sensitive research design.

Once you have identified a potential source of participants, the next task is to obtain permission to include them in your study. Obtaining access can range from trivially easy to nearly impossible. For example, to conduct field observation of families in a museum or a shopping mall, it is relatively easy to obtain permission from the management. Research in university settings is common, and procedures exist for gaining access to participants in the campus community. Research outside the university, however, may be more difficult. If you want to test a few children at the neighborhood elementary school, you may find yourself presenting a proposal to the teacher, the principal, and the school board. This time delay can extend your research for weeks or months. Medical settings present even more challenges, with approval needed from a multitude of review boards, possibly extending up to agencies of the state and federal government.

Here are a few suggestions that can smooth the review process. Prepare a brief prospectus of the project to give to the people in authority. The prospectus describes the essentials of your project. Be prepared to answer questions about your project. Successful researchers learn to convey their ideas in easily understood terms that are appropriate for the audience. If you show enthusiasm for your project, most people will be willing to participate.

Obtaining Consent

Obtaining consent from adult participants is rarely a problem because they are present during testing. However, when you are working with children, parents may not be on location. How should you go about obtaining informed consent under these circumstances?

Suppose you want to evaluate recent reports that listening to Mozart boosts IQ (Rauscher, Shaw, & Ky, 1993). You will need two groups of children to do a task of spatial reasoning such as assembling puzzles. One group will perform this task in a room with Mozart music. (Rauscher and colleagues used Mozart's sonata for two pianos in D major, K488.) A second group of children will perform this task in a room with no music. How should you go about obtaining informed consent?

Parental consent is best obtained in this situation with a letter. Schools vary, but the possibilities include mailing the letter to parents and receiving a reply by mail. Classroom teachers may be enlisted to write a short note to the parents introducing the project, and they also may be enlisted to assist in distribution and collection of the consent forms. You also may need to prepare versions of your consent materials in languages other than English, depending on the school population. Be prepared to send several letters home before replies are received. Your consent form may not be a top priority for busy families. When you have received sufficient consent forms, then you are ready to begin testing the children.

Notice the possibilities for violating the rules of good sampling inherent in this procedure. If only the smarter, more mature, or more motivated students manage to return their consent forms, this fact may affect the results. The problem is greatest when you need only a few children. In such situations, it is a good idea to send consent forms to all students, wait a week or two, then randomly select your sample from all the children who returned consent forms. This avoids the confounds associated with testing only the children who returned their forms promptly.

In our experience, the most effective technique is to engage the child's interest before the letters are distributed. The researcher should visit the class, introduce himself or herself, and talk a little about the study. For example:

```
Hi! I'm _____ from the University of _____. We're doing a
study to find out how second-graders solve puzzles. If you
want to be in the study, I'll take you to a special room, and
we'll play some puzzle games. But first you have to have your
parent's permission. I'm going to hand out a letter for you
to take to your parents. It will tell them about the study.
If it's okay with them, they'll sign the paper, and you
should bring that back to your teacher. Everyone who brings
back the letter saying it's okay with your parents will get
to play the puzzle games.
```

A personal approach can dramatically improve the return rate. In addition, the researcher can follow up with reminders or provide a small reward for children who return their forms. A word of caution about food: Parents often prefer that children not eat candy or sweets, and many children have food allergies. It is safest to use nonedible rewards such as stickers, pencils, or coupons that can be redeemed under parental supervision.

Figure 10.1 is a sample consent letter for this project. Letters should include these important features: (1) introduce the researcher and the nature of the project (a class project), (2) describe the task the students will perform in sufficient detail that parents can decide if there are any risks to their child, (3) estimate the time required for the task, (4) explain the student's right to refuse participation, (5) explain that results are confidential, (6) include phone numbers for parents to contact the researcher and the supervising professor, and (7) include an option for the parent to decline participation.

Young children would most likely not be given written information about the research because they are not proficient readers, but they would be given verbal information covering the same points included in the letter to their parents. Participants must be told the purpose of the study, their right of refusal, and their right to confidentiality, as in this script that might be used on the day of testing:

```
Hi again. Remember me? I'm _____ from the University of _____.
Your parents have agreed that you can be in our study, so I'd
like to tell you a little about it before we begin. We're
going to play a game trying to solve puzzles on these special
pages. You don't have to play the game if you don't want to,
and you won't get in trouble if you don't play. This isn't a
test, and we won't be giving you or your teacher a grade.
We'd like you to try hard to do a good job, though. Do you
want to play? Now I'll tell you the rules of the game. . . .
```

Dear Parent,

As part of a class project, students from the University of _____
will soon be conducting a study at your child's school. The project investigates how
children are affected by music when they study. Half of the children will solve puzzles
in a quiet setting, and half of the children will solve puzzles in a room with music
playing. The children will miss approximately 15 minutes of class time. Each child's
participation is voluntary, and your child will be told that he or she does not have to
take part. Most children enjoy playing the game because of the novelty and the
attention they receive, and the task is designed to be fun for children of this age.

If you approve of your child's participation, and your child agrees to be in the
study, your child's results are completely confidential. Because the purpose of the study
is to compare group averages, no results for individual children will be released to
parents or to school personnel.

Please indicate whether you approve of your child's participation by completing
the attached form and sending it to school in the envelope provided. We hope your
child will be able to take part in our study, and we thank you for your response. If you
have any questions about this study, please feel free to contact me at (phone number).
My professor, Dr. _____, can be reached in the Department of Family
Studies, University of _____, (phone number).

(Researcher's signature)

- -

Child's Name _____   Birthdate _____

_____ Yes, I give permission for my child to participate in the above-mentioned
research investigation. I understand that the information will be used for learning
purposes only and that no psychological evaluation is being conducted. I also
understand that the information is confidential and that my child's name will not be
used in discussing or writing about this project.

_____ No, I do not give permission for my child to participate.

_____   Date _____
Parent/Guardian's Signature

Figure 10.1   Sample parental consent letter

The investigator is obligated to answer any questions from parents or children prior to starting a research project. It is extremely important that children be given the opportunity to assent to their participation. You cannot force a child to play your game, even if their parents have signed a consent form. In all cases, respect the rights of children to make their own choices.

MANIPULATING THE INDEPENDENT VARIABLES

To manipulate an independent variable, you have to construct an operational definition of the variable (see Chapter 4). To operationalize a variable, you must turn a conceptual variable into a set of operations—specific instructions, events, and stimuli to be presented to the research participants. In addition, the independent and dependent variables must be introduced within the context of the total experimental setting. This has been called "setting the stage" (Aronson, Brewer, & Carlsmith, 1985).

Setting the Stage

In setting the stage, you usually have to do two things: (1) provide the participants with the informed consent information needed for your study, and (2) explain to them why the experiment is being conducted. Sometimes, the rationale given is completely truthful, although only rarely will you want to tell participants the actual hypothesis. For example, consider a study investigating own-race bias in recognition memory to see if adults remember faces of people of their own race better than those of other races (Lindsay, Jack, & Christian, 1991). White adults showed better recognition on White faces than on African American faces; for African Americans there was no difference in recognition across the races. This difference in perceptual skills would probably not have been detected if Lindsay et al. had explicitly stated the purpose of the study. To avoid any potential bias, the researchers might state their purpose in more general terms as an investigation of memory.

As noted in Chapter 2, participants sometimes are deceived about the actual purpose of the experiment. Deception is common in social psychological research, because researchers in this area find that people behave most naturally when they are unaware of the variable being manipulated. If participants know what you are studying, they may try to confirm the hypothesis, or they may try to "look good" by behaving in a socially acceptable way. As you plan the procedures for your study, remember that you will need to debrief the participants at the end of the experiment.

There are no clear-cut rules for setting the stage, except that the experimental setting must seem plausible to the participants. Nor are there any clear-cut rules for translating conceptual variables into specific operations. Exactly how the variable is manipulated depends on the variable, as well as the cost, practicality, and ethics of the procedures being considered.

Types of Manipulations

Straightforward Manipulation   Researchers are usually able to manipulate a variable with relative simplicity by presenting written or verbal material to the participants. Such a **straightforward manipulation** is sometimes referred to as an **instructional manipulation.** For example, Butler, Gross, and Hayne (1995) examined the use of drawing as a technique to assess memory for an event. Butler et al. assessed 5-year-old children's memories for a field trip to a fire station. One day after the event, children were asked to *tell* what happened on the trip or to *draw* what happened on the trip. By changing only one word in the instructions, Butler et al. manipulated the independent variable, test group. Children in the draw group reported more information than did children in the tell group. The facilitative effect of drawing on memory may be very useful in clinical settings to obtain information from children about traumatic events such as abuse.

Learning and memory studies commonly use instructional manipulations. Pressley and Brewster (1990) compared two instructional conditions. Half of the fifth- and sixth-grade students were instructed to use an imagery strategy to learn factual information about the 12 Canadian provinces; the remaining students were assigned to a no-strategy control condition. Students in the imagery group were given explicit instruction to imagine scenes depicting facts about each province, such as "Lots of blueberries are grown in New Brunswick" or "The biggest geese in Canada are in Manitoba." The imagery strategy was very effective, but only when students first learned to associate the name of each Canadian territory with an illustration of the territory. Pictures can improve learning of facts, but only after the picture content has been mastered.

A recent example of a straightforward manipulation is an investigation of the effect of warning labels for violent content of television programs (Bushman & Stack, 1996). The independent variable, type of warning label, was varied by presenting different written descriptions concerning the content of movies. The label condition included warnings from the network about violent content, warnings from the U.S. surgeon general that violence is harmful, informational labels about violent content, and a condition without labels. Contrary to what parents and politicians are hoping, the warning labels did not reduce interest in violent programs. College students were most likely to watch movies with the "surgeon general" warning about violence, perhaps as a kind of "forbidden fruit" response. The informational label was least likely to attract viewers to violent programs. Apparently, warning labels alone will not deter individuals from watching television programs and may actually have the undesirable effect of increasing viewership.

Most manipulations of independent variables are straightforward. Researchers may vary the difficulty of material to be learned, the level of motivation, the way questions are asked, characteristics of people to be judged, and a variety of factors in a direct manner.

Staged Manipulation   Other manipulations are less straightforward. Sometimes it is necessary to stage events that occur during the experiment to manipulate the independent variable successfully. When this occurs, the manipulation is called a **staged** or **event manipulation.** Staged manipulations are most frequently used for two reasons. First, the researcher may be trying to create some psychological state in the participants, such as frustration or a temporary lowering of self-esteem; second, a staged manipulation may be necessary to simulate some situation that occurs in the real world. For example, researchers might use a computer game that is impossible to solve, intentionally creating a stressful mood. A study of helping behavior might stage an incident such as dropping books, hearing a loud noise in the next room, or soliciting donations for a needy family as ways to engage the participants more fully.

In developmental research staged manipulations are often used to assess the quality of family interactions by asking the family to participate in two or more different events. Families may be asked to play a game, discuss an issue such as the effects of poverty (Brody, Stoneman, & Flor, 1996), or engage in their normal routine for mealtimes, schoolwork, and television viewing. Mothers may be observed interacting with their children during playtime and mealtime; they may also be observed in their home and in a laboratory setting (cf. Black, Hutcheson, Dubowitz, Starr, Jr., & Berenson-Howard, 1996; Crockenberg & Litman, 1991). All these different comparisons are event manipulations. The inclusion of multiple events or settings also contributes to the generalizability of the results.

Staged manipulations frequently employ a **confederate**—a person who poses as a participant but is actually part of the manipulation. Staged manipulations demand a great deal of ingenuity and even some acting ability. They are used to involve the participants in an ongoing social situation, which the individuals perceive not as an experiment but as a real experience. Researchers assume that the result will be natural behavior that truly reflects the feelings and intentions of the participants. However, such procedures allow for a great deal of subtle interpersonal communication that is hard to put into words; this may make it difficult for other researchers to replicate the experiment. Also, a complex manipulation is difficult to interpret. If many things happened during the experiment, what one thing was responsible for the results? In general, it is easier to interpret results when the manipulation is relatively straightforward. However, the nature of the variable you are studying sometimes demands complicated procedures.

Elaborate staging is unusual in research in human development research. One example is a study by Leichtman and Ceci (1995) that employed a confederate in a study of the effects of stereotypes and suggestions on preschoolers' memory for an event. In their "Sam Stone Study," a stranger named Sam Stone visited a preschool during storytelling time. Sam Stone said hello to the teacher, walked around the room, and left in about 2 minutes. Prior to Sam Stone's brief visit, one group of preschoolers were told a weekly story about Sam Stone. A research assistant at the day care centers casually presented the new Sam Stone story while playing with the children. Each story describes Sam Stone as a kind, but clumsy person, including comments such as "That Sam Stone is always getting into accidents and breaking things!" Following Sam Stone's visit, the children were interviewed several times. Incorrect information about Sam was given to the children in some of the interview questions—for example, that he had ripped a book or damaged a teddy bear. In a final interview, the children recalled Sam's visit. The most inaccurate reports were made by 3- and 4-year-old children who heard the misleading questions and the stereotyped information about Sam. In this stereotype plus suggestion condition, 72% of the children claimed that Sam Stone actually did rip the book or damage a teddy bear. This figure is alarmingly high and clearly indicates the power of suggestion on young children.

With their clever use of confederates, Leichtman and Ceci simulated the way children often learn information–through casual conversation. Ceci and his colleagues frequently use staged events in their work on the reliability of children's eyewitness testimony. Ceci, Ross, and Toglia (1987) utilized a 7-year-old confederate to deliver misleading postevent information to children. Bruck, Ceci, Francoeur, and Barr (1995) used an adult confederate to deliver misleading information to 5-year-olds about inoculations they received in a visit to their pediatrician. By using event manipulations, investigators can approximate the interviewing procedures that are commonly used in legal contexts and more accurately describe the complexities of children's memory for actual events.

Strength of the Manipulation

The simplest experimental design has two levels of the independent variable. In planning the experiment, the researcher has to choose these levels. A general principle to follow is to make the manipulation as strong as possible. A strong manipulation maximizes the differences between the two groups and increases the chances that the independent variable will have a statistically significant effect on the dependent variable.

To illustrate, suppose you hypothesize a positive linear relationship between attitude similarity and liking to test the old adage "birds of a feather flock together." In conducting the experiment you could arrange for teenage participants to encounter another person–a teenager working with you as a confederate. In one group the confederate and the participant would share similar attitudes; in the other group the confederate and the participant would be dissimilar. The independent variable is similarity, and liking is the dependent variable. Now you have to operationalize the similarity variable by deciding on the amount of similarity. How similar is "similar"? You could arrange for similar attitudes about music and school–but is that enough? Maybe the similar condition should be similar on music, school, politics, religion, and legalizing marijuana. Would that manipulation be strong enough? Figure 10.2 shows the hypothesized relationship between attitude similarity and liking at 10 different levels of similarity. Level 1 represents the least amount of similarity, and level 10 the greatest. To achieve the strongest manipulation, the participants in one group would encounter a confederate of level-10 similarity, and those in the other group would encounter a confederate of level-1 similarity. This would result in a 9-point difference in mean liking scores. A weaker manipulation, using levels 4 and 7, for example, would result in a smaller mean difference.

A strong manipulation is especially important in the early stages of research, when the researcher is most interested in demonstrating that a relationship does, in fact, exist. If the early experiments reveal a relationship between the variables, subsequent research can systematically manipulate the other levels of the independent variables to provide a more detailed picture of the relationship. In our hypothetical study of the effect of listening to Mozart music, we compared Mozart to no music for the strongest possible manipulation. If this contrast is significant,

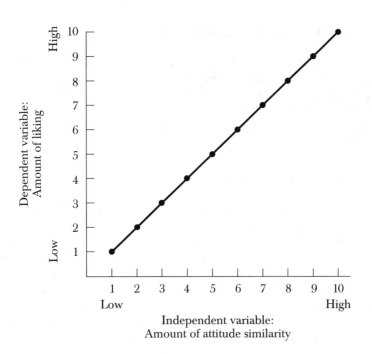

Figure 10.2
Relationship between
attitude similarity
and liking

then follow-up studies could compare different composers or different types of music.

The principle of using the strongest manipulation possible should be tempered by at least two considerations. First, the strongest possible manipulation may involve a situation that rarely, if ever, occurs in the real world. Suppose a researcher is interested in the effects of crowding on classroom learning and behavior. An extremely strong crowding manipulation may put so many students in a room that no one could move, which may result in a significant effect on a variety of behaviors. However, we wouldn't know if the results were similar to those occurring in more realistic, less crowded situations such as are commonly found in classrooms or offices.

A second consideration is ethics. A manipulation should be as strong as possible within the bounds of ethics. A strong manipulation of fear or anxiety, for example, might not be possible because of the potential physical and psychological harm.

Cost of the Manipulation

Cost is another factor in the decision about how to manipulate the independent variable. Researchers who have limited monetary resources may not be able to afford expensive equipment, salaries for confederates, or payments to participants in long-term experiments. Also, a manipulation in which participants must be run individually requires more of the researcher's time than a manipulation that allows running many individuals in a single setting. In this respect, a manipulation that uses straightforward presentation of written or verbal material is less costly than a complex, staged, experimental manipulation.

SELECTING DEPENDENT MEASURES

In previous chapters we have discussed various aspects of measuring variables. Self-report, behavioral, and physiological dependent measures were described in Chapter 4, with more information on designing self-report measures in Chapter 7. Reliability, validity, and reactivity of measures were also described in Chapter 4. Here, we discuss other issues that are particularly relevant to operationalizing the dependent variable in experimental research.

Sensitivity of the Dependent Measure

The dependent variable should be sensitive enough to detect differences between groups. For example, a measure of life satisfaction that asks adults "Are you satisfied with your life?" with a simple "yes" or "no" response alternative is less sensitive than one that asks "How satisfied are you with your life?" on a 5- or 7-point scale. With the first measure, people may tend to be nice and say "yes" regardless of their actual feelings. The second measure allows for a range of satisfaction; such a scale would make it easier to detect differences in the amount of life satisfaction.

The issue of **sensitivity** is particularly important when measuring human performance. Memory can be measured using recall, recognition, or reaction time; cognitive task performance might be measured by examining speed or number of errors during a proofreading task; physical performance can be measured through various motor tasks. Such tasks vary in their difficulty. Sometimes, a task is so easy that everyone does well regardless of the conditions that are manipulated. This results in what is called a **ceiling effect** (scores are at the top of the scale). Suppose you wish to test cognitive status in healthy, nonhospitalized retirement community residents by asking them to count from 1 to 100 and measuring their errors. Their performance would probably not differ significantly from that of a comparison group of younger adults. However, a more difficult task, such as counting backward from 582 by 3s, might reveal cognitive differences between the young and elderly adults. Conversely, a task that is too difficult can result in a **floor effect** (scores are at the bottom of the scale). Asking participants to perform mental multiplication with three-digit numbers would probably not reveal any meaningful differences between the young and elderly adults, because hardly anyone could do the task. Any time performance is at the top or the bottom of the scale of measurement, the researcher cannot be sure that a more sensitive measure would not have detected differences between the groups. To illustrate, consider a study of learning strategies (Dretzke & Levin, 1996). High school students were taught the "keyword" mnemonic strategy to learn facts about cities; for example, forming a mental picture of "ham" to remember "Hammondville." The mnemonic group outscored a control group on the city task. The next day the students were instructed to remember facts about presidents (five facts per president; for example, Jefferson was a skilled violinist and a landscape designer). Contrary to expectation, the mnemonic group did not score higher than the control group on the presidents task. One explanation is that the keyword method is ineffective and only works in particular situations. A better explanation is that the presidents task was simply too difficult. Scores were well under 50% correct, suggesting a floor effect. Dretzke and Levin revised the task to only three facts per president and obtained the expected advantage for the keyword method in a second experiment.

Ceiling and floor effects are particularly troublesome in developmental research when you are comparing individuals who differ substantially in age. For example, making a comparison on some aspect of cognitive development across the childhood years presents a challenge for the researcher. The cognitive development of a 10-year-old is extremely advanced compared to that of a typical 5-year-old. The older child has more experience with cognitive tasks and tends to have more memory skills and strategies to rely on when learning new material. If you present a list of 10 items to both age groups of children, you may get a ceiling effect in one group and a floor effect in the other group, eliminating any chance of identifying meaningful developmental differences. Age-appropriate tasks require careful selection. Another approach is to present a longer list to the older group and then convert scores to a percentage for a more equitable comparison.

Multiple Measures

It is often desirable to measure more than one dependent variable. One reason to use multiple measures stems from the fact that a variable can be measured in a variety of concrete ways, with different operational definitions (see Chapter 4). In a study of wellness, for example, you might measure the number of doctor visits, the number of medications, the use of vitamin and mineral supplements, dietary and sleeping habits, or perhaps physiological measures of blood pressure and heart rate. The independent variable is type of living arrangement, comparing elderly adults living alone versus living with a spouse. You would expect to find differences in wellness between these groups of individuals on several measures of wellness. One possible outcome is that elderly adults living alone may have more doctor visits, more medications, and poorer diets. This is useful because our confidence in the results is increased if the same results are found with a variety of operational definitions. You also may find that the type of living arrangement does not have any effect on some dependent measures—maybe blood pressure and heart rate do not vary as a function of living arrangement.

Taking multiple measurements in a single experiment using the multimethod approach is valuable when it is feasible to do so. However, it may be necessary to conduct a series of experiments to explore the effects of an independent variable on various behaviors.

Cost of Measures

Another consideration is cost—some measures may be more costly than others. Paper-and-pencil self-report measures are generally inexpensive, but measures that require trained observers or various equipment can become quite costly. Physiological recording devices are also expensive. Researchers need financial resources from the university or from outside agencies to carry out such research.

A study of television viewing behavior of children and adults by Anderson et al. (1986) mentioned in Chapter 6 was undoubtedly very costly. Home observations of television viewing were completed for 99 families. Equipment installed in each home (installation time 1.5 to 2 hours per unit) included two video cameras, a time-lapse video recorder, and electronic equipment to control the cameras and recorders. In some cases families had more than one television set, which required multiple installations of the recording equipment. Videotaping continued in each home for about 12 days, with videocassettes needed for continuous recording. If the researchers could only afford equipment to assess one family at a time, it would take them 3.25 years to collect the data. Granted, all 99 families did not have the equipment installed simultaneously, but even the cost of enough equipment to assess 3 or 4 families at the same time is quite high.

ADDITIONAL CONTROLS

In the simplest case the basic experimental design has two groups: (1) an experimental group that receives the manipulation, and (2) a control group that does not. Using a control group makes it possible to eliminate a variety of alternative explanations based on confounds such as history, maturation, statistical regression, and so on. Sometimes, additional control procedures may be necessary to address other types of alternative explanations. Different research problems may demand specific additional control groups.

Placebo Controls

In drug research one specific control group is called a placebo group. Consider an experiment investigating whether a drug improves the behavior of a group of hyperactive children. One group of children diagnosed as hyperactive receives the drug, and the other group does not. Now, suppose that the drug group shows an improvement. We don't know whether the improvement was caused by properties of the drug or by the expectations about the effect of the drug—what is called a **placebo effect.** You may recall Whalen et al.'s (1991) study described in Chapter 2 in which ADHD children expected that medication would improve their performance.

Merely administering a pill or an injection may be sufficient to cause an improvement in behavior. To control for this possibility, a **placebo control group** can be added. An inert, harmless substance is given to members of the placebo group; they do not receive the drug given to members of the experimental group. If the improvement results from the active properties of the drug, the participants in the experimental group should show greater improvement than those in the placebo group. If the placebo group improves as much as the experimental group, the improvement is a placebo effect. A solution is to use a **single-blind procedure** in which the participant is unaware of whether a placebo or the actual drug is being administered.

Experimenter Expectancies

Experimenters are usually aware of the purpose of the study and may develop expectations about how subjects should respond. These expectations can, in turn, bias the results. This general problem is called **experimenter bias** or **expectancy effects** (Rosenthal, 1966, 1967, 1969). Expectancy effects may occur whenever experimenters know which condition subjects are in, potentially biasing their observations. If the observers expect the drug to calm the hyperactive children, they may rate a given behavior as more calm than if it were seen in one of the children in the placebo group. For this reason, it is common that even the experimenters do not know which group is receiving the experimental drug and which the placebo. This is called a **double-blind procedure** because both the participant and the experimenter are uninformed about what condition the participant is actually in. In a double-blind, the participants and medications are coded by a researcher who does not make the observations. In this way, the observers remain uninformed about the actual conditions.

The importance of minimizing both the participant's and the experimenter's awareness of the expected results cannot be overestimated. A famous demonstration of how experimenter expectancy can bias the results was conducted by Rosenthal and Jacobson (1968). Their study, *Pygmalion in the Classroom,* demonstrates the power of self-fulfilling prophecies and the dangers of labeling children. Rosenthal and Jacobson gave first- and second-grade teachers the names of five students in each class who were supposedly identified as "rapid bloomers." In fact, these children had been selected randomly and did not necessarily have any special abilities or talents. Informing the teachers of the potential of these children created higher expectations, and the rapid bloomers did improve in reading achievement and IQ. There are several possible explanations for how the Pygmalion effect works. Because the teachers expected the rapid bloomers to perform better, perhaps the students received more praise for their successes. Teachers may pay more attention to the high-expectancy children, assisting them more when they do not understand material. The cumulative effect of this unconscious teacher expectancy bias could add up to a significant difference in the two groups of children, contributing to the better performance of the rapid bloomers. As parents and teachers know, children can live up to high expectations or just as easily fulfill negative expectations. Box 10.2 describes an experiment in which expectations did not conform to reality.

Attention Controls

Even if people are not aware of the purpose of the research, they are prone to change their behavior simply because they know they are being observed. As discussed in Chapter 4, a technical term for such behavior is *reactivity.* The most famous demonstration of how simply being studied can affect behavior took place in the Hawthorne, Illinois, manufacturing plant of the Western Electric Company in the late 1920s and early 1930s (Roethlisberger & Dickson, 1939). The researchers made a variety of changes in the workers' environment (e.g., both raising and lowering the level of illumination and temperature) to see what conditions would lead to increased production and employee satisfaction. The surprising finding was that production and satisfaction increased in every condition; after a while the researchers realized it was the workers' awareness that they were in a study that produced the results—not the experimental manipulations. The phenomenon has ever since been known as the **Hawthorne effect.** A possible remedy is to add an **attention control group** to the study that receives no treatment or a treatment that is not expected to produce an effect on the dependent measure. If

BOX 10.2   RESEARCH IN ACTION

Alzheimer's Disease

The concept of a "blind" study often extends to raters or observers in a study. To obtain unbiased measurements, it is important to have raters who are uninformed about the hypotheses of a study or the identity of participants. To illustrate this concept, consider an intriguing study of Alzheimer's disease, an illness associated with old age (Snowdon et al., 1996). About 60 years ago, a group of young women wrote autobiographical statements just before they took their vows to join an order of nuns, the School Sisters of Notre Dame. Now in their 80s, nearly one third have developed Alzheimer's disease, a rate comparable to that in the general population. Fourteen of the nuns have died, and autopsies determined the presence of Alzheimer's in some of the women. The researchers expected that education would serve as a protective factor against Alzheimer's, hypothesizing that nuns with college degrees would be less likely to develop the disease. As it turns out, their expectations were incorrect.

Raters blind to the Alzheimer's status of the nuns evaluated the autobiographical writings for idea density, a measure of how many ideas are in a piece of writing. To obtain accurate evaluations, it was essential for the raters to be uninformed about the health status of the nuns. The primary researchers could not do the coding because they had prior expectations about the nuns.

Content analysis showed that young nuns who wrote grammatically complex sentences packed with ideas remained free of Alzheimer's disease 60 years later. In contrast, nuns who wrote simple sentences later suffered from the dementia of Alzheimer's disease. This outcome was true regardless of the nuns' educational achievements. The results suggest that signs of Alzheimer's may be evident much earlier than previously theorized. Here are some examples of the writing from Sister A, who died of Alzheimer's and Sister B, who remains mentally healthy.

Sister A: I was born in Eau Claire, Wisconsin, on May 24, 1913, and was baptized in St. James Church.

Sister B: The happiest day of my life so far was my First Communion, which was in June nineteen hundred and twenty when I was but eight years of age, and four years later in the same month I was confirmed by Bishop D. D. McGavick.

Sister A: I prefer teaching music to any other profession.

Sister B: I visited the capitol in Madison and also the Motherhouse of the Franciscan Sisters of Perpetual Adoration at Duluth which visit increased my love for Notre Dame, because it was and is Notre Dame.

the treatment group shows a greater effect than the attention control group, then we can conclude that the result was not due to the Hawthorne effect.

It is more difficult to predict what will happen to children's behavior when they know they are being observed. Some children become uncharacteristically shy; others become shameless hams. For this reason, any time we single out a group of children to participate in an experimental treatment, there also should be a group that merely receives an equal amount of attention (without receiving the treatment). For example, Hudley and Graham (1993) designed an intervention to reduce aggressive behavior in third-, fourth-, and fifth-grade African American boys identified as aggressive. The curriculum consisted of 12 lessons developed to train aggressive boys *not* to infer hostile intent in the social behavior of their elementary school peers. An attention training group was included to control for the possibility that simply participating in any special program might alter the boys' aggressive behavior. The curriculum in the attention group also consisted of 12 lessons, but the topic was nonsocial problem-solving skills. The intervention successfully trained these highly aggressive youngsters to presume less hostile intent in hypothetical vignettes. In addition, teachers who were blind to their treatment condition also rated the boys' behavior as significantly less aggressive after the intervention program.

Maturation Control Group

A final control group that must be considered in developmental research is the maturation control group. In the Hudley and Graham (1993) study just discussed, one possible explanation for the results is that children had simply matured over the 4 months of the study. It could be that their social behavior improved at the end of the study as the result of natural maturational processes related to emotional and cognitive development—and not as a result of either the cognitive intervention or the increased attention resulting from participating in a study. A **maturation control group** is a group of participants who are the same age as the experimental participants at the beginning of a study. These participants are given the same pretest and posttest as the experimental group, but otherwise they do not participate in the study. If the treatment group shows a greater effect than the maturation control group, then we can conclude that the result was not due to maturation. As it turns out, Hudley and Graham also included a maturation control group in their study. Neither the attention control group nor the maturation control group showed significant changes in their presumptions of hostile intent and their reliance on aggressive behavior. The inclusion of these two control groups strengthens the researchers' confidence in the efficacy of cognitive retraining as a way to reduce childhood aggression.

DEBRIEFING

After all the data have been collected, a debriefing session usually is held. During debriefing, the researcher explains the purpose of the study and tells participants what kinds of results are expected; the practical implications of the results may also be discussed. The investigator has an ethical responsibility to inform participants, parents, or school personnel about the study. In some cases, researchers may contact participants later to inform them of the actual results of the study. This is the educational purpose of debriefing.

As discussed in Chapter 2, if participants have been deceived in any way, debriefing is required for ethical reasons. The researcher needs to explain why the deception was necessary so the participants appreciate the fact that deception was the only way to get the information on an important issue. The participants should leave the experiment without any ill feelings toward research in general, and they may even leave with some new insights into their own behavior or personality.

Debriefing children can be problematic. Recall from Chapter 2 that at times it is better not to debrief a child. One consideration involves the possibility of upsetting the child by revealing his or her true performance on an experimental task. Another consideration is that debriefing may inadvertently teach a child that adults lie and cannot be trusted. There are no definite rules about when to debrief. As the respected pediatrician Dr. Benjamin Spock advised parents, go with your instincts and you will make the right choice.

Researchers may ask the participants to refrain from discussing the study with others. Such requests typically are made when more people will be participating and they might talk with one another in classes or residence halls. People who have already participated are aware of the general purposes and procedures, and it is important that these individuals not provide expectancies about the study to potential future participants. Children have difficulty keeping information to themselves, and wise researchers design their studies accordingly. If you find that children's scores are improving dramatically as your study progresses, be suspicious that the cat is out of the proverbial bag.

The debriefing session can also provide an opportunity to learn more about what participants were thinking during the experiment. Such information can prove useful in interpreting the results and planning future studies. It may be helpful to find out whether the participants guessed the hypotheses. Ask how they interpreted the manipulation of the independent variable and what they were thinking when they completed the dependent measures. Even children can respond to questions such as these when phrased in developmentally appropriate language. They may actually take great delight in assuming the role of expert, retelling the experience from their point of view.

A word of warning about the validity of a post-experimental interview comes from Taylor and Shepperd (1996). A graduate student was recruited to fill in for a last-minute cancellation in a pilot study that involved deceptive feedback to participants on their performance on a task. When the experimenter stepped out of the room, the participants discussed the experiment and determined the nature of the deception. Later, when the experimenter explicitly asked if the participants were suspicious about the manipulation, no one admitted knowledge of the deception. Several important points are raised by the graduate student's fortuitous discovery of this procedural problem. First, never leave your participants unsupervised in group settings where they can discuss the experiment. Second, telling participants not to discuss the experiment may not be adequate. And third, carefully evaluate your debriefing procedures to increase the likelihood that participants will truthfully disclose their ideas and beliefs about the experiment.

RESEARCH PROPOSALS

After putting considerable thought into planning a study, the researcher writes a research proposal. A **research proposal** explains what you plan to study and the procedures that will be used. Such proposals are required as part of applications for research grants; ethics review committees require some type of proposal as well. You may be required to write a proposal as part of a course assignment. Plan on writing and rewriting the proposal; revisions are a valuable part of the process, allowing you to refine and organize your ideas. In addition, you can show the proposal to friends, colleagues, and professors who can provide useful feedback about the adequacy of your procedures and design. They may see problems that you did not recognize, or they may offer ways of improving the study.

The main body of a research proposal is similar to the introduction and method sections of a journal article (see Appendix A). Keeping in mind that the purpose of a proposal is to convince others of the worthiness of a project, explicit justification for the research and defense of the procedural details are essential for a proposal. A carefully crafted literature review points to inconsistencies or flaws in the existing literature that your study plans to address. Explain your reasoning carefully, defend the selection of your study sample, justify your manipulations and the operationalization of your variables. Proposals often include a brief results section that explains the purpose and logic of the analysis, showing how the statistical evaluation will address the hypotheses. Some funding agencies have very specific requirements for the components of a research proposal; you may be asked to submit many different sections other than the ones summarized here.

Estimating Costs

If your proposal is being submitted to a funding agency, you will need to provide a budget specifying where the money will be spent. Some instructors require cost estimation in a proposal as well—it can be very enlightening to find out just how expensive that longitudinal study will be! Research sometimes requires expensive laboratory equipment, computers, and standardized tests. In addition to equipment, there may be personnel costs associated with research assistants and expenses such as office supplies, postage, telephones, travel expenses, and photocopying. If participants are paid for their participation, the researcher must budget for this expense also. Even a token payment of $5 per person adds up very quickly.

Another cost to consider is time. Research projects range tremendously in the amount of time they take. Inexperienced researchers sometimes conceive projects that exceed their time and financial resources. Beginning researchers will be glad to know that relatively fast and easy projects are possible. Consider a recent study of children's knowledge about skin cancer and exposure to the sun (Kubar, Rodrigue, & Hoffmann, 1995). A questionnaire was distributed to three classes of fifth-grade children who responded to a total of 35 items about their knowledge of skin cancer, attitudes toward sun exposure, intentions to use sunscreen, and actual sunscreen use. The participants completed the materials as part of their regularly scheduled school activities. In one morning, all of the data could be collected. The only remaining task was for the researchers to tally the results and analyze the data.

Now compare that study to an observational study of social skills in developmentally delayed preschoolers conducted by Kopp, Baker, and Brown (1992). Developmental assessments were individually administered to 83 preschool children to match play groups on developmental age. Children were individually videotaped in play triads on two occasions. The addition of a second play session greatly extended the time required for the project because of the difficulty coordinating the availability of three children. The advantage of videotape is that many behaviors were coded from the play sessions. Tapes were coded for play activity, social behaviors, attention, affective behaviors, and regressive behaviors. However, the coding was extremely time-consuming, with a team of six coders working almost a year to score the play sessions. In fact, so many variables were measured that the researchers had to develop a coding manual specifying the definitions for each variable and their location in a multitude of computer files. The key point is to consider the time requirements of various procedures carefully and to select what is appropriate for your schedule.

PILOT STUDIES AND MANIPULATION CHECKS

When the researcher has finally decided on the specific aspects of the procedure, it is possible to conduct a **pilot study** in which the researcher does a "trial run" with a small number of participants. The pilot study will reveal whether participants understand the instructions, whether the total experimental setting seems plausible, whether any confusing questions are being asked, and so on. Pilot studies help to determine how much time it takes to run each participant through the procedure and debriefing. In other words, a pilot study helps the researcher "fine tune" the study. Another benefit is that the researcher gets a chance to practice the procedures in a pilot study; this practice reduces anxiety when running the actual participants and allows the researcher to standardize the procedures.

The pilot study also provides an opportunity for a manipulation check of the independent variable. A **manipulation check** is an attempt to directly measure whether the independent variable manipulation has the intended effect on the participants. Manipulation checks provide evidence for the construct validity of the manipulation (construct validity was discussed in Chapter 4). If you are manipulating anxiety, for example, a manipulation check will tell you whether members of the high-anxiety group really were more anxious than those in the low-anxiety condition. The manipulation check might involve a self-report of anxiety, a behavioral measure such as number of arm and hand movements, or a physiological measure such as heart rate. All manipulation checks ask whether the independent variable manipulation was in fact a successful operationalization of the conceptual variable being studied. Consider an example of a manipulation of physical attractiveness as an independent variable. In a study participants evaluate someone who is supposed to be perceived as attractive or unattractive. The manipulation check in this case could determine whether participants do rate the highly attractive person as more physically attractive.

Manipulation checks are particularly useful in the pilot study to determine if the independent variable manipulated is having the intended effect. They can also be used in the actual experiment to demonstrate the effectiveness of the manipulation. However, a manipulation check might not be included in the actual experiment if it would distract participants or reveal the purpose of the experiment.

A manipulation check has two advantages. First, if the check shows that your manipulation was not effective, you have saved the expense of running the actual experiment. You can turn your attention to changing the manipulation to make it more effective. For instance, if the manipulation check shows that neither the low-anxiety nor the high-anxiety group was very anxious, you can adjust the procedures to increase the anxiety in the high-anxiety condition.

Second, a manipulation check is advantageous if you get nonsignificant results—that is, if the results indicate that no relationship exists between the independent and dependent variables. A manipulation check can identify whether the nonsignificant results are due to a problem in manipulating the independent variable. Logically, if your manipulation is not successful, you will not obtain significant results. But what if the check shows that the manipulation was successful, and you still get nonsignificant results? Then you know that the similarity between your low-anxiety and high-anxiety groups is not due to a problem with the manipulation. If this happens, you will need to consider alternative explanations. Perhaps you had an insensitive dependent measure, or maybe there really is no relationship between the variables.

USING COMPUTERS TO CONDUCT RESEARCH

It is becoming easier and more common for researchers to use computers as a tool for manipulating independent variables and measuring behaviors. An individual sitting at a computer screen can be presented with written material or graphical displays that replace traditional methods such as printed materials, tachistoscopes (devices that vary the length of presentation of a stimulus), and slides. Researchers can ask questions on a computer monitor instead of using the traditional paper-and-pencil method. Computers can also be used to record response times and control physiological recording devices and other equipment.

Loftus, Levidow, and Duensing (1992) took full advantage of computer technology in their memory study of people attending a museum. As visitors entered the museum, a short film clip was displayed on a large TV screen in a prominent location. Loftus and colleagues set up their research computer as part of an interactive exhibit on memory. The computer screen displayed "Eyewitness Memory" on the screen, inviting museum visitors to answer questions about the movie clip. The computer was programmed to handle random assignment to experimental conditions, presentation of questions to participants, and debriefing. The computerized display tested almost 2,000 people. Imagine trying to test that many people using paper-and-pencil measures!

It has recently become possible to conduct research over the Internet. People connected to the Internet from anywhere in the world are potential participants in a research investigation. The extensive nature of these global linkages raises many unresolved issues such as the integrity of the data and the quality of the sample.

ANALYZING AND INTERPRETING THE RESULTS

After the data have been collected, the next step is to analyze them. Statistical analyses of the data are carried out to allow the researcher to examine and interpret the pattern of results obtained in the study. The statistical analysis helps the researcher decide whether a relationship actually exists between the independent and dependent variables. The logic underlying the use of statistics is discussed in Chapters 14 and 15. It is not the purpose of this book to teach statistical methods; however, the calculations involved in several statistical tests are provided in Appendix B.

COMMUNICATING RESEARCH TO OTHERS

The final step is to write a report that details why you conducted the research, how you obtained the participants, what procedures you used, and what you found. A description of how to write such reports is included in Appendix A. After you have written the report, what do you do with it? How do you communicate the findings to others? Research findings are most often submitted as journal articles or as papers to be read at scientific meetings. In either case, the submitted paper is reviewed by two or more knowledgeable individuals who decide whether the paper is acceptable for publication or presentation at the meeting.

Professional Meetings

Meetings sponsored by professional associations provide important opportunities for researchers to present their findings to other researchers and to the public. National and regional professional associations hold annual meetings at which professionals and students present their own studies and learn about the latest research being done by their colleagues. Sometimes verbal presentations are delivered to an audience in the form of a symposium or invited address. However, poster sessions are more common; researchers are assigned a large display board for a certain period of time. Those interested can view the poster and chat with the researchers about details of the study.

Holding conventions is perhaps the most important function of professional societies. Another important function is publication of scholarly journals. Some large and powerful organizations engage in political advocacy, attempting to influence the public or the government about specific issues of concern such as educational reform, health care programs for the elderly, or the effects of unemployment on the mental health of family members.

The Society for Research in Child Development (SRCD) illustrates a professional organization in action. SRCD is the major organization for researchers in child development from a variety of related disciplines, including anthropology, ethology, medicine, sociology, psychiatry, nursing, audiology, nutrition, special education, behavioral pediatrics, psychology, and other allied fields. Its members include the leading child researchers in the world. To give you an idea of the

---

BOX 10.3

Topics Presented at a Recent SRCD Convention

Panel 1. Infancy: Cognition and Communication
Panel 2. Infancy: Social and Emotional Processes
Panel 3. Perceptual, Sensory, Motor, and Psychobiological Processes
Panel 4. Infants and Toddlers at Risk (0–3 years)
Panel 5. Children at Risk (3+ years)
Panel 6. Adolescence and Life Course Development
Panel 7. Language
Panel 8. Cognition 1: Concepts, Space, Reasoning, Problem Solving
Panel 9. Cognition 2: Attention, Learning, Memory
Panel 10. Educational Issues: Intelligence, Learning or Language Disorders, Reading, Writing, Mathematics
Panel 11. Social Development and Behavior: Prosocial Behavior, Aggression, Play
Panel 12. Social Cognition
Panel 13. Affect
Panel 14. Family and Kinship Relations
Panel 15. Sociocultural and Ecological Contexts 1: Schools, Peers, and Media
Panel 16. Sociocultural and Ecological Contexts 2: Gender and Ethnicity
Panel 17. Atypical Development: Psychopathology, Sensory, Motor, or Mental Handicaps, Giftedness
Panel 18. History, Theory, and Interdisciplinary
Panel 19. Public Policy Issues
Panel 20. Methodology

---

breadth of interests of SRCD members, Box 10.3 lists the various panels of a recent SRCD convention. Note that the panels cover issues in infancy, early childhood, adolescence, families, and various applied topics.

Educators can join the American Educational Research Association (AERA). The American Sociological Association (ASA) is the major U.S. organization for sociologists, the American Anthropological Association (AAA) serves anthropologists, and the American Psychological Association (APA) and the American Psychological Society (APS) serve practitioners and researchers in all areas of psychology. In addition to these large, broadly based organizations, a number of smaller, more specific societies exist, such as the International Conference on Infant Studies. Researchers interested in life span issues can join the American Geriatrics Society or the Gerontological Society; those interested in family studies can join the National Council on Family Relations.

You may find that ideas discussed at conventions are preliminary, tentative, or "in progress." When scientists wish to put their results in more permanent form, they communicate their ideas in journals, books, and other scientific publications.

BOX 10.4

Designing and Conducting Research

1. Select an idea for research and develop hypotheses and predictions (see Chapter 3).

2. Choose a research method.

   Is your topic best suited for experimental research?

   Is a nonexperimental approach more appropriate, such as observational research, survey research, or archival research (see Chapters 7 and 8)?

3. Select a population and a sampling method.

   Who are you interested in testing? families? children? elderly? working mothers? divorced fathers? twins? first-generation immigrants?

   Do you need probability sampling or nonprobability sampling (see Chapter 8)?

   Where can you find these individuals?

   How can they be recruited?

   What are the procedures to get permission for the study?

   How will you obtain consent from the participants?

4. Operationalize the variables: How will the concepts be manipulated and measured?

   Will you use a straightforward (instructional) or staged (event) manipulation?

   Select the strongest manipulation possible.

Journal Articles

As we noted in Chapter 3, many journals publish research results. Nevertheless, the number of journals is small compared to the number of reports written; for this reason it is not easy to publish research. When a researcher submits a paper to a journal, two or more reviewers read the paper and recommend acceptance (often with the stipulation that revisions be made) or rejection. As many as 75% to 90% of papers submitted to the more prestigious journals are rejected. Many rejected papers are submitted to other journals and eventually are accepted for publication. Much research is never published. This isn't necessarily bad; it simply means that selection processes separate high-quality research from that of lesser quality.

Electronic Publication

A recent trend is for scientists to provide research reports on the World Wide Web. Some researchers include links to manuscripts, both finished and in progress, on their individual web pages. Electronic journals have been created where authors

Select a dependent variable with a range of possible values.

Watch for ceiling and floor effects: Don't make the measure too hard or too easy.

Will you include more than one dependent measure?

5. Are control groups needed to eliminate alternative explanations for the results?

Is a placebo group or a single-blind or double-blind procedure important for your study?

Is one group in your design spending extra time with the researcher or their teacher? If so, you need an attention control group.

Does your study last several months? If so, you may need a maturation control group to control for normal developmental progress.

6. What will be included in the debriefing session? Will participants be informed about any deception that may have occurred?

7. Write a research proposal that summarizes your design plans.

8. Obtain ethical approval from your university and possibly from the research site you selected.

9. Run a pilot study and debug the procedures.

10. Conduct the study.

11. Analyze the results.

12. Communicate the research results to other professionals. Submit a report to your instructor or a scholarly journal or make a presentation at a convention of your colleagues.

can "publish" papers without lengthy publication lags. Many are concerned that information on the Web has seldom gone through the peer review process that confers scientific respectability. As you know, anyone can put anything on the Web. In spite of this problem, scientists are excited about the Web's potential to increase people's access to information, to reduce publication lag, and to enable researchers to share technical information such as data archives. Efforts are needed to address the question of how to ensure scientific standards and quality in this new electronic environment.

SUMMARY

In this chapter we reviewed the practical matters that must be considered to conduct an actual research study. The discussion focused on experiments that use the simplest experimental design with a single independent variable. Box 10.4 summarizes the steps involved in designing and conducting research that we discussed in this chapter. Some of these steps occur simultaneously rather than in a step-by-step fashion.

Obtaining participants is one of the most challenging practical aspects of research. Once participants are identified, the researcher must decide how to set the stage with straightforward, instructional manipulations or staged, event manipulations. Some studies involve deception, and the researcher needs to provide appropriate debriefing in such cases. Sensitive dependent measures make it easier to detect differences between groups. Inappropriate selection of the dependent measure can lead to ceiling and floor effects. In some cases, multiple measures are especially useful to give a full picture of the phenomenon under study. A control group may be included in a research study to eliminate alternative explanations for the results. Depending on the research question, you may need a placebo group, attention control group, or maturation control group.

Research proposals help investigators plan their studies by estimating the costs, time, and materials involved. If the researcher is planning to apply for funding to support the research project, a proposal will be required. The process of writing the proposal helps organize ideas and refine the research.

Experienced researchers know the value of pilot studies, which are trial projects in which the instructions, procedures, apparatus, and so forth are tested with small numbers of participants. Pilot studies enable manipulation checks to ensure that the independent variables have the intended effect on the participants. The final step in conducting research is to communicate your findings to others. Professional meetings and journal publications provide opportunities for researchers to share their results.

KEY TERMS

attention control group	manipulation check	single-blind procedure
ceiling effect	maturation control	staged manipulation
confederate	group	(event manipulation)
double-blind procedure	pilot study	straightforward ma-
experimenter bias	placebo control group	nipulation (instruc-
(expectancy effects)	placebo effect	tional manipulation)
floor effect	research proposal	
Hawthorne effect	sensitivity	

REVIEW QUESTIONS

1. Think of a study in the area of family relations that you would be interested in conducting (e.g., How do younger and older couples adjust to living together? How do families maintain contact with grandparents and other extended family members? Does religious involvement promote mental health in parents and children?). How would you go about obtaining participants for your study? How would you obtain consent?

2. Describe how a straightforward manipulation of the independent variable differs from a staged manipulation.

3. What is the reason for selecting the strongest possible manipulation of the independent variable?

4. What is meant by the sensitivity of a dependent measure?

5. On the first test in your research methods class, students were very happy because they all got As. The teacher, however, says she is throwing out the scores. Students cry "No fair!" because they want to keep their As. How can the teacher defend her position? What is a possible problem here?

6. On the next test in your research methods class, students were not happy because they all got Fs. This time the teacher says there is nothing she can do. Students cry "No fair!" because they want better grades. How can the students defend their position? What is a possible problem here?

7. Distinguish between single-blind and double-blind procedures.

8. What is the reason for using a placebo control group? an attention control group? a maturation control group?

9. What information does the researcher tell participants during debriefing? What information can participants provide for the researcher?

10. What is the purpose of a pilot study?

11. What is a manipulation check? How does it help the researcher interpret the results of an experiment?

12. How do researchers communicate their findings after completing a study?

Practical Considerations in Conducting Research

This chapter presents some practical guidelines for conducting research. Working with participants is more than just "testing." An effective researcher is sensitive to the characteristics of the participants and the environment. We offer specific suggestions for working with infants, children, older adults, and children with special needs. However, we recognize that it is difficult to relay in words how to assess the participants in your research. Experience is the best teacher, and only through some experimentation of your own will you develop the skills needed to work with individuals in a research setting.

Many helpful suggestions for working with participants can be adapted from the fields of clinical psychology and counseling. In the clinical setting, the aim is to establish a therapeutic relationship; in research the goal is to establish a positive, cooperative relationship between participant and researcher. In addition, the developmental literature informs us about age-appropriate language development, understanding of self, memory skills, and cognitive, social, and emotional abilities.

THE ASSESSMENT PROCESS

The assessment process begins when the researcher first contacts the prospective participant for an interview, a survey, or an experiment. The participant may be unsure about what is expected, so it is important to put him or her at ease. Both adults and children may be apprehensive about the research process. At all times, researchers should be friendly yet maintain a professional manner. Treat the participant the way you wish your medical doctor would greet you when you go in for a checkup (instead of the abrupt, aloof, expeditious way we are too often treated). Greet the participant sincerely, and show genuine enthusiasm for his or her participation in your study. Overly friendly, extended conversations are not necessary—they serve only to take up excessive amounts of time (that's why the friendly doctor is always late for appointments!). Provide explanations for any questions to ensure that the participant understands what will happen in the course of the study.

Establishing Rapport

Establishing rapport with your participants is essential. Without the cooperation and confidence of the participants, the results do not reflect their true abilities. Maintain eye contact as you introduce yourself to participants. First impressions are very important; make sure they are positive. After introducing yourself to parents (use your first name), allow parents to introduce their young child, but introduce yourself to older children. Avoid using the word *doctor* when making introductions to minimize negative reactions associated with medical doctors.

With children, focus your attention on both the parent and the child. Parents will be assessing the researcher, and the child will look to the parent for cues about how to behave. Allow time for the child to become comfortable with you and to explore the surroundings. In a strange environment, children (and even adults) may become anxious and fearful. Some children are very outgoing and immediately comfortable around strangers; others may need a more extended period of time to relax. You will know that rapport has been successfully established when conversation flows easily.

To engage children in conversation, ask questions that require specific responses rather than open-ended vague comments. For example, "Do you like school?" may produce a mumbled "uh-huh." But a specific question such as "What are your favorite classes in school?" should produce more conversation. For younger children, ask questions about familiar things such as their age, pets, and favorite television programs. For older children, questions about friends, school, and social activities are effective. Developmental researchers should stay up to date on current events, children's fads, and trends in television shows and popular music to facilitate conversation about age-appropriate topics.

CHILDREN

Children of any age present unique problems. In an experimental study, a major challenge is to get children to do what you want them to—on your timetable. This is not always easily accomplished. Young children do not follow instructions well, so the researcher is usually satisfied with assessing what the child will do in reaction to a particular situation. Older children have a better understanding of what it means to be in an experiment, allowing more accurate assessment of their abilities. Adolescents are generally cooperative, and their verbal abilities and ability to reason abstractly make them ideal participants.

The Setting

The physical setting also contributes to building rapport. When testing children, the experimental setting should resemble a setting familiar to the child, with familiar objects and furnishings. And, of course, make sure your setup does not resemble a doctor's office! Children are easily distracted by objects, sounds, and other sources of stimulation in their surroundings; keep these to a minimum. If you are not using the observational window in your experimental playroom, consider hanging curtains to obscure the mirror. Children are easily engaged by objects that do not ordinarily attract an adult's attention. A colorful clipboard, stopwatch, or pencil will be more distracting than generic ones. Keep your experimental materials readily accessible but out of view until you are ready to use them.

Working With Children

Age-appropriate expectations for the child's behavior provide commonsense guidelines for research materials and procedures. Expect that infants less than 18 months old will explore experimental materials with their mouths. For this reason, small objects present a safety hazard. Stimulus materials will be thrown; make sure they are lightweight and unbreakable or firmly attached. Sterilize the objects in the experimental setting between sessions. Printed materials should be laminated or protected by plastic covers to prevent damage from smudgy little fingers.

Young children cannot read well enough to absorb a page of written instructions. They also do not process information well by listening passively to an experimenter reading a script. Some children do not respond well to an adult acting in a distant, clinically objective manner, which can easily happen to a researcher trying to adhere to the same script for all participants. More success results if the researcher is as natural as possible, openly warm and friendly, transmitting an impression that the activity is fun.

The researcher must be sensitive to the child's level of comprehension and explain the research so that each child understands what is expected. Age-appropriate language should be used, avoiding complex sentences and lengthy instructions. Most existing child instruments are geared to a third-grade reading level. It may take some experience for the researcher to learn to interpret a child's reaction to the instructions. Maintain eye contact with the child and ask frequently whether he or she understands what is expected. It is not sufficient merely to ask a general question such as "Do you understand?" because young children are poor at indicating their lack of knowledge (Flavell, Speer, Green, & August, 1981; Markman, 1977). Having the child repeat back or paraphrase what is expected is a better way to assess comprehension. It is sometimes necessary to explain a given concept in several alternative ways before a child grasps your intention. Precise terms may have to give way to language more appropriate to the child's level. For example, it is common to describe the experiment as a game you are going to play together. Students conducting research for a course assignment may enlist children's help by asking for help with their homework. One of our students using this approach recently was surprised when a precocious first grader replied, "I won't be able to help you with your homework. I'll go get my mom!"

Allow time for the child's response, adjusting to the speed of each individual child's temperament. Acknowledge the child's comments during the session, yet maintain focus on the task at hand should the child digress. Redirect the child's attention and resume the procedures as quickly as possible. Be playful and friendly with the child, yet maintain control of the situation. Watch for signs of boredom, fatigue, distress, or discomfort in the child's physical posture or tone.

Uniformity of understanding is the true goal of instructions to research participants, not uniformity of instructions. In addition to the instructions themselves, other conditions may have to be adjusted to suit the child's personality and developmental level. Some very young children can be tested by themselves; others may need a parent to be present for reassurance. If a parent must stay in the room, seat them in the background, out of the child's view. If the researcher is concerned that varying a factor such as presence or absence of parents may contaminate the results, this can be verified with a statistical analysis. The important thing is to test the child under conditions that make the child feel comfortable. Your goal is to elicit the child's best performance, not maintain rigid experimental control. With children, flexibility is essential. For example, the Peabody Picture Vocabulary Test-Revised (PPVT-R) is a measure of receptive vocabulary in which the child is instructed to indicate a diagram depicting a vocabulary word; we have successfully administered the PPVT-R with a resistant 4-year-old who stubbornly insisted on pointing to the pictures with her toes!

Infants

Infants are notoriously difficult to study because of the transitory nature of their behavioral states. The optimal state for testing infants is the quiet, alert state in which the infant is fully awake, with eyes wide open and little motor activity. This state of heightened alertness is well suited for exploring the environment. The problem is, infants may only spend a total of 2 to 3 hours a day in the quiet alert state when they are very young—and it is rarely all at one time in the middle of the day when you want to conduct your study! A typical scenario: You contact the parents and arrange a time when their infant is usually awake. Dad drives to the university—and the infant falls asleep in the car. When they arrive at the lab, the baby wakes up—but she is hungry. So Dad feeds the baby—and, you guessed it, the baby goes to sleep! The moral of the story is: Keep experimental sessions fairly short to maximize the chance of the baby's alertness. Some caretaking tricks may help as well. For example, an infant tends to be more alert in the upright position rather than lying down.

High rates of attrition are common with infancy studies because of drowsiness and fussiness. The babies who maintain the desired state and remain in the study may not represent typical infants. These infants tend to be more alert and less irritable, possibly limiting the generalizability of the results. An alternative interpretation is that the data represent the range of possible behavior, adding to our knowledge about infant abilities.

By the time an infant is about a year old, longer periods of alertness make research easier. However, at this time the infant is intensely interested in his or her surroundings and may be fascinated by the experimental apparatus, as well as by the experimenter's hair, glasses, or buttons. A toddler is awake even longer, but the added mobility of walking and running poses new challenges for getting the child to physically remain in the experimental session. As parents know, a toddler can run amazingly fast!

Preschoolers

Preschoolers have especially short attention spans and a limited understanding of the role of a research participant. They would much rather play a game with you than answer your silly questions. Researchers working with preschoolers commonly spend time playing with the children before testing, both to build rapport and to help the child acclimate to the surroundings. Do not abruptly remove the preschooler from an interesting pre-experimental activity; you will soon regret this! Use furniture designed for children, or conduct the experimental session on the floor so you are at the child's eye level.

Preschoolers have little interest in their performance and are likely to follow their own impulses about what they want to do. They are rarely concerned about giving the correct answer to questions. Praise for their efforts should maintain their interest in the task.

Young children are highly influenced by time of day and may become distracted as nap time or meal time approaches. Extreme weather also tends to excite children; so if your scheduled day is extremely windy or rainy, consider revising your plans. And by all means, have all children use the bathroom before beginning your research!

If the nature of your experimental task involves the child completing a task on his or her own (for example, playing a computer game or making a drawing), try to keep yourself "busy" with other materials such as a book or some paperwork. This will give the child privacy and diminish self-conscious feelings. If parents remain in the experimental room, they also should be "busy"; this is often a good opportunity for the parent to complete demographic measures or other parental questionnaires.

Elementary School-Aged Children

Elementary school-aged children can adapt their understanding of the teacher-student role to perform adequately in the research setting, but unexpected problems tend to occur nevertheless. Epidemics of childhood illnesses, field trips, or school events can make large segments of the school population unavailable without warning. Individual subjects can become sick or pull out a loose tooth during the experimental session. Schools usually lack space, and the "research facility" may wind up being a picnic table in the courtyard, a corner of the lunchroom, the back of the stage, or the nurse's office. Time of day is a concern for children in elementary school as well; they may become inattentive as recess or the end of the school day nears. Exciting upcoming events also have a strong effect on children; for this reason it is unwise to test children near holidays or at the end of the school year.

OLDER ADULTS

A major decision in gerontological research is operationally defining the age variable. Age can be defined based on (1) chronological age, (2) functional age, or (3) other categories such as retirement status or years of marriage.

Defining the Older Adult

Using a definition based on **chronological age,** older adults are defined as age 65 and over by the U.S. Bureau of the Census, with full Social Security benefits beginning at age 65. This provides some face validity for using 65 years old as a cut-off point. A second chronological age approach divides adults into **young-old** and **old-old.** There is no consensus on the age ranges for these categories; you may see young-old defined as 65–74 or 65–79 years, and old-old defined as 75+ or 80+ years. These age groups differ substantially in physical activity, health, and sensory deficits, providing logical categories for research. A third approach defines older adults on the basis of **functional age;** that is, according to self-maintenance abilities and the ability to engage in intellectual activity and work (Lindley, 1989). Schaie (1993) suggests classifying adults on variables such as educational level, income, years of marriage, retirement status, and length of retirement as substitutes for a reliance on chronological age. Research issues will guide your final decision about defining age.

Working With Older Adults

Avoid **ageism** in descriptions and assumptions about older adults. Carefully examine test instruments to ensure the item content and wording do not reflect an age bias. For example, family questionnaires inquiring about parent-child interactions are rarely appropriate for older adults. Consider also generational changes in definitions of terms. For an older adult, the term *family* may be restricted only to biological relatives; for younger adults the term *family* readily extends to biological and nonbiological family members.

Performance levels in the elderly may be affected by normal aging processes and do not necessarily represent "deficits." Timed tests put older adults at a disadvantage because of slower reaction times. Bahrick (1984) allowed flexible time limits in his study of long-term retention of Spanish because he was interested in measuring knowledge, not speed. Moreover, many older adults have not used test-taking skills for a while. Some individuals have difficulty with fine motor control of the hand and fingers due to health problems such as arthritis. It's a good idea to minimize the amount of writing required of older participants.

Normal aging processes also contribute to declining vision in many older adults. To compensate, use larger-sized print for written materials, or slowly read instructions to participants (although hearing loss may interfere with understanding). Color vision may also deteriorate; keep this in mind if your experiment requires color discrimination when presenting materials or making responses. More time may be needed to perform visual tasks, especially if the lighting conditions are changed during the experiment, such as lowering the lights to view a movie or slide presentation. Older adults also may have difficulty with their hearing; to compensate for this, minimize background noise in the experimental setting. As mentioned, oral instructions may be difficult to follow due to hearing loss. Present information at a slow pace to facilitate comprehension, and permit participants to ask for clarification to make sure the directions are clear.

Health status should be obtained as part of demographic questions about older participants. Without information on health status, you will be unable to distinguish behaviors associated with normative development from behaviors associated with chronic disease or disability. Such identification is essential to reduce emphasis on the "deficit" model of aging (Schaie, 1993). Age *differences* are not necessarily indicative of *declines.*

Allow adequate time for all phases of the research session. Even walking around the research setting may take more time for older adults. In contrast to young adults, older adults may wish to chat and socialize with the experimenter after the testing period. They also may be influenced by time of day, medication intervals, and proximity to meals or rest period. Be patient and sensitive to the needs of each individual, adjusting your research procedures accordingly. As always, the goal is to maximize performance, not maintain a strict experimental regimen.

On a practical note, elderly people often have transportation difficulties, so it may be necessary to provide transportation if the research takes place away from their residence. Field research presents a good option. Conduct your study in a location where older adults typically meet such as at social events, religious functions, or retirement communities.

FAMILIES

Married couples must juggle work and child care schedules, and they may not be available at the convenience of the researchers. This is one of the reasons that research on parents with daytime work schedules is so difficult to do. Researchers may need to travel to the home to make it easier for families to participate; evenings and weekends are obviously better for working parents. Include both parents in initial approaches to recruit families for participation. Although relatively few fathers participate in many family studies, it is important to give the father the option of agreeing to the research. This is especially true in many minority cultures in which respect for the father's traditional role as head of household is paramount.

Parent-child interactions are a good way to gain insight into family dynamics. Much research has been conducted that observes families in unstructured interaction or in a structured setting such as playing a game or discussing a particular issue. Family interactions may focus on a dyad of two family members, a triad involving three family members, or a single individual such as the youngest child or the father. Quantitative data offer detailed descriptions of the interaction, whereas qualitative data are useful to explain the context and pattern of the interaction.

Interviews may also be used. Direct observations describe how family members behave, but they cannot explain why a parent or child behaves in a particular way. Parental perceptions of their own behavior and of their child's behavior are good supplements to observational data. At times, the data from different sources yield different conclusions. Quittner and Opipari (1994) used three types of data to assess mother-child interactions with a healthy child and a chronically ill child: (1) home interviews, (2) self-report ratings of maternal behaviors, and (3) diaries. Differential treatment favoring the chronically ill child was only evident in the quantitative and qualitative data derived from the daily diaries. Mothers spent more time with their chronically ill child and viewed these interactions as more positive than interactions with their healthy child.

SPECIAL NEEDS CHILDREN

Exceptional children with limited cognitive and physical abilities present a number of challenges for the researcher. It is rare for a disability to occur in isolation; handicaps are more often multidimensional, including impairments in cognition, vision, hearing, speech, and possibly motor domains. A customized approach to assessment can accommodate their strengths and compensate for other areas of functioning. The need for a quiet, pleasant, distraction-free setting is particularly important for assessing children with special needs. For example, the visually impaired child is especially distracted by a novel environment (Simeonsson, 1986). If you are unable to conduct your research in a setting familiar to the child, plan on multiple sessions, using the first session to build rapport and allow the child to become acclimated to the new surroundings. Then, in a subsequent session you will be more likely to have a friendly, cooperative child who is willing to spend time with you.

Test instruments designed for use with normally developing children may not be valid for children with special needs. Carefully evaluate the type of response required by your testing instrument to be sure each child can respond appropriately. Consider whether the children can hear your instructions, see your visual stimuli, and make the needed responses. Can they communicate responses using speech? Can they write? Can they manipulate objects? It may be difficult to detect their true abilities if a disability limits performance.

DIVERSITY

It is very natural for a child to understand and trust an examiner of similar background. When possible, include an examiner, observer, or interviewer who is of the same race, language, and ethnicity as the participant. However, be careful that you do not inadvertently create a confound by covarying the background of the examiner with the sample tested.

Research relies almost exclusively on dependent measures and test instruments developed on middle-class, European American samples. Generalizing such measures to ethnic minority populations or to individuals from a culture of poverty may not be wise. Measures based on middle-class values do not operate the same way in a low-income minority population. For example, the HOME Inventory (Caldwell & Bradley, 1984) yields differential findings for children in different ethnic groups (Bradley et al., 1989; Sugland et al., 1995). Bradley et al. report cultural differences in the timing of parenting practices, with some cultures waiting longer to place demands on their children and provide cognitively stimulating play materials. Sugland et al. report more accurate evaluation of the home environment with European American children than with African American or Hispanic children. Cultural differences have also been found in the antecedents of attachment assessed with the Strange Situation (Harwood, 1992).

A shortage of published empirical research on African Americans (Graham, 1992) may in part be due to the unavailability of culturally validated instruments. Research on African American infants and older adults is particularly lacking, and

188

CHAPTER 11
Practical
Considerations
in Conducting
Research

◁ **BOX 11.1** ▷

Some Widely Used Measures in Developmental and Family Research

Infancy

Brazelton Neonatal Behavioral Assessment Scale (Brazelton, 1973)

HOME Inventory (Caldwell & Bradley, 1984)

Intelligence

Bayley Scales of Infant Development (Bayley, 1969)

Stanford Binet (4th ed.) (Thorndike, Hagen, & Sattler, 1985)

Wechsler Intelligence Scales (Wechsler, 1981, 1989, 1991)

WPPSI-R: Wechsler Preschool and Primary Scales of Intelligence (ages 3–8 yrs)

WISC-III: Wechsler Intelligence Scale for Children (ages 6–16 yrs)

WAIS-R: Wechsler Adult Intelligence Scale (ages 16–74 yrs)

Behavioral Control

Draw-A-Line, Walk-A-Line (Toner, Holstein, & Hetherington, 1977)

Matching Familiar Figures Test (Kagan, Rosman, Day, Albert, & Phillips, 1964)

Self-Concept

Coopersmith Self-Esteem Inventory (Coopersmith, 1967)

Harter Self-Concept Scale (Harter, 1982)

Pictorial Scale of Perceived Competence and Social Acceptance for Young Children (Harter & Pike, 1984)

Piers-Harris Self-Concept Scale (Piers-Harris, 1969)

Self-Esteem Rating Scale for Children (Chiu, 1987)

much of the available literature overemphasizes "deficits" rather than differences. Carefully examine your experimental materials for potential cultural bias, being especially sensitive to pejorative connotations of language.

TEST INSTRUMENTS

Box 11.1 lists some commonly used measures in human development and family relations. Many tests originally designed for adults have been adapted for use with children. However, the language and themes in adult tests are not always applicable for children and adolescents. This is especially true for children with cognitive deficits due to learning disabilities or mental retardation because they may

Empathy

Affective Situation Test for Empathy (Feshbach & Roe, 1968)

Empathy Test for Children and Adolescents (Bryant, 1982)

Moral Development

Defining Issues Test (Rest, 1979, 1986)

Sociomoral Reflection Measure (Gibbs, Widaman, & Colby, 1982)

Sex Roles

Bem Sex-Role Inventory (Bem, 1974)

Children's Personal Attributes Questionnaire (Hall & Halberstadt, 1980)

Personal Attributes Questionnaire (Spence & Helmreich, 1978)

Marital and Family Satisfaction

Dyadic Adjustment Scale (Spanier, 1976)

Family Environment Scale (Moos & Moos, 1981)

Locke-Wallace Marital Adjustment Scale (Locke & Wallace, 1959)

Life Satisfaction and Life Stress

Life Satisfaction Index (Neugarten, Havighurst, & Tobin, 1961)

Schedule of Recent Events (Holmes & Rahe, 1967)

Social Readjustment Rating Scale (Holmes & Rahe, 1967)

Adult Development

Research Instruments in Social Gerontology, Vol. 1: Clinical and Social Gerontology (Mangen & Peterson, 1982a)

Research Instruments in Social Gerontology, Vol. 2: Social Roles and Social Participation (Mangen & Peterson, 1982b)

not have the abilities to complete the assessment (La Greca, 1990). Carefully research any instrument you consider using in your study to be sure it has been validated on a sample similar to yours.

Devising Your Own Test or Using an Existing Measure

Sometimes the nature of the research question demands that a unique measure be devised. However, most of the time a previously developed measure is available. Thus, you probably would not devise your own intelligence test or marital satisfaction measure; such measures already have been developed by others and used in previous studies. Most important, existing measures have reliability and validity data, and you can compare your findings with prior research that uses the measure.

Using Self-Report Measures

Self-report has only recently been accepted as useful for child assessment because the child was previously viewed as an unreliable informant. For that reason, combined with the ease of obtaining information from parents, child self-report was not the prime choice. At times, however, you must obtain information directly from a child or adolescent rather than using observational methodologies or parental report. The most widely used self-report measures assess children's internal psychological states (e.g., fear, anxiety, depression, pain) and self-perceptions (e.g., self-concept, self-esteem).

Self-report measures provide a relatively low-cost method to obtain information directly from participants about their attitudes, beliefs, and behavior. However, self-report measures are not appropriate for all populations. Young children and the developmentally delayed may be challenged by many of the cognitive requirements of a self-report measure. First, respondents must be able to read or understand questions presented orally. Second, limited verbalization or ability to respond makes self-report measures inappropriate for speech-impaired or developmentally delayed children. Third, many questionnaires ask about prior events; respondents must be able to recall information from long-term memory. Fourth, the concept of "self" must be understood to answer self-report questions. Psychological understanding of personal social and emotional events does not develop until middle childhood, and the ability to reason abstractly about the self in hypothetical situations does not emerge until adolescence. Because of these developmental limitations, questions must be adjusted for age-appropriateness. For preschoolers and children in primary grades, use concrete questions about the self. Young children would have difficulty with a psychological question such as "Are you sad?" but could accurately answer a more concrete question such as "Do you cry?"

The same guidelines apply to questions about others. Children less than approximately 7 years old have limited person perception skills. Investigations of peer relations show that young children are poor informants about the behavior of their peers because they lack the cognitive or perceptual skills needed to recognize different types of social behavior. Even when young children can accurately describe the behavior of others, they usually cannot provide explanations or evaluations (Stone & Lemanek, 1990). For example, a young child might say that "Araceli gives me cookies" but would be unlikely to report that "Araceli is kind."

Unwarranted assumptions about children's developmental abilities can lead to validity problems for an educational or psychological instrument. Box 11.2 describes a study that evaluated the construct validity of an instrument designed to assess social competence in young children attending Head Start intervention programs. As you will see, researchers can be led to incorrect conclusions if they fail to take into account the cultural appropriateness of measures.

Using Rating Scales

Behavior rating instruments provide a reliable low-cost method for personality assessment. A parent can assess the behavior of their infant, preschooler, elementary school-aged child, or adolescent in a relatively short time by indicating

BOX 11.2 RESEARCH IN ACTION

Social Competence in Preschoolers—
Just How Many Is a Few?

The Pictorial Scale of Perceived Competence and Social Acceptance for Young Children (PSPCSA) was designed explicitly to assess self-perceptions of social competence in children ages 4 to 7 years (Harter & Pike, 1984). The measure was developed on a sample of White, middle-class preschoolers, leading Fantuzzo, McDermott, Manz, Hampton, and Burdick (1996) to question its utility on culturally diverse children. Using a pictorial format, children select pictures that reflect themselves; for example, "has a lot of friends to play with" or "doesn't have many friends to play with."

The PSPCSA assumes that young children have two key cognitive skills. One concept is the ability to distinguish between the following quantities: a few, hardly any, not very many, pretty many, a lot, and a whole lot. The second concept is the ability to recognize actions depicted in the pictures. For example, can the child distinguish a girl who is good at puzzles from a girl who is not good at puzzles?

Using 153 children enrolled in Head Start, Fantuzzo et al. found only 1 child who understood the key concepts essential to accurate responding with the PSPCSA. This methodological approach was apparently too sophisticated for the cognitive development of preschoolers. The developmental appropriateness of the PSPCSA format raises serious questions about its validity, indicating the need for further research to identify methods to obtain self-report information from culturally diverse samples of very young children.

ILLUSTRATION: Harter, S., & Pike, R., 1984. The Pictorial Scale of Perceived Competence and Social Acceptance for Young Children, *Child Development* 55, p. 1973. © Society for Research in Child Development, Inc. Used with permission.

the presence or absence of a particular behavior. Other persons can complete the rating forms; many checklists are designed for teachers. Ratings are usually based on an extended period of observation, so the rater needs sufficient knowledge of the person to be rated.

Ratings are preferred over self-report in several situations. As discussed earlier, some individuals cannot complete self-report measures due to cognitive or motor limitations. You also may want the caregiver's perspective to address your research questions. In addition, ratings may be less biased than self-report, which by definition may be very subjective.

Teachers are usually considered excellent raters. They have experience observing children of an age similar to the target child's and are familiar with typical behavior. Teachers can make fine distinctions between different types of behaviors and are particularly capable of judging qualitative aspects of children's behavior such as empathy (Coie & Dodge, 1988). However, they may be less accurate at quantitative features of behavior such as the frequency or rate of particular behaviors (Ladd & Profilet, 1996). Some of this bias may be related to oversampling attention-attracting behaviors.

Training observers to gather your rating data is another option. Multiple observers could observe the same child, allowing you to calculate interobserver reliability to ensure objective accuracy of the observations. However, observers tend to gather data during limited time intervals and, therefore, have a restricted sample of behavior. Because observer access to the diversity of behavior found in various school settings, such as playgrounds, lunchrooms, and hallways, is limited, their ratings may be inaccurate. In addition, the use of observers is usually a more costly approach for obtaining behavior ratings. Box 11.3 presents research that compared teacher and observer ratings of children's classroom behavior. Which source do you think is most accurate?

Ratings provided by both the teacher and a parent can yield divergent results. This is also true of ratings provided by both the mother and the father about the same child. The context of the home differs substantially from the context of the classroom, and, indeed, the child may behave differently in each setting. Thus, multiple raters provide valuable insight into the many patterns of behavior a child displays. Conflicting results do not pose a problem. As an example, consider a study of childhood anxiety in which parents and their adolescent twins rated the children's anxiety symptoms (Thapar & McGuffin, 1995). Parent ratings suggested a strong genetic component to anxiety; however, the twin ratings indicated that situations in the environment affected their anxiety. The divergent findings correspond to other findings that children report more internalizing symptoms and parents report more externalizing symptoms, highlighting the importance of both viewpoints.

SOURCES OF INFORMATION

There are many general reference books available to help locate test instruments that are commonly used in research. Here we discuss sources of information for five types of measures: (1) standardized tests, (2) self-report measures, (3) family measures, (4) personality measures, and (5) demographic measures.

Sources for Standardized Test Information

Sources of information about psychological tests include the *Mental Measurements Yearbook* (Kramer & Conoley, 1991) and *Test Critiques* (Keyser & Sweetland, 1991). These reference books are published periodically and contain descriptions and evaluations of many psychological tests.

BOX 11.3   RESEARCH IN ACTION

Teacher Ratings Versus Observer Ratings

The accuracy of teacher reports has been questioned because of potential biases associated with the personal relationship between the teacher and the child being studied. Weisz, Suwanlert, Chaiyasit, Weiss, Achenbach, and Trevathan (1988) report that Thai children were rated by their teachers as displaying more problem behavior than their American peers. This is surprising considering the Buddhist tradition in Thailand that emphasizes non-aggression, obedience, respect, and humility. Subsequent research (Weisz, Chaiyasit, Weiss, Eastman, & Jackson, 1995) compared teacher reports to reports provided by trained observers. The results are shown in the figure.

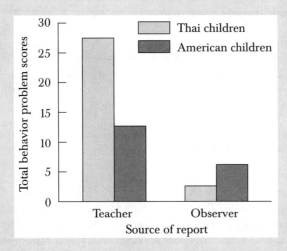

Based on teacher ratings, children in Thailand show twice as many problem behaviors as do American children. In sharp contrast, observer ratings show the opposite pattern, with American children scoring twice as high as Thai children. Note, also, the overall lower rate of behavior problems reported by observers.

Cultural values and expectations about child behavior clearly bias the teacher ratings. Thai teachers expect children to be well behaved in their classrooms and identify problem behavior more frequently than do American teachers. So, who is correct—the observers or the teachers? The observers were highly trained, yet their observations are restricted to a limited time period. The teachers have more extensive knowledge of the child's behavior, but they seem biased by personal and cultural expectations. The best answer is that multiple sources of information may be the only way to gain accurate information on children's behavior.

Mental Measurements Yearbook (MMY) is by far the most thorough publication, with 11 yearbooks published between 1938 and 1991. *MMY* is now available on CD-ROM; your library may have this resource available for computerized searching. *MMY* indexes all English-language standardized tests covering educational skills, personality, psychology, vocational aptitude, and related areas. Searching the electronic version of *MMY* is much easier than using the print versions, with many commands similar to those described earlier for searching *Psychological Abstracts*. For example, to locate a measure of self-esteem, you can search by test name (Piers-Harris Self-Concept Scale), concept (self-esteem and children), or scores field (to find out what information a test measures; for example, self-esteem in sc).

Sources for Self-Report Measures

Two good sources for self-report measures are Reed and Baxter (1992) and Miller's *Handbook of Research Design and Social Measurement* (1991). Reed and Baxter evaluate published indexes to psychological tests. Miller provides descriptions of many measures, including actual questions, scoring, information on reliability and validity, and references to locate the original publications for each measure.

Sources for Family Measures

An excellent sourcebook for measures of family-related variables is the *Handbook of Family Measurement Techniques* (Touliatos, Perlmutter, & Straus, 1990). The compendium includes nearly 1,000 instruments for the assessment of family functioning in five areas. The primary areas are: (1) dimensions of interaction, such as communication and family networks; (2) intimacy and family values, including marital relations, love, and sex; (3) parenthood; (4) roles and power; and (5) adjustment, including health, stress, and divorce. The handbook is designed with the researcher in mind, with detailed descriptions of each instrument.

A review of rating scales to assess parent–infant functioning (Munson, 1996) provides information on 17 measures developed by early intervention researchers and practitioners. Many instruments lack reliability and validity information, but you should be able to select an assessment instrument for a specific research purpose.

Sources for Personality Measures

Personality is a complex topic to study, requiring both quantitative and qualitative approaches. A major area of research in psychology has been development of quantitative measures of individual differences in psychological attributes such as intelligence, self-esteem, extraversion, and depression. Other tests focus on specific characteristics of a person such as self-esteem, social anxiety, and shyness. Still other measures focus on diagnosing psychological disorders, helping adolescents decide on possible careers, and screening applicants for jobs.

Sources for personality scales to use in your research include *Scales for the Mea-*

surement of Attitudes (Shaw & Wright, 1967) and *Measures of Personality and Social Psychological Attitudes* (Robinson, Shaver, & Wrightsman, 1991). These two source-books include many instruments, describing their reliability, validity, and scoring. Robinson et al. also include scales to measure aspects of personality such as sub-jective well-being, self-esteem, social anxiety, shyness, depression, and loneliness.

Qualitative approaches to understanding personality are being increasingly used as an alternative to quantitative research. For example, researchers are fo-cusing on narrative accounts of life histories to gain insights into the ways that personalities develop and are influenced by both common and unique idio-syncratic life events (Baumeister & Newman, 1994; Josselson & Lieblich, 1993). These accounts may come from various sources, including interviews and auto-biographical writings. They may be relatively unfocused accounts, or they may target particular parts of an individual's life such as personal relationships. Most important, such qualitative analyses may yield data that would be difficult to ob-tain with traditional personality measures, leading to a more complete under-standing of human behavior.

Sources for Demographic Measures

Demographic measures reflect aspects of a person such as gender, age, ethnic-ity, and socioeconomic status. The measurement of these variables is gaining importance for several reasons. First, the composition of the U.S. population is changing dramatically. The ethnic majority of the U.S. population is expected to be non-White by the middle of the 21st century. Second, the structure of the fam-ily is also changing, with social trends toward smaller family size, mother-only families, and working mothers. Third, descriptors of gender, ethnicity, race, and socioeconomic status are important social constructs that help explain develop-ment in different family, school, and neighborhood contexts.

Gender, age, and ethnicity are readily assessed using straightforward ques-tions. Following guidelines established by the U.S. Census Bureau, Entwisle and Astone (1994) recommend 5 basic groups: (1) non-Hispanic White, (2) Hispanic, (3) Black, (4) Native American, and (5) Asian and Pacific Islander. These can be expanded into the 14 categories shown in Table 11.1. Entwisle and Astone pro-vide questions that sort ethnicity into these 5 basic groups, in addition to catego-rizing Latinos into the 3 major Latino ethnic groups in the United States: Mexican, Puerto Rican, and Cuban. Federal standards for measuring race and ethnicity are currently being reviewed; therefore these categories are subject to revision (Her-nandez, 1997).

Race and ethnicity questions are usually answered by parents in interviews or in questionnaires. This information can be obtained easily at the time parental consent forms are completed. You may want to gather information about race and ethnicity from both parents and youngsters for some situations. For example, in cases of mixed-race parentage or recent immigration to the United States, it is useful to ascertain what racial group the child identifies with.

Guidelines for obtaining demographic information vary widely on just what information is needed to assess socioeconomic status. The traditional approach (Hauser, 1994) assesses socioeconomic status by measuring characteristics of one

TABLE 11.1 Ethnic Categories Used by U.S. Census Bureau

5 Categories	14 Categories
White	Non-Hispanic White
Black	Non-Hispanic Black
Hispanic	Puerto Rican
	Mexican
	Cuban
Asian and Pacific Islander	Japanese
	Chinese
	Hawaiian
	Filipino
	Vietnamese
	Korean
	Asian Indian
Native American	American Indian
	Other

adult in the household (the current term is "householder" not "household head"), preferably the father or father figure. Characteristics of the mother are used when a male is not present in the home. Socioeconomic status is determined by information on (1) education, (2) occupation, and (3) labor force status. Hauser prefers not to rely on income data because respondents frequently fail to reply to questions about income. In addition, income may not be an accurate index of economic well-being because it fluctuates. One advantage of relying on occupational status rather than income is that children and adolescents can reliably inform researchers about occupational data.

A potential problem with the traditional approach is overreliance on the concept of the two-parent family. This is clearly not the norm for many children. An alternative approach (Entwisle & Astone, 1994) assesses children's resources on three dimensions: financial capital, human capital, and social capital. **Financial capital** is measured by income from all sources; for example, investments, rent, unemployment, disability, Aid to Families with Dependent Children, and food stamps. **Human capital** is measured by maternal education. **Social capital** is indicated by the number of birth parents, stepparents, and grandparents in the home.

A third approach for determining socioeconomic status is offered by Hernandez (1997). In addition to describing historical demographic trends in the United States and current demographic statistics, Hernandez includes an excellent appendix with specific questions and wording formats to obtain accurate demographic measures of children's environments. The questions include most of the demographic variables mentioned earlier, with additional items on migration status ("Did you live in a different house one year ago?") and immigrant status.

These approaches to demographic measurement capture many features of diverse family backgrounds. Depending on your research concerns, you can adjust some of the items suggested in these resources to suit the population you are studying and the purpose of your research project.

SUMMARY

After careful planning and preparation, the opportunity to assess participants in your research project is often the "favorite" part of a research investigation. Working with infants, children, adolescents, and adults presents a variety of challenges for the researcher. Initially, rapport must be established to put participants at ease and gain their cooperation. Children may need time to relax in new surroundings and talk easily with new adults. Instructions should be adjusted to the developmental needs of each individual so that all participants have a uniform understanding of their role in the study.

Infants are difficult to test because of the large amount of time spent sleeping. Fussiness in infants contributes to a high rate of attrition in infancy studies. Toddlers have especially short attention spans and limited understanding of the role of a research participant. Elementary school children can adapt their understanding of the teacher-student role to cooperate well in the research setting. Adolescents are generally excellent participants.

Gerontological researchers define older adults on the basis of chronological age using 65 and over as a criterion. Some researchers divide older adults into categories of young-old and old-old. Another definition of older adults relies on functional age. Functional age defines older adults on the basis of abilities to live independently, work, and engage in intellectual activities. Normal aging processes can affect performance of older adults due to slower reaction times, declining vision, and hearing impairments. Obtaining information on the health status of older participants helps researchers distinguish between age differences and performance differences that may be attributable to these normal changes in sensory functioning.

Self-report measures can be used with children, although very young children may not be accurate informants due to their limited cognitive development. Rating scales completed by parents, teachers, or trained observers are a good alternative to self-report measures. However, different raters do not always agree with each other. Multiple raters may provide the best solution, providing information about a particular child in different contexts.

There are many sources for information on existing self-report measures, rating scales, family measures, and personality measures. However, test instruments developed on White, middle-class populations may not be appropriate for use with culturally diverse samples. Test instruments and test procedures should be examined for potential bias in descriptions and assumptions about older adults as well as potential cultural bias.

Changes in the nature of the U.S. population and the structure of the family are important reasons that developmental researchers need to obtain demographic measures of participants. Demographic characteristics include gender, age, ethnicity, race, and socioeconomic status. One way to measure socioeconomic status relies on information about the occupation and education of the father or "household head." Other approaches utilize information about the mother and additional household members to determine a family's socioeconomic status.

KEY TERMS

ageism
chronological age
demographic measures
financial capital

functional age
human capital
*Mental Measurements
Yearbook (MMY)*

social capital
young-old versus
old-old

REVIEW QUESTIONS

1. Describe several ways to establish rapport with children. How can the research setting contribute to establishing rapport?
2. What can researchers do to help young children understand directions for a research task?
3. What problems does an infant's behavioral state create for a researcher?
4. Describe some problems you may encounter working with preschoolers.
5. What is ageism?
6. Distinguish between age differences and age deficits.
7. List three ways that normal aging can affect the performance of an older adult on a written task.
8. Describe the problems associated with using self-report measures with children.
9. What are some reasons for using a teacher to rate children's behavior? What are some reasons for using a trained observer to rate children's behavior?
10. Name at least four demographic variables.
11. Distinguish between financial capital, human capital, and social capital.

CHAPTER 12

Factorial Designs

Thus far we have focused primarily on the simplest experimental design, in which one independent variable is manipulated with two levels and one dependent variable is measured. This simple design allows us to examine basic issues in research design, but the information provided is limited. Suppose you are interested in the reliability of children's eyewitness testimony. You might wish to learn whether older children differ from younger children in their memory for an event. You can design a simple experiment to compare the memory of two age groups of children, but you are probably interested in adding other variables to your design as well. Can children recall a stressful event as accurately as an everyday event? What happens to their memory over time? Are the children more accurate when using free recall or when responding to cued recall? Are children affected by who asks the questions and where the questioning takes place? To evaluate these important research issues, more complicated designs are needed. There are three ways to make an experiment more complex: (1) increasing the number of levels of an independent variable, (2) increasing the number of dependent variables, and (3) increasing the number of independent variables.

INCREASING THE NUMBER OF LEVELS
OF AN INDEPENDENT VARIABLE

In the simplest experimental design, there are only two levels of the independent variable. However, a researcher might want to design an experiment with more than two levels for several reasons. First, a design with only two levels of the independent variable cannot provide very much information about the exact form of the relationship between the independent and dependent variables. If there are only two levels of the independent variable, it is only possible to show linear relationships. For example, Figure 12.1 shows the outcome of a hypothetical experiment on the relationship between age and performance on a recall task. The solid line describes the results when there are only two levels of the independent variable, age (3-year-olds and 6-year-olds). Because there are only two levels, the

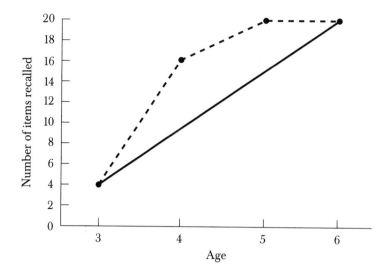

Figure 12.1
Comparison of hypo-
thetical outcomes
with two versus four
levels of the indepen-
dent variable

relationship can only be described with a straight line. We don't know for sure how 4- and 5-year-olds would do on the recall task. Based on the solid line, it looks like there is a gradual increase in recall across age. However, if you actually include groups of children who are 4 and 5 years of age, the relationship is not linear after all. The broken line shows the results when children 4 and 5 years old are added to the design. In this case, recall develops most rapidly between ages 3 and 4 and then levels off at the older ages. This result is a more accurate description of the relationship between age and memory recall.

An experiment that is designed to map out the exact relationship between variables is called a **functional design,** and it is intended to show how scores on the dependent variable change as a function of changes in the independent variable. For example, a parent may be interested in the functional relationship between amount of reward (none versus 25 cents, 50 cents, 75 cents, or 1 dollar) to number of homework problems completed.

Functional designs are especially important in developmental and aging research that focuses on understanding the way behavior changes with age. Remember, when using only two levels to the variable of age, only linear trends are exposed. Such evidence would be misleading and would obscure growth spurts and declines with age. This is an important factor to consider when selecting age groups for your research. If you choose ages that are widely separated, you may be limited in your conclusions about the behavior you are studying.

A second reason for increasing the number of levels of an independent variable is that an experimental design with only two levels of the independent variable cannot detect curvilinear relationships between variables (see Chapter 5). If a curvilinear relationship is predicted, at least three levels of the independent variable must be used. For example, many eyewitness memory experts believe that stress and memory are related in an inverted-U function (Deffenbacher, 1983; Loftus, 1979; see Christianson, 1992, for an opposing view). This hypothesized relationship is shown in Figure 12.2. It is theorized that both high- and low-stress events are not remembered well but that moderately stressful events are associated with high levels of recall accuracy. To test this hypothesis, all three levels of stress must be included in an experiment. If only low stress and high stress are included in an experiment, you cannot properly assess the theory.

Many such curvilinear relationships exist in the social sciences. For example, changes in the way we use memory strategies to learn new information are presumed to be curvilinear over the human life span: A young child's use of basic strategies such as rehearsal is less efficient than an adolescent's, which in turn is more efficient than an elderly adult's (Sugar & McDowd, 1992). Similarly, changes in fluid intelligence also appear to be curvilinear. Fluid intelligence tests are designed to assess the mechanical "hardware" of cognitive functioning such as working memory and basic perceptual processes. Fluid intelligence test performance increases with chronological age into adulthood, but may begin to decline as early as middle adulthood (Baltes, 1993, 1997). Marital satisfaction across the life span also has a curvilinear relationship, with highest satisfaction reported by newlyweds and aging couples. The lowest reports of marital satisfaction are associated with the postparental period of adulthood when children leave the home (Rollins, 1989).

Finally, researchers are frequently interested in comparing more than two groups. For example, a researcher may be interested in evaluating the effect of treatments for depression in the elderly. The researcher may compare three or four of the most popular treatments such as drug therapy, psychotherapy, behavior modification, and cognitive therapy. As another example, Barratt, Roach, Morgan, and Colbert (1996) examined the psychological adjustment of adolescent mothers by comparing four groups of mothers: adolescent mothers, adolescents who were not mothers, single adult mothers, and married adult mothers. Only by using comparison groups of adolescents and other mothers were Barratt et al. able to separate outcomes related to being a parent, being a parent at an early age, and being a parent outside of marriage. Results showed that adolescent mothers report greater enjoyment of life than adolescent nonmothers, perhaps as a result of a sense of identity associated with their role as mothers.

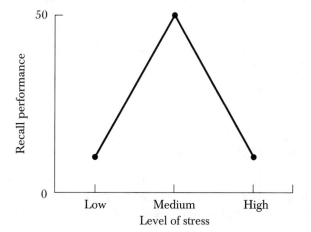

Figure 12.2
An inverted-U curvilinear relationship
NOTE: At least three levels of the independent variable are required to show curvilinear relationships.

INCREASING THE NUMBER OF DEPENDENT VARIABLES

A second way to make an experiment more complex is to add dependent variables. In this way the researcher can measure more than one aspect of the participant's behavior. Another approach is for the researcher to use more than one way to measure the same behavior. The use of multiple measures is very common today and is compatible with the multitrait, multimethod research approach described in Chapter 4.

For example, Luus, Wells, and Turtle (1995) included three dependent variables to assess the believability, confidence, and accuracy of a child witness. Studies of parent-child relationships may include a number of measures of language behavior (e.g., questions, positive comments, directives, negative comments) and physical activities (hugging, kissing, caretaking, and modeling behaviors). Each dependent variable provides useful information about the parent-child relationship. Investigation of changes in the visual system during the adult years may include measures of visual acuity, peripheral vision, and color vision. Such issues are important for determining if elderly drivers should continue to have driving privileges.

Another example is the Seattle Longitudinal Study, which uses a battery of intelligence measures to assess cognitive development in adulthood (Schaie & Willis, 1993). Abilities measured include inductive reasoning, perceptual speed, verbal memory, spatial ability, verbal ability, and numerical ability. These are all measures of "intelligence" but show different patterns of decline across adulthood. Four abilities decline starting as early as age 29 (inductive reasoning, perceptual speed, verbal memory, and spatial ability). Verbal ability and numerical ability resist decline better than the other cognitive skills, with decline delayed until approximately age 39 to 46. Only by using multiple measures can Schaie and Willis clarify the different dimensions of cognitive decline related to aging.

In some kinds of research, experiments are conducted with a primary dependent variable. Secondary dependent variables are included to provide collateral or converging information on the effects of the manipulated independent variable. For example, the number of correct responses is frequently used as the primary dependent variable in studies of memory development. Evaluation of the kinds of memory errors is frequently included as a secondary dependent variable to provide additional insights into the nature of the memory process being studied. The selection of dependent variables should always be determined by your hypotheses. Suggestions from current theory and the feasibility of collecting the additional information should also be considered when designing experiments.

INCREASING THE NUMBER OF INDEPENDENT VARIABLES: FACTORIAL DESIGNS

The third way that researchers make experiments more complex is by manipulating more than one independent variable in a single experiment. Researchers recognize that in any given situation a number of variables are operating to affect behavior, so they design experiments with more than one independent variable. Typically, two or three independent variables are manipulated simultaneously. This type of experimental design is a closer approximation of real-world conditions in which independent variables do not exist by themselves.

Factorial designs are designs with more than one independent variable (or *factor*). In a factorial design, all levels of each independent variable are combined with all levels of the other independent variables. The simplest factorial design has two independent variables, each with two levels. This kind of design is known as a 2×2 (two-by-two) factorial design.

To illustrate 2×2 factorial designs, consider an experiment used as a class project in a research methods course. The experiment is designed to evaluate age differences in children's eyewitness memory by comparing two age groups of children (6 years versus 10 years) on their memory for the content of a story. Children are read a story and then answer questions about the story. The questions are asked either immediately after the story or 1 week later. The first independent variable is age, with two levels—6 years and 10 years. The second independent variable is test interval, and it also has two levels—immediate and delayed. This 2×2 design results in four experimental conditions:

(1) 6-year-olds, immediate testing
(2) 6-year-olds, delayed testing
(3) 10-year-olds, immediate testing
(4) 10-year-olds, delayed testing

FACTORIAL NOTATION

A 2×2 design always has four groups. The general format for describing factorial designs is:

Number of levels of 1st independent variable	$\times$	Number of levels of 2nd independent variable	$\times$	Number of levels of 3rd independent variable

Factorial notation tells you three important things about the experimental design: (1) the number of independent variables, (2) the number of levels for each independent variable, and (3) the number of conditions in the design. To find out how many independent variables are in a factorial design, just count the number of digits in the factorial notation, ignoring the magnitude of the numbers. In factorial notation, each number represents one independent variable. In our 2×2 design there are two numbers, so we have two independent variables. To find out how many levels each independent variable has, look at the magnitude of each number. The size of each number in the 2×2 notation stands for the number of levels for each independent variable. For our design, each number is a 2, meaning there are 2 levels for each independent variable in the design. To find out how many conditions or groups are in the factorial design, use the "$\times$" to multiply the numbers. Thus, in our 2×2 design we have 2 times $2 = 4$ conditions.

Consider what happens if we want to expand our basic 2 × 2 factorial design. One logical addition is another testing interval—you may want to test children 4 weeks after the original story. How can you represent this design using factorial notation? We did not change the number of independent variables, so there are still only 2 numbers in the factorial notation. The number of levels of the second independent variable changes because now we have 3 levels for test interval (immediate, 1 week, and 1 month). The factorial notation now is 2 × 3 (2 age groups × 3 testing times). This creates a total of 6 experimental conditions. The design can be expanded easily with more independent variables. Adding gender to the design produces a 2 × 2 × 3 design (age × gender × time of testing), with 12 experimental conditions.

INTERPRETATION OF EFFECTS IN FACTORIAL DESIGNS

Factorial designs yield two kinds of information. The first is information about the effect of each independent variable taken by itself, which is called the **main effect** of an independent variable on the dependent variable. There is a main effect for each independent variable in a design, so our 2 × 2 design with two independent variables has two main effects. The second kind of information in a factorial design is called an **interaction effect.** An interaction effect indicates whether the effect of an independent variable depends on the level of another independent variable. In the 2 × 2 design, there is one interaction effect, representing the combined effects of the two independent variables on the dependent variable. Thus, in a 2 × 2 design there are three effects: two main effects and one interaction effect.

To illustrate main effects and interactions, we can look at the result of our experiment concerning children's memory. Table 12.1 illustrates a common method of presenting outcomes for the various groups in a factorial design. The numbers in each cell represent the mean number of questions answered correctly in the four conditions. These cell or group means indicate that, on average, 6-year-olds who were tested immediately answered 11 questions correctly; 10-year-olds who were tested immediately answered 14 questions correctly, and so on.

TABLE 12.1   Mean Number of Questions Answered Correctly in the Memory Experiment

Age Group (independent variable A)	Test Interval (independent variable B)		M (marginal mean for main effect of A)
	Immediate	Delayed	
6 years	11.0	4.0	7.5
10 years	14.0	12.0	13.0
M (marginal mean for main effect of B)	12.5	8.0	

Main Effects

A main effect is the influence each independent variable has by itself. In Table 12.1, the main effect of independent variable A, age, represents the overall effect that the child's age has on the dependent variable (number of questions answered correctly). Similarly, the main effect of independent variable B, test interval, is the effect of the different time intervals on the number of questions answered correctly.

The main effect of age examines the effect of the age independent variable by itself, without considering the second independent variable in this design. The main effect of age addresses these questions: What is the effect of age on performance, regardless of test interval? On average, do 6-year-olds and 10-year-olds differ in their performance on the questions? We can find out by looking at the marginal means in Table 12.1. We refer to these means as **marginal means** because they are shown in the margins of the table, outside the cell or group means. Marginal means are calculated to compare the overall performance of children in each age group. To do this, we need to average across the means shown in each row of the table. This calculation, shown below, will give you the average number of questions answered correctly for children in each age group.

$$M \text{ (age 6)} = \frac{11 + 4}{2} = 7.5$$

$$M \text{ (age 10)} = \frac{14 + 12}{2} = 13.0$$

You can see that, on average, the older children had more correct responses than the younger children. In this chapter we will examine the direction of the difference in the marginal means to determine main effects. Statistical tests discussed in Chapter 15 are needed to determine if this difference is a significant main effect.

Now let's turn to the main effect for the second independent variable in the design, the test interval. The main effect for test interval (variable B) examines the effect of the test interval independent variable by itself, without considering the other independent variable in this design, age. The main effect of test interval addresses these questions: What is the main effect of test interval performance, regardless of age? On average, do children differ in their memory performance when tested immediately and when tested 1 week after the story was read? Marginal means are calculated to compare the overall performance of children in each testing condition. To do this, we need to average the values shown in the columns of Table 12.1. This calculation, shown below, will give you the average number of questions answered correctly for children in each testing group.

$$M \text{ (immediate)} = \frac{11 + 14}{2} = 12.5$$

$$M \text{ (delayed)} = \frac{4 + 12}{2} = 8.0$$

The group means are added together and then divided by 2 to get the average. Two is used for the denominator because two numbers are being averaged. The marginal means show that, on average, the children in the immediate testing group had an overall score of 12.5 questions answered correctly, compared to 8.0 for children in the delayed testing group. Thus, in general, more errors occurred at the delayed testing interval. Again, a statistical test is needed to determine if this difference is statistically significant.

Interaction Effects

An interaction between independent variables indicates that the effect of one independent variable is different at each level of the other independent variable. An interaction tells us whether the effect of one independent variable depends on the particular level of the other. Is there an interaction in Table 12.1 such that the influence of age differs as a function of the test interval? Does immediate testing have the same impact on 6-year-olds and 10-year-olds? Does delayed testing have the same impact on the performance of both 6-year-olds and 10-year-olds?

When we say there is an interaction we mean that the outcome "depends" on a combination of the levels of the independent variables. The concept of interaction is common in many of your daily activities. For example, consider a typical student scenario. A major exam is scheduled for tomorrow. But as luck would have it, you don't get much sleep that night. If you are well rested, your test performance is likely to be very good on either multiple-choice or essay questions. However, what happens if you are not well rested? With a multiple-choice exam, your task is to select from the options written on the page—you can probably accomplish this with a minimum of sleep. But for an essay exam, your task is to develop a coherent, thoughtful, well-written reply, retrieving the content of your answer from your long-term memory. Without adequate rest, your memory skills may be seriously challenged. In this case, lack of sleep interacts with the type of exam, potentially spelling disaster for your GPA. The same concept applies when the druggist asks you what medications you are taking so she can look for possible drug interactions: The effect of each drug alone is not harmful, but when combined, the special combination may have a harmful side effect.

Interactions are very common in research because many independent variables do have different effects on different groups of participants. If an interaction exists, the main effects must be qualified somewhat. In our example, the main effects of age and test interval imply that greater accuracy is associated with greater age and immediate testing. However, a close examination of the cell means shows that the relationship is more complex.

Interactions can easily be seen when the group means for all conditions are presented in a graph. Figure 12.3 graphs the results of our memory experiment. The dependent variable, number of questions answered correctly, is placed on the vertical axis. One of the independent variables, age, is placed on the horizontal axis. The second independent variable, test interval, is represented by two different lines on the graph. The values on the graph are the *cell means* from Table 12.1. Interpreting interactions requires some practice. Although we cannot determine the significance of an interaction in this chapter, we can interpret the pattern of

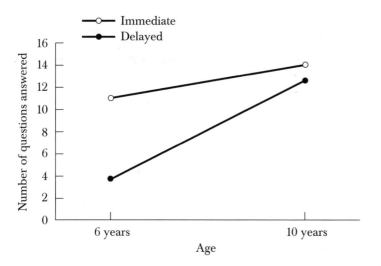

Figure 12.3
Interaction between
age and time of
testing

the relationship between the independent variables. First, look at the overall pattern. Are the lines on the figure parallel? If so, there is no interaction. In this case, the lines are not parallel. Clearly the lines would cross if extended further, indicating nonparallel lines. So, what is the nature of this interaction? A good approach to interpretation is to proceed systematically across the diagram, from left to right (or top to bottom). Starting on the left, which group has higher scores? For 6-year-olds, performance is higher with immediate testing. But how much higher are the scores? Immediate testing yields much higher scores than delayed testing for these 6-year-olds. Now, look at the means for the 10-year-olds on the right side of the figure. Which group has higher scores? Again, the immediate testing yields higher scores. But how much higher? For the 10-year-olds, the immediate testing scores are only slightly higher than the delayed testing scores. The fact that the difference between the means of the immediate and delayed testing groups is larger for 6-year-olds than for 10-year-olds indicates an interaction. In other words, the gap between the two testing intervals is larger at one age level than the other.

DESCRIBING MAIN EFFECTS AND INTERACTION EFFECTS

Main effects are determined by examining marginal means. (A helpful mnemonic device: both marginal and main effects begin with *m*.) Interaction effects are determined by examining cell means, which is easily done by making a graph of the cell means. We are now ready to write descriptions of the effects in our 2×2 factorial design.

Descriptions of main effects typically include the following items:

1. name the effect (e.g., the main effect of . . .)
2. state the direction of difference (more, less, same)
3. include the marginal means ($M = $) for each level

4. state the names for each level
5. specify the dependent variable

Combining this information into one sentence, we can now describe each main effect:

> The main effect of age indicates that, on average, 10-year-olds answered more questions correctly ($M = 13.0$) than did the 6-year-olds ($M = 7.5$).

> The main effect of test interval indicates that, on average, children answered more questions correctly on the immediate test ($M = 12.5$) than on the delayed test ($M = 8.0$).

Interaction descriptions are a bit more difficult because of the many different interactions that are possible. Descriptions of interaction effects typically include the following items:

1. name the effect (e.g., the interaction between independent variable #1 and independent variable #2)
2. state the pattern of the difference (described without numbers)
3. clarify the direction of differences with modifiers (e.g., nearly identical, much greater than, the opposite pattern)
4. state the names for each level
5. specify the dependent variable
6. refer to the figure (as seen in Figure 1 . . .)

Combining this information into one or two sentences, we can now verbally describe the interaction:

> As seen in Figure 12.3, the interaction between age and test interval indicates that for 6-year-olds substantially more questions are answered correctly on the immediate test than on the delayed test. However, for the 10-year-old children, performance is nearly identical under both conditions, with only a small decline in number of questions answered correctly on the delayed test.

POSSIBLE OUTCOMES OF 2 × 2 FACTORIAL DESIGNS

A 2×2 factorial design has two independent variables, each with two levels. When analyzing the results, there are several possibilities: (1) There may or may not be a significant main effect for independent variable A; (2) there may or may not be a significant main effect for independent variable B; and (3) there may or may not be a significant interaction between the independent variables. Figure 12.4 illustrates the eight possible outcomes for 2×2 factorial designs. For each outcome the means are given and then graphed. Note that on each graph the dependent variable is placed on the vertical axis and independent variable A is placed on the horizontal axis. Independent variable B is represented by two lines on the graph. The two means for level B_1 of independent variable B are plotted, and a line is drawn to represent this level of B. The two means for level B_2 are then plotted, and a second line is drawn to represent this level of B.

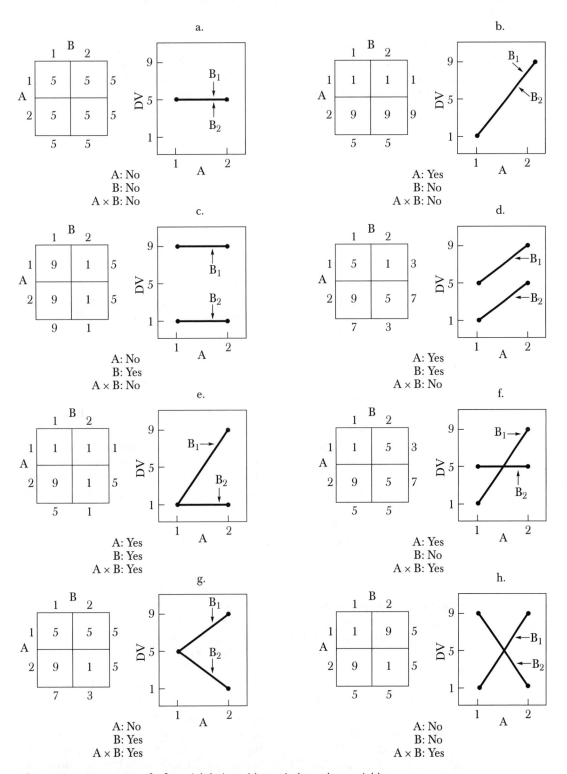

Figure 12.4   Outcomes of a factorial design with two independent variables

209

The means that are given in the figure are idealized examples; such perfect outcomes rarely occur in actual research. Nevertheless, you should study the graphs to determine for yourself why, in each case, there is or isn't a main effect for A, a main effect for B, and an A × B interaction.

The first four graphs (Figure 12.4a through 12.4d) illustrate outcomes in which there is no A × B interaction effect, and the last four graphs (Figure 12.4e through 12.4h) depict outcomes in which there is an interaction between A and B. When there is no interaction, the lines for B_1 and B_2 are parallel. In the first two graphs (Figure 12.4a and 12.4b), the lines representing B_1 and B_2 coincide, so only one line is shown. These parallel lines indicate that the nature of the relationship between independent variable A and the dependent variable is the same at B_1 as at B_2. An alternate way to conceptualize the absence of an interaction is in terms of differences: The difference between the group means for A_1 and A_2 at B_1 is *not* greater or less than the difference between the group means for A_1 and A_2 at level B_2.

Let's take a closer look at Figure 12.4d. First, we need to calculate marginal means. The numbers in the boxes are the group means for each condition. To find out if there is a main effect of A, we need to compare the marginal mean for A_1 to the marginal mean for A_2. For A_1 add $5 + 1$ and divide by 2, with the result of 3. We divide by 2 because there are 2 levels for the B independent variable. Then calculate the marginal mean for A_2 in the same way ($9 + 5 = 14$, then divide by 2). The result is 7, as shown in the figure. Compare the marginal mean for A_1 ($M = 3$) to the marginal mean for A_2 ($M = 7$). Are the values the same? If not, we assume that there appears to be a main effect for A (although we really need a statistical test to determine significance). Repeat the same procedure to obtain the marginal means for B_1 and B_2, but this time average the values down the columns. Compare the marginal means – are they the same? No, so we again assume there is a main effect for B. To determine if there is an interaction, look at the lines on the figure. Are they parallel? If yes, then we do *not* have an A × B interaction.

When the lines on the graph are not parallel, an interaction is present. Note than nonparallel lines cross on the graph or would cross if they were extended. Such outcomes indicate that the nature of the relationship is different, depending on the specific level of B. That is, the effects of independent variable A are different at each level of independent variable B. In some cases (e.g., Figure 12.4e and 12.4g) there is a strong relationship between the first independent variable and the dependent variable at one level of the second independent variable; however, there is no relationship or a weak relationship at the other level of the second independent variable. This pattern is also evident in the data from our memory experiment shown in Figure 12.3.

Let's take a closer look at Figure 12.4f. First, determine main effects. For independent variable A the marginal mean for A_1 ($M = 3$) is less than the marginal mean for A_2 ($M = 7$), indicating an apparent main effect. The marginal mean for B_1 ($M = 5$) is the same as the marginal mean for B_2 ($M = 5$), indicating no main effect for variable B. For the interaction, look at the pattern of the lines on the figure. Are the lines parallel? They are not parallel, indicating the presence of an interaction.

In other studies the interaction may indicate that an independent variable has opposite effects on the dependent variable, as shown in the last graph, Figure 12.4h. An interesting feature of this last graph is that neither independent variable has an effect by itself, with no main effects for A or B. Only when both variables are considered simultaneously does a relationship emerge such that A has strong (and opposite) effects depending on the particular level of B. This type of interaction is called a crossover interaction.

To make sure you understand these important graphs, test yourself. For each graph calculate the marginal means, and then cover the answers and draw a new set of graphs. This helps you make sure you understand how to label the variables in the figure. Then see if you can determine if there are main effects or an interaction for each one. If you have difficulty conceptualizing the graphs with the abstract labels A and B, use something you are more familiar with such as variables from the eyewitness experiment. Commonly used variables such as age and gender also may be used to make the examples more concrete, allowing you to describe the pattern of the main effects and the interaction more easily.

FURTHER CONSIDERATIONS IN FACTORIAL DESIGNS

Subject Variables

One common type of factorial design includes both experimental (manipulated) variables and selected (nonmanipulated) variables. These designs, sometimes called **IV × SV designs** (i.e., independent variable by subject variable) are common in the human development and family literature. Subject variables typically considered are age, sex, socioeconomic status, ethnic group membership, ability grouping, and clinical diagnostic category. As explained in Chapter 5, such variables cannot be directly manipulated because they are personal attributes of the participant.

The simplest IV × SV design includes one manipulated independent variable that has at least two levels and one subject variable with at least two levels. The eyewitness memory study we discussed earlier in this chapter is a good example of an IV × SV design. Children ages 6 and 10 years were compared on their memory either immediately after a story was read or 1 week later. Age is the subject variable because you cannot randomly assign children to be 6 years old or 10 years old—children will be selected for participation in one of these age groups based on a preexisting characteristic. The second independent variable, test interval, is manipulated because you can randomly assign the children to participate in testing that occurs immediately or at a delayed time interval.

The outcome of an IV × SV design is analyzed in the same way as other factorial designs, by calculating main effects and interaction effects. However, the interpretation is somewhat limited. You can make causal conclusions about the test interval because that variable is a true experimental independent variable—it is manipulated by the researcher, and participants can be randomly assigned to the immediate testing group or to the delayed testing group. If there is a main effect of test interval, you can safely conclude that the difference in memory performance was *caused* by the time interval.

However, when a variable is not randomly assigned, you cannot make causal conclusions. So, if there is a main effect of age, you cannot conclude that being 6 years old *caused* the child's performance. You can state that 6-year-olds answered fewer questions correctly, but you cannot make causal attributions. Because subject variables are not randomly assigned, you cannot be sure if age is the only thing that differs between the two age groups of participants—many experiential factors probably differ between these cohorts. A major rival explanation is that 10-year-old children have 4 more years of formal schooling than 6-year-olds, so the actual difference may be a result of "schooling." Other variables that correlate with age may also be responsible for any observed difference.

You probably recognized this particular IV × SV design as a cross-sectional design. Interpretation problems are a major limitation of cross-sectional designs, as discussed in Chapter 9. Cross-sectional designs describe developmental differences, not developmental change. It is possible to use the same individuals in both groups in an IV × SV design. In this case age is a repeated measure in a longitudinal design.

Factorial designs with both manipulated independent variables and subject variables offer a very appealing method for investigating many interesting research questions. Even though causal statements cannot be made about the nonmanipulated subject variable, adding a subject variable can make the study more valuable. For example, you can investigate the generalizability of a study by adding different age groups or ethnic groups to your design.

Designs With More Than Two Independent Variables

The 2 × 2 is the simplest factorial design. With this basic design, the researcher can arrange experiments that are more and more complex. One way to increase complexity is to increase the number of independent variables, as discussed earlier in the chapter. For example, we may extend the design of our basic eyewitness memory example by considering the influence the type of question may have on a child's recall; that is, children are interviewed using direct or misleading questions. Thus, our new design is a 2 × 2 × 2 factorial with factors of age (6 vs. 10 years), test interval (immediate vs. delayed), and type of question (direct vs. misleading). The dependent variable remains unchanged: the number of questions answered correctly. A 2 × 2 × 2 factorial is constructed in Table 12.2. The three-

TABLE 12.2   2 × 2 × 2 Factorial Design

Age	Type of Question	
	Direct	*Misleading*
	Immediate Testing	
6-year-olds		
10-year-olds		
	Delayed Testing	
6-year-olds		
10-year-olds		

factor design reveals information about the main effect of each independent variable acting alone, yielding three main effects. These are calculated in the same manner as in the 2×2, but more numerical values contribute to each marginal mean. The three-factor design also allows us to look at interactions. In the $2 \times 2 \times 2$ design, we can look at two-way interactions between (1) age and test interval, (2) age and type of question, and (3) test interval and type of question. We can also look at a three-way interaction that involves all three independent variables. Here we want to determine the nature of the interaction between two of the variables, depending on the particular level of the other variable. A frequently used analytic strategy is to decompose complex designs, thus viewing the $2 \times 2 \times 2$ factorial as two separate 2×2 designs. In this example, we have two separate 2 (age) $\times$ 2 (test interval) factorial designs, one for participants assigned to direct questions and one for participants assigned to misleading questions. Three-way interactions are rather complicated; fortunately you won't encounter too many of them in your preliminary explorations of human development research.

When students design experiments, sometimes they are tempted to include as many independent variables as they can think of in one study. A problem with this is that the design may become needlessly complex and require enormous numbers of participants. The $2 \times 2 \times 2$ design just discussed has 8 groups; a $2 \times 2 \times 2 \times 2$ has 16 groups; adding yet another independent variable with two levels means 32 groups would be required. The investigator is probably not interested in all of the main effects and interactions that may accompany such complex designs. Basic 2×2 factorial designs are very powerful when the investigator has carefully selected the independent variables to provide a good test of the hypotheses and has clear predictions for any interactions.

SUMMARY

The simplest experimental designs have only two levels of the independent variable. More complex experiments are created by increasing the levels of the independent variable, increasing the number of dependent variables, or increasing the number of independent variables. Factorial designs with more than one independent variable are used to answer many questions in research on human development and family relations. The simplest factorial design is a 2×2 design, in which there are two independent variables with two levels each. Main effects in factorial designs provide information about each independent variable by itself, and interaction effects provide information about the combined effect of the independent variables. An interaction indicates that the effect of one independent variable is different at the levels of the other independent variable.

Main effects are determined by examining marginal means; interaction effects are determined by examining cell means depicted in a figure. In a 2×2 factorial design, there are two main effects and one interaction effect. Significance of each effect is determined separately, so you may have significant main effects but no interaction in a particular study. Review Figure 12.4 for the possible outcomes of a 2×2 factorial design.

Factorial designs can include a combination of a manipulated variable and a selected subject variable such as age, ethnicity, or family status. These designs, called IV × SV designs, are commonly used to address developmental research questions. However, because the subject variable cannot be randomly assigned, causal conclusions about the nonmanipulated subject variable are not appropriate.

KEY TERMS

factorial designs	interaction effect	marginal mean
factorial notation	IV × SV design	
functional designs	main effect	

REVIEW QUESTIONS

1. Why would a researcher have more than two levels of an independent variable?
2. Identify some reasons for increasing the number of dependent variables in an experiment.
3. What is a factorial design? Why would a researcher use a factorial design?
4. For each design listed below, identify (1) the number of independent variables, (2) the number of levels for each independent variable, and (3) the number of conditions in the design.
   a. 3 × 2
   b. 3 × 3
   c. 2 × 3 × 4
   d. 2 × 2 × 2 × 2
5. What are main effects? How do you determine main effects?
6. What is an interaction? How do you know if a study has an interaction effect? What does a significant interaction tell us about main effects?
7. How many main effects and interaction effects are there in each design in question 4?
8. What items do you include when describing main effects? interaction effects?
9. Describe an IV × SV factorial design. How do subject variables limit the interpretation of a study?

CHAPTER 13

Assigning Participants to Conditions

In Chapter 12 we introduced factorial designs that allow researchers to simultaneously evaluate the effect of two or more independent variables. Such designs allow for greater approximation of real-world conditions in which independent variables do not exist by themselves. In this chapter we focus on procedures for assigning participants to conditions.

ASSIGNING PARTICIPANTS TO EXPERIMENTAL CONDITIONS

There are two basic ways of assigning participants to experimental conditions: independent groups designs and repeated measures designs. In an **independent groups design** participants are randomly assigned to experimental conditions so that each person participates in only one group. Using either simple random assignment or matched random assignment procedures, each individual participates in only one of the conditions in the experiment. This kind of study is also called a **between subjects design** because we are interested in comparing differences in behavior between different groups of participants. An alternative procedure is to have the same individuals participate in all of the groups, using a **repeated measures design.** Rather than assigning participants to only one experimental condition, a single group of individuals participates in more than one experimental condition. You can see why this is called a repeated measures design; participants are repeatedly measured on the dependent variable while taking part in each condition of the experiment. This kind of study is also called a **within subjects design** because the researcher is interested in evaluating the behavior within this group of participants.

To illustrate, let's simplify our memory experiment and use only 10-year-olds. The single independent variable, then, is time of testing (immediate vs. delayed). To conduct this experiment as an independent groups design, the children are randomly assigned to *either* the immediate testing *or* the delayed testing. To use the same independent variable in a repeated measures design, each child is tested both immediately *and* at the delayed time interval.

INDEPENDENT GROUPS DESIGNS

In an independent groups design different participants are assigned to the conditions in two ways: simple random assignment and matched random assignment.

Simple Random Assignment

The easiest method for assigning participants to different groups is **simple random assignment.** If there are two groups in the experiment, a possible randomization procedure is to flip a coin to assign each individual to one or the other group. If there are more than two groups, the researcher needs to use a table of random numbers to assign participants. A table of random numbers and instructions for using it are shown in Appendix C. The table is made up of a series of digits (0–99) that were arranged randomly by a computer. The researcher can use the arrangement of the numbers in the table to determine the group to which each participant will be assigned for the experiment. Random assignment will prevent any systematic biases, and the groups will be equivalent at the beginning of the experiment in terms of participant characteristics such as social class, intelligence, age, attitudes, and self-esteem.

Matched Random Assignment

A somewhat more complicated method of assigning participants to different groups is called **matched random assignment.** Matching procedures can be used when the researcher wants to ensure that the groups are equivalent on certain subject variables. Typically, the matching variable will be a characteristic that is strongly related to the dependent variable; for example, in a learning experiment participants might be matched on the basis of intelligence test scores.

When matched random assignment procedures are used, the first step is to obtain a measure of the matching variable from each individual. In our memory experiment, you may be concerned about the intelligence of the participants. You may need to administer an intelligence test to each participant. Or you can obtain grade point averages or standardized achievement test scores from existing school records. The second step is to rank order participants from highest to lowest on the basis of their scores on the matching variable. Now the researcher can form matched groups of participants that are approximately equal on the characteristic. If there are two experimental conditions, participants are matched in pairs. The two highest scores form the first pair, the next two form the second pair, and so on. With three experimental conditions, participants are matched in groups of three, with the three highest scores forming the first group. The third step is to randomly assign the members of each group to the conditions in the experiment.

Matched random assignment ensures that the groups are equivalent on the matching variable prior to the introduction of the independent variable manipulation. This assurance could be particularly important with small sample sizes because random assignment procedures are more likely to produce equivalent groups as the sample size increases. Matched random assignment, then, is most likely to be used when only a few participants are available or when financial constraints limit the number of individuals in the experiment.

Matching results in a greater ability to detect a statistically significant effect of the independent variable. This is because it is possible to account for individual differences in response to the independent variable. Suppose you conduct an experiment in which the independent variable is written versus audio presentation of materials for a history lesson on space travel. The dependent variable is students' scores on a test of facts from the history lesson. When you examine the results, you may find that the average ability to recall is different in the two groups. You may also find that, within each group, the students' test scores vary; participants do not respond with the same score even though they were in the same experimental condition. With simple random assignment, we don't know why this variability exists; it is merely called "error" or unexplained variance in the scores. With matched random assignment to groups, however, we can account for much of the variability within each group by using appropriate statistical techniques. If intelligence is related to the ability to remember material, we can statistically identify the extent to which individual differences in reactions to the written or audio presentation of material are attributed to intelligence. The ability to explain the variability in the test scores reduces the amount of "error." When error or unexplained variability is reduced, we are more likely to find that the differences in the means are statistically significant.

These issues of variability and statistical significance are discussed further in Chapter 14 and Appendix B. The main point here is that matching on a variable makes it more likely that a statistically significant difference between groups will be found in an experiment. However, matching procedures can be costly and time-consuming because they require measuring participants on the matching variable prior to the experiment. Such efforts are worthwhile only when the matching variable is strongly related to the dependent measure and you know that the relationship exists prior to conducting your study. For these reasons, matched random assignment is used less frequently than simple random assignment.

To illustrate the importance of matching, consider an intervention study of children having difficulty learning to read. Hatcher, Hulme, and Ellis (1994) developed three reading intervention strategies to improve the reading skills of poor readers: reading instruction alone, phonological training alone, or a combination of reading instruction and phonological training. Phonological training instructs children about the sounds of words. Careful prescreening identified 7-year-olds who were having reading problems. Hatcher et al. then used matched random assignment procedures to assign children to the intervention groups or a control group that did not receive any instruction. Children were matched on reading ability, IQ score, gender, and age. Only by such careful matching on variables related to reading ability could the researchers be confident that the four groups were equivalent when the interventions began. This initial equivalence greatly strengthens their conclusions that the most effective method for improving reading skills is an instructional approach that includes both reading instruction and phonological training.

REPEATED MEASURES DESIGNS

In a repeated measures design participants are assigned to more than one experimental condition. Consider an experiment to investigate vision in older drivers. The visual system changes over time, contributing to difficulties with dynamic vision, a visual process used when reading signs or other moving objects (Gilmore, Wenk, Naylor, & Stuve, 1992). Computers are programmed to display information scrolling vertically down the screen the way movie credits are displayed. The computer screen shows words or traffic signs so the researcher can compare processing of two types of items in the visual display. The dependent variable is the number of items correctly identified. In an independent groups design, one group is shown the words to identify and a second group is given the traffic signs to identify. In a repeated measures design, the same participants first identify the words and then they identify the signs. One group of older drivers is recruited for the study, and they are repeatedly measured on the dependent variable when they participate in each condition of the experiment.

Advantages and Disadvantages of Repeated Measures Designs

The repeated measures design has several advantages. An obvious one is that fewer research participants are needed because each individual participates in all conditions. When participants are scarce or when it is costly to run each individual in the experiment, a repeated measures design may be preferred. In much research on adult perception, for instance, extensive training of participants is necessary before the actual experiment can begin. Such research often involves only a few individuals who participate in all conditions of the experiment.

An additional advantage of repeated measures or within subjects designs is that they are extremely sensitive to finding differences between groups. Because participants in the various groups are identical in every respect (they are the same people), error variability due to subject differences (e.g., intelligence, personality, past experiences) is minimized. As with the matched random assignment procedure described earlier, the error variance or unexplained variability in the scores can be more readily identified, which results in a more powerful statistical test. The principle is the same as with matching designs, but participants are not just matched on a single characteristic—they are identical on all characteristics. As a result, we are much more likely to detect an effect of the independent variable on the dependent measure. Despite these advantages, repeated measures designs have limitations. These include: (1) order effects, (2) carry-over effects, and (3) demand characteristics.

Order effects are a major problem with a repeated measures design because the different conditions must be presented in a particular sequence. In the study of elderly drivers, suppose that identification of signs is better than identification of words. Although this result could be caused by manipulation of the type of item in the visual display, the result could also simply be an order effect—the order of presenting the treatments affects the dependent variable. Thus, more proficient identification of signs could be attributed to the fact that the sign condition is second in the order of presentation.

There are several types of order effects. Order effects that are associated simply with the passage of time include practice effects and fatigue effects. A **practice effect** is an improvement in performance as a result of repeated practice with a task. A **fatigue effect** is a deterioration in performance as the research participant becomes tired, bored, or distracted. Time-related order effects are possible whenever there is a sequence of tasks to perform. For example, suppose you ask a child to play a videogame for half-hour periods under different conditions each time (e.g., different rewards for good performance or different amounts of distraction). The child playing the game for the first time might show a practice effect, with scores improving over time, but the child who is familiar with the game might show a fatigue effect, with scores deteriorating as boredom or weariness sets in. A possible remedy for practice effects is to give the participants extensive practice before the experiment begins. In this way, when the experiment begins, participants are more proficient at the task and understand the procedure fully. Fatigue effects can be minimized by keeping the experiment interesting and relatively brief. This is especially true with individuals who may tire or become inattentive easily such as young children and the elderly.

Carry-over effects occur when the effects of the first treatment are still present when the next treatment is given, potentially influencing the response to the second treatment. Because of their nature, the effects of certain manipulations tend to persist. Suppose a researcher investigating stress-reduction techniques recruits a group of employed, single parents. Condition A is physical exercise; condition B is relaxation training. The dependent variable is a measure of stress reduction, perhaps a physiological measure or a self-report of stress ratings. When the parents participate in the physical exercise condition first, side effects (including fatigue or exhilaration from the endorphins) can affect the outcome of the relaxation training. However, if the order of participation is reversed, the carry-over effects are not the same. Starting with relaxation training is unlikely to create the side effects associated with intense physical activity. In this way, the carry-over effect from condition A to condition B is not the same as from B to A.

A **contrast effect** is a special kind of carry-over effect that occurs when the response to the second condition in the experiment is altered because the two conditions are contrasted to one another. In a study of eyewitness credibility, suppose the independent variable is "details in eyewitness testimony," with levels of high detail and low detail. If participants first read a court transcript of a child's testimony containing few details about an abusive event, the more detailed testimony may seem even more detailed and credible to participants. In addition, reading the high-detail testimony first may subsequently cause participants to view the low-detail testimony as even less credible than they normally would.

A possible remedy to minimize carry-over effects is to increase the time interval between treatments. By allowing additional time between condition A and condition B, the effects of the first condition should diminish. For instance, the participants could be tested on different days. Another alternative, of course, is to use an independent groups design.

Demand characteristics are also a problem in a repeated measures design. Experimenters prefer not to inform participants about the specific hypotheses being studied or the exact purpose of the research. However, in a repeated measures design participants may guess the hypothesis because they are participating in multiple experimental conditions. This problem is one of demand characteristics, in which certain aspects of the experiment provide clues that enable the participant to discern the experimenter's hypothesis. If this happens, people may behave differently in later parts of the experiment. This creates a threat for both internal validity and construct validity. It is usually more difficult for participants to figure out the true purpose of an experiment in an independent groups design.

Counterbalancing in Repeated Measures Designs

In a repeated measures design, order effects can be controlled by **counterbalancing** the order of the conditions. With complete counterbalancing, all possible orders of presentation are included in the experiment. In the example of elderly drivers identifying words and signs, half of the participants would be randomly assigned to the words–signs order, and the other half would be assigned to the signs–words order. This design is illustrated as follows:

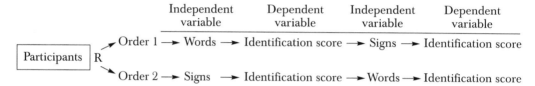

By counterbalancing the order of conditions it is possible to determine the extent to which order is influencing the results. In the elderly drivers example, you would know if the greater recall in the signs condition is consistent for both orders; you would also know the extent to which a practice effect is responsible for the results.

Counterbalancing principles can be extended to experiments with three or more groups. With three groups there would be 6 possible orders ($3! = 3 \times 2 \times 1 = 6$); with four groups the number of possible orders increases to 24 ($4! = 4 \times 3 \times 2 \times 1 = 24$); and so on. You would need a minimum of 24 participants to present each order, and you would need 48 participants to have just two participants per order. In practice, with four or more groups the order of presentation is either randomized across subjects, or a partially counterbalanced design is used. Otherwise, it wouldn't be feasible to conduct all the potential orders. One solution is to choose a subset of possible orders from the complete set of 24 and then assign participants randomly to one of these possible orders. The object is to design the experiment in such a way that any potential effects of order are distributed evenly across the participants in the various conditions.

ASSIGNING PARTICIPANTS TO GROUPS IN FACTORIAL DESIGNS

So far we have discussed assigning participants to designs with only one independent variable. In factorial designs, participants can be assigned on a between subjects basis or a within subjects basis for each independent variable or factor. These two types of assignment procedures have important implications for the number of participants necessary to complete the experiment. We can illustrate this fact by looking at a 2 × 2 factorial design. The design can be completely independent groups (or between subjects), completely repeated measures (or within subjects), or a **mixed factorial design**—that is, a combination of between and within subjects.

Independent Groups In a 2 × 2 factorial design, there are two independent variables. Consider our hypothetical study of elderly drivers in which we compared identification accuracy of words and signs presented on a moving vertical display. Let's add a second independent variable, speed of presentation, with levels of fast and slow. If we want a completely independent groups design, participants are assigned to each independent variable on a between subjects basis, and each person participates in only one level. For type of item, the adults see *either* words *or* signs. For speed of presentation, the items are *either* fast *or* slow. You will have four different groups of adults under four different experimental conditions: (1) words displayed fast, (2) words displayed slow, (3) signs displayed fast, and (4) signs displayed slow.

If you want to have 10 participants in each condition, you will need a total of 40 different participants for this independent groups factorial design. This can be determined by multiplying the number of groups times the number of participants in each group (4 groups of participants × 10 adults per group). This is shown in the first panel of Figure 13.1.

Repeated Measures In a completely repeated measures design, the same individuals participate in *all* conditions. For each independent variable in the elderly drivers study, adults are assigned to both levels of the variable. For type of item, the adults see both words *and* signs on the computer screen. For speed of presentation, the items are both fast *and* slow. You will have one group of adults who participate in all four experimental conditions.

Independent groups design (A and B = between subjects)

A	B: 1		B: 2	
1	S_{1}	S_{6}	S_{11}	S_{16}
	S_{2}	S_{7}	S_{12}	S_{17}
	S_{3}	S_{8}	S_{13}	S_{18}
	S_{4}	S_{9}	S_{14}	S_{19}
	S_{5}	S_{10}	S_{15}	S_{20}
2	S_{21}	S_{26}	S_{31}	S_{36}
	S_{22}	S_{27}	S_{32}	S_{37}
	S_{23}	S_{28}	S_{33}	S_{38}
	S_{24}	S_{29}	S_{34}	S_{39}
	S_{25}	S_{30}	S_{35}	S_{40}

Repeated measures design (A and B = within subjects)

A	B: 1		B: 2	
1	S_{1}	S_{6}	S_{1}	S_{6}
	S_{2}	S_{7}	S_{2}	S_{7}
	S_{3}	S_{8}	S_{3}	S_{8}
	S_{4}	S_{9}	S_{4}	S_{9}
	S_{5}	S_{10}	S_{5}	S_{10}
2	S_{1}	S_{6}	S_{1}	S_{6}
	S_{2}	S_{7}	S_{2}	S_{7}
	S_{3}	S_{8}	S_{3}	S_{8}
	S_{4}	S_{9}	S_{4}	S_{9}
	S_{5}	S_{10}	S_{5}	S_{10}

Mixed factorial design (A = between subjects, B = within subjects)

A	B: 1		B: 2	
1	S_{1}	S_{6}	S_{1}	S_{6}
	S_{2}	S_{7}	S_{2}	S_{7}
	S_{3}	S_{8}	S_{3}	S_{8}
	S_{4}	S_{9}	S_{4}	S_{9}
	S_{5}	S_{10}	S_{5}	S_{10}
2	S_{11}	S_{16}	S_{11}	S_{16}
	S_{12}	S_{17}	S_{12}	S_{17}
	S_{13}	S_{18}	S_{13}	S_{18}
	S_{14}	S_{19}	S_{14}	S_{19}
	S_{15}	S_{20}	S_{15}	S_{20}

Figure 13.1 Number of participants required to have 10 participants in each condition

If you want to have 10 participants in each condition, you will need a total of 10 different participants for this repeated measures factorial design. This can be determined by multiplying the number of groups times the number of participants in each group (1 group × 10 adults per group). This type of design in which performance is evaluated within the group is shown in the middle panel of Figure 13.1.

This design offers considerable savings in the number of participants required. In deciding whether to use a completely repeated measures assignment procedure, however, the researcher would have to consider the disadvantages of repeated measures designs. In addition, not all variables can be assigned on a repeated measures basis for ethical or practical reasons. For example, subject variables do not lend themselves to within subjects assignment—a participant cannot be assigned to a two-parent family for one condition and a single-parent family for the next condition.

Mixed Factorial Design A factorial design that uses independent groups procedures and repeated measures procedures in the same design is a mixed factorial design (or mixed subjects factorial design). In our 2 × 2 study one variable is assigned on a between subjects basis, and the second variable is assigned on a within subjects basis. For type of item, the adults see words *or* signs on the computer screen. For speed of presentation, the items are both fast *and* slow. (The design can also be mixed by assigning type of item as a within subjects variable and speed of presentation as the between subjects variable.) The important thing is to have one variable assigned using each procedure—one between and one within in this 2 × 2 case.

How many adults do you need to recruit for this design? If you want 10 participants in each condition, you will need a total of 20 different participants for this mixed factorial design. Using the same formula, this can be determined by multiplying the number of groups times the number of participants in each group (2 groups × 10 adults per group). This type of design is shown in the third panel of Figure 13.1. There are two groups because 10 participants are assigned to level 1 of the independent groups variable, and then they will receive both levels of the speed variable. Another 10 participants are assigned to level 2 of the independent groups variable, and they also will receive both levels of the speed variable.

CHOOSING BETWEEN INDEPENDENT GROUPS AND REPEATED MEASURES DESIGNS

Repeated measures designs have two major advantages over independent groups designs: (1) a reduction in the number of participants required to complete the experiment, and (2) greater control over participant differences and, thus, greater power to detect an effect of the independent variable. As noted previously, in certain areas of research, these advantages are very important. However, the disadvantages of repeated measures designs and the need to deal with these are usually sufficient reasons for researchers to use independent groups designs.

A very different consideration in whether to use a repeated measures design concerns generalization to conditions in the "real world." In actual, everyday situations, we sometimes encounter events in an independent groups fashion when we encounter only one condition without a contrasting comparison. However, you will frequently be interested in the sequence of events because real life resembles a series of events that occur in a repeated measures fashion (Greenwald, 1976). In the study of stress reduction, you may be interested in knowing what the effects are of each sequence: Is it better to do physical activity before or after relaxation? You may have other questions about physical activity: Would it be a good idea to do physical activity before you study? Or should you study first and exercise later? A within subjects design allows you to address these issues. You can probably think of many other events in life that generate questions about a series of events. In a child abuse case, should the prosecution open with testimony from the child victim, or should the child's testimony follow the testimony of the other witnesses? A repeated measures design may be appropriate to investigate legal issues such as these because actual jurors consider the testimony of more than one witness. If you are investigating age discrimination in the workplace, a repeated measures design would be appropriate because personnel administrators typically consider several applicants when making hiring and promotion decisions. Whether to use an independent groups or repeated measures design is influenced by participant availability, need for statistical precision, and the nature of the phenomenon under investigation.

EXAMPLES OF HUMAN DEVELOPMENT RESEARCH QUESTIONS

Problems studied in human development and family relations often require the use of complex factorial designs or multiple dependent variables. In this section, we consider three examples: age group comparisons, special populations, and family variables.

Age Group Comparisons

Developmental research is concerned with explaining the changes that occur with age. Age is frequently included as an independent variable. Individuals from one age group are compared with those from a different age group. Researchers using this design typically are testing a theory that predicts an interaction between age and the manipulated independent variable. Age is included as a variable in such experiments because some psychological, educational, social, or biological process is hypothesized to differ in the age groups studied.

Friedman, Tzukerman, Wienberg, and Todd (1992) used a $2 \times 2 \times 2 \times 2$ between subjects factorial design to investigate changes in the perception of interpersonal power over the life span. The participants included young adults (mean age 33.2 years) and older adults (mean age 62.3 years) who were residents of either a kibbutz or a city in Israel. The adults were shown a picture of a young couple that is part of the Thematic Apperception Test—a projective measure of personality—and asked to write a story about the characters. Raters then evaluated the interpersonal power of female and male characters in the stories. The independent variables were age (younger or older adults), residence (kibbutz or city), sex of participant, and sex of story character. The primary dependent variable was the

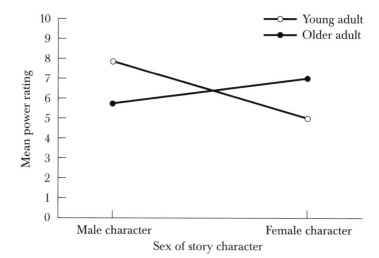

Figure 13.2
Interaction between
age of adult and sex
of story character

rating of interpersonal power for the character in the story, with values ranging from 2 to 10. The results yielded a significant interaction between age and sex of story character. This interaction is shown in Figure 13.2. For younger adults, the male characters were seen as more powerful than the female characters. In contrast, for the older adults, the opposite pattern emerged, with female characters described as more powerful than the male characters. Friedman et al. conclude that the shift in perceived power with increasing age occurs in both the city and the kibbutz, generalizing earlier findings of the shift in power across cultures.

Special Populations

Age may not always be the primary variable of interest in human development research. For example, differences in ability level, social status, or family background may be the focus of research. In such studies the researcher is often testing a hypothesis that some treatment or independent variable has differential effects (i.e., an interaction) for the groups studied. A mixed subjects factorial design used by Landau, Lorch, and Milich (1992) evaluated the visual attention of boys with attention-deficit hyperactivity disorder (ADHD). The ADHD boys were compared to a control group of normally developing boys. Each child viewed short videotapes of educational programming under one of two conditions. In one viewing condition toys were available as potential distracters in the room, whereas in the other viewing condition no toys were present. The researchers measured the amount of time that the boys spent attending the TV. The researchers used a 2×2 mixed factorial design, with a selected between subjects variable, boys' group status (ADHD and normal), and a within subjects variable, viewing condition (toys present and toys absent). The dependent variable was the percentage of visual attention to the television. The study was designed to evaluate a hypothesis concerning attention. Do ADHD boys have difficulty with sustained attention or selective attention? If the problem is related to global, sustained attention, they should be less attentive under both viewing conditions, and there would be no

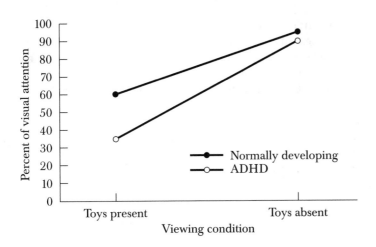

Figure 13.3
Interaction between
viewing condition
and group

interaction. Alternatively, if the ADHD boys have difficulty with selective attention, they should differ from the normal boys only when the distracting toys are
available. You probably recognize this second option as a test of an interaction
because there is a possibility that the ADHD boys might behave differently at the
different levels of the viewing condition variable.

The results are shown in Figure 13.3. When no distractions were present, the
ADHD boys attended at a level similar to that of the normal boys. The only difference in visual attention emerged when the appealing toys were present in the
environment. This suggests that a major difference between ADHD and normal
children is related to selective attention. A second dependent variable assessed
the children's recall of the program content and indicated a trend in the data for
greater recall in the boys in the control group. This suggests that the diminished
attention to the TV program can have important practical significance, with implications for a child's learning.

Family Variables

The traditional, two-parent nuclear family is declining in prevalence in the United
States. One alternative family structure that is increasing is lesbian and gay parenting. Limited research has been done on planned lesbian families. Flaks, Ficher,
Masterpasqua, and Joseph (1995) evaluated the functioning of 15 lesbian-mother
families who were raising children born to them via donor insemination. A carefully matched control group of heterosexual-parent families was recruited who
also had children ages 3 to 9 years old. Children were matched on sex, age, and
birth order. Parents were matched on race, educational level, and parental income. The design was a 2×2 factorial with selected independent variables of
parental sexual orientation and gender of the child. The dependent variables included the children's IQ scores and measures of the children's behavior problems
and social competence. No main effects for parental sexual orientation were found
on any of the child variables. Children of lesbian parents and heterosexual parents performed equally well in the areas of intellectual functioning and behavioral

adjustment. No gender differences were found, and there were no interactions between parental sexual orientation and gender. The researchers concluded that boys and girls who are being raised by lesbian mothers are psychologically healthy, a conclusion that has broad legal implications.

The outcome of this family study illustrates the importance of basic research. The results of this carefully constructed study can be applied to the concerns of the legal system, informing judges and legislators of the positive parenting outcomes that are possible in nontraditional families. The study also illustrates the importance of research that finds no differences between experimental conditions—sometimes it is meaningful to establish equality between diverse individuals and focus on the commonalties inherent in development.

SUMMARY

In this chapter we discussed the two major ways people can participate in experiments. In independent groups (also called between subjects) designs, each person participates in only one group. Simple random assignment is a typical means for assigning participants to groups. Matched random assignment is a more complex method that is less common than simple random assignment. Participants are matched on the basis of characteristics that are strongly related to the dependent variable.

In repeated measures (or within subjects) designs, individuals participate in more than one experimental condition. Repeated measures studies often can be conducted with fewer participants and have reduced error variability because subject differences are minimized. However, researchers must be on the lookout for the susceptibility to order effects, carry-over effects, and demand characteristics that can occur when people participate in more than one condition of the study.

Counterbalancing is a technique used to control for order effects that occur when individuals participate in more than one condition. Repeated participation may lead to improved performance as a result of practice or to poorer performance as a result of fatigue. With complete counterbalancing, all possible orders of presentation are included in the experiment. With two experimental conditions (A and B), half of the participants start with condition A and follow with condition B; the remaining participants begin with condition B and follow with condition A. More elaborate procedures for partial counterbalancing may be needed with complex designs.

KEY TERMS

between subjects design	independent groups	practice effect
carry-over effects	design	repeated measures
contrast effect	matched random	design
counterbalancing	assignment	simple random
demand characteristics	mixed factorial design	assignment
fatigue effect	order effects	within subjects design

REVIEW QUESTIONS

1. Distinguish between a between subjects design and a repeated measures design.
2. Distinguish between simple random assignment and matched random assignment. When would a researcher use the matched random assignment procedure? What are the advantages of this design?
3. What are the advantages of using a repeated measures design? What are the disadvantages?
4. How does counterbalancing control order effects?
5. In a 2×2 factorial design, assume you want 12 participants per condition. How many different participants do you need for a
   a. completely between subjects design?
   b. completely repeated measures design?
   c. mixed factorial design?
6. Consider the 2×3 factorial design in the diagram. Independent variable A has two levels, A_1 and A_2. Independent variable B has 3 levels, B_1, B_2, and B_3. There are six conditions, represented by the numbers in each box.

	B_1	B_2	B_3
A_1	1	2	3
A_2	4	5	6

Using the numbers in each box to identify each condition, what conditions would a person be assigned to in a

a. completely between subjects design? (For variable A, individuals are assigned to either level A_1 or level A_2; for variable B, individuals are assigned to either level B_1 or B_2 or B_3.)
b. completely within subjects design? (Individuals are assigned to level A_1 and A_2 as well as level B_1, B_2, and B_3.)
c. mixed factorial design, with independent variable A as the between subjects factor and independent variable B as the within subjects factor?
d. mixed factorial design, with independent variable A as the within subjects factor and independent variable B as the between subjects factor?

CHAPTER 14 ◆

Understanding Research Results

After completing a research study, the next task is to analyze the data. Statistics allow you to summarize and describe the data so others can understand the findings. In this chapter we introduce some basic ideas about statistics. The goal is to introduce the terminology and logic of statistics so you can interpret statistical information in articles you read and possibly summarize data from your own studies. Chapter 15 introduces statistical tests. Specific calculations for a variety of statistics are provided in Appendix B. Recall from Chapter 4 that the measurement scale that is used to measure a variable determines the types of statistics that are appropriate and the conclusions that can be drawn about the meaning of a particular score on a variable.

ANALYZING THE RESULTS OF RESEARCH INVESTIGATIONS

Most research focuses on the study of relationships between variables. Depending on the way the variables were studied, there are three basic ways of describing the results: (1) comparing group percentages, (2) correlating scores of individuals on two variables, and (3) comparing group means.

Comparing Group Percentages

Suppose you want to know whether males and females differ in their views on mandatory retirement. In your study you ask males and females whether they would vote "yes" in support of mandatory retirement legislation or whether they would be opposed to such legislation. To describe your results, you will need to calculate the percentage of males and females who favor mandatory retirement. Suppose you tested 50 females and 50 males and found that 40 of the females and 30 of the males replied "yes." In describing your findings, you would report that 80% of the females support mandatory retirement in comparison to 60% of the males. Thus, a relationship between gender and support for mandatory retirement appears to exist. Note that we are focusing on percentages because the retirement variable is nominal; supporting or opposing legislation are simply two different categories. After describing your data, the next step would be to perform a statistical analysis to determine if there is a statistically significant difference. Statistical significance is discussed later in this chapter.

Correlating Individual Scores

A second type of analysis is needed when you do not have distinct groups of participants. Instead, individuals are measured on two variables, and each variable has a range of numerical values. In Chapter 15 we will consider an analysis of data on the relationship between health status and happiness. Are elderly citizens who are in better health happier than their peers with health problems?

Comparing Group Means

Much research is designed to compare the mean responses of two or more groups of participants on a measured variable. To illustrate, let's start with some fictitious data from a project concerning the benefits of sports participation. Twenty 14-year-old girls were selected from an alternative high school for students who were having difficulty in school. The girls were randomly assigned to one of two groups: intramural sports after school versus aerobic exercise classes. After 4 weeks, the school principal (blind to the condition the girls were assigned to) reported the number of times the girls had been referred to her office for discipline.

In this case you would be interested in comparing the mean number of discipline referrals in the two conditions to determine if the girls who participated in intramural sports had fewer referrals than the girls in the aerobics condition. Hypothetical data from such an experiment are presented in Table 14.1. After completing an experiment, it is important to understand your results by carefully describing your data. We begin by constructing frequency distributions.

Table 14.1 Discipline Referral Scores in a Hypothetical Experiment on Sports Participation

	Intramural Sports	Aerobics
	1	3
	2	4
	2	5
	3	5
	3	5
	3	5
	4	6
	4	6
	4	6
	5	7
ΣX	31.00	52.00
$\bar{X}$	3.10	5.20
s^2	1.43	1.29
s	1.20	1.14
N	10	10

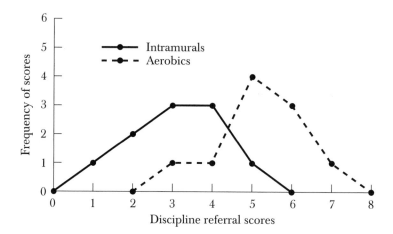

Figure 14.1
Frequency polygons
illustrating the
distribution of
scores in Table 14.1

FREQUENCY DISTRIBUTIONS

When analyzing results, it is useful to start by constructing a **frequency distribution** of the data. A frequency distribution indicates the number of participants who received each possible score on a variable. Frequency distributions of exam scores are familiar to most college students—they tell how many students received a given score on an exam. Along with the number of individuals associated with each response, it is useful to examine the percentage associated with this number.

Frequency Polygons

Frequency distributions can be depicted in a **frequency polygon** such as Figure 14.1, which presents the data from the sports participation experiment. These two frequency polygons—one for each group—show how many girls received each score on the dependent variable, number of discipline referrals. The horizontal axis (or abscissa) represents the different scores that were possible on the dependent measure, ranging from 0 to 8. The vertical axis (or ordinate) represents the number of girls who received each score. The solid line represents the intramurals group, and the dotted line is for the aerobics group. Thus, in the intramurals group, no students received zero referrals, one student was referred once, two students were referred twice, and so on.

Histograms

Histograms, or **bar graphs**, are an alternative method of presenting a frequency distribution. In a histogram, a bar is drawn for each possible score on the measure; the height of the bar depicts the number of persons who received that score. Figure 14.2 illustrates a histogram for the distribution of scores in Table 14.1. The histogram is just a different way to present the same information shown in the polygons. Notice that if you connected the center of each bar with a line you would have the polygons shown in Figure 14.1.

What can you tell by examining these frequency distributions? First, you can directly observe how the participants responded. You can see what scores are most

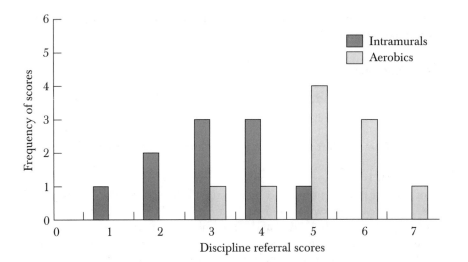

Figure 14.2
Histogram illustrating the distribution of scores in Table 14.1

frequent (find the highest peak in the polygon or the tallest bar in the histogram), and you can look at the shape of the distribution of scores. You can tell if there are any "outliers"–scores that are unusual, unexpected, or very different from the scores of other participants. In our hypothetical experiment it looks like the scores in the aerobics group tend to be higher than those in the intramural group, as indicated by the higher peak and the cluster of scores on the higher end of the horizontal axis.

DESCRIPTIVE STATISTICS VERSUS INFERENTIAL STATISTICS

There are two kinds of statistics, descriptive statistics and inferential statistics. **Descriptive statistics** allow researchers to make precise statements about the data, summarizing information about the groups. As implied by the name, descriptive statistics describe the participants' responses on the dependent measures. **Inferential statistics** are used to make a judgment about the data, inferring that the pattern of results observed on the sample applies to the larger population. Inferential statistics are necessary because the results of a given study are based on data obtained from a single sample of research participants. Researchers rarely, if ever, study entire populations; the findings are based on sample data. Would the results hold up if the experiment were conducted repeatedly, each time with a new sample? Inferential statistics allow researchers to make statements about populations.

DESCRIPTIVE STATISTICS

Two descriptive statistics are needed to summarize the data. A single number can be used to describe the central tendency, or how subjects scored overall. Another number describes the variability, or how widely the distribution of scores is spread. The two numbers summarize the information contained in a frequency distribution. Procedures for calculating measures of central tendency and variability are in Appendix B.

Central Tendency

Measures of **central tendency** provide information about the typical score in a sample, telling us what the sample is like as a whole. There are three measures of central tendency: the mean, the median, and the mode. (For those who use mnemonics: They all start with "m" and have something to do with the "middle" of the distribution.)

The **mean** is the most commonly used measure of central tendency. The mean of a set of scores is obtained by adding all the scores and dividing by the number of scores. It is symbolized as $\bar{X}$ (a capital X with a bar on top) and in scientific reports it is abbreviated as M. The mean is an appropriate indicator of central tendency only when scores are measured on an interval or ratio scale, because the actual values of the numbers are used in calculating the statistic. In Table 14.1, we can see that the mean score for the girls in the aerobics group is 5.20, and the mean for the intramural sports group is 3.10. Note that the Greek letter Σ (sigma) in Table 14.1 is a statistical notation for summing a set of numbers. Thus ΣX is shorthand for "sum of the values in a set of scores."

The **median** is the score that divides the group in half, with 50% scoring below and 50% scoring above the median. The median is obtained by arranging the scores in order of their magnitude; the median will be the score in the middle. With an odd number of scores, the median is easy to determine. With an even number of scores (as in our example in Table 14.1), the median falls halfway between the two middle scores. The median for the intramural group is 3, and for the aerobics group the median is 5. In scientific reports, the median is abbreviated as Mdn. The median is appropriate when scores are measured on an ordinal scale because the median takes into account only the rank order of the scores.

The **mode** is the most frequent score, the one that occurs the most in the distribution. The mode is the only measure of central tendency that is appropriate when a nominal scale is used. The mode simply indicates the most frequently occurring value in the distribution. There are two modal values for the intramural group, 3 and 4. The mode in the aerobics group is 5. You can find the mode by scanning down the list of scores in Table 14.1, but an easier way is to look at the frequency polygons or histograms. The modal score in each distribution will have the highest peak.

Variability

We can also determine how much **variability** exists in a set of scores. A measure of variability is a number that characterizes the amount of spread in a distribution of scores. One measure of variability is the **standard deviation,** which is represented by the symbol s. The standard deviation indicates the average deviation of scores from the mean. In scientific reports it is abbreviated as SD. The standard deviation is derived by first calculating the **variance,** symbolized as s^2 (the standard deviation is the square root of the variance). When the standard deviation is small, the mean provides a good description of the data because the scores do not vary much around the mean. In contrast, when scores are widely dispersed around the mean, the standard deviation is large, and the mean does not describe the data well. For the aerobics group, the standard deviation is 1.14, which tells us that most scores in that condition lie 1.14 units above and below the mean, that is, between 4.06 and 6.34 (5.20 − 1.14 = 4.06; 5.20 + 1.14 = 6.34). Together, the mean and the standard deviation provide a great deal of information about the distribution. Note that, as with the mean, the calculation of the standard deviation uses the actual values of the scores; thus, the standard deviation is appropriate only for interval and ratio scale variables.

Another measure of variability is the **range,** which is simply the difference between the highest score and the lowest score. The range for both the aerobics and the intramurals group is 4. You may also see the range reported with two numbers, the low and high values. Using this approach, the range for the intramural group is 1–5; for the aerobics group the range is 3–7. This is more informative because a range of a particular size can be obtained from a variety of beginning and end points. The range is the least useful of the measures of central tendency because it looks at extreme values without considering the variability in the set of scores.

GRAPHING RELATIONSHIPS

Graphing relationships between variables was discussed briefly in earlier chapters. Recall that line graphs and bar graphs were used in Chapter 12 to illustrate the concept of interactions in 2 × 2 factorial designs. Both line and bar graphs are frequently used to express relationships between levels of an independent variable. Figure 14.3 illustrates the graphing of the means for the sports participation study. Figure 14.3a is a line graph; Figure 14.3b shows the same data using a

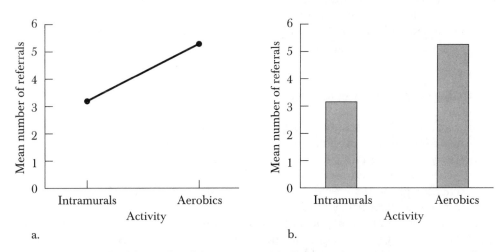

Figure 14.3 Graph of the results of the sports participation experiment: (a) line graph, (b) bar graph

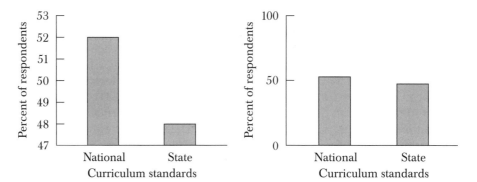

Figure 14.4
Two ways to graph
the same data

bar graph. In both graphs we see that the mean number of referrals for discipline problems is lower in the intramural sports group than in the aerobics group.

It is interesting to note a common trick that is sometimes used by scientists and all too commonly by advertisers. The trick is to exaggerate the distance between points on the measurement scale to make the results appear more dramatic than they really are. Suppose, for example, that a survey reports that 52% of the respondents support national education standards advocated by Goals 2000, and 48% prefer that individual states continue to determine curriculum standards. How should political action committees present these results? Figure 14.4 shows a bar graph of the most honest method, as well as one that is considerably more dramatic. The moral of the story is that it is always wise to look carefully at the numbers on the scales depicted in graphs.

Graphing the means provides an idea of the relationship between the experimental groups on the dependent variable. The computation of descriptive statistics such as the mean and the standard deviation also helps the researcher understand the results by describing characteristics of the sample. The results are based on sample data that are presumed to be representative of the population from which the sample was drawn (see sampling in Chapter 8). If you want to make statements about the populations from which samples were drawn, it is necessary to use inferential statistics.

INFERENTIAL STATISTICS

In our hypothetical study of sports participation, the intramural group had fewer discipline referrals. Would the same pattern be true for other samples of students? Can you infer that the differences observed in one study apply to other groups? We tested one sample of 14-year-olds. Would the same results be obtained on another sample of 14-year-olds? Are we confident that the means of the aerobics and intramural sports groups are sufficiently different to infer that the difference would be obtained in an entire population? The scores only differ by a few points. Is that difference large enough to conclude that sports participation has a positive effect on discipline? Or is it possible that the difference occurred just by chance alone? Inferential statistics allow us to arrive at such conclusions.

Much of the previous discussion of experimental design centered on the importance of making sure that the groups are equivalent in every way except the independent variable manipulation. Equivalency of groups is achieved by experimentally controlling all other variables or by randomization. The assumption is that if the groups are equivalent, any differences in the dependent variable must be due to the effect of the independent variable.

This assumption is usually valid. However, it is also true that the difference between any two groups will almost never be zero. In other words, there will be some difference in the sample means, even when all of the principles of experimental design are utilized. This happens because we are dealing with samples rather than populations. Random or chance error will be responsible for some difference in the means even if the independent variable had no effect on the dependent variable.

The point is that the difference in the sample means reflects true difference in the population means (i.e., the effect of the independent variable) plus random error. Inferential statistics allow researchers to make inferences about the true difference in the population on the basis of the sample data. Specifically, inferential statistics give the probability that the difference between means reflects random error rather than a real difference.

One way of thinking about inferential statistics is to use the concept of reliability that was introduced in Chapter 4. Recall that reliability refers to the stability or consistency of scores; a reliable measure will yield the same score over and over again. Inferential statistics allow researchers to assess whether the results of a study are reliable. Would the same results be obtained if the study were repeated again and again? You could, of course, repeat your study many times, each time with a new sample of research participants. However, this is not practical. Instead, inferential statistics are used to tell you the probability that your results would be obtained if you repeated the study on many occasions.

Hypothesis Testing

Statistical inference usually begins with a formal statement of the null hypothesis and a research (or alternate) hypothesis. The **null hypothesis,** traditionally symbolized as H_0, states that the population means are equal. This means that the independent variable has no effect on the dependent variable. Any difference between the means is due only to random error, not to some systematic effect of the independent variable.

The **research hypothesis,** traditionally symbolized as H_1, states that the population means are not equal. This means that the independent variable has an effect on the dependent variable; only by having an effect will the group means turn out to be different because the groups were equivalent at the beginning.

In our example on sports participation, the null and research hypotheses are:

H_0 (null hypothesis): The population mean of the intramural sports group is equal to the population mean of the aerobics group.

H_1 (research hypothesis): The population mean of the intramural sports group is not equal to the population mean of the aerobics group.

Essentially, the null hypothesis states that $M_1 = M_2$, and the research hypothesis implies that $M_1 \neq M_2$. Notice that the research hypothesis does not state a direction for the effect; it does not state that the aerobics group will have more or fewer referrals. The nondirectional, generic form of the research hypothesis simply states that there is a difference between the means.

The logic of the null hypothesis is this: If we can determine that the null hypothesis is incorrect, we reject the null hypothesis, and then we accept the research hypothesis as correct. Rejecting the null hypothesis means that the independent variable had an effect on the dependent variable. Formal hypothesis testing begins with an assumption that the null hypothesis is true. Then inferential statistics are used to establish if this hypothesis accurately represents the relationship between the independent variable and the dependent variable.

The null hypothesis is used because it is a very precise statement—the population means are exactly equal. This permits us to know the exact probability of the outcome of the results occurring if the null hypothesis is correct. Such precision isn't possible with the research hypothesis, so we infer that the research hypothesis is correct only by rejecting the null hypothesis. The null hypothesis is rejected when there is a very low probability that the obtained results could be due to random error. This is what is meant by **statistical significance** or a **significant result.** Significance indicates that there is a low probability that the difference between the obtained sample means was due to random error. Significance, then, is a matter of probability.

Probability

Probability is the likelihood of the occurrence of some event or outcome. We all use probabilities frequently in everyday life. For example, if you say that there is a high probability that you will get an A in this course, you mean that there is a high likelihood that this will occur. Your probability statement is based on specific information, such as your grades on examinations. The weather forecaster says there is a 10% chance of rain today; this means that the likelihood of rain is very low. A gambler gauges the probability that a particular horse will win a race on the basis of the past performance of that horse.

Probability in statistical inference is used in much the same way. We want to specify the probability that an event (in this case, a difference between means in the sample) will occur if there is no difference in the actual population. The question is, what is the probability of obtaining this result if only random error is operating? If this probability is very low, we reject the possibility that only random or chance error is responsible for the obtained difference in means. A low probability means that we have a "real" difference between our groups.

Let's look at our sports participation example again. The aerobics group has a mean of 5.20 referrals; the intramurals group has a mean of 3.10 referrals. Do these means differ because of random error, or does participation in sports have a significant effect on girls, improving their school behavior? We need to know the probability of means of this size occurring. If there is a low probability of these means occurring, then we have a statistically significant effect. A low probability

Table 14.2 Hypothesis Testing and Probability

Significant results imply:	*Nonsignificant results imply:*
Low probability (or p level)	High probability (or p level)
Unlikely to occur due to chance or random error	Likely to occur due to chance or random error
"Real" (reliable) effect	"Chance" effect
Reject H_0	Accept H_0
Groups differ from each other $M_1 \neq M_2$	Groups are not different $M_1 = M_2$
Independent variable has an effect on the dependent variable	Independent variable has no effect on the dependent variable

means that it is unlikely the means occurred due to chance alone; the means occurred due to a "real" effect. We then reject the null hypothesis because the groups are not identical after all. On a practical level, this would suggest that we might want to encourage participation in extracurricular activities to influence academic performance and diminish school dropouts. Conversely, the difference between 5.20 and 3.10 may be a result of "chance" or random error. If there is a high probability that the means occurred due to chance alone, the null hypothesis is supported. This means we do not have a "real" effect, and the intramurals program did not make any changes in the girls' behavior at school. Table 14.2 summarizes the implications of obtaining significant and nonsignificant results.

Probability: The Case of the Gifted Baby

The use of probability in statistical inference can be understood intuitively from a simple example. Suppose that a friend claims that she has taught her gifted 1-year-old daughter to read by using flash cards. You decide to test your friend's claim by testing her baby with the flash cards. A different word is presented on each card, and the baby is told to point to the corresponding object presented on a response card. In your test you use 10 different words, presented in a random order. The response card contains pictures of the 10 objects named on the flash cards. Your task is to determine if the baby's responses reflect random error (guessing) or whether the answers indicate that something more than random error is occurring. The null hypothesis in your study is that only random error is operating; the baby cannot read. The research hypothesis is that the number of correct answers shows more than just random or chance guessing; the baby can read (or possibly, the baby has learned to associate the correct objects with the different colors used as backgrounds on the flash cards).

You can easily determine the number of correct answers to expect if the null hypothesis is correct. Just by guessing, the baby should get 1 out of 10 answers correct (10%). If in the actual experiment more than 1 correct is obtained, can you conclude that the data reflect something more than just random guessing?

Suppose the baby gets two correct answers. Then you probably conclude that only guessing is involved, because you recognize that there is a high probability that there would be two correct answers. Even though only one correct response is expected under the null hypothesis, small deviations away from the expected one correct answer are highly likely.

Suppose, though, that the baby gets seven correct answers. Then you might conclude that the results indicate more than random guessing. Your conclusion is based on your intuitive judgment that an outcome of 70% correct is very unlikely. At this point, you would decide to reject the null hypothesis and state that the result is significant. A significant result is one that is very unlikely if the null hypothesis is correct. It looks like the baby may be a genius after all!

How unlikely does an event have to be before we decide it is significant? A decision rule is determined prior to collecting the data. The probability or p level required for significance is called the **alpha level.** The most common alpha level used is .05. The outcome of the study is considered significant when there is a .05 or less probability of obtaining the results—that is, there are only five chances out of 100 that the results were due to random error. Because of the small likelihood that random error is responsible for the obtained results, the null hypothesis is rejected.

Sampling Distributions

You may have been able to judge intuitively that obtaining seven correct on the 10 trials is very unlikely. Fortunately, we don't have to rely on intuition to determine the probabilities of different outcomes. Table 14.3 shows the probability of actually obtaining each of the possible outcomes in the gifted baby example. An outcome of one correct answer has the highest probability of occurrence. Also, as intuition indicates, an outcome of two correct is highly probable, but an outcome of seven correct has a very low probability of occurrence and can be considered highly unlikely.

The probabilities shown in Table 14.3 were derived from a probability distribution called the *binomial distribution;* all statistical significance decisions are based on probability distributions such as this one. Such distributions are called **sampling distributions.** The sampling distribution is based on the assumption that the null hypothesis is true; in the gifted baby example, the null hypothesis is that the baby is only guessing and should therefore get 10% correct. If you were to conduct the study over and over again, the most frequent finding would be 10%. However, because of the random error possible in each sample, there is a certain possibility associated with other outcomes. Outcomes that are close to the expected null hypothesis value of 10% are very likely. However, outcomes further from the expected result are less and less likely if the null hypothesis is correct. When the baby gets seven correct responses, the probability of this occurring is so small if the null hypothesis is true that you are forced to reject the null hypothesis. Obtaining seven correct does not really belong in the sampling distribution specified by the null hypothesis that the baby cannot read—you must be sampling from a different distribution (one in which the baby may actually read!).

All statistical tests rely on sampling distributions to determine the probabil-

Table 14.3 **Exact Probability of Each Possible Outcome of the Gifted Baby Experiment With 10 Trials**

Number of Correct Answers	Probability
10	.0000
9	.0000
8	.0000
7	.0000
6	.0001
5	.0015
4	.0112
3	.0574
2	.1937
1	.3874
0	.3487

ity that the results are consistent with the null hypothesis. When it is highly unlikely that the null hypothesis is correct (usually a .05 probability or less), the researcher decides to reject the null hypothesis and therefore accepts the research hypothesis.

ISSUES IN DECISION MAKING

Inferential statistics allow us to make decisions about the null hypothesis. The decision to reject the null hypothesis is based on probabilities rather than on certainties. The decision is made without direct knowledge of the true state of affairs in the population because you only tested a sample of individuals from the population, not every member of the population. Thus, the decision might not be correct; errors may result from the use of inferential statistics. When your alpha level is .05, you are rejecting the null hypothesis when there is less than a 5% chance that the results occurred due to chance—but that implies you will be incorrect in your decision 5% of the time. In fact, 5% of the time the results were due to chance only, not a "real" effect as your decision rule would suggest. Unfortunately, you do not know when you are making an incorrect decision.

A decision matrix is presented in Figure 14.5. The left side of the matrix displays your decision about the null hypothesis based on the sample of participants you assessed. Recall that statistical decisions are always about the null hypothesis, so there is no need to be concerned about the research hypothesis at this point. You have only two choices: (1) reject the null hypothesis, or (2) accept the null hypothesis. The top of the matrix displays the state of affairs in the population. You cannot know what is really true in the population because you did not test everyone. However, there are only two possible choices in the population: (1) the null hypothesis is true, or (2) the null hypothesis is false. From the matrix, you can see that there are two kinds of correct decisions and two kinds of errors that occur in statistical inference.

Population

		Null hypothesis is true	Null hypothesis is false
Decision	Reject the null hypothesis	Type I Error	Correct Decision
	Accept the null hypothesis	Correct Decision	Type II Error

Figure 14.5
Decision matrix:
Type I and Type II
errors

Correct Decisions

One correct decision occurs when we reject the null hypothesis (the null hypothesis is false) based on our sample data and, in fact, the null hypothesis is really false in the population. We conclude that the population means are not equal, implying that there is a "real" effect in our sample. Based on the probabilities associated with our results, we reached a correct decision. It appears that the independent variable has an effect on the dependent variable.

The other correct decision occurs when we accept the null hypothesis (null hypothesis is true) and, in fact, the null hypothesis is really true in the population. We conclude that the population means are equal, implying that there is no difference between the groups in our experiment. We correctly decide that the independent variable has no effect on the dependent variable because the means are equivalent in the population.

Type I and Type II Errors

A **Type I error** is made when we decide to reject the null hypothesis, claiming it to be false, when the null hypothesis is actually true. Our conclusion is that the population means are not equal when they actually are equal. We decide there is an effect of the independent variable on the dependent variable when, in fact, no effect exists. A Type I error occurs when we incorrectly reject a null hypothesis that is actually true.

The probability of a Type I error is determined by the significance or alpha level. When the alpha level is set at .05, the probability of making a Type I error is also .05. Recall that a .05 probability level means that we reject the null hypothesis when the outcome is likely to occur due to chance less than 5 times out of 100. However, it is these 5 chance occurrences that are candidates for Type I errors. The probability of making a Type I error can be reduced by changing the alpha level. With the alpha set lower, at .01 for example, the chance of making a Type I error is reduced because we can reject the null hypothesis only 1 out of 100 times. With a lower incidence of possible rejections, there are fewer oppor-

Population

	Null is true (innocent)	Null is false (guilty)
Reject the null (find guilty)	Type I Error	Correct Decision
Accept the null (find innocent)	Correct Decision	Type II Error

Decision

Figure 14.6
Decision matrix for a juror

tunities to make an error of rejection. Similarly, if we increase the alpha level to .10 (as we might in exploratory research), we increase the likelihood of making a Type I error.

A **Type II error** occurs when the null hypothesis is accepted although in the population the null hypothesis is actually false. Based on our sample data, we decide that the population means are equal, when in fact they are not equal. A Type II error occurs when we incorrectly accept a null hypothesis that is actually false.

The probability of making a Type II error is not directly specifiable, although the significance level is an important factor. If we set a very low significance level (e.g., $p = .0001$), we decrease the chances of a Type I error but at the same time we increase the chances of a Type II error. With a low p level, we make it very difficult to reject the null hypothesis (only 1 out of a 1,000 times), so we will be accepting the null hypothesis more often. With more opportunities to accept the null, we have more opportunities to accept the null hypothesis in error—a Type II error.

Examples of Type I and Type II Errors

The decision matrix used in statistical analyses can be applied to the kinds of decisions people frequently make in everyday life. For example, consider the decision made by a juror in a criminal trial for elder abuse. As is the case with statistics, a decision must be made on the basis of evidence: Is the defendant innocent or guilty? The decision rests with individual jurors and does not necessarily reflect the true state of affairs because we have no way of knowing whether the person really is innocent or guilty of abuse.

The juror's decision matrix is illustrated in Figure 14.6. The easiest way to understand the decision matrix is to identify the null hypothesis first because all statistical inference concerns the null hypothesis. The null hypothesis is that the defendant is innocent (i.e., the person is equivalent to other persons). Next, consider the decision the juror makes—the juror makes a decision about guilt or innocence. Rejecting the null hypothesis means deciding that the defendant is guilty; she has committed elder abuse. Accepting the null hypothesis means

Population

		Null is true (no operation needed)	Null is false (operation needed)
Decision	Reject the null (operate)	Type I Error	Correct Decision
	Accept the null (do not operate)	Correct Decision	Type II Error

Figure 14.7
Decision matrix for
a doctor

deciding that the defendant is innocent; she has not committed elder abuse. These decisions are shown on the left side of the matrix. Finally, look at the top of the matrix. The "true" state of affairs is described here. The defendant may actually be innocent (null hypothesis is true) or guilty (null hypothesis is false).

There are two correct decisions and two kinds of errors. The juror is correct in sending a guilty person to prison and is also correct in setting an innocent person free. The errors are more problematic. A Type I error occurs when the juror finds the defendant guilty when the person is really innocent of elder abuse. In this case the legal system has sent an innocent person to jail. A Type II error occurs when the juror finds the defendant innocent when in fact the person actually committed elder abuse. In this case a guilty person has escaped punishment. In our society Type I errors by jurors are generally considered to be more serious than Type II errors. Thus, before finding someone guilty, the jurors are asked to make sure that the person is guilty "beyond a reasonable doubt" or to consider that "it is better to have a hundred guilty persons go free than to find one innocent person guilty."

The decision that a doctor makes to operate or not operate on a patient provides another illustration of how a decision matrix works. The matrix is shown in Figure 14.7. Here, the null hypothesis is that no operation is necessary (the patient is equivalent to other people). The decision is whether to reject the null hypothesis (the patient is not equivalent to other people) and perform surgery or to accept the null hypothesis and not perform the surgery. In reality the surgeon is faced with two possibilities: Either the surgery is unnecessary (the null hypothesis is true), or the patient will die without the surgery (a dramatic case of the null hypothesis being false). Which error is more serious in this case? Most doctors would believe that not operating on a patient who really needs the operation—making a Type II error—is more serious than making the Type I error of performing surgery on someone who does not really need it.

You might try to construct a decision matrix for other problems. For example, consider the evaluation of a home pregnancy test. Many individuals select such a test to provide a preliminary indication of pregnancy prior to consulting a physician. However, the tests are not 100% accurate. The null hypothesis is that the woman is "not pregnant." A Type I error is an error of rejection—you incorrectly decide that she is pregnant. A Type II error is an error of acceptance—you incorrectly decide that she is not pregnant. Which error is more costly, a Type I error or a Type II error?

Choosing a Significance (Alpha) Level

Researchers traditionally have used either a .05 or a .01 alpha or **significance level** in the decision to reject the null hypothesis. If there is less than a .05 or a .01 probability that the results occurred because of random error, the results are said to be significant. However, there is nothing magical about a .05 or a .01 significance level. The significance level chosen merely specifies the probability of a Type I error if the null hypothesis is rejected. The significance level chosen by the researcher usually is dependent on the consequences of making a Type I versus a Type II error. As previously noted, for a juror, a Type I error is more serious than a Type II error; for a doctor, however, a Type II error may be more serious. Box 14.1 describes a decision faced by an AIDS researcher.

Researchers generally believe that the consequences of making a Type I error are more serious than those associated with a Type II error. If the null hypothesis is rejected, the researcher might publish the results in a journal, and the results might be reported by others in textbooks or in newspaper or magazine articles. Researchers don't want to mislead people or risk damaging their reputations by publishing results that aren't reliable and so cannot be replicated. This problem can be especially serious in applied research because consumers may adopt procedures or recommendations based on reported statistical significance. Thus, researchers want to guard against the possibility of making a Type I error by using a very low significance level (.05 or .01).

Researchers want to be very careful to avoid Type I errors when their results may be published. However, in certain circumstances, a Type I error is not serious. For example, if you were engaged in pilot or exploratory research, your results would be used primarily to decide whether your research ideas were worth pursuing. In this situation, it would be a mistake to overlook potentially important data by using a conservative significance level. In exploratory research, a significance level of .10 may be appropriate for deciding whether to do more research. How the researcher intends to use the results influences both the significance level and the consequences of a Type I or Type II error.

INTERPRETING NONSIGNIFICANT RESULTS

Although "accepting the null hypothesis" is convenient terminology, it is important to recognize that researchers are not generally interested in accepting the null hypothesis. With few exceptions, research is generally designed to show that a relationship between variables exists rather to demonstrate that variables are unrelated. More important, **nonsignificant results** are difficult to interpret. There may be problems associated with (1) the probability of the outcome, (2) the procedure, (3) the alpha level, and (4) the sample size.

First, it isn't possible to specify the probability that you could be wrong in the

BOX 14.1   RESEARCH IN ACTION

Medical Decisions

The director of a study of children infected with the AIDS virus discovered that children receiving monthly doses of immunoglobulin (IG) were significantly healthier than children receiving a placebo. The new treatment could help 20,000 children in the United States infected with the AIDS virus, as well as the 2,000 HIV-infected babies born each year (Toufexis, 1991). The dilemma: How should she inform the medical community of the breakthrough?

Using traditional channels of communication, the results would be published in medical journals such as the *New England Journal of Medicine* or the *Journal of the American Medical Association.* Unfortunately, this publication avenue often creates a delay of more than a year. In that time, patients may lose their lives without the new treatment. Finding a way to get the information to the medical community faster might help patients. Conservative critics contend that time is needed to allow peers to verify the results and evaluate the study thoroughly.

So what should the director do? The decision matrix that appears in this box indicates the consequences of each decision. The null hypothesis is that the IG treatment is ineffective such that children with IG are equivalent to children without IG. If she makes the wrong decision, children may be given a treatment that doesn't work (Type I error), or children may lose their lives if they do not receive the treatment (Type II error). Viewed in this way, the director easily made her decision. The results were released at a press conference and in overnight letters to physicians to alert the medical community to the new treatment.

	Null is really true: IG is an effective treatment	*Null is really false:* IG is not an effective treatment
Director rejects the null hypothesis. She decides that the evidence indicates IG is effective. *Publish now*	Type I error *Outcome:* Children are given an ineffective treatment because of early publication.	Correct decision *Outcome:* Children's lives are saved because of early publication.
Director accepts the null hypothesis. She decides the evidence is not clear enough to publish now, preferring to allow peer review of her study. *Publish later*	Correct decision *Outcome:* No hopes are raised unnecessarily, no wasted effort. Delay publication to allow further study.	Type II error *Outcome:* Children do not receive the treatment because of delayed publication and may lose their battle with AIDS.

decision to accept the null hypothesis. Second, a single study might not show significant results even when a relationship between the variables in the population does exist. For example, a researcher might fail to uncover a reliable difference by providing unclear instructions to the participants, by having a very weak manipulation of the independent variable, or by using a dependent measure that is unreliable and insensitive. When nonsignificant results are obtained, the researcher must reexamine all aspects of the procedure to try to discover if something went wrong in the design and execution of the study.

Third, nonsignificant results may also be produced by being very cautious in choosing the alpha level. If the researcher uses a significance level of .001 in deciding whether to reject the null hypothesis, there isn't much chance of a Type I error. However, a Type II error is possible because the researcher has decreased the chances of wrongly rejecting the null hypothesis. In other words, a meaningful result is more likely to be overlooked when the significance level is very low.

Fourth, a small sample size might also cause a researcher to wrongly accept the null hypothesis. A general principle is that the larger the sample size the greater the likelihood of obtaining significant results. This is because large sample sizes give more accurate estimates of the actual population than do small sample sizes. In any given study, the sample size may be too small to permit detection of a significant result.

This is not meant to imply that researchers should always use huge samples. A very large sample size (for example, 200 participants in each group) might enable the researcher to find a significant difference between means. However, this difference, even though statistically significant, might have very little *practical significance*. For example, if an expensive new hair loss treatment significantly reduces average hair loss in men with "male pattern baldness" by 1%, it might not be practical to use the technique despite the evidence for its effectiveness. In such cases there can be a statistically significant effect, but the effect size will be very small.

The key point is that nonsignificant results do not necessarily indicate that the null hypothesis is correct. Nonsignificant results are very much like the legal verdict of "not guilty" in a criminal trial. We do not know if the defendant is actually innocent or if the defendant is guilty, but the prosecution presented a poor case. Not finding significant results is not the same as establishing that an effect does not exist. When you fail to obtain significant results, further evidence is needed. The research project should be conducted again with refined procedures. Perhaps a larger sample of participants should be tested in a follow-up study. If evidence from repeated studies shows no relationship between the variables of interest, then the researcher may be more willing to accept the hypothesis that no relationship exists. Box 14.2 describes an $80 million community health project, the Fort Bragg study, that failed to yield significant results, raising many questions about the research design.

QUANTITATIVE VERSUS QUALITATIVE RESULTS

The discussion in this chapter focuses on quantitative data—numerical values that represent the participants' behavior. Data from research such as naturalistic

BOX 14.2   RESEARCH IN ACTION

The Fort Bragg Demonstration Project

In an effort to determine the cost and effectiveness of mental health systems for children and adolescents, the Fort Bragg Demonstration Project was launched in 1990 for the 42,000 child and adolescent dependents of military personnel at Fort Bragg, North Carolina. Five years and $80 million later, data analysis supports the null hypothesis: There is no significant difference in outcome between the two health care approaches. Needless to say, a great deal of attention has been devoted to examining reasons for the absence of a difference. Mental health professionals who favor managed health care are a bit unwilling to say that a very expensive comprehensive approach to mental health care is no more effective than the fragmented services provided by independent community professionals.

Possible reasons for the null effects have been proposed by Bickman (1996) and Sechrest and Walsh (1997). The program was implemented properly, the independent and dependent variables were carefully defined, data analysis techniques were sufficiently powerful to detect significant differences, and the population served by the demonstration project did not differ from any other population of families with children. By examining issues related to internal validity, construct validity, statistical conclusion validity, and external validity, the unavoidable conclusion is that the experimental mental health care program is ineffective and should not be implemented at other locations. In this era of managed health care, such null findings highlight the need for applied community research by the health care industry before implementing large-scale changes in health care.

observation, surveys, and interviews may be coded into quantitative categories to allow comparison of percentages for a set of variables. By coding the data in this way, inferential statistics can be used to evaluate the results. Coding may also be used to identify categories for qualitative interpretation, not to count the frequency of behaviors. Much qualitative data in the form of field notes or in-depth interviews are not easily adapted to quantitative coding and statistical inference. As a result, qualitative researchers cannot extend their results from a sample to a population. However, that does not present much of a problem because qualitative research is not intended to describe the larger population. Researchers rely on qualitative approaches to provide detailed descriptions of the individual context; thus, inferential statistics are not needed to achieve the research goal.

SUMMARY

Understanding research outcomes is important for researchers and consumers of research findings. Both descriptive and inferential analyses are used. Frequency distributions of the data depicted in a frequency polygon or a histogram help you gain an impression of the data. Descriptive statistics allow researchers to summarize information about the data. Measures of central tendency such as the mean, median, and mode describe how subjects scored overall. Measures of variability such as the standard deviation, variance, and range describe the distribution of the scores around the mean.

Because the data collected in studies are based on a sample of people drawn from a larger population, inferential statistics are needed to inform the researcher about the likelihood of a particular outcome occurring on an entire population. Inferential statistics allow the researcher to infer, on the basis of the sample data, that observed differences are reliable and hold true for the more general population.

Statistical inference begins with hypothesis testing procedures. There are two kinds of hypotheses: A null hypothesis states that the population means are equal; a research hypothesis states that the population means are different. Statistical analysis allows us to test the null hypothesis, determine a probability associated with its occurrence, and reject the null hypothesis if the outcome is statistically significant.

Because inferential statistics are based on probability, researchers can make mistakes when deciding to reject or accept the null hypothesis. A Type I error is made when we incorrectly reject the null hypothesis when, in fact, the null hypothesis is true. A Type II error occurs when we incorrectly accept the null hypothesis when, in fact, the null hypothesis is false. In experimental research, a Type I error is typically viewed as more serious than a Type II error because the researcher wants a high degree of confidence that the differences observed are not due to chance. The significance level selected by the researcher indicates the number of times out of 100 that the researcher will make a Type I error and incorrectly reject the null hypothesis. With a .05 significance level, 5 Type I errors will be made out of 100; this level of imprecision is considered acceptable for most research purposes.

If significant differences are not found for an independent variable, the researcher may wish to accept the null hypothesis that the groups do not actually differ. However, accepting the null hypothesis should only be done after repeated failures to observe a systematic difference with well-designed and carefully controlled research investigations.

KEY TERMS

alpha level	median	significance level
central tendency	mode	standard deviation
descriptive statistics	nonsignificant results	statistical significance
frequency distribution	null hypothesis	(significant result)
frequency polygon	probability	Type I error
histogram (bar graph)	range	Type II error
inferential statistics	research hypothesis	variability
mean	sampling distribution	variance

REVIEW QUESTIONS

1. What is a frequency distribution?

2. Distinguish a frequency polygon from a histogram. Be able to construct both types of graphs.

3. What is a measure of central tendency? Distinguish between the mean, median, and mode.

4. What is a measure of variability? Define the standard deviation and the range.

5. Why are inferential statistics necessary?

6. When does the researcher decide to reject the null hypothesis?

7. What is meant by statistical significance?

8. Distinguish between Type I and Type II errors. How does your significance level affect the probability of making a Type I error?

9. Suppose that you work for the child social services agency in your county. Your job is to investigate instances of possible child neglect or abuse. After collecting evidence from a variety of sources, you must decide whether to leave the child in the home or place the child in protective custody. Specify the null hypothesis and the research hypothesis. Draw a decision matrix for this example. What constitutes a Type I and Type II error? Is a Type I or Type II error more serious in this situation?

10. Discuss some reasons a researcher might fail to detect significant differences or relationships.

CHAPTER 15

Statistics

Different statistical tests allow us to use probability to decide whether to reject the null hypothesis. In this chapter we will examine the *t* test, the *F* test, and correlational techniques. The *t* **test** is used to examine whether two groups are significantly different from each other. In the hypothetical experiment on sports participation from the last chapter, a *t* test is appropriate because we are asking whether the mean of the intramural group differs from the mean of the aerobics group. The *F* test is a more general statistical test that can be used to ask whether there is a difference among three or more groups, or to evaluate the results of factorial designs (discussed in Chapter 12). Correlation coefficients assess the strength of the relationship between two variables. A summary of some of the statistical tests developed for the more common research designs is provided at the end of this chapter. Appendix B describes the calculation of many of these statistics.

To use a statistical test, you must first specify the null hypothesis and the research hypothesis that you are evaluating. In Chapter 14 we specified the null and research hypotheses for the sports participation experiment. You must also specify the significance level that you will use to decide whether to reject the null hypothesis. As noted, researchers generally use a significance level of .05.

THE *t* TEST

A value of *t* is calculated from the obtained data and evaluated in terms of the sampling distribution of *t*, which is based on the null hypothesis. If the obtained *t* has a low probability of occurrence (.05 or less), then the null hypothesis is rejected, and the results are significant. The *t* value is a ratio of two aspects of the data—the difference between the group means and the variability within groups. The ratio may be described as follows:

$$t = \frac{\text{Between group difference}}{\text{Within group variability}}$$

The between group difference is simply the difference between your obtained means. Under the null hypothesis, you expect this value to be zero because the null hypothesis states that the groups are equal. The value of t increases as the difference between your sample means increases. The greater the t value that is obtained (i.e., the larger the between group difference relative to within group variability), the greater the likelihood that the results will be significant.

The within group variability is the amount of variability of scores about the mean. The denominator of the t formula is essentially an indicator of the amount of random error in your sample. Recall from Chapter 14 that s (the standard deviation) and s^2 (the variance) are indicators of how much scores deviate from the group mean. The logic of the t test is that the difference in the group means reflects the effect of the independent variable on the dependent variable. In contrast, the within group variability cannot be accounted for directly and is referred to as "error" in the sense that we don't know why individuals within each group differ in their responses to the independent variable.

A concrete example of a calculation of a t test should help clarify these concepts. The formula for the t test for two groups with equal (or nearly equal) numbers of participants in each group is

$$t = \frac{\overline{X}_1 - \overline{X}_2}{\sqrt{\dfrac{s_1^2}{N_1} + \dfrac{s_2^2}{N_2}}}$$

The numerator of the formula is simply the difference between the means of the two groups. In the denominator, we first divide the variance (s^2) of each group by the number of subjects in the group and add these together (N_1 = number in first group, N_2 = number in second group). We then find the square root of the result. This yields an estimate of the overall amount of variability within the groups.

When this formula is applied to the data from the sports participation example in Table 14.1, we find:

$$t = \frac{5.2 - 3.1}{\sqrt{\dfrac{1.289}{10} + \dfrac{1.433}{10}}}$$

$$= \frac{2.1}{\sqrt{.1289 + .1433}}$$

$$= 4.025$$

Thus, the t value calculated from the data is 4.025. Try the calculation yourself. If you do not get the same answer, be sure that you do the calculations in the correct order. Small variations are generally attributable to rounding errors.

In a scientific paper, this statistic would be reported in the following form:

$$t(18) = 4.02, p < .05$$

Is this a significant result? A computer program analyzing the results would immediately tell you the probability of obtaining a t value of this size with a total sample size of 20. Without such a program, however, you can refer to a table of

BOX 15.1   RESEARCH IN ACTION

Happiness in Elderly Citizens

Kehn (1995) examined the impact of variables such as living arrangements and independence on the overall happiness of 98 elderly citizens living in the community. Using a survey, Kehn obtained self-report measures of happiness, living arrangements, marital status, use of transportation, and other demographics such as number of children and grandchildren. Kehn used *t* tests to evaluate the happiness scores (ranging from 1 = very low, to 5 = very high).

Married adults ($M = 3.98$) were significantly happier than unmarried adults ($M = 3.45$), $t(96) = 3.36$, $p < .01$. In addition, adults living alone ($M = 3.63$) were happier than adults living with their children ($M = 3.19$), $t(73) = 2.015$, $p < .05$. Elderly adults prefer not to live with their children, possibly due to lack of privacy and loss of independence. The elderly who depend on others for transportation for their errands were not as happy ($M = 3.29$) as those who maintain independence by driving, walking, or using public transportation ($M = 3.75$), $t(96) = 2.186$, $p < .05$.

The *t* test is the appropriate statistic for these analyses because the happiness dependent variable is measured on an interval scale, and the two comparison groups were independent (see Table 15.2). You should be able to decode important features of the statistical phrases. For example, did you notice that all 98 participants were not included in the comparison of adults living alone and living with their children? The degrees of freedom is different here because some adults lived with their spouses. The significance levels also differed, as indicated by $p < .01$ and $p < .05$. Which one shows a lower probability of occurring by chance?

"critical values" of *t,* such as Table C.3 in Appendix C. We will discuss the use of the appendix tables in detail in Appendix B. Before going any further, you should know that the obtained result is significant. Using a significance level of .05, the critical value from the sampling distribution of *t* is 2.101. Any *t* value greater than or equal to 2.101 has a .05 or less probability of occurring under the assumptions of the null hypothesis. Because our obtained value is larger than the critical value, we can reject the null hypothesis and conclude that the difference in means obtained in the sample reflects a true difference in the population. An example of research that used the *t* test to analyze the results is described in Box 15.1.

Statistical Phrases

Let's take a closer look at the **statistical phrase** $t(18) = 4.02$, $p < .05$. You have seen many such phrases in results sections of journal articles. Once you know what the elements in the phrase are, reading the results becomes much easier. You do not need to know how to calculate all the different statistics that you read about, but it does help to know what all those symbols and numbers represent. All statistical phrases have the same basic structure, consisting of the following four components: (1) the statistic, (2) degrees of freedom, (3) the obtained value of the statistic, and (4) the significance level.

$$ t \quad (18) \quad = \quad 4.02 \quad p < .05 $$

Symbol for statistic	Degrees of freedom		Obtained value of statistic	Significance level

The first symbol represents the statistic; in this case the t test is represented by a lowercase t. Later in the chapter we will look at the analysis of variance, which is represented by a capital F. The correlation coefficient is represented by a lower-case r. There are many different symbols (e.g., χ^2 for Chi-square), but in all cases they represent the statistic the researcher used for that particular analysis. We will look at other statistics later in the chapter.

The second entry in the statistical phrase, the number in parentheses, is the **degrees of freedom** for the statistical test. Degrees of freedom (df) are related to sample size. When comparing two means, the degrees of freedom are equal to $N_1 + N_2 - 2$, or the total number of participants in the groups minus the number of groups. In our experiment, the degrees of freedom would be $10 + 10 - 2 = 18$. The degrees of freedom are the number of scores free to vary once the means are known. To illustrate the concept, imagine we have three numbers that add up to 10. The first number is 2; the second number is 4. What is the third number? The third value cannot vary; once the first two are determined, the final number is fixed. So in this set of three values only two are free to vary. Degrees of freedom depend on the number of participants or the number of data values. Determining degrees of freedom for each statistic is explained further in Appendix B. To help you understand statistical results, you need to know that the number in parentheses represents the degrees of freedom. A larger df indicates a large sample size; a smaller df indicates a small sample size.

The third entry in the statistical phrase is the obtained value of the statistic. This value is calculated from the data in the experiment. Researchers report their statistical values so readers can evaluate the results more fully.

The final entry in the statistical phrase is the significance level. As discussed earlier, a computer program analyzing the results would automatically calculate the p level for you. Some journal articles publish exact probabilities for a finding, such as $p = .03$ or $p = .62$. The p level can be very informative. For example, p values that are almost significant (between .05 and .10) may suggest something of theoretical interest to the reader. Significant effects are indicated by small p values (e.g., $p < .01$ or $p < .001$). Values that fail to reach traditional significance levels use the greater than symbol (e.g., $p > .10$). This means that the probability that the results are due to chance alone is *more* than 10 times out of 100. If the results could be due to chance that often, researchers do not consider the findings significant.

ANALYSIS OF VARIANCE: THE F STATISTIC

The **analysis of variance,** or F **test,** is an extension of the t test. The analysis of variance is a more general statistical procedure than the t test. When a study has only one independent variable with two groups, F and t are virtually identical—

the value of F equals t^2 in this situation. However, analysis of variance is also used when there are more than two levels of an independent variable and when a factorial design with two or more independent variables has been used. Thus, the F test is appropriate for the simplest experimental design, as well as for the more complex designs discussed in Chapter 12.

The F statistic is a ratio of two types of variance (hence the term *analysis of variance*). **Systematic variance** is the deviation of the group means from the grand mean, which is the mean score of all subjects in all groups. Systematic variance is small when the difference between group means is small and increases as the group mean differences increase. Systematic variance is analogous to the "between group difference" in the numerator of the t test. Another term for systematic variance is *between group variance*. **Error variance** is the deviation of the individual scores in each group from their respective group means. Error variance is analogous to the "error" term in the denominator of the t test and is called *within group variance*. Thus, the F ratio is conceptually similar to the t test, consisting of a ratio of between group differences to within group variability.

$$F = \frac{\text{Systematic variance}}{\text{Error variance}} = \frac{\text{Between group variance}}{\text{Within group variance}}$$

As you may recall from our discussion of complex designs in Chapter 12, when 2 × 2 factorial designs are used, three effects must be explained: main effect of independent variable A, main effect of independent variable B, and the A × B interaction effect. When a 2 × 2 design is analyzed, the analysis of variance has three F values, one for each effect in the factorial design. Now you need three of everything in your statistical arsenal: three null hypotheses, three obtained values of F, three decisions about significance, and three statistical phrases to report the effects. You can see that the analysis of variance is more complex than the t test, although the logic is identical.

To illustrate, we can extend our sports participation study to include a gender comparison by adding a group of 20 boys who also participate in intramural sports or aerobic exercise after school. This expands the design from a comparison of two groups to a 2 × 2 factorial design with between subjects factors of type of activity

Table 15.1   Sports Participation Study With a Gender Comparison

Mean Number of Discipline Referrals			
	Gender		
Type of activity	Girls	Boys	Mean
Intramurals	3.10	4.10	3.60
Aerobics	5.20	8.00	6.60
Mean	4.15	6.05	

Analysis of Variance Summary Table			
Source	df	MS	F ratio
Gender	1	90.000	65.59
Activity	1	36.100	26.31
Gender × Activity	1	8.100	5.90
Error	36	1.372	
$p < .05$			

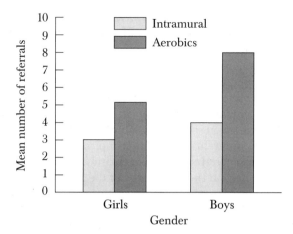

Figure 15.1
Gender × activity
interaction

(intramural, aerobics) and gender (male, female). This design will have three effects: (1) a main effect of type of activity, (2) a main effect of gender, and (3) an interaction between activity and gender. The upper portion of Table 15.1 presents the descriptive statistics for the four groups; the lower portion presents the F ratios associated with each of the effects in a 2×2 design. Looking first at the marginal means, it appears that boys ($M = 6.05$) had more discipline referrals than girls ($M = 4.15$). The intramurals group ($M = 3.60$) had fewer referrals than the aerobics group ($M = 6.60$). An interaction is indicated because the difference between the activity conditions is larger for boys (4.10 vs. 8.00) than for girls (3.10 vs. 5.20). This can be confirmed by drawing a figure of the results, such as Figure 15.1.

The F statistics in the lower portion of the table allow us to verify our impressions of the results based on descriptive statistics. Similar to the t test, the F test must exceed a critical value to be significant. For this example, with a probability level of .05, the critical F value is 4.08. Each of the obtained F values calculated on our data exceed this critical value, which indicates that the main effects and the interaction effect are all significant. Thus, we can reject the corresponding null hypotheses for the three effects. In a scientific paper, the F statistic for the Gender × Activity interaction would be reported in the following form: $F(1, 36) = 5.90, p < .05$.

The analysis of variance summary table in the lower panel of Table 15.1 includes columns of information labeled df (degrees of freedom) and MS (mean square). There are degrees of freedom associated with each effect in the model as well as with the error term. The mean square for the main effect of gender, activity, and the interaction is the estimate of the systematic variance for each effect. The mean square for "error" estimates the error variance from the study. Recall that the F statistic is a ratio of two variances, systematic variance/error variance. Thus, you can compute the F statistic by dividing the estimate of systematic variance by error variance. You might try it to see how simple the logic of analysis of variance really is. The calculation of the mean square is a bit more complex; formulas are provided in Appendix B.

The degrees of freedom listed in the table are useful to locate the critical value for a significant F ratio. Notice there are two degrees of freedom for the F statistic, one for the numerator and one for the denominator. Because sample size influences the detection of significant differences, it is harder to obtain significant F values with small samples. This means that you need a larger F ratio to reject the null hypothesis when small samples are used. Further information on analysis of variance is given in Appendix B, and Appendix C.4 lists critical values of F.

CORRELATION COEFFICIENT

A correlation coefficient is a statistic that describes how strongly variables are related to one another. As mentioned in Chapter 4, the values of a correlation coefficient can range from -1.00 to $+1.00$. The plus and minus signs indicate whether there is a positive or negative linear relationship between the variables. The absolute size of r (ignoring the sign) indicates the strength of the relationship: The nearer r is to 1.00 (plus or minus), the stronger the relationship (positive or negative). A correlation of 0.00 indicates that there is no relationship at all. A 1.00 correlation is sometimes called a perfect relationship, because the two variables go together in a perfect fashion. In research, however, perfect relationships are extremely rare.

Data from studies examining similarities of intelligence test scores among siblings illustrate the connection between the magnitude of a correlation coefficient and the strength of a relationship. The relationship between IQ scores of identical twins is very strong (correlation of .86), demonstrating a strong similarity of test scores in these pairs of individuals. The correlation for fraternal twins is less strong, with a value of .60. The correlation among nontwin siblings raised together is .47, and the correlation among nontwin siblings reared apart is .24 (cf. Bouchard & McGue, 1981).

There are many different types of correlation coefficients. Each coefficient is calculated somewhat differently depending on the measurement scale that applies to the two variables. We will focus on the Pearson product-moment correlation coefficient, which is symbolized by r.

Indexing the Strength of a Relationship

The **Pearson r correlation coefficient** is appropriate when the values of both variables are on an interval or ratio scale. A correlation coefficient begins with a pair of scores from each participant. Thus, each individual has two scores, one for each of the variables. Table 15.2 shows fictitious data for 10 elderly adults (age 70+) who were measured on two variables, happiness and health. Happiness scores ranged from 0 (very low) to 5 (very high) on a self-report happiness index. An overall rating of health, ranging from 0 to 100, was obtained from each adult's primary care physician. Using a correlation coefficient, we can address the research question: Are health and happiness related to one another? Do the variables go together in a systematic fashion?

Using the mathematical formula for the Pearson r described in Appendix B, we can calculate the value of r. The correlation for the data in Table 15.2 is .881, indicating a strong, positive relationship. This means that for elderly adults, higher ratings of happiness are associated with higher ratings of health.

Table 15.2 Pairs of Scores for 10 Participants on Ratings of Happiness and Health (Fictitious Data)

ID Number	Happiness Rating	Health Score
01	2	75
02	5	90
03	1	50
04	4	95
05	3	75
06	5	85
07	2	70
08	3	70
09	1	60
10	4	80

Graphing Correlations With Scatterplots

The data in Table 15.2 can be visualized in a **scatterplot** in which each pair of scores is plotted as a single point in a diagram. A correlation represents the relationship between two dependent measures; one variable is placed on the horizontal axis and the other variable on the vertical axis. Then each pair of scores is plotted. Figure 15.2 shows scatterplots for a perfect positive relationship $(+1.00)$ and a perfect negative relationship (-1.00). You can easily see why these relationships are perfect: The scores on the two variables fall on a straight line that is on the diagonal of the diagram. Each person's score on one variable goes perfectly with his or her score on the other variable. If we know an individual's score on one of the variables, we can predict exactly what his or her score will be on the other variable.

The scatterplots in Figure 15.3 show patterns of correlations you are more likely to encounter in exploring research findings. The first diagram shows pairs of scores with a positive correlation of $+.65$; the second diagram shows a negative relationship, $-.77$. The data points in these two scatterplots reveal a general pattern of either a positive or negative relationship, but there is scatter (variability) in the scores. You can make a general prediction in the first diagram that the

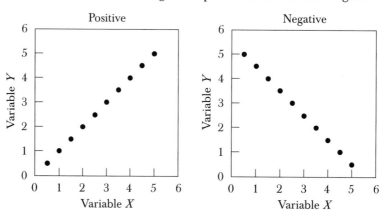

Figure 15.2
Scatterplots of perfect (±1.00) relationships

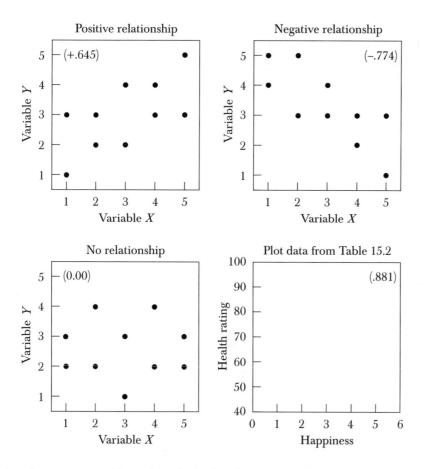

Figure 15.3
Scatterplots
depicting patterns
of correlation

higher the score on one variable, the higher the score will be on the second variable. To confirm this, take a look at value 1 on variable X (the horizontal axis) in the positive scatterplot. Looking up, you will see that two individuals had a score of 1. One of these had a score of 1 on variable Y (the vertical axis), and the other had a score of 3. The data points do not fall on the perfect diagonal. This variability represents scatter from the straight line illustrated in Figure 15.2.

The third diagram shows a scatterplot in which there is absolutely no correlation ($r = 0.00$). The points fall all over the diagram in a completely random pattern. Thus, scores on variable X are not related to scores on variable Y.

The fourth diagram has been left blank so that you can plot the scores from the data in Table 15.2. The horizontal X axis has been labeled for the happiness variable, and the vertical Y axis has been labeled for the health variable. To complete the scatterplot, plot the scores for each of the 10 participants. Find the score on the happiness variable, then go up until you reach that person's health score. A point placed there will describe the score on both variables. There will be 10 points on the finished scatterplot, one for each pair of scores.

Using the mathematical formula for the Pearson r described in Appendix B, the correlation coefficient calculated from these data shows that there was a positive relationship between happiness and health, $r = .88$. In other words, elderly adults who reported lower levels of happiness have poorer health. As happiness increases, so does health. Higher levels of happiness are associated with better health. Knowing about someone's feelings of happiness tells us something about their health. Although these data are fictitious, they are consistent with actual research findings (Kehn, 1995).

INTERPRETING CORRELATIONS

Interpreting a correlation begins by examining the size of the correlation—is it small, medium, or large? The sign, positive or negative, indicates if you have a positive linear relationship or a negative linear relationship. Other important considerations are: (1) restriction of the range, (2) curvilinear relationships, (3) significance of a correlation, and (4) the third variable problem.

Restriction of the Range

It is important that the researcher sample from the full range of possible values of both variables. If the range of possible values is restricted, the magnitude of the correlation coefficient is reduced. For example, if the range of health status is restricted to adults who report minimal health problems, you will not get an accurate picture of the relationship between happiness and health. The reason for needing a full range of values is the same as the reason for needing a strong manipulation when conducting an experiment (see Chapter 10). In both cases, it is easier to detect a relationship when low and high values of the variable are represented.

The problem of **restriction of the range** occurs when the individuals in your sample are very similar or homogeneous. If you are studying age as a variable, for instance, testing only 6- and 7-year-olds will reduce your chances of finding age effects. Likewise, trying to study the correlates of intelligence will be almost impossible if everyone in your sample is very similar in intelligence (e.g., the senior class of a prestigious private college).

Curvilinear Relationships

The Pearson product-moment correlation coefficient r is designed to detect only linear relationships. If the relationship is curvilinear, as in the scatterplot shown in Figure 15.4, the correlation coefficient will not indicate the existence of a relationship. The correlation coefficient calculated from the data in the figure shows $r = 0.00$, although it is clear that the two variables are in fact related.

When the relationship is curvilinear, other statistics are necessary to determine the strength of the relationship. Because a relationship may be curvilinear, it is important to construct a scatterplot in addition to looking at the magnitude of the correlation coefficient. The scatterplot is valuable because it gives a visual indication of the shape of the relationship. Scatterplots can be generated by most computer programs for statistical analysis.

Significance of a Correlation Coefficient

The Pearson r correlation coefficient is a descriptive statistic, providing information about the strength of the relationship between two variables. However, there

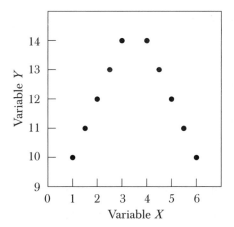

Figure 15.4
Scatterplot of a
curvilinear relation-
ship ($r = 0.00$)

remains the issue of whether the correlation is statistically significant. As with the inferential statistics t and F, a Pearson r can be subjected to a formal hypothesis test to determine significance. In this case, the null hypothesis is that the variables are not correlated, $r = 0.00$. The procedures for calculating a Pearson r and determining significance are provided in Appendix B. The correlation based on our hypothetical happiness–health data would be considered highly significant, $r(8) = .881$, $p < .01$. Notice that correlations are also reported using statistical phrases, including the same elements as previously described. The number in parentheses is the degrees of freedom. For a correlation df is defined as $N - 2$, the number of pairs of scores minus 2.

Correlations are often presented in a correlation matrix such as the one shown in Table 15.3. The data are based on a collaborative study investigating the relationship between aspects of the child's home environment and cognitive development in the first three years (Bradley et al., 1989). The dependent measures are listed down the left side of the matrix: (1) mother's education, (2) socioeconomic status (SES), (3) score on the HOME inventory at age 12 months (the HOME inventory assesses the quality of stimulation in the home), and (4) IQ at age 36 months. Although the matrix may look confusing, it is really just a condensed way to present multiple correlation coefficients. In the Bradley et al. study their table actually included eight variables; much larger correlation matrices are very common.

To interpret this information, you need to know what the elements in the matrix represent. The numbers across the top row represent each of the variables listed in the left column. The first value in the table (.69) is the correlation between mother's education and variable 2, socioeconomic status. The next value (.46) is the correlation between mother's education and variable 3, HOME score at age 12 months. Notice there are no values on the diagonal. The value that would go in the first position is the correlation between mother's education and mother's education. How strongly are these two variables related—perfectly, of course. This is not meaningful information and is omitted from the matrix. Also, the lower quadrant is omitted because it would duplicate information in the upper quadrant above the diagonal. All of these correlation coefficients are significant, $p < .05$.

Table 15.3   Correlation Matrix

Variable	1	2	3	4
1. Mother's education	—	.69	.46	.49
2. SES		—	.52	.47
3. HOME (12 months)			—	.53
4. IQ (36 months)				—

NOTE: *N*s vary from 366 to 785. SES = socioeconomic status; HOME = Home Observation for Measurements of the Environment Inventory. All correlations are significant at the .05 level. SOURCE: Based on Bradley et al., 1989.

Spurious Correlations and the Third Variable Problem

Recall that a correlation does not identify causality; a correlation only indicates that two variables are related. Thus, we can say that happiness and health are related, yet we have not identified a causal relationship. We cannot say that better health causes happiness; nor can we say that happiness causes people to be healthy. As discussed in Chapter 5, the observed relationship may actually be caused by a third variable. For example, it is possible that a third variable such as activity level is actually responsible for both happiness and health. Adults who are more active may be happier as well as healthier; thus, their activity level may actually be causing both of the variables we measured in our hypothetical study.

PARTIAL CORRELATION AND THE THIRD VARIABLE PROBLEM

Researchers face the third variable problem in correlational research when some uncontrolled third variable may be responsible for the relationship between the two variables of interest. The problem doesn't exist in experimental research because extraneous variables are controlled either by keeping the variables constant or by using randomization. A technique called **partial correlation** provides a way of statistically controlling third variables. A partial correlation is a correlation between the two variables of interest, with the influence of the third variable removed from, or "partialed out" of, the original correlation.

Suppose a researcher finds that the correlation between residential crowding and school grades among elementary schoolchildren is −.50 (the greater the crowding, the lower the grades in school). One potential third variable that may be operating is social class, which may be responsible for both crowding and school grades. The use of partial correlations involves measuring participants on

Figure 15.5
Two partial correlations between crowding and school grades

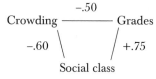

Partial correlation between crowding and school grades is −.09

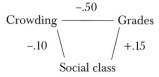

Partial correlation between crowding and school grades is −.49

the third variable in addition to the two primary variables. Thus, the researcher has to conceptualize possible third variables in advance and measure participants on all the variables—crowding, school grades, and social class.

When a partial correlation between crowding and school grades is calculated, with social class removed from the relationship, we can determine whether the original correlation is substantially reduced. Is our original correlation of −.50 lowered very much when the influence of social class is removed? If it is, this means that social class did contribute to the relationship, acting as a third variable. Figure 15.5 shows two different partial correlations. In both, there is a −.50 correlation between crowding and grades. However, the first partial correlation between crowding and school grades drops to −.09 when social class is statistically controlled, suggesting that social class accounts for a large portion of the observed relationship. In the second example, the partial correlation between crowding and school grades remains high (−.49) even when the influence of social class is removed. This indicates that social class does not affect the relationship between crowding and school grades. The outcome of the partial correlation depends on the magnitude of the correlations between the third variable and the two variables of primary interest.

In research articles you may read about partial correlations, particularly to remove the effect of social class. An example is a study comparing cognitive and motor abilities of male preschoolers with alcoholic fathers (COA, children of alcoholics) to a control group recruited from the community (Noll, Zucker, Fitzgerald, & Curtis, 1992). Despite rigorous attempts to match the comparison group on social class, the families were not equivalent on socioeconomic status. Initial comparisons between the groups of young boys indicated that the COA were significantly delayed in developmental functioning, fine motor skills, and personal and social skills. However, after adjusting for differences in social class and the home environment, only one significant difference remained. It turns out that COA differ from the control boys only in delayed personal and social skills. This is an important modification of the first analysis and demonstrates the important relationship between socioeconomic status and early child development.

CORRELATION COEFFICIENTS AND THE CORRELATIONAL METHOD

There is a very confusing aspect of the term *correlation* as it has been used over many years by researchers in the behavioral sciences. We have reviewed the distinction between the experimental and correlational methods of studying relationships among variables (see Chapter 5). We have seen that a correlation coefficient functions as an index of the strength of relationships between variables. One might expect that researchers use correlation coefficients only in conjunction with the correlational method, because the term *correlation* is common to both. However, this is not correct. The term *correlational method* refers to a nonexperimental study, whereas *correlation coefficient* refers to an index of the strength of the relationship between two variables irrespective of whether the experimental or correlational method was used.

This confusion arises because historically the results of most studies using the correlational method have been analyzed using Pearson r correlation coefficients. However, researchers have become aware that correlation coefficients should always be used as an index of strength of relationships in both correlational and experimental research. The result is that more and more researchers are reporting correlation coefficients in both correlational and experimental research. The term *effect size* increasingly is being used to refer to all such correlation coefficients.

EFFECT SIZE

Effect size refers to the magnitude of the association between variables. Findings of an experiment can be statistically significant yet represent an effect of very little strength. Use of this term eliminates some of the confusion over the terms *correlation* and *correlational method*. The Pearson r correlation coefficient is one indicator of effect size; it indicates the strength of the linear association between two variables. In an experiment with two or more treatment conditions, some other types of correlation coefficients can be calculated to indicate the magnitude of the effect of the independent variable on the dependent variable. For example, in our experiment on the effects of sports participation on discipline referrals, we compared the means of two groups. In addition to knowing the means, it is valuable to know the effect size. An effect size correlation coefficient can be calculated for the sports participation and discipline referrals study. The effect size value is .68. The formula for calculating the effect size for a t test is:

$$\text{Effect size } r = \sqrt{\frac{t^2}{t^2 + df}}$$

Thus, using the obtained value for t from our example ($t = 4.023$) and 18 degrees of freedom, we find

$$\text{Effect size } r = \sqrt{\frac{(4.025)^2}{(4.025)^2 + 18}} = \sqrt{\frac{16.201}{34.201}} = .688$$

An increasing number of researchers are reporting effect size in the results section; you can interpret effect size the same way you interpret other correlation coefficients. The advantage of reporting effect size is that it provides us with a scale of values that is consistent across all types of studies. The values range from 0.00 to 1.00, irrespective of the variables used, the particular research design selected, or the number of participants studied. In addition, effect size provides valuable information that is not available from inferential statistics. For additional information on effect size, see Rosenthal (1991).

ADVANCED CORRELATIONAL TECHNIQUES

More sophisticated statistical tools that rely on correlations include: (1) regression equations, (2) multiple correlation, and (3) structural equation models.

Regression Equations

It is often useful to predict a person's future behavior or performance on the basis of some currently available indicator. This rationale is used in developing tests to determine whether to admit a student to college, whether a child should be enrolled in honors classes in school, or even whether a couple should reconsider a decision to get married.

Regression equations are used to predict a person's score on one variable when that person's score on another variable is already known. They are essentially "prediction equations" that are based on known information about the relationship between the two variables. For example, after discovering that happiness and health are related, a regression equation may be calculated that predicts someone's health based only on information about their happiness.

The general form of a regression equation is:

$$Y = a + bX$$

where Y is the score we wish to predict, X is the known score, a is a constant, and b is a weighting adjustment factor that is multiplied by X (the weight is necessary because X and Y are measured on different scales). In our happiness–health example, the folllowing regression equation is calculated from the data:

$$Y = 99 + (-8)X$$

Thus, if a person scores 2 on the happiness measure (X), we can insert that into the equation and predict that $Y = 99 + (-16)$, or that the health score will be 83. Through the use of regression equations such as these, colleges can use SAT scores to predict college grades.

When researchers or practitioners are interested in predicting some future behavior (called the **criterion variable**) on the basis of a person's score on some other variable (called the **predictor variable**), it is first necessary to demonstrate that there is a reasonably high correlation between the criterion and predictor variables in a sample of individuals. Research is conducted to formulate a regression equation from one sample of participants, and then the equation can be utilized to make predictions about other individuals. Children at high risk for various developmental or school problems can be identified at a young age if we know that a relationship exists between two variables. For example, students who do not complete high school tend to be older than their classmates (due to grade retention, perhaps) and also tend to be aggressive (Cairns, Cairns, & Neckerman, 1989). Our criterion variable is school dropout. Adolescents at risk for school dropout can be identified by examining a predictor variable such as their chronological age. In this way, predictions can identify students in need of redirection toward school completion.

Multiple Correlation

So far we have focused on the correlation between two variables at a time. Researchers recognize that a number of different variables may be related to a given behavior. A technique called **multiple correlation** is used to combine a number of predictor variables to increase the accuracy of prediction of a given criterion variable.

A multiple correlation is the correlation between a combined set of predictor variables and a single criterion variable. Taking all of the predictor variables into account usually permits greater accuracy of prediction than if any single predictor is considered alone. Thus, in our school dropout example, we can use both chronological age and aggression as predictors of early school dropout. Other risk factors associated with school dropout include GPA, extracurricular involvement, socioeconomic status, and popularity (Mahoney & Cairns, 1997). A combination of these variables can yield a more accurate prediction of students at risk for early dropout. The multiple correlation is usually higher than the correlation between any one of the predictor variables and the criterion variable.

The multiple correlation coefficient is symbolized as R, and it can range from 0.00 to $+1.00$. Larger values of R indicate greater accuracy of predicting the criterion variable from the predictor variables.

Structural Equation Models

Recent advances in statistical theory and methods have resulted in techniques for testing structural equation models (SEM) of relationships among variables using the correlational method. Although these methods are beyond the scope of this book, you should be aware that they exist because of their increasing prominence in reports of developmental data. A good introduction to SEM is provided by Biddle and Marlin (1987). A **structural model** is a theoretical model that describes how variables are related to one another. Thus, a popular term for conducting the statistical analysis is *causal modeling.* However, the more general term is *structural modeling,* because the techniques allow researchers to test how well data from a set of measured variables fit a theoretical "structure" among variables. Structural modeling is particularly well suited for longitudinal research, allowing developmentalists to make causal statements about the relationship between independent and dependent variables over several waves of data collection.

Models are usually expressed in the form of path diagrams, with a complex

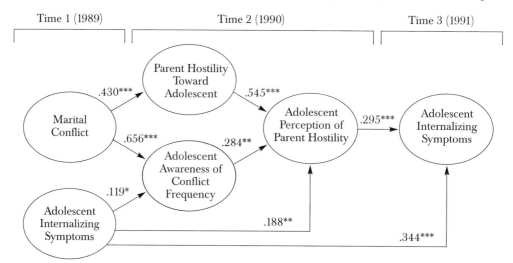

Figure 15.6 Structural model adapted from Harold and Conger (1997), Child Development 68, 333–350. © 1997 Society for Research in Child Development, Inc.

pattern of squares, circles, and ovals. Arrows leading from one variable to another depict paths that relate the variables in the model. Coefficients on the paths are similar to the weights derived in the regression equations described previously. These numbers represent the strength of the relationship between the variables. Figure 15.6 depicts a causal model examining the impact of marital conflict on adolescents (Harold & Conger, 1997). The model shows the relationship between the variables at three points in time. There is a direct path from adolescent internalizing symptoms (depression, anxiety, hostility) at Time 1 to adolescent internalizing at Time 3, indicating continuity in these symptoms across time. The influence of marital conflict, however, is indirect. Marital conflict (assessed at Time 1) affects the adolescent's internalizing symptoms through the other variables in the model. Marital conflict affects the parent-child relationship, leading to parental hostility toward the adolescent and a heightened awareness of the marital conflict. A hostile perception of the parents is created, and this hostility then contributes directly to the adolescent's internalizing symptoms of depression, anxiety, and hostility. The model supports the hypothesis that conflict between parents creates an aversive environment, which contributes to adverse consequences for adolescents. Research that develops structural models such as this enables researchers to better understand complex networks of relationships among variables.

SELECTING STATISTICAL TESTS

Many statistical tests have been developed for different research designs. The appropriateness of a particular test of significance depends on the design and the type of measurement scales employed for studying the variables. Recall from Chapter 4 that there are four measurement scales: (1) nominal, in which the values have no numerical properties; (2) ordinal, in which the values are only meaningful as a ranked order; (3) interval, in which the values are arranged along a continuum of equal intervals; and (4) ratio, in which there is a true zero point on the scale of values.

Table 15.4 provides guidelines for selecting appropriate tests for some of the more common experimental designs used in human development and family

Table 15.4 Common Statistical Tests

Scale of Measurement	Assignment to Conditions	One Independent Variable: Two Groups Only	One Independent Variable: Three or More Groups	Two or More Independent Variables
Nominal		Chi-square χ^2	Chi-square χ^2	Chi-square χ^2
Ordinal	Independent groups	Mann-Whitney U test	Kruskal-Wallis H test	No appropriate test is available
	Repeated measures or matched groups	Wilcoxon's T or the sign test	Friedman T test	No appropriate test is available
Interval or ratio	Independent groups	t test or one-way analysis of variance	One-way analysis of variance	Analysis of variance
	Repeated measures or matched groups	Correlated t test		Analysis of variance

BOX 15.2 RESEARCH IN ACTION

High School Students in Japan, China, and the United States

Cross-national differences in academic achievement have been well established in a series of studies conducted by researchers at the University of Michigan (Stevenson, Chen, & Lee, 1993; Stevenson, Lee, Chen, & Lummis, 1990; Stevenson, Lee, Chen, Stigler, Hsu, & Kitamura, 1990). East Asian students outperform American students, especially in math and science achievement. In an attempt to explain these academic differences, Fuligni and Stevenson (1995) interviewed 11th-grade students in Minneapolis, Taipei (Taiwan), and Sendai (Japan) about the ways they use their time. The amount of time students spent in academic, work, and leisure activities was compared. A one-way analysis of variance is appropriate to analyze these data because: (1) the dependent variable (time) was measured on a ratio scale, (2) three groups were compared, and (3) the groups were independent (see Table 15.4).

Outside school, students in China spent significantly greater amounts of time ($M = 25.5$ hrs) in academic activities such as studying, taking lessons, and reading for pleasure than students from Japan ($M = 17.2$ hrs) or the United States ($M = 15.4$ hrs). In contrast, students in the United States spent more time in leisure activities such as extracurricular school activities, dating, and socializing with friends. The means for time spent with friends were 18.4 hours in the United States, 8.8 hours in Taiwan, and 12.4 hours in Japan. The F statistics for all of these comparisons were significant at $p < .01$.

So what do these teenagers do with their friends? A chi-square analysis compared the percentage of students who participated in various activities with their friends. Chi-square is the appropriate statistic for comparing these percentages because the data are measured on a nominal scale. The students' responses simply represent categories of behavior. American students more frequently attended parties, dances, movies, and concerts, whereas Chinese and Japanese students were more likely to spend their time with friends in informal activities, hanging out at home, talking on the phone, or studying together. The chi-square values for all of these comparisons were significant at $p < .001$.

relations. Choosing the appropriate test depends on the four characteristics about the design: (1) the number of groups of participants, (2) the number of independent variables, (3) assignment to conditions (independent groups or repeated measures), and (4) the scale of measurement. A statistical text should be consulted for a complete description of statistical tests and guidelines for their selection. Appendix B provides computational illustrations for many of the tests included in the table.

Researchers use more than one statistical test for their research because typical studies include multiple dependent measures. Box 15.2 describes a research

One of the reasons students in the United States spend more time dating and with friends is related to finances. Students in the United States had significantly more spending money each month from jobs and allowances. The means for U.S., Chinese, and Japanese students were $205, $90, and $85 respectively, $F(2, 561) = 53.24$, $p < .001$.

Overall, these results indicate a pattern of greater time spent in school and academic activities for the East Asian students, with the U.S. students engaging in a great deal more leisure activity. But does this have an impact on their academic achievement? To address this issue, Fuligni and Stevenson calculated a series of correlation coefficients, with each one assessing the strength of the relationship between two dependent measures (e.g., the mathematics score and time spent studying, the mathematics score and time spent working, and so on). In all three countries, time spent studying positively correlated with math scores; logically, the more you study, the better your academic performance. Time spent with friends, working, and watching television correlated negatively with the math scores in all three countries, suggesting that these activities may interfere with time for academic studies. The negative correlation between time spent with friends and mathematics scores was highest in the United States, $r = -.34$, $p < .001$. Students in the United States also reported that such activities interfered with their schoolwork.

The analyses support your intuitive conclusions about why students in the United States fare poorly on cross-national comparisons. Academic pursuits are not the major focus for American high school students, who spend a good deal of their time in nonacademic activities. However, it would be misleading to conclude that students in China and Japan spend all of their free time on academics—they do engage in a variety of recreational and social activities, just not to the extent typical of teenagers in the United States. The results reflect the cultural context in each country, with Japan and China emphasizing the importance of academic pursuits for adolescents, whereas the United States places more value on peer and work activities.

project that used descriptive statistics, chi-square, analysis of variance, and correlations for different aspects of their data.

COMPUTER ANALYSIS OF DATA

Many computer programs calculate statistics. Sophisticated statistical analysis software packages make it easy to calculate statistics for any data set. Descriptive and inferential statistics are obtained quickly, the calculations are accurate, and

	group	refscore
1	1	3
2	1	5
3	1	4
4	1	3
5	1	1
6	1	3
7	1	4
8	1	2
9	1	4
10	1	2
11	2	6
12	2	5
13	2	5
14	2	7
15	2	4
16	2	5
17	2	6
18	2	3
19	2	6
20	2	5

Figure 15.7
Data matrix in SPSS
for Windows

	A	B
1	Intramurals	Aerobics
2	1	3
3	2	4
4	2	5
5	3	5
6	3	5
7	3	5
8	4	6
9	4	6
10	4	6
11	5	7
12		
13		

Figure 15.8
Excel method of
data input

t-Test: Two-Sample Assuming Equal Variances		
	Intramurals	Aerobics
Mean	3.10	5.20
Variance	1.433	1.289
Observations	10	10
Pooled Variance	1.361	
Hypothesized Mean Difference	0	
df	18	
t Stat	−4.025	
P(T<=t) one-tail	0.000	
t Critical one-tail	1.734	
P(T<=t) two-tail	0.001	
t Critical two-tail	2.101	

Figure 15.9
Output for a *t* test
using Excel

information on statistical significance is provided in the output. Computers also facilitate graphic displays of data.

Some of the major statistical software programs are SPSS, SAS, Minitab, Systat, and BMDP; other programs may be used on your campus as well. Many people do most of their statistical analyses using a spreadsheet program such as Excel. You will need to learn the specific details of the computer system used at your college or university. No one program is better than another; they all differ in the appearance of the output and the specific procedures needed to input data and execute the statistical test. However, the general procedures for doing analyses are quite similar in all of the statistics programs.

The first step in doing the analysis is to enter the data. Suppose you want to input the data in Table 14.1, the sports participation and discipline referral experiment. Data are entered into columns. It is easiest to think of data for computer analysis as a matrix with rows and columns. Data for each research participant are the rows of the matrix. The columns contain each participant's scores on one or more measures, and an additional column may be needed to indicate a code to identify which condition the individual was in (e.g., group 1 or group 2). A data matrix in SPSS for Windows is shown in Figure 15.7. The numbers in the "group" column indicate whether the individual is in group 1 (intramurals) or group 2 (aerobics), and the numbers in the "refscore" column are the discipline referral scores from Table 14.1.

Other programs may require somewhat different methods of data input. For example, in Excel, it is usually easiest to set up a separate column for each group, as shown in Figure 15.8.

The next step is to provide instructions for the statistical analysis. Again, each program uses somewhat different steps to perform the analysis; most require you to choose from various pull-down menu options. When the analysis is completed, you are provided with output that shows the results of the statistical procedure you performed. You will need to learn how to interpret the output. Figure 15.9 shows the output for a *t* test using Excel.

When you are first learning to use a statistical analysis program, it is a good idea to practice with some data from a statistics text to make sure that you get the same results. This will ensure that you know how to properly input the data and request the statistical analysis.

SUMMARY

Many statistical tests have been developed for different research designs. The t test is used to examine whether two groups are significantly different from one another. The analysis of variance, or F test, extends the logic of the t test to compare more than two groups. Analysis of variance is appropriate when there are more than two levels of an independent variable and when a factorial design is used. The analysis of variance compares the variability between groups (systematic variance) to variability within groups (error variance). Statistical results are formally presented in statistical phrases such as $t(19) = 9.74, p < .001$, which include the statistical symbol, the degrees of freedom, the obtained value of the statistic, and the significance level.

A correlation coefficient is a statistic that describes the strength of a relationship between two variables. One of the most commonly used correlation coefficient statistics is the Pearson product-moment correlation coefficient, symbolized as r. A correlation coefficient can range from 0.00 to ± 1.00. A positive correlation indicates a positive relationship between the variables; a negative correlation indicates a negative relationship. Scatterplots are useful to visually inspect the relationship between variables; curvilinear relationships can be detected with scatterplots.

Partial correlation is a technique for statistically controlling a third variable. This method allows you to estimate the strength of the relationship between two variables with the influence of a third variable removed from the correlation.

Advanced statistical techniques use correlations for regression equations, multiple correlation, and structural equation modeling. Regression equations predict a person's future behavior or performance from a score on another variable. This approach is commonly used in college admissions, for example, to predict your college GPA from your high school GPA. A multiple correlation, symbolized as R, examines the relationship between one variable (e.g., college GPA) and a set of other variables (e.g., high school GPA, SAT scores, and high school extracurricular activities). Structural models are theoretical models developed from a set of data that describe how variables are causally related to one another. Developmental researchers rely on structural models to better understand the relationship among a large set of variables.

KEY TERMS

analysis of variance (F test)	effect size	Pearson r correlation coefficient
criterion variable	error variance	predictor variable
degrees of freedom	multiple correlation	regression equation
	partial correlation	

restriction of the range   statistical phrase   systematic variance
scatterplot   structural model   *t* test

REVIEW QUESTIONS

1. What factor determines whether a *t* test or an *F* test is the appropriate statistical test?
2. Define systematic variance and error variance.
3. The results of a statistical test are listed below. Arrange the information in a statistical phrase.
     Value of *t* calculated from the raw data: 3.10
     Degrees of freedom: 18
     Probability level: .01
4. What does it mean if results are significant at the .001 level? Which outcome shows a lower probability of occurring by chance, $p < .001$ or $p < .01$?
5. Dr. Kapp studied the addictive effects of the "information superhighway" by comparing the time college students spend on the Internet to the number of hours doing school assignments on the computer. She tabulated the number of minutes students spent in two activities: (1) surfing the Internet, and (2) using word processing programs.
     a. What is the independent variable?
     b. What is the dependent variable?
     c. What inferential statistic is appropriate to analyze the data?
6. Based on a pilot study, Dr. Kapp noticed gender differences in the way students use computers, so she added a second independent variable to her design and collected additional data on computer use in males and females. What inferential statistic is appropriate to analyze the data?
7. What is a correlation coefficient? What do the size and sign of the correlation coefficient tell us about the relationship between the variables?
8. What is a scatterplot? What happens if the scatterplot shows a curvilinear relationship?
9. What is the purpose of a partial correlation?
10. What is the difference between the correlational method and a correlation coefficient?
11. Define effect size.
12. What is a regression equation? How would an employer or school psychologist use a regression equation?
13. What is the purpose of structural modeling?

CHAPTER 16

Generalizability

In this chapter we will consider the problem of generalization of research findings. Can the results of a completed research project be generalized beyond the group of participants in the study? Do the results apply to other participant populations, other age groups, other times, or other ways of manipulating or measuring the variables? Recall that internal validity refers to the adequacy of the procedures and design of the research; external validity is the extent to which the findings may be generalized. Internal validity is of primary importance because we are not very interested in findings that are the result of a weak design with low internal validity. Ideally, however, a study should have external validity as well.

External validity is valuable for several reasons. Recall from Chapter 1 that the goals of the scientific method are to describe, predict, explain, and understand behavior. Only with generalizable results can such explanation and understanding be achieved. External validity allows social scientists to develop general principles that guide behavior and development. Without **generalizability,** research results are extremely limited and have minimal theoretical or practical value.

GENERALIZATION AS A STATISTICAL INTERACTION

The problem of generalization can be thought of as an interaction in a factorial design (see Chapter 12). An interaction occurs when a relationship between variables exists under one condition but not another, or when the nature of the relationship is different in one condition than in another. Thus, if you question the generalizability of a study that used only males, you are suggesting that an interaction between gender and the treatment occurred. Suppose, for example, that a study examines the relationship between crowding in residential neighborhoods and delinquency among adolescent males. If the study reports that males engage in more delinquency in crowded, densely populated areas, you might then question whether the results are generalizable to adolescent females.

Figure 16.1 shows four potential outcomes of a hypothetical study on crowding and delinquency that tested both males and females. In each graph, the relationship between crowding and delinquency for males has been maintained, with higher levels of delinquency associated with more crowded neighborhoods. In Graph A there is no interaction—the behavior of males and females is virtually identical. Thus, the results of the original all-male study could be generalized to female adolescents. In Graph B, there is also no interaction; the effect of neighborhood crowding is identical for males and females. However, in this graph males engage in more delinquent behavior than females. Although such a difference is interesting, it does not limit generalization because the overall pattern of the relationship between crowding and delinquency is present for both male and female adolescents.

Graphs C and D do show interactions. In both, the original results with males cannot be generalized to females. In Graph C there is no relationship between neighborhood crowding and delinquent behavior for females. Females display the same low level of delinquency regardless of how crowded the neighborhood might be. The answer to the generalization question "Is this true for females?" is a definite no. In Graph D the interaction tells us that a positive relationship between crowding and delinquency exists for males but that a negative relationship exists

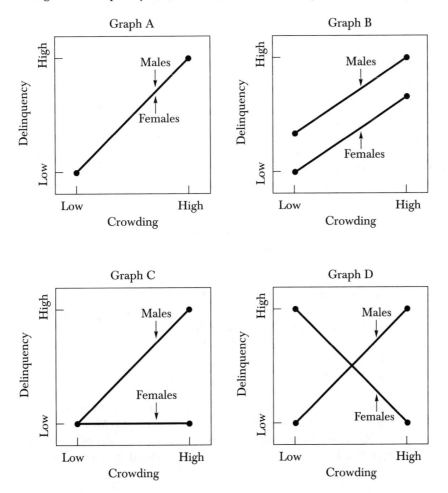

Figure 16.1
Outcomes of a hypothetical experiment on crowding and delinquency
NOTE: The presence of an interaction indicates that the results for males cannot be generalized to females.

for females, with females engaging in high levels of delinquent behavior in a less crowded neighborhood. Thus, you cannot generalize the results for males to females in these situations.

Researchers can address generalization issues that stem from the use of different populations by including type of participant as a variable in the study. By including variables such as gender, age, or ethnic group in the design of the study, the results may be analyzed to determine whether there are interaction effects like the ones illustrated in Figure 16.1.

THE IMPORTANCE OF REPLICATIONS

The best way to address external validity is through **replication.** Fundamentally, generalizability is a question of how well the results of a study apply to another group of people, perhaps of a different age or a different ethnic group. By repeating the results of a single study, you can overcome problems of generalization. There are two types of replications to consider: exact replications and conceptual replications.

Exact Replications

An **exact replication** is an attempt to replicate precisely the procedures of a study to see if the same results are obtained. Conducting the same experiment in a rural community and in an industrial town involves different settings and different types of participants, yet the same procedures are employed. If the same pattern of results is obtained in these replications, the researcher can be reasonably confident that the findings are not unusual. Although it is not possible to positively establish external validity, confidence is greatly increased with each successive replication.

A researcher who obtains an unexpected finding will frequently attempt a replication to make sure that the finding is reliable. If you are starting your own work on a problem, you may try to replicate a crucial study to make sure that you understand the procedures and can obtain the same results. Often, exact replications occur when a researcher builds on the findings of a prior study. For example, suppose you were intrigued by the research mentioned in Chapter 10 that listening to Mozart raises IQ (Rauscher et al., 1993). First, you might attempt to replicate the procedures used in the original study, using the same musical piece, for the same amount of time. IQ would be measured by the same instrument, abstract reasoning tests from the Stanford-Binet intelligence scale.

You might also consider expanding on the original research. Rauscher et al. used a Mozart sonata; what are the effects of other composers or other types of music? Researchers in New Zealand (Stough, Kerkin, Bates, & Mangan, 1994) attempted to replicate the Rauscher et al. findings by using the Mozart sonata and dance music. IQ scores were assessed with a different instrument, Raven's Advanced Progressive Matrices. With these modified procedures, Stough et al. find no facilitative effect of music on spatial IQ scores, leading them to conclude that "this would not be a profitable area for future research" (p. 695). But did they perhaps overstate their conclusion?

A single failure to replicate doesn't reveal much. It is unrealistic to assume, on the basis of a single failure to replicate, that the previous research is invalid. Failures to replicate share the same interpretation problems as nonsignificant results (see Chapter 14). A failure to replicate could mean that the original results are invalid, but it could also mean that the replication attempt was flawed. For example, if the replication is based on the procedure as reported in a journal article, it is possible that the article omitted an important aspect of the procedure. For this reason, it is usually a good idea to contact the researcher to obtain detailed information on all of the materials that were used in the study.

Repeated failures to replicate do lead to reconsideration of the original findings. Eventually, we may conclude that the original results were a fluke—a Type I error was made in the statistical analysis. This is especially likely when unsuccessful attempts to replicate employ not only the original procedures but different procedures as well.

Conceptual Replications

The use of different procedures to replicate a research finding is called a **conceptual replication.** Conceptual replications are even more important than exact replications in furthering our understanding of behavior.

In most research the goal is to discover whether a relationship between conceptual variables exists. Thus, the Rauscher et al. study examined the effect of music on learning by playing a musical piece before testing spatial IQ. Another conceptual approach would be to assess spatial IQ of children who take music lessons. This conceptual replication has been conducted by researchers at the University of California, Irvine (Rauscher et al., 1997). Preschoolers who took piano lessons once a week for a year scored 34% higher on puzzle-solving tests than children in a control group who received computer lessons, singing lessons, or no special instruction. This is an important extension of the original findings, underscoring the potential value of musical instruction in schools.

Another example of the value of replication is recent work on attachment. Chisholm and her colleagues (Chisholm, 1997; Chisholm, Carter, Ames, & Morison, 1995) investigated the development of attachment in Romanian orphans who were adopted early in infancy (before age 4 months) and later in infancy (after spending at least 8 months in an orphanage). The children adopted later in infancy were more likely to show atypical forms of insecure attachment (52% of later adoptees vs. 17% of early adoptees). The timing of adoption appears to be critical in the development of a secure attachment to a caregiver. A conceptual replication of this study was conducted by other attachment researchers (Dozier & Stovall, 1997) who evaluated attachment in children placed in foster care at varying ages during infancy. The pattern of findings is consistent with the work on adopted children; the most severe attachment problems occurred with infants who entered foster care at 8 months or older. This is an important extension of the Chisholm study, replicating a similar finding with different procedures and a different assessment procedure.

In a conceptual replication, the same independent variable is manipulated in a different way (and possibly the dependent variable is measured in a different way also). Such conceptual replications are extremely important in the social sciences because the specific manipulations and measures are usually operational definitions of complex variables. A crucial generalization question is whether the relationship holds when other ways of manipulating or measuring the variables are studied. Do different types of alternate caregiver relationships such as adoption or foster care by relatives lead to the same disruption in attachment reported by Chisholm (1997) and Dozier and Stovall (1997)? When conceptual replications produce similar results, our confidence in the generalizability of relationships between variables is greatly increased.

In sum, replication, exact or conceptual, provides important evidence about the generalizability of a finding. The ability to precisely replicate the findings of a study or to extend the findings of a study by employing different procedural approaches enhances the theoretical importance of a finding. Replication studies are a fruitful avenue for research, adding substantially to our knowledge about development.

GENERALIZING TO OTHER PARTICIPANT POPULATIONS

The results of an experiment should be evaluated for how well they generalize to other participant populations. A researcher interested in breaking the cycle of teen pregnancy is unlikely to test all pregnant teenagers. Instead, a sample of girls is recruited. Results obtained on the sample of girls are then generalized to the larger population. This extension of the findings is possible only if the sample is, in fact, representative of the larger group. Random sampling from the population is the best way to ensure that a representative sample has been employed, yet researchers almost never use random sampling to select from the general population. As we noted in earlier chapters, individuals who participate in research are usually selected because they are available. This nonrandom selection of participants creates a "convenience" sample rather than a random sample. Such a convenience sample may differ on important participant characteristics that limit the generality of results and limit our ability to make rational conclusions about development. Important participant characteristics include volunteer status, educational level, age, and diversity issues such as gender, ethnicity, race, and social status. Let's examine how some of these factors affect generalizability.

Volunteers

One important way that participants differ from nonparticipants is that most research participants are volunteers. For example, you may ask people at a homeowner's association to participate in a study of marital interaction or invite residents in a retirement community to take part in a study examining attitudes toward managed health care. Volunteers differ in important ways from nonvolunteers (Rosenthal & Rosnow, 1975). Volunteers tend to be more highly educated, more in need of approval, and more social; they also tend to have a higher socio-economic status. Consider what happens when you need children for a study—the parents must "volunteer" their children. This creates a nonrandom sample that is potentially biased by characteristics of the parents.

Educational Level: College Students

At many colleges introductory psychology students are required either to volunteer for experiments or to complete an alternative project. The students tend to be freshmen and sophomores (Sears, 1986) who are young and possess the characteristics of late adolescence: a sense of self-identity that is still developing, social and political attitudes that are in a state of flux, a high need for peer approval, and unstable peer relationships. They also are intelligent, have high cognitive skills, and know how to win approval from authority. This pool of participants is handy if you are studying developmental issues that involve late adolescence and the transition to early adulthood, but it is misleading to assume that these young adults are representative of the general population.

Age Group

Generalization can be limited by the age of participants in a study. A study conducted on 18-year-old, middle-class college students may not generalize to other participants. Thus, an age-comparative study that compares these "adults" to children or older adults does not use a random or representative sample of adults, seriously limiting the study. Cross-sectional research can address issues of generalizability, with each different age group representing a built-in replication. For example, in the eyewitness testimony literature, investigators repeatedly find that participants perform better on direct questions than on misleading questions. This has been replicated on preschoolers, elementary school-aged children, and adults (Ceci & Bruck, 1993). Thus, the pattern of results generalizes well across age groups. The difference, of course, is in the level of performance. A preschooler does not provide correct answers to as many questions as a school-aged child, who in turn does not provide as many correct answers as an adult.

Studies of aging typically include people with more financial resources, higher levels of education, better jobs, and better health. Such individuals are easier to locate and more readily agree to participate in research projects. This contributes to a middle-class bias in the aging research, a problem common to child and adolescent research as well. Adult men have been studied more than adult women, focusing on psychosocial transitions such as the mid-life crisis and retirement. In Chapter 9 we discussed the problems inherent in longitudinal studies of adults; the representativeness of the sample often diminishes across the course of the study so that by the time the study is completed, the remaining participants are primarily middle class. This naturally imposes serious limitations to the generalizability of the findings.

In addition, age-comparative studies should carefully consider the health status of each sample. There are problems inherent in applying findings from a healthy sample of adults who reside in the community to a sample of institutionalized adults with a variety of physical and mental health concerns. For these reasons, it is essential to assess the health status of participants in any study, as well as the more commonly requested demographic information.

Diversity

Diversity addresses variables such as gender, race, ethnicity, culture, and socioeconomic status. Sometimes researchers use a sample that is disproportionately male or female, or primarily European American, or middle class simply because this is convenient or the procedures seem better suited to one group. Given the possible differences between individuals of different backgrounds, the results of such studies may not be generalizable. Even basic memory abilities may vary across individuals from diverse backgrounds. A recent literature search of memory studies (Herrmann & Guadagno, 1997) suggests that socioeconomic status and memory performance are positively related, with higher memory performance associated with participants of higher socioeconomic status. Denmark, Russo, Frieze, and Sechzer (1988) provide an example of studies on contraception practices that use only females because of stereotypical assumptions that only females are responsible for contraception. They also point out several other ways that gender bias may arise in research, including confounding gender with age or job status and selecting response measures that are gender-stereotyped. Their paper offers several suggestions for avoiding such biases.

Until recently, diversity was not a main focus of analysis in human development research, as evidenced by content analyses of journals and textbooks (Graham, 1992; Lerner, 1995; MacPhee, Kruetzer, & Fritz, 1994; McLoyd & Randolph, 1985). However, the heterogeneity of the population of the United States cannot be overlooked, strengthening the need for research that informs us about the needs and strengths of different ethnic groups. In 1995, 31% of children were non-White; this proportion is expected to increase to 60% by 2030 (Hernandez, 1997). In some states (e.g., California, Texas, and New Mexico) the majority of youth will be from minority groups by the year 2000. Some of America's problems disproportionately affect minority children, necessitating more research to identify normative developmental processes among minority children and their families.

Families of divergent racial, ethnic, and immigration history may differ in their customs, behaviors, and attitudes toward child care, education, the role of the child in the family, and the role of parents. Thus, it is inappropriate to presume that research based on European American, middle-class, two-parent families will generalize to other populations (García-Coll et al., 1996; Steinberg, Dornbusch, & Brown, 1992). Middle-class values may not be culturally relevant for minority groups, and it is particularly important to avoid interpretation of differences as deficits. To complicate matters, ethnicity and income are confounded with family structure, as many single African American mothers are raising their children in poverty. Researchers in the developmental sciences have a social responsibility to be sensitive to such issues, making generalizations to other groups only after adequate research.

In Defense of Middle-Class White Families in Developmental Research

Far too much of the developmental literature is based on middle-class White nuclear families in cities and towns where universities are located. It is easy to criticize this research on the basis of participant characteristics, yet criticism by itself does not mean that the research necessarily is flawed. Although we need to be concerned about the potential problems of generalizability, we should also keep two things in mind when thinking about this issue. First, criticisms of the use of any particular type of participant, such as middle-class families, should be backed with good reasons why a relationship would not be found with other types of participants. Second, remember that replication of research studies provides a safeguard against limited generalizability. Studies should be replicated using other groups of participants, in other cultural settings.

Research in cognitive development offers excellent examples of generalization across ethnic groups. Using a noun-pair learning task, Kee and Rohwer (1973) assessed the learning efficiency of second-grade children from four ethnic groups: Black, Chinese American, Spanish American, and White. No differences in performance emerged, demonstrating equivalence across diverse ethnic backgrounds. Recent research by Saccuzzo, Johnson, and Guertin (1994) evaluated the information processing skills of gifted and nongifted African American, Latino, Filipino, and White children. Gifted children in all ethnic groups were superior across four different measures of elementary information processing abilities (e.g., reaction time, inspection time), and older children performed better than younger children. However, no significant ethnic differences emerged on the battery of tasks, providing support for the view that giftedness is independent of ethnic background.

Researchers have become more sensitive to these issues. There is a growing literature of research on the role of gender, ethnicity, race, and culture in determining behaviors and cognitions. This research is providing the data necessary to develop theories that include the influence of these variables.

GENERALIZING TO OTHER EXPERIMENTERS

The person who actually conducts the experiment is the source of another generalization problem. In most research only one experimenter is used, and rarely is much attention paid to the personal characteristics of the experimenter (McGuigan, 1963). The main goal is to make sure that any influence the experimenter has on participants is constant throughout the experiment. There is always the possibility, however, that the results are generalizable only to certain types of experimenters. Participants may behave differently with male and female experimenters. A fine example of the use of multiple experimenters is a study by Rubin (1975), who sent several male and female experimenters to the Boston airport to investigate self-disclosure. The experimenters revealed different kinds of information about themselves to both male and female travelers and recorded the passengers' return disclosures. One solution to the problem of generalizing to other experimenters is to use two or more experimenters, preferably both male and female, to conduct the research. Experimenter gender can then be an independent variable in the experiment, allowing statistical evaluation of the effect. Another solution is to conduct replication studies; if the same pattern of results is obtained with male experimenters in one study and female experimenters in a subsequent study, this increases our confidence in the generality of the findings.

The race of the experimenter, observer, interviewer, rater, or clinician also merits consideration as a factor that may limit generalizability. Unfortunately, content analyses of the representation of African Americans in published articles (Graham, 1992) indicate the race of the individual who actually collects the data is mentioned less than half of the time. According to Graham, there currently is no substantial evidence that White experimenters have negative influences on African American participants. However, we are uncertain about possible influences and should take a conservative approach by minimizing the opportunities for such a threat to external validity. It is currently unclear what effect a White experimenter might have on an African American child asked to perform tasks such as reading aloud, indicating their classroom friends, or rating their likelihood of getting a good job.

GENERALIZING TO OTHER SETTINGS

Research conducted in a laboratory setting has the advantage of experimenter control over most extraneous variables. Laboratory findings about fundamental educational, psychological, and developmental issues have been widely applied to settings outside the laboratory. The question arises, however, whether the artificiality of the laboratory setting limits the ability to generalize what is observed in the laboratory to real-life settings. One method of counteracting laboratory artificiality is to conduct field experiments, discussed in Chapter 5. In a field experiment, the researcher manipulates the independent variable in a natural setting—a school, a local playground, or a nursing home, for example. In theory, a field experiment will provide more ecologically valid results.

Mundane and Experimental Realism

Aronson, Brewer, and Carlsmith (1985) point out that even field experiments can be contrived and artificial, having little real-world relevance. They propose a better distinction: mundane realism versus experimental realism. **Mundane realism** refers to whether the experiment bears similarity to events that occur in the real world. Research with high mundane realism should also have good external validity. **Experimental realism** refers to whether the experiment has an impact on the participants, involves them, and makes them take the experiment seriously. Aronson et al. point out that experimental and mundane realism are separate, independent dimensions. An experiment may have considerable mundane realism (being very similar to real life) but may be totally boring and uninvolving and, thus, lack experimental realism. Consider two examples:

Example 1: In a helping study an experimenter drops some pencils outside a building on the high school campus and waits to see whether anyone stops to help pick them up. The dependent variable is the helping by observers of the "accident." This study would possess considerable mundane realism but little experimental realism.

Example 2: In another helping experiment high school students are seated in individual cubicles that are interconnected via an intercom system. During the course of the study, the individual hears another (supposed) participant having an epileptic seizure and must decide whether to help the person (Darley & Latané, 1968). This study has relatively little mundane realism but a great deal of experimental realism.

Other experimental procedures, in both laboratory and field settings, may rate either high or low on both mundane and experimental realism. Experiments that are low on both mundane realism (bearing little similarity to real-world events or tasks) and experimental realism (failing to engage the participants' interest) are not likely to yield valuable results. The key point here, however, is that laboratory experiments are not automatically artificial; even when an experiment lacks mundane realism, it may be very realistic in terms of experimental realism.

Mutual Benefits of Lab and Field Research

Aronson et al. (1985) also point out that it is unwise to consider laboratory or field experiments in isolation. Conducting research in both laboratory and field settings provides the greatest opportunity for advancing our understanding of development. A good example is research on cooperative learning (Slavin, 1986, 1991) that has been used to promote integration in the classroom. Students of different races and different ability levels work as teams and are rewarded for team performance. This encourages members of the team to support and encourage one another. The "jigsaw method" of instruction (Aronson, Stephan, Sikes, Blaney, & Snapp, 1978) uses a similar approach to reduce conflict among ethnic and racial groups in a school setting. The effectiveness of these techniques in reducing intergroup conflict has been demonstrated in both laboratory and field settings.

EVALUATING GENERALIZATIONS: LITERATURE REVIEWS AND META-ANALYSIS

Researchers have traditionally drawn conclusions about the generalizability of research findings by conducting literature reviews. In a literature review a reviewer reads a number of studies that address a particular topic. Selecting all of the articles on a topic is not possible; the reviewer may limit selection based on time of publication (for example, articles published in the last decade) or some other criterion such as age of participants (for example, only adults over age 60). The reviewer then writes a paper summarizing findings that are strongly supported by the research (e.g., obtained across numerous conceptual replications), findings that are less strongly supported (e.g., reported by only a few researchers), and findings that are puzzling because of contradictory results (e.g., results obtained in some studies but not others). A literature review often includes a table condensing the results from the numerous studies. The table identifies the study, the participants, key features of the design, and the pattern of results. By consulting the table, readers can quickly compare the studies under review. In addition, the reviewer may integrate the findings into a theoretical framework.

Literature reviews provide valuable information because they organize many studies on a topic and point to areas in which there are well-established findings and others in which more research needs to be done. A literature review can be very helpful when you are beginning research in an area and want to know what has already been researched. Ceci and Bruck (1993) summarized the literature on the reliability of children's eyewitness testimony, delineating the historical background and clearly identifying the strengths and weaknesses in the existing literature. In a special issue of *Child Development* (Vol. 61, 1990) devoted to research on minority children, McLoyd (1990) reviews the literature on the impact of poverty on Black families. In a review of three decades of memory training studies with children, Bjorklund, Miller, Coyle, and Slawinksi (1997) report the surprising finding that after learning a new memory strategy, children are frequently utilization deficient, producing the strategy but failing to obtain increased memory performance.

The conclusions in a traditional literature review are based on the subjective impressions of the reviewer. There is nothing wrong with this practice; however, another technique for comparing a large number of studies in an area has emerged in recent years. This technique is meta-analysis (Durlak & Lipsey, 1991; Rosenthal, 1991). You are likely to see references to meta-analytic studies as you become more familiar with human development research.

In a **meta-analysis** the researcher combines the actual results from a number of existing studies. The analysis consists of a set of statistical procedures that combine statistics such as t values, standardized scores, and p values. The statistical procedures involve standardizing the results of each study in terms of an effect size. The effect size is an index of the magnitude of the relationships reported in the studies. By transforming the results of the various studies to a common base, the findings in various studies can be compared quantitatively even if they initially employed different statistics (e.g., r, t, or F). Instead of relying on subjective judgments obtained in a traditional literature review, statistical conclusions can be drawn in a meta-analysis. The important point here is that meta-analysis is a method for determining the reliability of a finding by examining the results from many different studies.

An example of a meta-analysis is a study by Wells and Rankin (1991) on the relationship between broken homes and delinquency. The researchers located 50 published studies dealing with juvenile delinquency, crime, single parenthood, divorce, and family separation. They then applied appropriate statistical techniques to combine and compare the different results. The meta-analysis found that the prevalence of delinquency is 10 to 15% higher in broken homes than in intact homes. However, the relationship is strongest for minor crimes and relatively weak for serious criminal behavior such as theft and interpersonal violence. In addition, no gender or racial differences were found. Wells and Rankin attribute much of the variation in earlier studies to the use of small convenience samples that were unrepresentative of the population, a problem we discussed in Chapter 7. These are important additions to our knowledge about juvenile delinquency and suggest important directions for additional research.

The information obtained from a meta-analysis such as the one conducted by Wells and Rankin is very informative. In a traditional literature review it would be very difficult to provide the type of general conclusion that was reached with the meta-analysis. Anyone would find it difficult to integrate the results of so many studies with different experimental designs, subject types, and measures. In fact, if you read all the studies on juvenile delinquency and divorce, and someone asked you the simple question "Does divorce lead to juvenile delinquency?" you would find it very difficult to provide a direct answer to this question. Meta-analysis provides an answer to this question and is a valuable tool to assess the strength of findings obtained across diverse research projects.

There are limits to meta-analysis. A meta-analysis cannot be conducted when very few studies are available on a particular topic. New research areas that are just being investigated such as the benefits of school uniforms do not lend themselves to the meta-analytic approach. Not all studies report enough information to calculate the effect size. In addition, meta-analysis applies only to quantitative data. Qualitative research approaches such as field observation, open-ended interviews, or case studies cannot be incorporated in a meta-analytic review. Also, variation in the quality of studies should be accounted for in some way; a weak design does not merit the same weight as a well-designed study. Despite these potential sources of bias, meta-analysis has been favorably compared to the traditional literature review (Beaman, 1991).

USING RESEARCH TO CHANGE COMMUNITIES AND FAMILIES

In a presidential address to the American Psychological Association in 1969 George Miller discussed "psychology as a means of promoting human welfare." He spoke of "giving psychology away." Miller was addressing the broadest issue of generalizability, taking what we know about human behavior and allowing it to be applied by many people in all areas of everyday life. Two research programs by David Riley at the University of Wisconsin exemplify this aspect of generalizability (Riley, Meinhardt, Nelson, Salisbury, & Winnett, 1991; Riley, 1997).

The *School-Age Child Care Project* addressed the issue of latchkey children. Riley's first attempts to educate the public about the risks of unsupervised children created no impact, primarily because people questioned the external validity of research conducted in locations such as Los Angeles and Philadelphia for their communities in Wisconsin. To counteract this, Riley collaborated with community members to collect information on how much time elementary school children spent unsupervised on school days in each community and presented the reports to local residents and business leaders. As a result of his work, communities responded to the need for after-school child care by adding school-age programs, intergenerational care projects, telephone warm-lines for unsupervised children, and family education programs. Replications in 12 other states indicate the generalizability of the program to other participants, other researchers, and procedural variations modified for different cultures. For example, tribal elders of the Cherokee and Creek-Muscogee Indians supported an after-school program to teach children traditional stories, dances, and crafts.

The second program, *Parenting the First Year,* is an intervention for new parents.

Parents receive free newsletters in the mail each month about developmental changes, health, nutrition, and safety issues specifically tailored for their child's age. For example, parents of a 5-month-old receive a newsletter that describes the physical, mental, and social skills of 5-month-olds. The newsletters are available in Spanish and English and are written at a fifth-grade reading level so most adults can understand the information. The response to the newsletters has been overwhelmingly positive; over 40,000 families received the newsletters in 1996. The program is expanding to a prenatal newsletter and *Parenting the Second & Third Year*. Newsletter articles are also available on their Web site <http://www.uwex.edu/ces/flp/parenting>.

By "giving away" information about child care, parenting, and developmental milestones, these programs have been extremely successful. Through innovative programs designed to share research with families and children, basic research can be applied to help promote human welfare. Despite all the potential problems of generalizing research findings that were highlighted in this chapter, the evidence suggests that we can generalize our findings to many aspects of our lives.

SUMMARY

External validity refers to the extent to which results generalize beyond the circumstances that were studied. Generalizability allows researchers to make inferences about the research findings to other populations or settings. One way to address external validity is by conducting replication studies. An exact replication is an attempt to copy the procedures of an earlier study. Although a single replication failure may not be important, repeated failures to replicate usually lead to a reconsideration of the earlier findings. A conceptual replication investigates the same variables but uses different procedures or different operational definitions. Extending findings beyond the specific method of the original study is essential for increasing construct validity. For this reason, conceptual replications are even more important than exact replications.

The results of an experiment should be evaluated for how well they generalize to other participant populations. Potential generalizability problems occur when participants are selected on the basis of convenience rather than using random sampling. Possible biases occur because volunteer participants differ from individuals who do not volunteer. College students differ from other adults in a variety of ways. Generalizability is often limited by the age and socioeconomic status of participants. Diversity issues such as gender, race, and ethnicity also merit careful consideration when generalizing research findings.

External validity may also be affected by the research setting. Laboratory findings do not always apply to real-life settings, in part due to the artificial lab environment. Mundane realism refers to the degree to which the experimental events are similar to things people normally experience. Experimental realism refers to the impact an experimental situation has on participants. Lab experiments that engage the participants fully can provide meaningful, generalizable results.

Generalizability can be examined by conducting a literature review of existing studies. Literature reviews identify empirical evidence that supports or contradicts a particular hypothesis or theory. A more objective way to evaluate existing research is a statistical technique called meta-analysis. Meta-analysis evaluates effect sizes to assess the strength of findings in diverse research studies.

KEY TERMS

conceptual replication   generalizability   replication
exact replication   meta-analysis
experimental realism   mundane realism

REVIEW QUESTIONS

1. Define external validity.
2. Distinguish between an exact replication and a conceptual replication. What is the value of a conceptual replication?
3. Why should a researcher be concerned about generalizing to other populations of participants? What are some of the problems researchers might confront when generalizing to other populations?
4. What is the source of the problem of generalizing to other experimenters? How can this problem be solved?
5. Distinguish between mundane and experimental realism.
6. What is a literature review? What is a meta-analysis?

APPENDIX A ◆

Writing Research Reports

This appendix presents the information you will need to prepare a written report of your research for a course and for possible publication in a professional journal. We will consider the specific rules that should be followed in organizing and presenting research results. These rules are a great convenience for both the writer and the reader. They provide structure for the report and a uniform method of presentation, making it easier for the reader to understand and evaluate the report.

Specific rules vary from one discipline to another. A rule for presenting research results in psychology may not apply to the same situation in, for example, sociology research. Also, the rules may vary depending on whether you are preparing the report for a class, a thesis, or submission to a journal. Fortunately, the variation is usually minor, and the general rules of presentation are much the same across disciplines and situations.

The format presented here for writing research reports is drawn from the *Publication Manual of the American Psychological Association* (fourth edition, 1994). APA style is used in many journals in psychology, child development, family relations, and education. If you are concerned about specific rules for a particular journal, consult a recent issue of that journal. You may purchase a copy of the *Publication Manual* through your bookstore or directly from the American Psychological Association (APA Order Department, P.O. Box 2710, Hyattsville, MD 20784-0710; 1-800-374-2721). APA has also published a student workbook and training guide for the *Publication Manual* (Gelfand & Walker, 1990). Other useful sources for preparing papers are brief books by Rosnow and Rosnow (1995) and Sternberg (1993). Kazdin (1995) also offers an excellent summary of guidelines for preparing research reports for publication.

The fourth edition of the APA manual is a major revision and was guided by principles of "specificity and sensitivity." First, papers should be written at a level of specificity and detail that will allow others to replicate the research. Second, papers should be free of inappropriate language that might be interpreted as biased and insensitive. The manual also includes new manuscript preparation guidelines that take advantage of the features of word processing software. Throughout this appendix, examples that are intended to appear as you would type them in your papers appear in a `typewriter font`; this convention is also used in the APA manual.

WRITING STYLE

In any format for preparing your report, writing style is important. A poorly written report that is difficult to understand is of no value (and almost certainly will bring you a poor grade!). Also, a good paper should be neatly typed and free of spelling and typographical errors.

Clarity

Clarity in writing is essential. Be precise and clear in presenting ideas. It is often a good idea to think about your intended audience. It is helpful to direct your paper to an audience that is unfamiliar with your general topic and the methods you used to study the topic. Eliminate jargon that most readers will not comprehend. Sometimes a researcher will develop an abbreviated notation for referring to a specific variable or procedure. Such abbreviations may be convenient when communicating with others who are directly involved in the research project, but they are confusing to the general reader. However, you should assume that the reader has a general familiarity with statistics and hypothesis testing. Statistical outcomes can usually be presented without defining terms such as the *mean, standard deviation,* or *significance.* These are only general guidelines, however. Rosnow and Rosnow (1995) point out that when your intended audience is your instructor you should pay close attention to what the instructor has to say about expectations for the paper!

The entire report should have a coherent structure. Ideas should be presented in an orderly, logical progression to facilitate understanding. If you write your report for someone who is just being introduced to your ideas and research findings for the first time, you will be more likely to communicate clearly with the reader.

One method for producing a more organized report is to use an outline. Many writers plan a paper by putting their thoughts and ideas into outline form (computer word processing programs usually have features that facilitate outlining). The outline then serves as a writing guide. This method forces writers to develop a logical structure before writing the paper. Other writers prefer to use a less structured approach for the first draft. They then try to outline what has been written. If the paper does not produce a coherent outline, the organization needs to be improved.

Paragraphs should be well organized. It is a good idea for a paragraph to contain a topic sentence. Other sentences within a paragraph should be related to the topic sentence and develop the idea in this sentence by elaborating, expanding, explaining, or supporting the idea in the topic sentence. Additionally, avoid one-sentence paragraphs. If you find such paragraphs in your paper, expand the paragraph, include the idea in another paragraph, or delete the concept.

After completing the first draft of your paper, it is a good idea to let it sit for a day or so before you reread it. Carefully proofread the paper, paying attention to grammar and spelling. Some grammatical considerations are described here, and you can also use a computer word processor to check your spelling and grammar. After you make changes and corrections, you may want to get feedback from others. Find one or more people who will read your report critically and suggest improvements. Be prepared to write several drafts before you have a satisfactory finished product.

Acknowledging the Work of Others

It is extremely important to clearly separate your own words and ideas from those obtained from other sources. If you use a passage drawn from an article or book, make sure the passage is presented as a direct quotation. There is nothing wrong with quoting another author as long as you acknowledge your source. Never present another person's idea as your own. This is plagiarism and is inexcusable.

Sometimes writers are tempted to fill a paper with quotes from other sources or to quote another paper at great length (e.g., several paragraphs or more). This practice is distracting and counterproductive. Be direct, and use your own descriptions and interpretations while at the same time acknowledging your sources. If you have any questions about how to properly include material from source articles in your own paper, consult your instructor.

Active Versus Passive Voice

Many writers rely too much on the passive voice in their reports, perhaps because they believe that the passive voice makes their writing seem more "scientific." Consider the following sentences:

It was found by Yee and Johnson (1996) that adolescents prefer. . . .

Participants were administered the test after a 10-minute rest period.

Participants were read the instructions by the experimenter.

Now try writing those sentences in a more active voice. For example:

Yee and Johnson (1996) found that adolescents prefer. . . .

Participants took the test after a 10-minute rest period.

I read the instructions to the participants.

Prose that seems stilted using the passive voice is much more direct when phrased in the active voice. It is, of course, possible for the active voice to become distracting if used too much. "I" in particular can become awkward if it begins too many sentences. A good practice is to vary sentence constructions.

Biased Language

APA style is guided by the principles of specificity and sensitivity. Be sensitive to the possibility that your writing might convey a bias, however unintentional, regarding gender, sexual orientation, and ethnic or racial group. As a general principle, be as specific as possible when referring to groups of people. For example, referring to the participants in your study as "Korean Americans and Vietnamese Americans" is more specific and accurate than "Asians." Also, be sensitive to the use of labels that might be offensive to members of certain groups. In practice, this means that you refer to people using the terms that these people prefer. Also, avoid implicit labels such as saying "The lesbian sample, in contrast to the sample of normal women" or "We tested groups of autistics and normals." The latter phrase could be written as "We tested people with autism and without autism."

The APA manual has numerous examples of ways of being sensitive to gender, racial and ethnic identity, age, sexual orientation, and disabilities. The term *gender* refers to males and females as social groups. Thus, gender would be the proper term to use in a phrase such as "gender difference in average salary." The term *sex* refers to biological aspects of men and women; for example, "sex fantasies" or "sex differences in the size of certain brain structures." The use of gender pronouns can be problematic. Do not use *he, his, man, man's,* and so on when both males and females are meant. Sentences can usually be rephrased or specific pronouns deleted to avoid linguistic biases. For example, "The worker is paid according to his productivity" can be changed to "The worker is paid according to productivity" or "Workers are paid according to their productivity." In the first case, the *his* was simply deleted; in the second case, the subject of the sentence was changed to plural. Do *not* try to avoid sexist language by simply substituting *s/he* whenever that might appear convenient.

There are certain rules when referring to racial and ethnic groups. The names of these groups are capitalized and never hyphenated; for example, Black, White, African American, Latino, Asian, Asian American. The manual also reminds us that the terms that members of racial and ethnic groups use to describe themselves may change over time, and there may be a lack of consensus about a preferred term. Currently, for example, both Black and African American are generally acceptable. Depending on a number of factors, participants may prefer to be called Hispanic, Latino, Chicano, or Mexican American. You are urged to use the term most preferred by your participants.

The APA manual includes a great deal of information and numerous examples to encourage sensitivity in writing reports. The best advice is to review your papers for possible problems at least once prior to your final draft. If you have any questions about appropriate language, consult the manual and others whose opinions you respect.

Typing and Word Processing

You will eventually have to prepare a typed copy of your paper. In APA style, the paper should be *entirely double-spaced.* The margins for text should be *at least 1 inch* on all four sides of the page; in the example paper, all margins are set at 1.25 inches. Page headers are set approximately .5 inch from the top of the page. All pages are numbered except for figure pages at the end of the paper. Paragraphs are indented 5 to 7 spaces (use the tab function, not the space bar). Contractions are not used in APA-style writing. Words should never be hyphenated at the end of a line; lines should be a little short or a little long rather than breaking a word. This is easily accomplished in word processing programs. Such details used to be called typing rules; in the era of word processing, they become rules for printing.

Many students use word processing computer programs to prepare their papers: With a computer, you can improve your writing and submit a high-quality paper far more easily. If you are not already using a word processor, consider purchasing your own computer system or at least investigate word processing facilities on your campus. When you use a word processor, your writing is no longer typed copy but simply characters on a computer screen. Correcting, revising, moving, and deleting text is no longer a chore; such changes are easily made on the computer screen using the word processing program. Writing several drafts of a paper is easy because you don't have to retype the paper each time you wish to make a change.

Many word processing programs also include writing tools such as a spell check, thesaurus, grammar analysis, and outliner (if not, separate writing tool programs can be used with the word processor). The spelling checker examines your paper for spelling errors and even suggests possible corrections for misspelled words; the thesaurus feature allows you to examine possible alternative words to express an idea. Grammar programs analyze the grammar and readability of your paper; such programs look for sentences that are too long, words that might be difficult to understand, and simple grammatical mistakes. Finally, an outlining tool can facilitate the process of making an outline and help you better plan your actual paper.

Word processors also allow many advanced printing options such as justification of text against the margins, different type styles and type sizes, italics, boldface, and other features that make the paper resemble an actual published report. Never use full justification of text; set justification to the left margin only. Use a font that is of normal size and appearance (10 or 12 characters per inch and Courier, Times Roman, or Arial), and use the same font throughout. When submitting papers for publication, do not use boldface type. Always underline any text that you would italicize in a published paper (pay attention to the use of underlining in the headings and references in the examples given later in the appendix). When you are preparing a paper for a class or a thesis, using the boldface and italics capability of a word processing program may be acceptable; your instructor will provide you with guidelines for your situation. Finally, you need to have only one space between a period that ends a sentence and the beginning of the following sentence; this practice makes the paper look more attractive when using a proportional font and saves a step when publishing the paper.

ORGANIZATION OF THE REPORT

A research report is organized into five major parts: Abstract, Introduction, Method, Results, and Discussion. References must be listed using a particular format. The report may also include tables and figures used in presenting the results. We will consider the parts of the paper in the order prescribed by APA style. Refer to the sample paper at the end of this appendix as you read the material that follows.

Title Page

The first page of the paper is the title page. It is a separate page and is numbered page 1. Note in the example paper that the title page does in fact list the title; however, there are other important items of information as well.

At the top of the title page is a page header. The page header includes a short title, consisting of the first two or three words of the title of your paper, and a page number. These should be typed so the page number is flush to the right margin of the paper. If you are using a word processor, use the page header feature to create a header that prints approximately halfway between the text of the paper and the top of each page (in the sample paper, the header is set for .5 inch from the top). Do not try to manually type a page header and page number at the top of every page of your paper; instead use the page header function of your word processing program. The page header appears on every page of your paper except the figure pages. The page header provides a heading for your readers; more important, if the pages get separated accidentally, it will be easy for the reader to put them together again in proper order.

The first line of the title page will be the *running head* for publication; it is typed flush against the left margin and appears as follows (note that all letters in the running head are capitalized): The running head is an abbreviated title and should be no more than 50 characters (letters, numbers, spaces) in length. If the paper is published in a journal, the running head is printed as a heading at the top of pages to help readers identify the article. The running head is used for publication purposes and appears only once; the page header, in contrast, is used by readers of your paper and appears on every page. Do not confuse the running head and the page header. In the sample paper, the short title is "Experience"—a short description drawn from the first few words of the title of the paper. However, the running head is "WATER-LEVEL TASK"—which is longer than the short title and more descriptive of the content of the paper. The remainder of the title page consists of the title, author byline, and institutional affiliation. All are centered on the page.

The title should be fairly short (usually no more than 12 to 15 words) and should inform the reader of the nature of your research. A good way to do this is to include the names of your variables in the title. For example, the following titles are both short and informative:

Effect of Anxiety on Mathematical Problem Solving

Memory for Faces Among Elderly and Young Adults

Sometimes a colon in the title will help to convey the nature of your research or even add a bit of "flair" to your title, as in:

Cognitive Responses in Persuasion: Affective and Evaluative Determinants

Comparing the Tortoise and the Hare: Gender Differences and Experience in Dynamic Spatial Reasoning Tasks

Another method of titling a paper is to pose the question that the research addresses. For example:

Do Rewards in the Classroom Undermine Intrinsic Motivation?

Does Occupational Stereotyping Still Exist?

Abstract

The abstract is a brief summary of the research report and typically runs 100 to 120 words in length (no more than 900 characters including spaces and punctuation marks). The purpose of the abstract is to introduce the article, allowing readers to decide if the article appears relevant to their own interests. The abstract should provide enough information so that the reader can decide whether to read the entire report, and it should make the report easier to comprehend when it is read.

Although the abstract appears at the beginning of your report, it is easiest to write the abstract last. Read a few abstracts and you will get some good ideas for how to condense a full-length research report down to 8 or 10 information-packed sentences. A very informative exercise is to write an abstract for a published article, and then compare your abstract to the one written by the original authors.

Abstracts generally include a sentence or two about each of the four main sections in the body of the article. First, from the *introduction* section, state the problem under study and the primary hypotheses. Second, from the *method* section, include information on the characteristics of the participants (e.g., number, age, sex, and any special characteristics) and a brief summary of the procedure (e.g., self-report questionnaires, direct observation, repeated measurements on several occasions). Third, from the *results* section, describe the pattern of findings for major variables. This is typically done by reporting the direction of differences without relying on numerical values. APA guidelines recommend including statistical significance levels, yet few authors comply (Ono, Phillips, & Leneman, 1996). We suggest that you rely on guidelines provided by your instructor. From the *discussion* section, the implications of the study are commonly abstracted. Informative comments about the findings are preferred to general statements such as "the implications of the study are addressed" (Kazdin, 1995).

The abstract is typed on a separate page and is numbered page 2. The word *Abstract* is centered at the top of the page. The abstract is always typed as a single paragraph in a "block" format with no paragraph indentation.

Introduction

The introduction section begins on a new page (page 3), with the title of your report typed at the top of the page. Note that the author's name doesn't appear on this page; this allows a reviewer to read the paper without knowing the name of the author. The introduction section presents the specific problem under study, describes the research strategy, and presents the predicted outcomes of the research. After reading the introduction, the reader should know why you decided to do the research and how you decided to go about doing it. In general, the introduction progresses from broad theories and findings to specifics of the current research.

There are three components to the introduction, although no formal subsections are utilized. The components are: (1) the problem under study, (2) the literature review, and (3) the rationale of the present study.

The introduction should begin with an opening statement of the *problem under study*. In two or three sentences give the reader an appreciation of the broad context and significance of the topic being studied (Bem, 1981; Kazdin, 1995). Specifically state what problem is being investigated. This is worthwhile if it can be done; it helps readers, even those who are unfamiliar with the topic, understand and appreciate why the topic was studied in the first place.

Following the opening statement, the introduction provides a description of past research and theory. This is called the *literature review*. An exhaustive review of past theory and research is not necessary (if there are major literature reviews of the topic, you would of course refer the reader to the reviews). Rather, you want to describe only the research and theoretical issues that are clearly related to your study. State explicitly how this previous work is logically connected to your research problem. This tells the reader why your research was conducted and shows the connection to prior research.

The final part of the introduction tells the reader the *rationale* of the current study. Here you state what variables you are studying and what results you expect. The links between the research hypothesis, prior research, and the current research design are shown by explaining why the hypotheses are expected.

Method

The method section begins immediately after you have completed the introduction (on the same page if space permits). This section provides the reader with detailed information about how your study was conducted. Ideally, there should be enough information in the method section to allow a reader to replicate your study.

The method section is typically divided into a number of subsections. Both the order of the subsections and the number of subsections vary in published articles. Decisions about which subsections to include are guided by the complexity of the investigation. The sample paper in this appendix uses 3 subsections: *Participants, Materials,* and *Procedure.* Some of the most commonly used subsections are discussed next.

Overview   If the experimental design and procedures used in the research are complex, a brief overview of the method should be presented to help the reader understand the information that follows.

Participants   A subsection on the participants or respondents is always necessary. The number and nature of the participants should be described. Age, sex, ethnicity, and any other relevant characteristics should be described. Special characteristics of participants are described, such as first-born children, adolescent children of alcoholics, student teachers, parents of hyperactive boys. State explicitly how participants were recruited and what incentives for participation might have been used. The number of individuals in each experimental condition also can be included here.

Apparatus   An apparatus subsection may be necessary if special equipment is used in the experiment. The brand name and model number of the equipment may be specified; some apparatus may be described in detail. This information would be included if it is needed to replicate the experiment.

Procedure   The procedure subsection tells the reader exactly how the study was conducted. One way to report this information is to describe, step by step, what occurred in the experiment. Maintain the temporal sequence of events so the reader is able to visualize the sequence of events the participants experienced.

The procedure subsection tells the reader what instructions were given to the participants, how the independent variables were manipulated, and how the dependent variables were measured. The methods used to control extraneous variables also should be described. These would include randomization procedures, counterbalancing, and special means that were used to keep a variable constant across all conditions. Finally, the method of debriefing should be described. If your study used a nonexperimental method, you would still provide details on exactly how you conducted the study and the measurement techniques you used.

It is up to you to decide how much detail to include here. Use your own judgment to determine the importance of a specific aspect of the procedure and the amount of detail that is necessary for the reader to clearly understand what was done in the study. If any detail might be important in a replication of the study, it should be included.

Other Subsections   Other subsections should be included if needed for clear presentation of the method. For example, a subsection on "testing materials" might be necessary instead of an "apparatus" subsection. Other sections are customized by the authors to suit their study. A recent volume of *Child Development* (Volume 68) included sections titled "Overview of Procedure," "Reliability and Validity," "Measures," "Timing of Assessments," and "Demographic and Socioeconomic Characteristics," with some articles having only 2 subsections (Flavell, Green, Flavell, & Grossman, 1997) and a more complex article using 15 subsections in the Method (Kochanska, 1997).

Results

In the results section, present the results as clearly as possible. The results section is a straightforward description of your analyses. Do not explain your findings in the results section. This is very tempting, but save that discussion for the next section of the paper.

Be sure to state the alpha (probability) level that you used in making decisions about statistical significance: This will usually be .05 or .01 and only requires a simple sentence such as "an alpha level of .05 was used for statistical analyses."

Present your results in the same order that your predictions are stated in the introduction section of the paper. If a manipulation check was made, it should be presented before the major results are described.

The content of your results section will vary according to the type of statistical test performed and the number of analyses you conducted. However, every results section includes some basic elements. If applicable, describe any scoring or coding procedures performed on the data to prepare them for analysis. This is particularly important when coding qualitative data. (Sometimes data transformations are included in a subsection of the Method.) State which statistical test was performed on the data (*t* test, *F* test, correlation). Justify the selection of a particular statistical comparison to address your hypothesis. Be sure to summarize each finding in words as well as including the results of statistical tests in the form of statistical phrases (see Chapter 15).

The results should be stated in simple sentences. For example, the results of the sports participation experiment described in Chapter 14 might be expressed as follows:

```
As predicted, girls in the intramurals group were referred
for discipline problems significantly less than girls in the
aerobics group, t(18) = 4.025, p < .01. The mean referral
score in the intramurals group was 3.10, and the aerobics
group mean was 5.20.
```

These two sentences inform the reader of the general pattern of the results, the obtained means, and the statistical significance of the results (note the placement of the results of the statistical phrase that includes the symbol for the *t* test, degrees of freedom, and significance level).

If the results are relatively straightforward, they can be presented entirely in sentence form. If the study involved a complex design, tables and figures may be needed to clarify presentation of the results.

Tables and Figures   Tables are generally used to present large arrays of data. For example, a table might be useful in a design with several dependent measures; the means of the different groups for all dependent measures would be presented in the table. Tables are also convenient when a factorial design has been used. For example, in a $2 \times 2 \times 3$ factorial design, a table could be used to present all 12 means.

Figures are used when a visual display of the results would help the reader understand the outcome of the study. Figures may be used to illustrate a significant interaction or show trends over time.

In APA style, tables and figures are not presented in the main body of the manuscript. Rather, they are placed at the end of the paper. Each table and figure appears on a separate page. A table or figure is noted in the text by referring to a table or figure number and describing the content of the table or figure. Never make a reference to the placement of the figure because the placement is determined by the typesetter. In the results section make a statement such as "As shown in Figure 2, the aerobics group . . ." or "Table 1 presents the demographic characteristics of the participating families." Describe the important features of the table or figure rather than using a generic comment such as "See Figure 3."

Do not repeat the same data in more than one place. An informative table or figure supplements, not duplicates, the text. Using tables and figures does not diminish your responsibility to clearly state the nature of the results in the text of your report.

When you are writing a research report for a purpose other than publication—for example, to fulfill a course or degree requirement—it may be more convenient to place each figure and table on a separate page within the main body of the paper. Because rules about the placement of tables and figures may vary, check on the proper format before writing your report.

Discussion of the Results   It is usually *not* appropriate to discuss the implications of the results in the results section. However, the results and discussion section may be combined if the discussion is brief and greater clarity is achieved by the combination.

Discussion

The discussion section is the proper place to discuss the implications of the results. One way to organize the discussion is to begin by summarizing the original purpose and expectations of the study, then state whether the results were consistent with your expectations. If the results do support your original ideas, you should discuss how your findings contribute to knowledge of the problem you investigated. You will want to consider the relationship between your results and past research and theory. If you did not obtain the expected results, discuss possible explanations. The explanations would be quite different, of course, depending on whether you obtained results that were the opposite of what you expected or the results were nonsignificant.

It is often a good idea to include your own criticisms of the study. Many published articles include limitations of the study. Try to anticipate what a reader might find wrong with your methodology. For example, if you used the correlational method, you might point out problems of cause and effect and possible extraneous variables that might be operating. Sometimes there may be major or minor flaws that could be corrected in a subsequent study (if you had the time, money, and so on). You can describe such flaws and suggest corrections. If there are potential problems generalizing your results, state the problems and give reasons why you think the results would or would not generalize.

The results will probably have implications for future research. If so, you should discuss the direction that research might take. It is also possible that the results have practical implications—for example, for child rearing or improving learning in the classroom. Discussion of these larger issues is usually placed at the end of the discussion section. Finally, you will probably wish to have a brief concluding paragraph that provides "closure" to the entire paper.

Students generally find that writing the discussion section is the most challenging. The guidelines for the discussion section are less structured than guidelines for the other sections of an APA paper, allowing flexibility in content.

Support your explanations with citations to prior research, and tie your study to the broader theoretical context. The goal is to interpret, evaluate, and discuss the findings in a logical, coherent manner.

References

The list of references begins on a new page. The references must contain complete citations for all sources mentioned in your report. Do not omit any sources from the list of references; also, do not include any sources that are not mentioned in your report. The exact procedures for citing sources within the body of your report and in your list of references are described later in Appendix A. Follow the examples in recent publications; APA format was revised in 1994, and therefore older books and journal articles do not utilize the appropriate format.

Appendix

An appendix is rarely provided in manuscripts submitted for publication. The APA *Publication Manual* notes that an appendix might be appropriate when necessary material would be distracting in the main body of the report. Examples of appendixes include a sample of a questionnaire or survey instrument, a complex mathematical proof, or a long list of words used as stimulus items. An appendix (or several appendixes) is much more appropriate for a student research project or a thesis. The appendix might include the entire questionnaire that was used, a new test that was developed, or other materials employed in the study. Check with your instructor concerning the appropriateness of an appendix for your paper. If an appendix is provided, it begins on a new page with the word *Appendix* centered at the top.

Author Note

An author note may be provided. The author note typically begins with a paragraph that gives the department affiliations of the authors (this is necessary only for papers with multiple authors or when an author's current affiliation has changed since the study was completed). Another paragraph may give details about the background of the study (e.g., that it is based on the first author's master's thesis) and acknowledgments (e.g., grant support, colleagues who assisted with the study, and so on). A final paragraph begins with "Correspondence concerning this article should be addressed to . . ." followed by the mailing address of the person designated for that purpose. An author note will probably be unnecessary for class research reports. Author note begins on a new page.

Footnotes

Footnotes, if used, are not typed in the body of the text. Instead, all footnotes in the paper are typed on one page at the end of the paper. Avoid using footnotes unless they are absolutely necessary. They tend to be distracting to readers, and the information can and should be integrated into the body of the paper.

Tables

Each table should be on a separate page. As noted previously, APA style requires placement of the table at the end of the paper, but for a class you may be asked to place your tables on separate pages within the body of the paper. A sample table is included in the sample paper at the end of Appendix A. In preparing your table, allow enough space so that the table does not appear cramped in a small portion of the page. Areas of the table are defined by typed horizontal lines (do not use vertical lines). Give some thought to the title so that it accurately and clearly describes the content of the table. You may wish to use an explanatory note in the table to show significance levels or the range of possible values on a variable. Before you make up your own tables, examine the tables in a recent issue of one of the journals published by the American Psychological Association.

Figures

There are two special APA style rules for the placement and preparation of figures: (1) Figures are placed after the tables in the papers, and (2) a separate page containing the figure captions is provided before the figures. However, either or both of these rules may not be necessary for student reports or theses. You may be asked to place each figure on a separate page at the appropriate point in the body of the text, and you may not need a figure caption page (this is only for the convenience of typesetting and printing the paper). Also, if you are following true APA style, there is no page number or short title on the figure pages (the figure number is written on the back of the figure in pencil).

If you are preparing your figure by hand, it is a good idea to buy graph paper with lines that do not photocopy (a photocopy of the graph is turned in with your final report). Lines are drawn using black ink and a ruler (alternatively, you can use press-on type and rules, available at a graphics supply store). In deciding on the size of the figure, a good rule is that the horizontal axis should be about 5 inches wide, and the vertical axis should be about 3.5 inches long. Both the vertical and the horizontal axes must be labeled. Dependent and criterion variables are placed on the vertical axis. Independent and predictor variables are placed on the horizontal axis (see Chapter 4).

Instead of preparing your graphs by hand, consider using computer graphics software. You may have access to such software in your word processing or spreadsheet program. Graphics software makes preparation of graphs easier and reduces the frustration that arises when you make mistakes.

Remember that the purpose of a figure is to increase comprehension of results by having a graphical display of data. If the graph is cluttered with information, it will confuse the reader and will not serve its purpose. Plan your graphs carefully to make sure that you are accurately and clearly informing the reader. If you become interested in the topic of how to display information in graphs and charts, two books by Tufte (1983, 1990) are recommended. Tufte explores a variety of ways of presenting data, factors that lead to clarity, and ways that graphs can deceive the reader.

Summary: Order of Pages

To summarize, the organization of your paper is as follows:

1. Title page (page 1)
2. Abstract (page 2)
3. Pages of text (start on new page 3)
   a. Title at top of first page begins the introduction
   b. Method
   c. Results
   d. Discussion
4. References (start on new page)
5. Appendix (start on new page if included)
6. Author note (start on new page if included)
7. Footnotes (start on new page if included)
8. Tables, with table captions (each table on a separate page)
9. Figure captions (all captions together on one separate page)
10. Figures (each figure on a separate page)

You should now have a general idea of how to structure and write your report. The remainder of Appendix A focuses on some of the technical rules that may be useful as you prepare your own research report.

THE USE OF HEADINGS

Papers written in APA style use one to five levels of headings. Most commonly, you will use "level 1" and "level 3" headings, and you may need to use "level 4" headings as well. These are:

(Level 1)		Centered Heading
(Level 3)	Margin Heading	
	The text begins indented on a new line.	
(Level 4)	Paragraph heading. The heading is indented	
	and the text begins on the same line.	

Level 2 and level 5 headings will not be described because they are used in more complex papers in which multiple experiments are presented.

Level 1, or centered, headings are used to head major sections of the report: Abstract, Title (on page 3), Method, Results, Discussion, References, and so on. Level 1 headings are typed with uppercase and lowercase letters (i.e., the first letter of each word is capitalized).

Level 3, or margin, headings are used to divide major sections into subsections. Level 3 headings are typed flush to the left margin, with uppercase and lowercase letters (i.e., the first letter of each word is capitalized). For example, the Method section is divided into at least two subsections: Participants and Procedure. The correct format is

```
                         Method
Participants
        The description of the participants begins on a new
line.
Procedure
        The procedure is now described in detail.
```

Level 4, or paragraph, headings are used to organize material within a subsection. For example, the Procedure subsection might be broken down into separate categories for describing instructions to participants, the independent variable manipulation, measurement of the dependent variable, and debriefing. Each of these would be introduced through the use of a paragraph heading.

Paragraph headings begin on a new line, indented five spaces. The first word begins with a capital letter; the remaining words are all typed in lowercase letters. The heading ends with a period. The entire heading including the period is underlined. All information that appears between a paragraph heading and the next heading (of any level) must be related to the paragraph heading.

CITING AND REFERENCING SOURCES

Citation Style

Whenever you refer to information reported by other researchers, you *must* accurately identify the sources. APA journals use the author-date citation method: The author name(s) and year of publication are inserted at appropriate points. The citation style depends on whether the author names are part of the narrative or are in parentheses.

One Author   When the author's name is part of the narrative, include the publication date in parentheses immediately after the name:

```
Markman (1991) found that marital discord can lead to
constructive resolution of conflict.
```

When the author's name is not part of the narrative, the name and date are cited in parentheses at the end of an introductory phrase or at the end of the sentence:

```
In one study (Markman, 1991), couples learned to
discuss. . . .

It has been reported that couples have lower rates of
divorce and marital violence after problem-solving
intervention (Markman, 1991).
```

Two Authors When the work has two authors, both names are included in each reference citation. The difference between narrative and parenthetical citations is in the use of the conjunction "and" and the ampersand "&" to connect authors' names. When the names are part of a sentence, use the word "and" to join the names of two authors. When the complete citation is in parentheses, use the "&" symbol:

> Harris and Marmer (1996) reported that fathers in poor and welfare families are less involved with their adolescent children than fathers in nonpoor families.

> Fathers in poor and welfare families are less likely to spend time with their adolescent children than fathers in nonpoor families (Harris & Marmer, 1996).

Three to Five Authors When a report has three to five authors, all author names are cited the first time the reference occurs. Thereafter, cite the first author's surname followed by the abbreviation *et al.* ("and others") along with the publication date. The abbreviation may be used in narrative and parenthetical citations:

First citation

> Abernathy, Massad, and Romano-Dwyer (1995) reported that female adolescents with low self-esteem are more likely to smoke than their peers with high self-esteem.

> Research suggests that low self-esteem is one reason teenage girls are motivated to smoke (Abernathy, Massad, & Romano-Dwyer, 1995).

Subsequent citations

> Abernathy et al. (1995) also examined the relationship between smoking and self-esteem in adolescent males.

> For males, there is no relationship between smoking and self-esteem, suggesting gender-specific motivations for initiating smoking in adolescence (Abernathy et al., 1995).

Another question about subsequent citations is whether to include the publication date each time an article is referenced. Within a paragraph, you do *not* need to include the year in subsequent citations as long as the study cannot be confused with other studies cited in your report.

First citation

> In a recent study of reaction times, Yokoi and Jones (1998) found. . . .

Subsequent citations within a paragraph

```
Yokoi and Jones also reported that. . . .
```

When subsequent citations are in another paragraph or in another section of the report, the publication date should be included.

Six or More Authors   Occasionally you will reference a report with six or more authors. In this case, use the abbreviation *et al.* after the first author's last name in *every* citation. Although you would not list all author names in the text, the citation in the references section of the report should include the names of all authors.

References With No Author   When an article has no author (e.g., some newspaper or magazine articles), cite the first two or three words of the title in quotation marks, followed by the publication date:

Citation in reference list

```
Parental smoking kills 6,200 kids a year, study says. (1997,
July 15). Orange County Register, p. 11.
```

Citation in text

```
In an article on smoking ("Parental smoking," 1997),
data. . . .
```

Multiple Works Within the Same Parentheses   A convenient way to cite several studies on the same topic or several studies with similar findings is to reference them as a series within the same parentheses. When two or more works are by the same author(s), report them in order of year of publication, using commas to separate citations:

```
Schaie and Willis (1986, 1993) found. . . .

Past research (Schaie & Willis, 1986, 1993) indicates. . . .
```

When two or more works by different authors are cited within the same parentheses, arrange them in alphabetical order and separate citations by semicolons:

```
Investigations of families in economic distress consistently
report that girls react with internalization problems
whereas boys respond with externalization problems (Conger,
Ge, Elder, Lorenz, & Simons, 1994; Flanagan & Eccles, 1993;
Lempers, Clark-Lempers, & Simons, 1989).
```

Reference List Style

The APA *Publication Manual* specifies different reference formats for journal articles, books, chapters in books, technical reports, convention presentations, dissertations, and videos, among many others. Only a few of these are presented here. When in doubt about how to construct a reference, consult the APA manual (especially pages 174–222). The general format for a reference list is:

1. The references are listed in alphabetical order by first author's last name. Do not categorize references by type (i.e., books, journal articles, and so on).
2. The first line of each reference is indented as if it were the first line of a paragraph. You might think of each reference as a different paragraph.
3. Elements of a reference (authors' names, article title, publication data) are separated by periods.

Notice the spacing in the typing of authors' names in the examples.

When the paper is typeset for publication in the journal, the citation will appear differently than it does in the manuscript. A reference in the manuscript might appear as follows:

```
Hammond, J. M. (1995). Multiple jeopardy or
multiple resources? The intersection of age, race, living
arrangements, and education level and the health of older
women. Journal of Women & Aging, 7, 5-24.
```

However, when published it would appear as follows:

Hammond, J. M. (1995). Multiple jeopardy or multiple resources? The intersection of age, race, living arrangements, and education level and the health of older women. *Journal of Women & Aging, 7,* 5–24.

Format for Journal Articles   Most journals are organized by volume and year of publication (e.g., Volume 20 of *Health and Social Work* consists of journal issues published in 1995). A common confusion is whether to include the journal issue number in addition to the volume number. The rule is simple: If the issues in a volume are paginated consecutively throughout the volume, *do not* include the journal issue number. If each issue in a volume begins with page 1, the issue number should be included. Specific examples are shown below.

In the reference list, both the name of the journal and the volume number are underlined. Also, only the first letter of the first word in article titles is capitalized (except proper nouns and the first word after a colon or question mark). Here are some examples.

One author—no issue number

```
Newby, T. J. (1991). Classroom motivation strategies:
Strategies of first-year teachers. Journal of Educational
Psychology, 83, 195-200.
```

Two authors—use of issue number

```
Greenwald-Robbins, J., & Greenwald, R. (1994).
Environmental attitudes conceptualized through developmental
theory: A qualitative analysis. Journal of Social Issues,
50(3), 29-47.
```

Format for Books   When a book is cited, the title of the book is underlined. Only the first word of the title is capitalized; however, proper nouns and the first word after a colon or question mark are also capitalized. The city of publication and the publishing company follow the title. If the city is not well known, include the U.S. Postal Service two-letter abbreviation for the state (e.g., AZ, NY, MN, TX).

One-author book

> Uba, L. (1994). <u>Asian Americans: Personality patterns, identity, and mental health.</u> New York: The Guilford Press.

One-author book—second or later edition

> McAdoo, H. P. (1988). <u>Black families</u> (2nd ed.). Newbury Park, CA: Sage.

Edited book

> Huston, A. H. (Ed.). (1991). <u>Children in poverty: Child development and public policy.</u> New York: Cambridge University Press.

Format for Articles in Edited Books   For edited books, the reference begins with the names of the authors of the article, not the book. The title of the article follows. The name(s) of the book editor(s), the book title, the inclusive page numbers for the article, and the publication data for the book follow, in that order. Only the book title is underlined, and only the first letters of the article and book titles are capitalized. Here are some examples.

One editor

> Brown, A. L., & Campione, J. C. (1994). Guided discovery in a community of learners. In K. McGilly (Ed.), <u>Classroom lessons: Integrating cognitive theory and classroom practice</u> (pp. 229-270). Cambridge, MA: MIT Press.

Two editors

> Bates, J., Bayles, K., Bennett, D., Ridge, B., & Brown, M. (1991). Origins of externalizing behavior problems at eight years of age. In D. Pepler & K. Rubin (Eds.), <u>The development and treatment of childhood aggression</u> (pp. 93-120). Hillsdale, NJ: Erlbaum.

Chapter from book in multivolume series

> Kagan, J. (1992). Temperamental contributions to emotion and social behavior. In M. S. Clark (Ed.), <u>Review of personality and social psychology: Vol. 14. Emotion and social behavior</u> (pp. 99-118). Newbury Park, CA: Sage.

Format for "Popular Articles"   The reference styles shown next should be used for articles from magazines and newspapers. As a general rule, popular press articles are used sparingly (e.g., when no scientific articles on a topic can be found or to provide an example of an event that is related to your topic).

Magazine – continuous pages

> Begley, S. (1995, March 27). Gray matters. Newsweek, 125, 48-54.

Newspaper – no author

> 10-year-old is youngest to graduate from college. (1994, June 6). Orange County Register, p. 15.

Newspaper – discontinuous pages

> Cole, K. C. (1995, May 1). Way the brain works may play role in bias, experts say. Los Angeles Times, pp. A1, A18.

Format for Papers and Poster Sessions Presented at Conferences   Occasionally you may need to cite an unpublished paper or poster session that was presented at a professional meeting. Here are two examples:

Paper

> Kee, D. W., McBride, D., Neale, P., & Segal, N. (1995, November). Manual and cerebral laterality in hand-discordant monozygotic twins. Paper presented at the annual meeting of the Psychonomics Society, Los Angeles, CA.

Poster session

> Roach, M. A., Barratt, M. S., & Miller, J. F. (1997, April). Maternal adaptation over time to children with Down Syndrome and typically developing children. Poster session presented at the annual meeting of the Society for Research in Child Development, Washington, DC.

ABBREVIATIONS

Abbreviations are not extensively used in APA-style papers. They can be distracting because the reader must constantly try to translate the abbreviation into its full meaning. However, APA style does allow for the use of abbreviations that are accepted as words in the dictionary (specifically, Webster's *Collegiate Dictionary*). These include IQ, REM, ESP, and AIDS.

Certain well-known terms may be abbreviated when it would make reading easier, but the full meaning should be given when first used in the paper. Examples of commonly used abbreviations are:

MMPI	Minnesota Multiphasic Personality Inventory
STM	short-term memory
CS	conditioned stimulus
RT	reaction time
CVC	consonant-vowel-consonant
ANOVA	analysis of variance

Statistical terms are sometimes used in their abbreviated or symbol form. These are always underlined in a manuscript. For example:

$\underline{M}$	mean
$\underline{SD}$	standard deviation
$\underline{Mdn}$	median
$\underline{df}$	degrees of freedom
$\underline{n}$	number of individuals in a group or experimental condition
$\underline{N}$	total number of participants or respondents
$\underline{p}$	probability (significance) level
$\underline{SS}$	sum of squares
$\underline{MS}$	mean square
$\underline{F}$	value of F in analysis of variance
$\underline{r}$	Pearson correlation coefficient
$\underline{R}$	multiple correlation coefficient

Finally, certain abbreviations of Latin terms are regularly used in papers. Some of these abbreviations and their meanings are:

cf.	compare
e.g.	for example
etc.	and so forth
i.e.	that is
viz.	namely
vs.	versus

SOME GRAMMATICAL CONSIDERATIONS

Transition Words and Phrases

One way to produce a clearly written research report is to pay attention to how you connect sentences within a paragraph and connect paragraphs within a section. The transitions between sentences and paragraphs should be smooth and consistent with the line of reasoning. Some commonly used transition words and phrases and their functions are described in this section.

Adverbs Adverbs can be used as introductory words in sentences. However, you must use them to convey their implied meanings.

Adverb	Implied meaning
(Un)fortunately	It is (un)fortunate that. . . .
Similarly	In a similar manner. . . .
Certainly	It is certain that. . . .
Clearly	It is clear that. . . .

One adverb that is frequently misused as an introductory or transition word is *hopefully*. *Hopefully* means "in a hopeful manner," *not* "it is hoped that. . . ."

Incorrect: Hopefully, this is not the case.

Correct: I hope this is not the case.

Words Suggesting Contrast Some words and phrases suggest a contrast or contradiction between what was written immediately before and what is now being written:

Between sentences	Within sentences
By contrast,	whereas
On the other hand,	although
However,	but

The words in the left list refer to the previous sentence. The words in the right list connect phrases within a sentence; that is, they refer to another point in the same sentence.

Words Suggesting a Series of Ideas Words and phrases that suggest that information after the transition word is related or similar to information in the sentence are:

First	In addition	Last	Further
Second	Additionally	Finally	Moreover
Third	Then	Also	Another

Words Suggesting Implication These words and phrases indicate that the information following the transition word is implied by or follows from the previous information:

Therefore	If . . . then
It follows that	Thus
In conclusion	Then

When you use transition words, be sure that they convey the meaning you intend. Sprinkling them around to begin sentences leads to confusion on the reader's part and defeats your purpose.

Troublesome Words and Phrases

"That" Versus "Which"   *That* and *which* are relative pronouns that introduce subordinate clauses and reflect the relationship of the subordinate clause to the main clause. *That* clauses are called restrictive clauses and are essential to the meaning of the sentence; *which* clauses are nonrestrictive and simply add more information. Note the different meanings of the same sentence using *that* and *which:*

> The mice that performed well in the first trial were used in the second trial.

> The mice, which performed well in the first trial, were used in the second trial.

The first sentence states that only mice that performed well in the first trial were used in the second. The second sentence states that all the mice were used in the second trial and they also happened to perform well in the first trial.

"While" Versus "Since"   *While* and *since* are subordinate conjunctions that also introduce subordinate clauses. To increase clarity in scientific writing, the APA manual suggests that *while* and *since* should be used only to refer to time. *While* is used to describe simultaneous events, and *since* is used to refer to a subsequent event:

> The participants waited together while their personality tests were scored.

> Since the study by Elder (1974), many studies have been published on this topic.

The APA manual suggests other conjunctions to use to link phrases that do not describe temporal events. *Although, whereas,* and *but* can be used in place of *while,* and *because* should be substituted for *since.*

> *Incorrect:* While the study was well designed, the report was poorly written.

> *Correct:* Although the study was well designed, the report was poorly written.

"Effect" Versus "Affect"   A common error in student reports is the incorrect use of *effect* and *affect. Effect* is a noun that is used in scientific reports to mean "what is produced by a cause," as in the sentence: "The movie had a strong effect on me." *Affect* can be a noun or a verb. As a noun it means emotion, as in "The patient seemed depressed but she displayed very little affect." As a verb it means "to have an influence on," as in "The listeners' responses were affected by the music they heard."

> *Incorrect:* The independent variable effected their responses.

> *Correct:* The independent variable affected their responses.

Incorrect: The independent variable had only a weak affect on the partici-pants' behavior.

Correct: The independent variable had only a weak effect on the partici-pants' behavior.

Singular and Plural   The following words are often misused. The left list shows singular nouns requiring singular verb forms. The right list contains plural nouns that must be used with plural verbs.

Singular	*Plural*
datum	data
stimulus	stimuli
analysis	analyses
phenomenon	phenomena
medium	media
hypothesis	hypotheses
schema	schemata

Probably the most frequently misused word is *data.*

Incorrect: The data *was* coded for computer analysis.

Correct: The data *were* coded for computer analysis.

REPORTING NUMBERS AND STATISTICS

Virtually all research papers report numbers: number of participants, number of groups, the values of statistics such as *t, F,* or *r.* Should you use numbers (e.g., *"43"*), or should you use words (e.g., *"forty-three"*)? The general rule is to use words when expressing the numbers zero through nine but numbers for 10 and above. There are some important qualifications, however.

If you start a sentence with a number, you should use words even if the num-ber is 10 or larger (e.g., *"Eighty-five student teachers participated in the study."*). Start-ing a sentence with a number is often awkward, especially with large numbers. Therefore, you should try to revise the sentence to avoid the problem (e.g., *"The participants were 85 students enrolled in teaching credential classes."*).

When numbers both above and below 10 are being compared in the same sentence, use numerals for both (e.g., *"Participants read either 8 or 16 paragraphs."*). However, this sentence contains an appropriate mix of numbers and words: *"Par-ticipants read eight paragraphs and then answered 20 multiple-choice questions."* The sen-tence is correct because the paragraphs and the questions are different entities and so are not being compared.

When reporting a percentage, always use numerals followed by a percent sign except when beginning a sentence. This is true regardless of whether the number is less than 10 (e.g., *"Only 6% of the computer games appealed to females."*) or greater than 10 (e.g., *"When using this technique, 85% of the participants improved their performance."*).

Always use numbers when describing ages (e.g., *"5-year-olds"*), points on a scale (e.g., *"a 3 on a 5-point scale"*), units of measurement (e.g., *"the children stood 2 m from the target"*), sample size (e.g., *"6 girls and 6 boys were assigned to each study condition"*), and statistics (e.g., *"the mean score in the no model group was 3.10"*). An odd but sensible exception to the word-number rule occurs when two different types of numbers must appear together. An example is *"Teachers identified the most aggressive fifteen 7-year-olds."* This sentence avoids an awkward juxtaposition of two numbers.

Finally, you need to know about presenting statistical results within your paper. As noted previously, statistical terms are abbreviated and underlined (e.g., $\underline{M}$, $\underline{r}$, $\underline{t}$, $\underline{F}$). In addition, when reporting the results of a statistical significance test, provide the name of the test, the degrees of freedom, the value of the test statistic, and the probability level. Here are two examples of sentences that describe statistical results:

```
As predicted, participants in the high anxiety condition
took longer to recognize the words (M = 2.63) than did the
individuals in the low anxiety condition (M = 1.42), t(20)
= 2.34, p < .05.

Job satisfaction scores were significantly correlated with
marital satisfaction, r(50) = .38, p < .05.
```

If your printer cannot produce a particular symbol, you may draw it in with black ink. Pay attention to the way statistics are described in the articles you read. You will find that you can vary your descriptions of results to best fit your data and presentation, as well as vary your sentence constructions.

CONCLUSION

When you have completed your research report, you should feel proud of your effort. You have considered past research on a problem, conducted a research project, analyzed the results, and reported the findings. Such a research effort may result in a publication or a presentation at a convention. This is not the most important part of your research, however. What is most important is that you have acquired new knowledge and that your curiosity has been aroused so you will want to learn even more.

SAMPLE PAPER

The remainder of this appendix consists of a typed manuscript of a paper that was published in a professional journal. This is intended to be a useful guide when you write and organize your own reports in APA style. The margin notes point out important elements of APA style. Read through the manuscript, paying particular attention to the general format, and make sure you understand the rules concerning page numbering, section headings, citing references, and the format of tables and figures. Writing your first research report is always a difficult and challenging task. It will become easier as you read the research of others and practice by writing reports of your own.

The sample paper by Ross Vasta, Deirdre Rosenberg, Jill A. Knott, and Christine E. Gaze is a longer version of an article published in *Psychological Science* (1997, Vol. 8, pp. 336–339). Certain modifications were made to illustrate various elements of APA style. The authors graciously gave permission to reprint the paper in this form.

Experience   1

Running head: WATER-LEVEL TASK

Experience and the Water-Level Task Revisited:

Does Expertise Exact a Price?

Ross Vasta

State University of New York, Brockport

Deirdre Rosenberg

Rochester Institute of Technology

Jill A. Knott and Christine E. Gaze

State University of New York, Brockport

Each page has a header with the first 2 or 3 words from the title and page number. Place the page number 5 spaces after the page identification.

The running head is a short title at the top of each page of the printed article. Place the running head at the left margin, in capital letters. Maximum length is 50 characters.

Center the title in uppercase and lowercase letters. Authors' names are placed one double-spaced line below the title, centered. The institutional affiliation is typed on the next double-spaced line.

The title is usually 10 to 12 words.

Double-space the entire paper.

Use uniform margins of at least 1 inch on the top, bottom, right, and left of all pages.

SOURCE: From *Psychological Science,* Vol. 8, No. 4, July 1997. Reprinted with permission of Cambridge University Press.

Abstract begins on a
new page.

The word "Abstract" is
centered on the page,
in uppercase and
lowercase letters.

The abstract is typed in
block format, with no
paragraph indentation.

The abstract is usually
about 120 words in
length.

In the abstract, use
digits for all numbers to
conserve space (except
at the beginning of a
sentence).

Abstract

A recently published study (Hecht & Proffitt, 1995) reported
that adults in Munich, Germany, whose occupations involved
considerable experience with liquids in containers were less
accurate on Piaget's water-level task than were comparable
adults in other occupations. The present study attempted to
replicate that experiment with a North American sample, but
using tighter controls. The resulting data and conclusions
contrast with those of the original study and indicate,
instead, that individuals in occupations that provide much
experience with liquids in containers (bartenders, waiters,
and waitresses) are, in fact, more accurate than individuals
of equivalent gender, age, and education in control
occupations (salespeople, clerical workers) on two versions
of the water-level task. The data are discussed in terms of
both the impact and limits of experience on spatial-task
performance.

Experience   3

Experience and the Water-Level Task Revisited:
Does Expertise Exact a Price?

Piaget's water-level task (Piaget & Inhelder, 1948/1956) has provided psychology with one of its more fascinating and intriguing puzzles. In the 30 years since Rebelsky (1964) reported that many of her graduate and undergraduate students--especially females--did not know that the surface of a liquid remains horizontal when its container is tilted, dozens of experiments have investigated this problem. Yet today it remains unclear why so many adults, who encounter liquids in tilted containers virtually every day of their lives, somehow fail to note this seemingly obvious physical principle (Vasta & Liben, 1996).

In a recent study, Hecht and Proffitt (1995) added another surprising twist to this puzzle when they reported that adults whose occupations involve considerable experience with liquids in containers (viz., bartenders and waitresses in Munich, Germany) performed even less accurately on the water-level task than did comparable groups of adults in other occupations. These data are obviously counterintuitive in that it is commonly believed that greater experience in an area leads to greater knowledge about the area--which, in turn, should facilitate problem solving in the area when that becomes necessary. People who spend hours each day attending to liquids in containers, therefore, should be much more likely than most other people to appreciate the invariant horizontality of liquid surfaces or at least should be better able to generate the correct response when faced with the

Page 3 begins the main body of the paper, including introduction, method, results, and discussion.

Center the title of the paper, in uppercase and lowercase letters. Double-space and begin typing the text of the paper.

Paragraphs are indented five to seven spaces using the tab function.

Use the author's last name and date for reference citations. (The citation of Piaget & Inhelder is unusual because it has two dates: 1948 is the year of the original publication, and 1956 is the year the work was republished.)

Use the "&" symbol when authors' names are within parentheses. Use "and" when authors' names are part of the text.

Standard Latin abbreviations such as "viz." are used only within parentheses. When the terms are part of the text, use the English translation of the terms (viz. = namely).

Left-justify the paper so the words are aligned with the left margin, but the length of each line varies at the right margin.

water-level task. That they cannot, and that they in fact do worse than people without such experience, is an assault on this widely held belief.

The researchers' explanation for their findings grows directly out of their theoretical model, which posits that the water-level problem can be cognitively represented by adopting either an environment-relative reference system-- which promotes the correct solution to the problem--or an object-relative reference system--which biases the subject toward an incorrect solution (McAfee & Proffitt, 1991). According to the authors, "people whose occupations entail extensive experience with liquid-filled containers might be more inclined to adopt an object-relative perspective" (p. 91). The study thus is notable not simply because the findings were unexpected but also because it purports to provide important evidence as to why the water-level task poses such a vexing challenge to many adults.

To evaluate the validity of the study's conclusions, it is important to consider that the Hecht and Proffitt study falls into the category called quasi-experimental research (Campbell & Stanley, 1966; Cook & Campbell, 1979). Because their variable of major interest was occupation, the participants of the research could not, of course, have been randomly assigned to each job and then given years of experience working at it. (Nor could they have been randomly assigned to the categories male and female, the other variable of some interest in the experiment.) Instead, quasi-experimental research requires that investigators simply identify extant groups of participants (e.g.,

Use double quotations to include short quotations (less than 40 words) in the text of the paper. Include the page number in parentheses.

Underline words that will appear in italics when typeset.

Arrange multiple citations that occur at the same place in the text in the order they appear in the reference list. Use a semicolon to separate citations.

Experience   5

bartenders, waitresses, etc.) who embody the different
levels or categories of the variables under study. The
paramount concern attending this sort of research involves
ensuring that the groups differ only on the variable(s) of
interest (i.e., occupation) and not on any other variable(s)
that could potentially account for differences found between
groups. In true experimental designs this problem is
normally handled by the random assignment of participants,
which presumably distributes all of the other variables
unsystematically across conditions. However, when that
technique is not available, as here, considerable care must
be taken to assure that the groups are as equivalent as
possible beyond the variable under study.

Let us examine how successful Hecht and Proffitt (1995)
were at manipulating the primary variable of interest,
occupation. Their stated goal involved selecting
"professions that assured different degrees of experience
with surface orientation" (p. 92). In what we will term the
high-experience groups, bartenders were selected because
most of their work time is spent pouring beer (draft and
bottled), as well as measuring, pouring, shaking, and
stirring drinks of other kinds. Waitresses were used because
they spend much of their time carrying drinks (as many as
five mugs in each hand, for the Munich waitresses) and
serving them to customers.

The control occupations, ideally, should have been
selected according to two criteria. Inasmuch as these groups
constituted the low-experience level of the variable, their
relative exposure to liquids in containers should be

Use "we" only to refer to yourself and your co-authors (do not use "we" if you are the only author). Avoid the use of the editorial "we" that refers to a generic group. Instead, use an appropriate term such as "people," "humans," or "researchers."

considerably less. In addition, to avoid the potential
problems inherent in quasi-experimental designs, the groups
should differ only on the experience variable and be
otherwise comparable on all other factors.

   One of the control occupations was bus driver. This job
seems well chosen in that these men undoubtedly devoted
little of their work time to dealing with liquids in
containers. The other low-experience occupation was
housewife. Here, the wisdom of the choice is less obvious.
The typical woman participating in the experiment was
described as "54 years old on average . . . [and who] cared
for a household with several children and devoted most of
her time to the family" (p. 92). As such, it is reasonable
to expect that these women spent some portion of their
normal day involved in cooking, washing dishes, pouring and
serving drinks to the family, and other routine activities
that involve liquids. Conceptualizing this group as
low-experience, therefore, would seem questionable. This
problem is underscored by the researchers' finding that,
when compared directly, the performance of housewives and
waitresses was not significantly different. A better choice
for the second control occupation, then, would have been
preferred.

   The present research attempted to replicate, with a
North American sample, Hecht and Proffitt's study, but with
an improved methodology. One improvement was that males and
females were represented in all occupations. Bartender and
server[1] were again selected as the high-experience (with
liquids in containers) occupations. Salesperson and clerical

Brackets are used to enclose material that is inserted in a quotation.

The final paragraph of the introduction presents the purpose of the present study.

Content footnotes are used infrequently in APA format. The placement of the footnote is indicated by a superscript, using Arabic numerals. The footnote is typed on a separate page later in the manuscript.

Experience   7

worker were chosen to represent low-experience occupations.
The latter occupations were selected because they
(a) involved no job-related experience with liquids in
containers, (b) were sufficiently common occupations to
guarantee access to ample participants, (c) permitted us
to include male and female participants in all four
occupations, and (d) were easy to equate with the
high-experience groups (in terms of both means and ranges)
on the variables of age and education, another improvement
over the original study. Finally, the high-experience groups
were matched for years on the job (means and ranges), with a
minimum of 5 years required.

Method

Participants

The group that was selected for inclusion in the study
comprised 80 adults (see Procedure): 10 males and 10 females
in each of four occupations--bartender, server, salesperson,
and clerical worker. The demographic characteristics of
these participants are presented in Table 1. Participants
were recruited from businesses in the metropolitan area of a
medium-size city (population = approximately 750,000) in the
Northeast.

Materials

The problems and questions were prepared as a booklet.
On the first page, participants signed a consent form that
assured their participation was voluntary and anonymous.
The form was then detached and kept separate from the
participant's data. The form also explained that the
research concerned people's judgments of liquids.

Seriation of items within a paragraph or sentence is indicated with lowercase letters typed in parentheses.

The Method section begins immediately after the introduction (no new page). The word "Method" is centered, in uppercase and lowercase letters, and not underlined.

Subsection headings (e.g., Participants) are typed in uppercase and lowercase letters. They are placed flush to the left margin, are underlined, and stand alone on the line.

Refer to tables and figures in the text of the paper. The table is typed on a separate page later in the manuscript.

The three problems were on separate pages. Problem 1 (Figure 1a) was the same problem used by Hecht and Proffitt (1995, p. 93, Figure 2). The instructions, printed above the problem, were as identical as possible to those described by the original researchers (which were not reported verbatim, presumably because they were in German). The instructions read:

> Think of the drawing below as a glass of water that is being held perfectly still by an invisible hand, so that the water in it is at rest. Note that the glass is being held above the table and that the drawing is a side view of the glass, so that a single line is appropriate to indicate the water level. Draw a line representing the surface of the water, so that it touches the point marked on the right side of the glass.

Problem 2 was a more common version of the water-level task (Figure 1b). We included it to ensure that the findings by Hecht and Proffitt (1995) were not a function of the manner in which participants were asked to perform the problem. Printed instructions above the problem read "Figure A shows a bottle with some water in it. In Figure B the bottle has been tilted. Draw a line to show how the water would look."

On the next page, participants' understanding of the invariance (horizontality) principle was assessed verbally with a multiple-choice question in which the stem and answers read "When a container with water is tilted to the right, the water line in the container will be

Figures and tables, when used, must be mentioned in the text.

Type quotations of 40 or more words in block format, without quotation marks. Indent the block five spaces from the left margin.

Experience   9

horizontal (—), will slant downward (\), or will slant
upward (/)."

   Problem 3, on the page that followed, involved
predicting how water would look if poured from one container
to another of a different shape. (We report no data on this
problem in this article.)

   On the final page, participants provided demographic
and employment information. The data solicited included
gender, age, years of experience at the job, number of hours
worked per week, any other current employment, any previous
experience as a bartender or waiter/waitress, highest year
of schooling completed, and any prior familiarity with the
water-level problem.

Procedure

   The data were collected over an 11-week period.
Participants were tested individually at their places of
work by one of the three junior authors, who each tested
approximately equal numbers in the four occupations. As
individuals were tested, their demographic and employment
data only were given to the senior author whose job it was
to determine when the eight groups were sufficiently
equivalent on the variables of age, education, and, for the
high-experience occupations, years of job experience. When
he decided that the means and ranges of these variables were
comparable across the eight groups, the senior author halted
the data collection and, only afterward, gained access to
the performance data. This procedure ensured that the nature
of the individuals' performance in no way influenced the
final selection of participants to be included in the study.

Note that the word
"data" is plural; thus,
"the data were"
(not was).

The Results section does not begin on a new page; the heading is typed in uppercase and lowercase letters, centered, and not underlined.

The authors used optional subsection headings to present the material in the Results section. The title of each heading depends on the particular study. Subsection headings are typed flush at the left margin, underlined. Major terms are capitalized.

Give all authors' names in the first citation. When there are three or more authors, use "et al." for subsequent citations.

The first time an abbreviation is used, write out the term completely and place the abbreviation in parentheses. Later in the paper use the abbreviation without additional explanation.

To achieve the goal of having eight groups of 10 participants with equivalent demographic data, 124 adults had to be tested. Participants were not included in the final group of 80 if (a) they had prior familiarity with the water-level task ($\underline{n}$ = 3), (b) they had previously been servers or bartenders but were currently in one of the low-experience occupations ($\underline{n}$ = 8), (c) they were bartenders or servers who had fewer than 5 years of experience or worked only part-time ($\underline{n}$ = 7), or (d) their age or education lay outside the range that eventually emerged as equivalent across the eight groups ($\underline{n}$ = 26).

Results

Scoring

The water-level task drawings (Problems 1 and 2) were scored using a transparent protractor overlay to determine the number of degrees each drawing deviated from horizontal, as has been done previously (Vasta, Belongia, & Ribble, 1994; Vasta, Lightfoot, & Cox, 1993).

Analyses

The mean deviations from horizontal on Problem 1, the replication water-level task, for males and females in each of the four occupations are presented in Figure 2. A 4 (Occupation) x 2 (Gender) analysis of variance (ANOVA) revealed main effects for occupation, $\underline{F}$(3, 72) = 3.01, $\underline{p}$ < .05, and gender, $\underline{F}$(1, 72) = 4.05, $\underline{p}$ < .05, with no interaction. As seen in Figure 2, bartenders and servers were more accurate than salespersons and clerical workers. Follow-up analyses indicated no differences in accuracy for occupations within the high- and low-experience conditions and so the data were combined across the occupations. A 2 (Experience) x 2 (Gender) ANOVA was performed, producing both a main effect for job experience, $F(1, 76) = 9.19$, $p < .01$, and a main effect for gender, $F(1, 76) = 4.22$, $p < .05$, with no interaction. Contrary to the findings of Hecht and Proffitt (1995), subjects in the high-experience occupations were more accurate ($M = 6.9$) than those in the low-experience occupations ($M = 14.5$). Predictably, males ($M = 8.12$) were more accurate than females ($M = 13.27$).

A similar pattern emerged from the data of Problem 2, shown in Figure 3. The 4 (Occupation) x 2 (Gender) ANOVA in this case resulted in a borderline main effect for occupation, $F(3, 72) = 2.22$, $p < .10$, and a significant effect for gender, $F(1, 72) = 7.58$, $p < .01$, with no interaction. Follow-up analyses again indicated that the occupations did not differ within job experience categories. A 2 (Experience) x 2 (Gender) ANOVA revealed main effects for experience, $F(1, 76) = 6.63$, $p < .01$, and gender, $F(1, 76) = 7.96$, $p < .01$, with no interaction. As with Problem 1, subjects in the high-experience occupations were more accurate ($M = 6.25$) than those in the low-experience occupations ($M = 10.97$), and males ($M = 6.02$) were more accurate than females ($M = 11.2$).

The same pattern of results was found when the drawings were scored in terms of the number of subjects whose water lines fell within a predetermined criterion range. When the criterion was set at $5°$, the data of more adults in the high-experience occupations than in the

When presenting statistical copy, the name of the statistical test is underlined and followed by the degrees of freedom in parentheses. Note the spacing. If your word processor does not have a necessary symbol, write the symbol in black ink.

Most statistical symbols are underlined (e.g., F, t, M, p, df).

The term "subjects" is appropriate when discussing results.

low-experience occupations fell within this range (Problem 1: 55% vs. 37.5%; Problem 2: 55% vs. 47.5%, respectively). Even larger differences emerged when the range was set at $10°$ (Problem 1: 77.5% vs. 47.5%; Problem 2: 87.5% vs. 57.5%, respectively).

As has been found before, subjects who demonstrated knowledge of the invariance principle were significantly more accurate on Problem 1, $\underline{F}(1, 78) = 9.97$, $\underline{p} < .01$, and Problem 2, $\underline{F}(1, 78) = 19.7$, $\underline{p} < .01$.

Discussion

It is clear from the present results that expertise gained from job-related experience with liquids in containers does not exact a price on water-level task performance. In fact, the data support quite the opposite conclusion. In contrast to the findings of Hecht and Proffitt (1995), subjects in our high-experience occupations (bartender, server) were significantly more accurate than comparable participants in the control occupations (salesperson, clerical worker). This effect was found for both males and females and was apparent on both versions of the water-level task.

The conclusion drawn from these data can be asserted with greater confidence than the conclusion from the original study, as the present research was more carefully controlled. While using precisely the same task and overall procedures of the earlier study, our design included males and females in each occupation and, more important, essentially equated the eight groups on the variables of age, education, and job experience (for the high-experience

The Discussion section immediately follows the Results section. The heading is typed in uppercase and lowercase letters, centered, and not underlined.

Experience   13

condition). The performance differences found between the high- and low-experience conditions, therefore, at least cannot be attributed to differences in any of these variables, increasing the likelihood that it was indeed the nature of the participants' work that produced the main effect.

Whether the starkly different patterns of findings and levels of performance (e.g., the mean errors for the Munich waitresses and bartenders were about 21° and 14°, respectively, whereas the corresponding means for the American sample were 7° and 4°) obtained by the two studies involved any or all of these extraneous variables, however, remains unclear. Other possibilities also exist. Certainly we must at least raise the question of cultural differences between the two samples. While it seems unlikely that adults in Germany would approach the water-level task in a qualitatively different manner, or would derive very different sorts of expertise from their bartending and waitressing experiences, these possibilities cannot be entirely discounted without additional research.

Regardless of the reasons for the different outcomes, the present results are important in their own right in that they bolster two previous sets of findings regarding the impact of experience on spatial-task performance. First, our data align with previous reports that performance on the water-level task is positively related to vocational aspirations and training in both adolescents (De Lisi & McGillicuddy-De Lisi, 1988) and adults (Robert & Harel, 1996). While direction-of-effect issues must be considered in all of these studies, the findings nevertheless are consistent with an experiential analysis, in which greater exposure to the components of a process leads to a better understanding of its underlying principles. The present data, however, also support research indicating that experience may have its limits. Robert and Harel (1996) have reported that although the spatial-task performance of students in natural sciences programs surpassed that of students in social sciences programs, women continued to perform less accurately than men in both areas. These results closely parallel our findings, in that the accuracy of female bartenders and servers on the first two problems was higher than that of female sales and clerical workers but remained significantly below that of the high-experience males (see Baenninger & Newcombe, 1995; and Vasta, Knott, & Gaze, 1996, for more on this issue).

In conclusion, the provocative and counterintuitive results reported by Hecht and Proffitt (1995) remain difficult to explain in light of the present research. If job-related expertise does, in fact, alter adults' cognitive perspective on the water-level task, as they claim, then subsequent demonstrations of that phenomenon are needed.

Experience   15

References

Baenninger, M., & Newcombe, N. (1995). Environmental input to the development of sex-related differences in spatial and mathematical ability. Learning and Individual Differences, 7, 363-379.

Campbell, D. T., & Stanley, J. C. (1966). Experimental and quasi-experimental designs for research. Chicago: Rand McNally.

Cook, T. D., & Campbell, D. T. (1979). Quasi-experimentation: Design and analysis issues for field settings. Chicago: Rand McNally.

De Lisi, R., & McGillicuddy-De Lisi, A. V. (1988). Individual differences in adolescents' horizontality representation: Associations with vocational major and gender. Merrill-Palmer Quarterly, 34, 437-449.

Hecht, H., & Proffitt, D. R. (1995). The price of expertise: Effects of experience on the water-level task. Psychological Science, 6, 90-95.

McAfee, E. A., & Proffitt, D. R. (1991). Understanding the surface orientation of liquids. Cognitive Psychology, 23, 483-514.

Piaget, J., & Inhelder, B. (1956). The child's conception of space. London: Routledge & Kegan-Paul. (Original work published 1948)

Rebelsky, F. (1964). Adult perception of the horizontal. Perceptual and Motor Skills, 19, 371-374.

Robert, M., & Harel, F. (1996). The gender difference in orienting liquid surfaces and plumb lines: Its robustness, its correlates, and the associated knowledge of

References begin on a new page. Each reference is a separate paragraph, with the first line indented five to seven spaces.

These references contain journal articles (Baenninger & Newcombe) and books (Campbell & Stanley).

This reference is for a book originally published in 1948 and then republished in 1956.

Experience   16

simple physics. Canadian Journal of Experimental Psychology,
50, 280-314.

     Vasta, R., Belongia, C., & Ribble, C. (1994).
Investigating the orientation effect on the water-level
task: Who? When? and Why? Developmental Psychology, 30,
893-904.

     Vasta, R., Knott, J. A., & Gaze, C. E. (1996). Can
spatial training eliminate the gender differences on the
water-level task? Psychology of Women Quarterly, 20,
549-567.

     Vasta, R., & Liben, L. S. (1996). The water-level task:
An intriguing puzzle. Current Directions in Psychological
Research, 5, 1-7.

     Vasta, R., Lightfoot, C., & Cox, B. D. (1993).
Understanding gender differences on the water-level problem:
The role of spatial perception. Merrill-Palmer Quarterly,
39, 391-414.

Experience   17

Author Note

Ross Vasta, Department of Psychology; Deirdre
Rosenberg, Department of School Psychology; Jill A. Knott,
Department of Psychology; Christine E. Gaze, Department of
Psychology.

Special thanks are given to Norman Frisch for preparing
the artwork.

Address correspondence to the first author at
Department of Psychology, SUNY Brockport, Brockport, New
York 14420. Electronic mail may be sent via Internet to
rvasta@acspr1.acs.brockport.edu.

The heading is
centered, in uppercase
and lowercase letters.

Indent each paragraph
of the author note.

The first paragraph
states the authors'
names and department
affiliations.

The second
paragraph includes
acknowledgments such
as grants that provided
financial support for the
study and colleagues
who assisted with the
study.

The third paragraph
provides addresses
for correspondence,
frequently ending with
an electronic mail
address.

The heading is centered, in uppercase and lowercase letters.

Indent the first line of each footnote five to seven spaces. Footnotes are double-spaced and numbered in the order they appear in the manuscript.

```
                                              Experience    18

                            Footnote
           ¹Professionals in this occupation prefer the
gender-neutral term server, and so we have adopted it here.
```

Experience   19

Table 1

Demographic Variables Characterizing Participants Selected

for Inclusion in the Research

Occupation and gender	n	Age	Education	Job experience
Bartender				
Female	10	34.1	14.0	11.4
		(24-46)	(12-16)	(5-20)
Male	10	33.0	14.2	10.3
		(26-43)	(12-16)	(5-20)
Server				
Female	10	32.7	14.0	11.9
		(23-49)	(12-16)	(5-30)
Male	10	32.3	14.3	11.9
		(24-46)	(12-16)	(5-20)

(table continues)

Each table is typed on a new page. Use Arabic, not Roman, numerals to number your tables.

Type the title of the table flush to the left margin, underlined, with major terms capitalized.

Note that only horizontal lines are used to separate sections of the table.

Double-space the entire table, including the title, headings, and notes.

Headings in the table are typed in sentence style, with only the first letter of the first word in capitals.

Design your table to fit your data. The table does not need to span across the entire page.

If the table does not fit on one page, do not single-space or use smaller type fonts to reduce the size of the table. Instead, type (table continues) in the bottom right-hand corner of the page.

When a table extends beyond one page, repeat the column heads at the top of the next page.

Notes are placed below the table. General notes provide information about the table. Notes may also provide specific information about an entry in the table or indicate the probability of statistical results.

Experience   20

Occupation and gender	n	Age	Education	Job experience
Clerical worker				
Female	10	33.8	14.3	- -
		(26-49)	(13-16)	
Male	10	34.3	14.1	- -
		(28-44)	(12-16)	
Salesperson				
Female	10	33.8	14.7	- -
		(26-47)	(12-16)	
Male	10	33.8	14.2	- -
		(25-44)	(12-16)	

Note. Values for age, education, and job experience represent means (and ranges) in years.

Experience   21

Figure Captions

<u>Figure 1.</u> The two tasks used in the study. Problem 1 (a) is identical with the problem used by Hecht and Proffitt (1995); Problem 2 (b) is a more conventional version of the water-level task.

<u>Figure 2.</u> Mean degrees of deviation and standard errors on Problem 1 for male and female participants in the four occupations.

<u>Figure 3.</u> Mean degrees of deviation and standard errors on Problem 2 for male and female participants in the four occupations.

Begin the figure captions on a new page. Center the heading, in uppercase and lowercase letters.

Begin each caption flush at the left margin, underlining the figure number to begin each figure caption. Capitalize only the first word and any proper nouns in the caption. Do not indent.

Place each figure on a
separate page.

Pages on which figures
are drawn are not
numbered, nor is there
a page identification. To
identify the figure, write
the figure number in
pencil on the back of
the page.

This diagram is Figure 1.

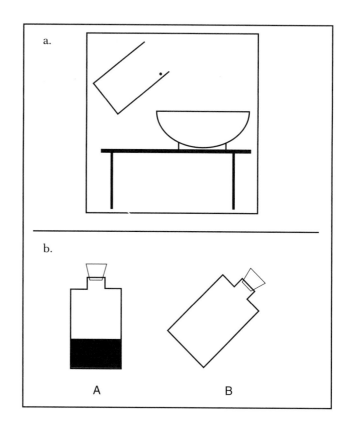

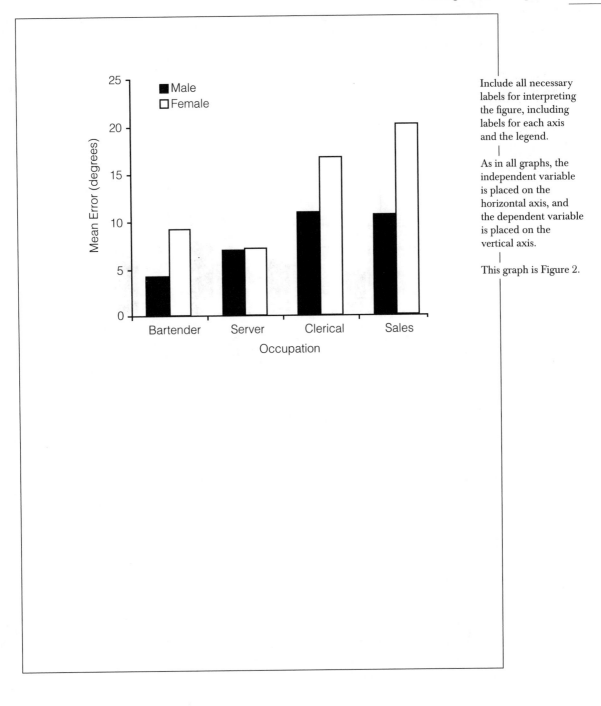

Include all necessary labels for interpreting the figure, including labels for each axis and the legend.

As in all graphs, the independent variable is placed on the horizontal axis, and the dependent variable is placed on the vertical axis.

This graph is Figure 2.

Draw figures carefully
and make sure
everything is accurate.

Always use black ink for
figures.

This graph is Figure 3.

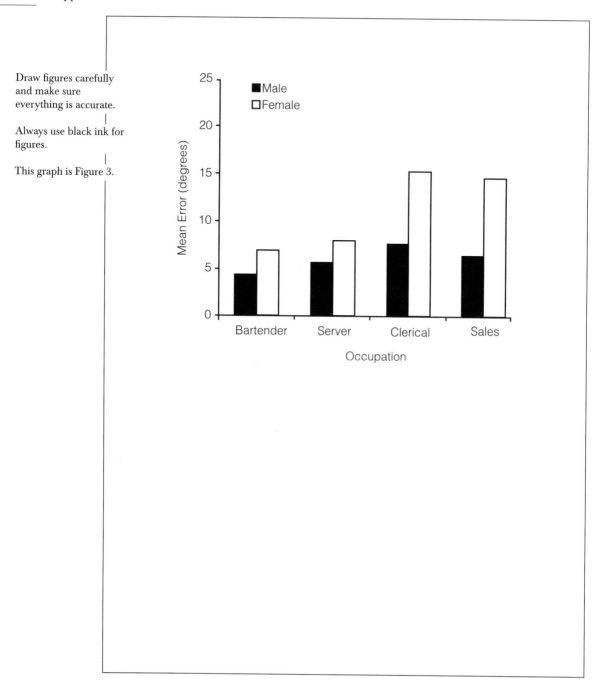

APPENDIX B ◆

Statistical Tests

The purpose of this appendix is to provide the formulas and calculational procedures for analysis of data. All possible statistical tests are not included, but a variety of tests that should be appropriate for many of the research designs you might use are given.

We will examine both descriptive and inferential statistics. Before you study the statistics, however, you should review the properties of measurement scales described in Chapter 4. Remember that there are four types of measurement scales: nominal, ordinal, interval, and ratio. Nominal scales have no numerical properties, ordinal scales provide rank-order information only, and interval and ratio scales have equal intervals between the points on the scale. In addition, ratio scales have a true zero point. You will also recall from Chapter 15 that the appropriate statistical analysis is determined by the type of design and by the measurement scale that was used in the study. As we proceed, the discussion of the various statistical tests will draw to your attention the relevant measurement scale restrictions that apply.

The examples here use small and simple data sets so the calculations can be easily done by hand using a calculator. However, you will find that the calculations become tedious and that you are more likely to make errors when working with large data sets and when you have to perform many statistical analyses in your study. Computer programs to perform statistical analyses have been developed to make the process easier and to reduce calculation errors.

DESCRIPTIVE STATISTICS

With a knowledge of the types of measurement scales, we can turn to a consideration of statistical techniques. We can start with two ways of describing a set of scores: central tendency and variability.

TABLE B.1   Descriptive Statistics for a Set of Scores

Score	Descriptive Statistic
1	Mode = 5
2	
4	Median = 5
4	
5	$\bar{X} = \dfrac{\Sigma X}{N} = 4.5$
5	
5	
6	Range = 6
6	
7	
$\Sigma X = 45$	$s^2 = \dfrac{\Sigma(X - \bar{X})^2}{N-1} = \dfrac{\Sigma X^2 - N\bar{X}^2}{N-1} = \dfrac{233 - 202.5}{9} = 3.338$
$\Sigma X^2 = 233$	$s = \sqrt{s^2} = 1.84$
$N = 10$	

Measures of Central Tendency

A measure of central tendency gives a single number that describes how an entire group scores as a whole, or on the average. Three different central tendency measures are available: the mode, the median, and the mean.

The Mode   The mode is the most frequently occurring score. Table B.1 shows a set of scores and the descriptive statistics that are discussed in this section. The most frequently occurring score in these data is 5: No calculations are necessary to find the mode. The mode can be used with any of the four types of measurement scales. However, it is the only measure of central tendency that can be used with nominal scale data. If you are measuring gender and find there are 100 females and 50 males, the mode is "female" because this is the most frequently occurring category on the nominal scale.

The Median   The median is the score that divides the group in half: 50% of the scores are below the median and 50% are above the median. When the scores have been ordered from lowest to highest (as in Table B.1), the median is easily found. If there is an odd number of scores, you simply find the middle score. (For example, if there are 11 scores, the sixth score is the median, since there are 5 lower and 5 higher scores.) If there is an even number of scores, the median is the midpoint between the two middle scores. In the data in Table B.1, there are 10 scores, so the fifth and sixth scores are the two middle scores. To find the median, we add the two middle scores and divide by 2. Thus, in Table B.1, the median is

$$\frac{5 + 5}{2} = 5$$

The median can be used with ordinal, interval, or ratio scale data. It is most likely to be used with ordinal data, however. This is because calculation of the median considers only the rank ordering of scores and not the actual size of the scores.

The Mean   The mean does take into account the actual size of the scores. Thus, the mean is based on more information about the scores than either the mode or the median. However, it is appropriate only for interval or ratio scale data.

The mean is the sum of the scores in a group divided by the number of scores. The calculational formula for the mean can be expressed as

$$\bar{X} = \frac{\Sigma X}{N}$$

where $\bar{X}$ is the symbol for the mean. In this formula, X represents a score obtained by an individual, and the Σ symbol indicates that scores are to be summed or added. The symbol ΣX can be read as "sum of the Xs" and simply is an indication that the scores are to be added. Thus, ΣX in the data from Table B.1 is

$$1 + 2 + 4 + 4 + 5 + 5 + 5 + 6 + 6 + 7 = 45$$

The N in the formula symbolizes the number of scores in the group. In our example, $N = 10$. Thus, we can now calculate the mean:

$$\bar{X} = \frac{\Sigma X}{N} = \frac{45}{10} = 4.5$$

Measures of Variability

In addition to describing the central tendency of the set of scores, we want to describe how much the scores vary among themselves. How much spread is there in the set of scores?

The Range   The range is the highest score minus the lowest score. In our example, the range is 6. The range is not a very useful statistic, however, because it is based on only two scores in the distribution. It doesn't take into account all of the information that is available in the entire set of scores.

The Variance and Standard Deviation   The variance, and a related statistic called the standard deviation, uses all the scores to yield a measure of variability. The variance indicates the degree to which scores vary about the group mean. The formula for the variance (symbolized as s^2) is

$$s^2 = \frac{\Sigma(X - \bar{X})^2}{N - 1}$$

where $(X - \bar{X})^2$ is an individual score, X, minus the mean, $\bar{X}$, and then squared. Thus, $(X - \bar{X})^2$ is the squared deviation of each score from the mean. The Σ sign indicates that these squared deviation scores are to be summed. Finally, dividing by $N - 1$ gives the mean of the squared deviations. The variance, then, is the mean of the squared deviations from the group mean. (Squared deviations are used because simple deviations would add up to zero. $N - 1$ is used in most cases for statistical purposes because the scores represent a sample and not an entire population. As the sample size becomes larger, it makes little difference whether N or $N - 1$ is used.)

The data in Table B.1 can be used to illustrate calculation of the variance. $(X - \bar{X})^2$ is equal to

$$(1 - 4.5)^2 + (2 - 4.5)^2 + (4 - 4.5)^2 + (4 - 4.5)^2 + (5 - 4.5)^2 +$$
$$(5 - 4.5)^2 + (5 - 4.5)^2 + (6 - 4.5)^2 + (6 - 4.5)^2 + (7 - 4.5)^2 = 30.50$$

The next step is to divide $\Sigma(X - \bar{X})^2$ by $N - 1$. The calculation for the variance, then, is

$$s^2 = \frac{\Sigma(X - \bar{X})^2}{N - 1} = \frac{30.50}{9} = 3.388$$

A simpler calculational formula for the variance is

$$s^2 = \frac{\Sigma X^2 - N\bar{X}^2}{N - 1}$$

where ΣX^2 is the sum of the squared individual scores, and $\bar{X}^2$ is the mean squared. You can confirm that the two formulas are identical by computing the variance using this simpler formula (remember that ΣX^2 tells you to square each score and then sum the squared scores). This simpler formula is much easier to work with when there are many scores because each deviation doesn't have to be calculated.

The standard deviation is the square root of the variance. Because the variance uses squared scores, the variance doesn't describe the amount of variability in the same units of measurement as the original scale. The standard deviation (s) corrects this problem. Thus, the standard deviation is the average deviation of scores from the mean.

STATISTICAL SIGNIFICANCE TESTS

This section describes several statistical significance tests. All of these tests are used to determine the probability that the outcome of the research was due to the operation of random error. All use the logic of the null hypothesis discussed in Chapter 14. We will consider three significance tests in this section: the chi-square test, the Mann-Whitney U test, and the analysis of variance, or F test.

Chi-Square (χ^2)

The chi-square (Greek letter chi, squared) test is used when dealing with nominal scale data. It is used when the data consist of frequencies—the number of subjects who fall into each of several categories.

Chi-square can be used with either the experimental or correlational method.

TABLE B.2   Data for Hypothetical Study on Hand Dominance: Chi-Square Test

Sex of Subject	Hand Dominance			Row Totals
	Right	*Left*	*Ambidextrous*	
Male	$O_1 = 15$	$O_2 = 30$	$O_3 = 5$	50
	$E_1 = 25$	$E_2 = 20$	$E_3 = 5$	
Female	$O_4 = 35$	$O_5 = 10$	$O_6 = 5$	50
	$E_4 = 25$	$E_5 = 20$	$E_6 = 5$	
Column Totals	50	40	10	$N = 100$

Computations:

Cell number	$\dfrac{(O - E)^2}{E}$	
1	4.00	
2	5.00	
3	0.00	
		$\chi^2 = \sum \dfrac{(O - E)^2}{E}$
4	4.00	
5	5.00	$= 18.00$
6	0.00	
	$\Sigma = 18.00$	

It is used in conjunction with the experimental method when the dependent variable is measured on a nominal scale. It is used with the correlational method when both variables are measured on nominal scales.

Example   Suppose you want to know whether there is a relationship between gender and hand dominance. To do this, you sample 50 males and 50 females and ask whether they are right-handed, left-handed, or ambidextrous (use both hands with equal skill). Your data collection involves classifying each person as male or female and as right-handed, left-handed, or ambidextrous.

Fictitious data for such a study are presented in Table B.2. The frequencies labeled as "O" in each of the six cells in the table refer to the number of male and female subjects who fall into each of the three hand-dominance categories. The frequencies labeled "E" refer to frequencies that are expected if the null hypothesis is correct. It is important that each subject falls into only one of the cells when using chi-square (that is, no subject can be counted as both male and female or both right- and left-handed).

The chi-square test examines the extent to which the frequencies that are actually observed in the study differ from the frequencies that are expected if the null hypothesis is correct. The null hypothesis states that there is no relationship between sex and hand dominance: Males and females do not differ on this characteristic.

The formula for computing chi-square is

$$\chi^2 = \sum \frac{(O - E)^2}{E}$$

where O is the *observed* frequency in each cell, E is the *expected* frequency in each cell, and the symbol Σ refers to summing over all cells. The steps in calculating the value of X^2 are

Step 1: Arrange the observed frequencies in a table such as Table B.2. Note that in addition to the observed frequencies in each cell, the table presents row totals, column totals, and the total number of observations (N).

Step 2: Calculate the expected frequencies for each of the cells in the table. The expected frequency formula is

$$E = \frac{\text{Row total} \times \text{Column total}}{N}$$

where the row total refers to the row total for the cell, and the column total refers to the column total for the cell. Thus, the expected frequency for cell 1 (male right-handedness) is

$$E_1 = \frac{50 \times 50}{100} = 25$$

The expected frequencies for each of the cells are shown in Table B.2 below the observed frequencies.

Step 3: Calculate the quantity $(O - E)^2/E$ for each cell. For cell 1, this quantity is

$$\frac{(15 - 25)^2}{25} = \frac{100}{25} = 4.00$$

Step 4: Find the value of X^2 by summing the $(O - E)^2/E$ values found in step 3. The calculations for obtaining X^2 for the example data are shown in Table B.2.

Significance of Chi-Square   The significance of the obtained X^2 value can be evaluated by consulting a table of critical values of X^2. A table of critical X^2 values is presented as Table C.2 in Appendix C. The critical X^2 values indicate the value that the *obtained* X^2 must equal or exceed to be significant at the .10 level, the .05 level, and the .01 level.

To be able to use the table of critical values of X^2 as well as most other statistical tables, you must understand the concept of *degrees of freedom* (*df*). The critical value of X^2 for any given study depends on the degrees of freedom. Degrees of freedom refers to the number of scores that are free to vary. In the table of categories for a chi-square test, the number of degrees of freedom is the number of cells in which the frequencies are free to vary once we know the row totals and column totals. The degrees of freedom for chi-square is easily calculated:

$$df = (R - 1)(C - 1)$$

where R is the number of rows in the table and C is the number of columns. In our example in Table B.1, there are two rows and three columns, so there are 2 degrees of freedom. In a study with three rows and three columns, there are 4 degrees of freedom, and so on.

In order to use Table C.2, find the correct degrees of freedom and then determine the critical value of X^2 necessary to reject the null hypothesis at the chosen significance level. With 2 degrees of freedom, the obtained X^2 value must be *equal to* or *greater than* the critical value of 5.991 to be significant at the .05 level. There is only a .05 probability that a X^2 of 5.991 would occur if only random error is operating. Because the obtained X^2 from our example is 18.00, we can reject the null hypothesis that there is no relationship between sex and hand dominance. (The chi-square was based on fictitious data, but it would be relatively easy for you to determine for yourself whether there is in fact a relationship.)

Concluding Remarks   The chi-square test is extremely useful and is used frequently in all of the behavioral sciences. The calculational formula described is generalizable to expanded studies in which there are more categories on either of the variables. One note of caution, however: When both variables have only two categories, so that there are only two rows and two columns, the formula for calculating chi-square changes slightly. In such cases, the formula is

$$X^2 = \sum \frac{(|O - E|) - .5)^2}{E}$$

where $|O - E|$ is the absolute value of $O - E$, and .5 is a constant that is subtracted for each cell.

Analysis of Variance (*F* Test)

The analysis of variance, or *F* test, is used to determine whether there is a significant difference between groups that have been measured on either interval or ratio scales. The groups may have been formed using either the experimental or the correlational method; the important thing is that at least an interval scale measure was used. The analysis of variance may be used with either independent groups or repeated measures designs. Procedures for calculating *F* for both types of designs are presented.

Analysis of Variance: One Independent Variable

To illustrate the use of the analysis of variance, let's consider a hypothetical experiment on physical distance and self-disclosure. You think that people will reveal more about themselves to an interviewer when they are sitting close to the interviewer than they will when sitting farther away. To test this idea, you conduct an experiment on interviewing. Participants are told that interviewing techniques are being studied. Each participant is seated in a room; the interviewer comes into the room and sits at one of three distances from the participant: close (2 feet, or .61 meter), medium (4 feet, or 1.22 meters), or far (6 feet, or 1.83 meters). The distance chosen by the interviewer is the independent variable manipulation. Participants are randomly assigned to the three distance conditions, and the interviewer's behavior is constant in all conditions. The interview consists of a number of questions, and the dependent variable is the number of personal, revealing statements made by the participant during the interview.

Table B.3   Data for Hypothetical Experiment on Distance and Self-Disclosure: Analysis of Variance

Distance (A)		
Close (A1)	Medium (A2)	Far (A3)
33	21	20
24	25	13
31	19	15
29	27	10
34	26	14
$T_{A1} = 151$	$T_{A2} = 118$	$T_{A3} = 72$
$n_{A1} = 5$	$n_{A2} = 5$	$n_{A3} = 5$
$\bar{X}_{A1} = 30.20$	$\bar{X}_{A2} = 23.60$	$\bar{X}_{A3} = 14.40$
$\Sigma X_{A1}^2 = 4{,}623$	$\Sigma X_{A2}^2 = 2{,}832$	$\Sigma X_{A3}^2 = 1{,}090$
$T_{A1}^2 = 22{,}801$	$T_{A2}^2 = 13{,}924$	$T_{A3}^2 = 5{,}184$

$$SS_{TOTAL} = \Sigma X^2 - \frac{G^2}{N} = (4{,}623 + 2{,}832 + 1{,}090) - \frac{(151 + 118 + 72)^2}{15}$$

$$= 8{,}545 - 7{,}752.07$$

$$= 792.93$$

$$SS_A = \Sigma \frac{T_a^2}{n_a} - \frac{G^2}{N} = \left[\frac{(151)^2}{5} + \frac{(118)^2}{5} + \frac{(72)^2}{5} \right] - 7{,}752.07$$

$$= 8{,}381.80 - 7{,}752.07$$

$$= 629.73$$

$$SS_{ERROR} = \Sigma X^2 - \Sigma \frac{T_a^2}{n_a} = 8{,}545 - 8{,}381.80$$

$$= 163.20$$

Fictitious data for such an experiment are shown in Table B.3. Note that this is an independent groups design with five participants in each group. The calculations of the systematic variance and error variance involve computing the *sum of squares* for the different types of variance.

Sum of Squares   Sum of squares stands for the *sum of squared deviations from the mean.* Computing an analysis of variance for the data in Table B.3 involves three sums of squares: (1) SS_{TOTAL}, the sum of squared deviations of each individual score from the grand mean; (2) SS_A, the sum of squared deviations of each of the group means from the grand mean; and (3) SS_{ERROR}, the sum of squared deviations of the individual scores from their respective group means. The "A" in SS_A is used to indicate that we are dealing with the systematic variance associated with independent variable *A*.

The three sums of squares are deviations from a mean (recall that we calculated such deviations earlier when discussing the variance in a set of scores). We could calculate the deviations directly with the data in Table B.3, but such calculations are hard to work with, so we will use simplified formulas for computational purposes. The computational formulas are

$$SS_{TOTAL} = \Sigma X^2 - \frac{G^2}{N}$$

$$SS_A = \Sigma \frac{T_a^2}{n_a} - \frac{G^2}{N}$$

$$SS_{ERROR} = \Sigma X^2 - \Sigma \frac{T_a^2}{n_a}$$

You might note here that $SS_{TOTAL} = SS_A + SS_{ERROR}$. The actual computations are shown in Table B.3.

SS_{TOTAL}   The formula for SS_{TOTAL} is

$$\Sigma X^2 - \frac{G^2}{N}$$

ΣX^2 is the sum of the squared scores of all subjects in the experiment. Each of the scores is squared first and then added. Thus, for the data in Table B.3, ΣX^2 is $33^2 + 24^2 + 31^2$ and so on until all of the scores have been squared and added. If you are doing the calculations by hand or with a pocket calculator, it may be convenient to find the ΣX^2 for the scores in each group and then add these up for your final computation. This is what we did for the data in the table. The G in the formula stands for the grand total of all the scores. This involves adding up the scores for all subjects. The grand total is then squared and divided by N, the total number of subjects in the experiment. When computing the sum of squares, you should always keep the calculations clearly labeled. You can simplify later calculations by referring to these earlier ones. Once you have computed SS_{TOTAL}, SS_A can be calculated.

SS_A   The formula for SS_A is

$$\Sigma \frac{T_a^2}{n_a} - \frac{G^2}{N}$$

The T_a in this formula refers to the total of the scores in group a of independent variable A. (T_a is a shorthand notation for ΣX in each group [recall the computation of ΣX from our discussion of the mean]. The T_a symbol is used to avoid having to deal with too many Σ signs in our calculational procedures.) The a is used to symbolize the particular group number; thus, T_a is a general symbol for T_1, T_2, and T_3. Looking at our data in Table B.3, $T_1 = 151$, $T_2 = 118$, and $T_3 = 72$. These are the sums of the scores in each of the groups. After T_a has been calculated, T_a^2 is found by squaring T_a. Now, T_a^2 is divided by n_a, the number of subjects in group a. Once the quantity T_a^2/n_a has been computed for each group, the quantities are summed as indicated by the Σ symbol.

Notice that the second part of the formula, G^2/N, was calculated when SS_{TOTAL} was obtained. Because we already have this quantity, it needn't be calculated again when computing SS_A. After obtaining SS_A, we can now compute SS_{ERROR}.

TABLE B.4   Analysis of Variance Summary Table

Source of Variance	Sum of Squares	df	Mean Square	F
A	SS_A	$a - 1$	SS_A/df_A	MS_A/MS_{ERROR}
Error	SS_{ERROR}	$N - a$	SS_{ERROR}/df_{ERROR}	
Total	SS_{TOTAL}	$N - 1$		
A	629.73	2	314.87	23.15
Error	162.20	12	13.60	
Total	792.93	14		

SS_{ERROR}   The formula for SS_{ERROR} is

$$\Sigma X^2 - \sum \frac{T_a^2}{n_a}$$

Both of these quantities were calculated above in obtaining SS_{TOTAL} and SS_A. To obtain SS_{ERROR}, we merely have to find these quantities and perform the proper subtraction.

As a check on the calculations, we can make sure that $SS_{TOTAL} = SS_A + SS_{ERROR}$.

The next step in the computation of the analysis of variance is to find the *mean square* for each of the sums of squares. We can then find the value of F. The necessary computations are shown in an analysis of variance summary table in Table B.4. Constructing a summary table is the easiest way to complete the computations.

Mean Squares   After obtaining the sum of squares, it is necessary to compute the mean squares. Mean square stands for the *mean of the sum of the squared deviations from the mean* or, more simply, the mean of the sum of squares. The mean square (MS) is the sum of squares divided by the degrees of freedom. The degrees of freedom are determined by the number of scores in the sum of squares that are free to vary. The mean squares are the variances that are used in computing the value of F.

From Table B.4, you can see that the mean squares that concern us are the mean square for A (systematic variance) and the mean square for error (error variance). The formulas are

$$MS_A = SS_A/df_A$$

$$MS_{ERROR} = SS_{ERROR}/df_{ERROR}$$

where $df_A = a - 1$ (the number of groups minus one) and $df_{ERROR} = N - a$ (the total number of subjects minus the number of groups).

Obtaining the F Value   The obtained F is found by dividing MS_A by MS_{ERROR}. If only random error is operating, the expected value of F is 1.0. The greater the F value, the lower the probability that the results of the experiment were due to chance error.

Significance of F   To determine the significance of the obtained F value, it is necessary to compare the obtained F to a critical value of F. Table C.4 in Appendix C shows critical values of F for significance levels of .10, .05, and .01. To find the critical value of F, locate on the table the degrees of freedom for the numerator of the ratio (the systematic variance) and the degrees of freedom for the denominator of the F ratio (the error variance). The intersection of these two degrees of freedom on the table is the critical F value.

The appropriate degrees of freedom for our sample data are 2 and 12 (see Table B.4). The critical F value from Table C.4 is 3.89 for a .05 level of significance. For the results to be significant, the obtained F value must be equal to or greater than the critical value. Because the obtained value of F in Table B.4 (23.15) is greater than the critical value, we conclude that the results are significant and reject the null hypothesis that the means of the groups are equal in the population.

Concluding Remarks   The analysis of variance for one independent variable with an independent groups design can be used when there are two or more groups in the experiment. The general formulas described are appropriate for all such designs. Also, the calculations are the same whether the experimental or the correlational method is used to form the groups. The formulas are also applicable to cases in which the number of subjects in each group is not equal (although you should have approximately equal numbers of subjects in the groups).

When the design of the experiment includes more than two levels of the independent variable (as in our example experiment, which had three groups), the obtained F value doesn't tell us whether any two specific groups are significantly different from one another. One way to examine the difference between two groups in such a study is to use the formula for SS_A to compute the sum of squares and the mean square for the two groups (the df in this case is $2 - 1$). When doing this, the previously calculated MS_{ERROR} should be used as the error variance term for computing F. More complicated procedures for evaluating the difference between two groups in such designs are available, but these are beyond the scope of this book.

Analysis of Variance: Two Independent Variables

In this section, we will describe the computations for analysis of variance with a factorial design containing two independent variables. The formulas apply to an $A \times B$ factorial design with any number of levels of the independent variables. The formulas apply only to a completely independent groups design with different subjects in each group, and the number of subjects in each group must be equal. Once you understand this analysis, however, you should have little trouble understanding the analysis for more complicated designs with repeated measures of unequal numbers of subjects. With these limitations in mind, let's consider example data from a hypothetical experiment.

The experiment uses a 2 IV $\times$ 2 SV factorial design. Variable A is the type of instruction used in a course, and variable B is the intelligence level of the students. The students are classified as of either "low" or "high" intelligence on

TABLE B.5   Data for Hypothetical Experiment on the Effect of Type of Instruction and Intelligence Level on Exam Score: Analysis of Variance

	Intelligence (B)	
	Low (B1)	*High (B2)*
Traditional lecture (A1)	75	90
	70	95
	69	89
	72	85
	68	91
	$T_{A1B1} = 354$	$T_{A1B2} = 450$
	$\Sigma X^2_{A1B1} = 25{,}094$	$\Sigma X^2_{A1B2} = 40{,}552$
	$n_{A1B1} = 5$	$n_{A1B2} = 5$
	$\bar{X}_{A1B1} = 70.80$	$\bar{X}_{A1B2} = 90.00$

$T_{A1} = 804$
$n_{A1} = 10$
$\bar{X}_{A1} = 80.40$

Individualized method (A2)	85	87
	87	94
	83	93
	90	89
	89	92
	$T_{A2B1} = 434$	$T_{A2B2} = 455$
	$\Sigma X^2_{A2B1} = 37{,}704$	$\Sigma X^2_{A2B2} = 41{,}439$
	$n_{A2B1} = 5$	$n_{A2B2} = 5$
	$\bar{X}_{A2B1} = 86.80$	$\bar{X}_{A2B2} = 91.00$

$T_{A2} = 889$
$n_{A2} = 10$
$\bar{X}_{A2} = 88.90$

	$T_{B1} = 788$	$T_{B2} = 905$
	$n_{B1} = 10$	$n_{B2} = 10$
	$\bar{X}_{B1} = 78.80$	$\bar{X}_{B2} = 90.50$

the basis of intelligence test scores and are randomly assigned to one of two types of classes. One class uses the traditional lecture method; the other class uses an individualized learning approach with frequent testing over small amounts of material, proctors to help individual students, and a stipulation that students master each section of material before going on to the next section. The information presented to students in the two classes is identical. At the end of the course, all students take the same test, which covers all of the material presented in the course. The score on this examination is the dependent variable.

Table B.5 shows fictitious data for such an experiment, with 5 subjects in each condition. This design allows us to evaluate three effects—the main effect of *A*, the main effect of *B*, and the *A* × *B* interaction. The main effect of *A* is whether one type of instruction is superior to the other; the main effect of *B* is whether high-intelligence students score differently on the test than do low-intelligence students; the *A* × *B* interaction examines whether the effect of one independent variable is different depending on the particular level of the other variable.

The computation of the analysis of variance starts with calculation of the sum of squares for the following sources of variance in the data: SS_{TOTAL}, SS_A, SS_B, $SS_{A \times B}$, and SS_{ERROR}. The procedures for calculation are similar to the calculations performed for the analysis of variance with one independent variable. The

TABLE B.6   Computations for Analysis of Variance With Two Independent Variables

$SS_{TOTAL} = \Sigma X^2 - \dfrac{G^2}{N}$ $= (25{,}094 + 40{,}552 + 37{,}704 + 41{,}439)$

$$- \dfrac{(354 + 450 + 434 + 455)^2}{20}$$

$= 144{,}789 - 143{,}312.45$

$= 1{,}476.55$

$SS_A = \dfrac{\Sigma T_a^2}{n_a} - \dfrac{G^2}{N}$ $= \dfrac{(804)^2 + (889)^2}{10} - 143{,}312.45$

$= 143{,}673.70 - 143{,}312.45$

$= 361.25$

$SS_B = \dfrac{\Sigma T_b^2}{n_b} - \dfrac{G^2}{N}$ $= \dfrac{(788)^2 + (905)^2}{10} - 143{,}312.45$

$= 143{,}996.90 - 143{,}312.45$

$= 684.45$

$SS_{A \times B} = \dfrac{\Sigma T_{ab}^2}{n_{ab}} - \dfrac{G^2}{N} - SS_A - SS_B = \dfrac{(354)^2 + (450)^2 + (434)^2 + (455)^2}{5}$

$$- 143{,}312.45 - 361.25 - 684.45$$

$= 144{,}639.40 - 143{,}312.45 - 361.25 - 684.45$

$= 281.25$

$SS_{ERROR} = \Sigma X^2 - \dfrac{\Sigma T_{ab}^2}{n_{ab}}$ $= 144{,}789 - 144{,}639.40$

$= 149.60$

numerical calculations for the example data are shown in Table B.6. We can now consider each of these calculations.

SS_{TOTAL}   The SS_{TOTAL} is computed in the same way as the previous analysis formula. The formula is

$$SS_{TOTAL} = \Sigma X^2 - \dfrac{G^2}{N}$$

where ΣX^2 is the sum of the squared scores of all subjects in the experiment, G is the grand total of all of the scores, and N is the total number of subjects. It is usually easiest to calculate ΣX^2 and G in smaller steps by calculating subtotals separately for each group in the design. The subtotals are then added. This is the procedure followed in Tables B.5 and B.6.

SS_A   The formula for SS_A is

$$SS_A = \dfrac{\Sigma T_a^2}{n_a} - \dfrac{G^2}{N}$$

where ΣT_a^2 is the sum of the squared totals of the scores in each of the groups of independent variable A, and n_a is the number of subjects in each level of independent variable A. When calculating SS_A, we only consider the groups of independent variable A without considering the particular level of B. In other words, the totals for each group of the A variable are obtained by considering all subjects in that level of A, irrespective of which condition of B the subject may be in. The quantity of G^2/N was previously calculated for SS_{TOTAL}.

SS_B   The formula for SS_B is

$$SS_B = \frac{\Sigma T_b^2}{n_b} - \frac{G^2}{N}$$

SS_B is calculated in the same way as SS_A. The only difference is that we are calculating totals of the groups of independent variable B.

$SS_{A \times B}$ The formula for $SS_{A \times B}$ is

$$SS_{A \times B} = \frac{\Sigma T_{ab}^2}{n_{ab}} - \frac{G^2}{N} - SS_A - SS_B$$

The sum of squares for the $A \times B$ interaction is computed by first calculating the quantity ΣT_{ab}^2. This involves squaring the total of the scores in each of the ab conditions in the experiment. In our example experiment in Table B.5, there are four conditions; the interaction calculation considers *all* of the groups. Each of the group totals is squared, and then the sum of the squared totals is obtained. This sum is divided by n_{ab}, the number of subjects in each group. The other quantities in the formula for $SS_{A \times B}$ have already been calculated, so the computation of $SS_{A \times B}$ is relatively straightforward.

SS_{ERROR}   The quantities involved in the SS_{ERROR} formula have already been calculated. The formula is

$$SS_{ERROR} = \Sigma X^2 - \frac{\Sigma T_{ab}^2}{n_{ab}}$$

These quantities were calculated previously, so we merely have to perform the proper subtraction to complete the computation of SS_{ERROR}.

At this point, you may want to practice calculating the sums of squares using the data in Table B.5. As a check on the calculations, make sure that $SS_{TOTAL} = SS_A + SS_B + SS_{A+B} + SS_{ERROR}$.

After obtaining the sums of squares, the next step is to find the mean square for each of the sources of variance. The easiest way to do this is to use an analysis of variance summary table like Table B.7.

Mean Square   The mean square for each of the sources of variance is the sum of squares divided by the degrees of freedom. The formulas for the degrees of freedom and the mean square are shown in the top portion of Table B.7, and the computed values are shown in the bottom portion of the table.

Obtaining the F Value   The F value for each of the three sources of systematic variance (main effects for A and B, and the interaction) is obtained by dividing the

TABLE B.7   Analysis of Variance Summary Table: Two Independent Variables

Source of Variance	Sum of Squares	df	Mean Square	F
A	SS_A	$a - 1$	SS_A/df_A	MS_A/MS_{ERROR}
B	SS_B	$b - 1$	SS_B/df_B	MS_B/MS_{ERROR}
$A \times B$	$SS_{A \times B}$	$(a - 1)(b - 1)$	$SS_{A \times B}/df_{A \times B}$	$MS_{A \times B}/MS_{ERROR}$
Error	SS_{ERROR}	$N - ab$	SS_{ERROR}/df_{ERROR}	
Total	SS_{TOTAL}			
A	361.25	1	361.25	38.64
B	684.45	1	684.45	73.20
$A \times B$	281.25	1	281.25	30.08
Error	149.60	16	9.35	
Total	1,476.55	19		

appropriate mean square by the MS_{ERROR}. We now have three obtained F values and can evaluate the significance of the main effects and the interaction.

Significance of F   To determine whether an obtained F is significant, we need to find the critical value of F from Table C.4 in Appendix C. For all of the Fs in the analysis of variance summary table, the degrees of freedom are 1 and 16. Let's assume that a .01 significance level for rejecting the null hypothesis was chosen. The critical F at .01 for 1 and 16 degrees of freedom is 8.53. If the obtained F is larger than 8.53, we can say that the results are significant at the .01 level. By referring to the obtained Fs in Table B.7, you can see that the main effects and the interaction are all significant. We'll leave it to you to interpret the main effect means and to graph the interaction. If you don't recall how to do this, you should review the material in Chapter 12.

Analysis of Variance: Repeated Measures and Matched Subjects

The analysis of variance computations considered thus far have been limited to independent groups designs. This section considers the computations for analysis of variance of a repeated measures or a matched random assignment design with one independent variable.

Fictitious data for a hypothetical experiment using a repeated measures design are presented in Table B.8. The experiment examines the effect of a job candidate's physical attractiveness on judgments of the candidate's competence. The independent variable is the candidate's physical attractiveness; the dependent variable is judged competence on a 10-point scale. Subjects in the experiment view two videotapes of different females performing a mechanical aptitude task that involved piecing together a number of parts. Both females do equally well, but one is physically attractive whereas the other is unattractive. The order of presentation of the two tapes is counterbalanced to control for order effects.

The main difference between the repeated measures analysis of variance and the independent groups analysis described earlier is that the effect of subject differences becomes a source of variance. There are four sources of variance

TABLE B.8   Data for Hypothetical Experiment on Attractiveness and Judged Competence: Repeated Measures Analysis of Variance

Subjects (or Subject Pairs)	Condition (A)		T_s	T_s^2
	Unattractive Candidate (A1)	Attractive Candidate (A2)		
S#1	6	8	14	196
S#2	5	6	11	121
S#3	5	9	14	196
S#4	7	6	13	169
S#5	4	6	10	100
S#6	3	5	8	64
S#7	5	5	10	100
S#8	4	7	11	121
	$T_{A1} = 39$	$T_{A2} = 52$		$\Sigma T_s^2 = 1067$
	$\Sigma X_{A1}^2 = 201$	$\Sigma X_{A2}^2 = 352$		
	$n_{A1} = 8$	$n_{A2} = 8$		
	$\overline{X}_{A1} = 4.88$	$\overline{X}_{A2} = 6.50$		

$$SS_{TOTAL} = \Sigma X^2 - \frac{G^2}{N} = (201 + 352) - \frac{(39 + 52)^2}{16}$$

$$= 553 - 517.56$$

$$= 35.44$$

$$SS_A = \frac{\Sigma T_a^2}{n_a} - \frac{G^2}{N} = \frac{(39)^2 + (52)^2}{8} - 517.56$$

$$= 528.13 - 517.56$$

$$= 10.57$$

$$SS_{SUBJECTS} = \frac{\Sigma T_s^2}{n_s} - \frac{G^2}{N} = \frac{1067}{2} - 517.56$$

$$= 533.50 - 517.56$$

$$= 15.94$$

$$SS_{ERROR} = SS_{TOTAL} - SS_A - SS_{SUBJECTS} = 35.44 - 10.57 - 15.94$$

$$= 8.93$$

in the repeated measures analysis of variance, and so four sums of squares are calculated:

$$SS_{TOTAL} = \Sigma X^2 - \frac{G^2}{N}$$

$$SS_A = \frac{\Sigma T_a^2}{n_a} - \frac{G^2}{N}$$

$$SS_{SUBJECTS} = \frac{\Sigma T_s^2}{n_s} - \frac{G^2}{N}$$

$$SS_{ERROR} = SS_{TOTAL} - SS_A - SS_{SUBJECTS}$$

TABLE B.9   Analysis of Variance Summary Table: Repeated Measures Design

Source of Variance	Sum of Squares	df	Mean Square	F
A	SS_A	$a - 1$	SS_A/df_a	MS_A/MS_{ERROR}
Subjects	$SS_{SUBJECTS}$	$s - 1$	–	
Error	SS_{ERROR}	$(a - 1)(s - 1)$	SS_{ERROR}/df_{ERROR}	
Total	SS_{TOTAL}	$N - 1$		
A	10.57	1	10.57	8.26
Subjects	15.94	7	–	
Error	8.93	7	1.28	
Total	35.44	15		

The calculations for these sums of squares are shown in the lower portion of Table B.8. The quantities in the formula should be familiar to you by now. The only new quantity involves the calculation of $SS_{SUBJECTS}$. The term T_s^2 refers to the squared total score of each subject—that is, the squared total of the scores that each subject gives when measured in the different groups in the experiment. The quantity ΣT_s^2 refers to the sum of these squared totals for all subjects. The calculation of $SS_{SUBJECTS}$ is completed by dividing ΣT_s^2 by n_s and then subtracting by G^2/N. The term n_s refers to the number of scores that each subject gives. Because our hypothetical experiment has two groups, $n_s = 2$, the total for each subject is based on two scores.

An analysis of variance summary table is shown in Table B.9. The procedures for computing the mean squares and obtaining F are similar to our previous calculations. Note that the mean square and F for the subjects' source of variance are not computed. There is usually no reason to know or care whether subjects differ significantly from one another. The ability to calculate this source of variance does have the advantage of reducing the amount of error variance—in an independent groups design, subject differences are part of the error variance. Because there is only one score per subject in the independent groups design, it is impossible to estimate the influence of subject differences.

You can use the summary table and the table of critical F values to determine whether the difference between the two groups is significant. The procedures are identical to those discussed previously.

Analysis of Variance: Conclusion

The analysis of variance is a very useful test that can be extended to any type of factorial design, including those that use both independent groups and repeated measures in the same design. The method of computing analysis of variance is much the same regardless of the complexity of the design. A section on analysis of variance as brief as this cannot hope to cover all of the many aspects of such a general statistical technique. You should now, however, have the background to compute an analysis of variance and to understand the more detailed discussions of analysis of variance in advanced statistics texts.

CORRELATION AND EFFECT SIZE

Finally, we will examine calculations for measures of correlation and effect size; these are indicators of the strength of association between variables. These are very important measures because they provide a common metric number that can be used in all types of studies. These numbers range from 0.00, indicating no relationship, to 1.00; correlations above .50 are considered to be indicative of very strong relationships. In much research, expect correlations between about .25 and .50. Correlations between about .10 and .25 are weaker, but correlations of this size can be statistically significant with large sample sizes; they can also be important for theoretical and even practical reasons.

Effect Size for the Chi-Square Statistic

The chi-square (X^2) test was described previously. In addition to determining whether there is a significant relationship, you want an indicator of effect size to tell you the strength of association between the variables. This is obtained by calculating a phi coefficient, symbolized as ϕ. Phi is computed after obtaining the value of chi-square. The formula is

$$\phi = \sqrt{\frac{X^2}{N}}$$

Thus, the value of ϕ for the sex and hand-dominance study analyzed previously (see Table B.2) is

$$\phi = \sqrt{\frac{18.00}{100}} = \sqrt{.18} = .42$$

Because the significance of the obtained chi-square value has already been determined from Table C.2 in Appendix C, no further significance testing is necessary.

Effect Size for the F Statistic

After computing an analysis of variance and evaluating the significance of the F statistic, you need to examine effect size. Rosenthal (1991) provides the following formula for calculating the effect size r:

$$\text{Effect size } r = \sqrt{\frac{F}{F + df_{ERROR}}}$$

We can easily calculate the effect size for the value of F obtained in the experiment on interpersonal distance and disclosure (see Table B.4). The value of F was 23.15, and the degrees of freedom for the error term was 12. Effect size, then, is

$$\text{Effect size } r = \sqrt{\frac{23.15}{23.15 + 12}} = \sqrt{.6586} = .81$$

Pearson Product-Moment Correlation Coefficient

The Pearson product-moment correlation coefficient (r) is used to find the strength of the relationship between two variables that have been measured on interval scales.

Example Suppose you want to know whether travel experiences are related to knowledge of geography. In your study, you give a 15-item quiz on North American geography, and you also ask how many states and Canadian provinces participants have visited. After obtaining the pairs of observations from each participant, a Pearson r can be computed to measure the strength of the relationship between travel experience and knowledge of geography.

Table B.10 presents fictitious data from such a study along with the calculations for r. The calculational formula for r is

$$r = \frac{N\Sigma XY - \Sigma X \Sigma Y}{\sqrt{N\Sigma X^2 - (\Sigma X)^2}\sqrt{N\Sigma Y^2 - (\Sigma Y)^2}}$$

where X refers to a subject's score on variable X, and Y is a subject's score on variable Y. In Table B.10, the travel experience score is variable X, and the geography knowledge score is variable Y. In the formula, N is the number of paired observations (that is, the number of participants measured on both variables).

The calculation of r requires a number of arithmetic operations on the X and Y scores. ΣX is simply the sum of the scores on variable X. ΣX^2 is the sum of the squared scores on X (each score is first squared and then the sum of the squared scores is obtained). The quantity $(\Sigma X)^2$ is the square of the sum of the scores: The total of the X scores (ΣX) is first calculated, and then this total is squared. It is important not to confuse the two quantities, ΣX^2 and $(\Sigma X)^2$. The same calculations are made, using the Y scores, to obtain ΣY, ΣY^2, and $(\Sigma Y)^2$. To find ΣXY, each participant's X score is multiplied by the score on Y; these values are then summed for all subjects. When these calculations have been made, r is computed using the formula for r given previously.

At this point, you may wish to examine carefully the calculations shown in Table B.10 to familiarize yourself with the procedures for computing r. You might then try calculating r from another set of data, such as the happiness and health ratings shown in Table 15.2.

Significance of r To test the null hypothesis that the population correlation coefficient is in fact 0.00, we consult a table of critical values of r. Table C.5 in Appendix C shows critical values of r for .10, .05, and .01 levels of significance. To find the critical value, you first need to determine the degrees of freedom. The *df* for the significance test for r is $N - 2$. In our example study on travel and knowledge, the number of paired observations is 10, so the *df* = 8. For 8 degrees of freedom, the critical value of r at the .05 level of significance is .632 (plus or minus). The obtained r must be greater than the critical r to be significant. Because our

TABLE B.10   Data for Hypothetical Study on Travel and Knowledge of Geography: Pearson r

Subject Identification Number	Travel Score (X)	Knowledge Score (Y)	XY
01	4	10	40
02	6	15	90
03	7	8	56
04	8	9	72
05	8	7	56
06	12	10	120
07	14	15	210
08	15	13	195
09	15	15	225
10	17	14	238
	$\Sigma X = 106$	$\Sigma Y = 116$	$\Sigma XY = 1{,}302$
	$\Sigma X^2 = 1{,}308$	$\Sigma Y^2 = 1{,}434$	
	$(\Sigma X)^2 = 11{,}236$	$(\Sigma Y)^2 = 13{,}456$	

$$\text{Computation: } r = \frac{N\Sigma XY - \Sigma X \Sigma Y}{\sqrt{N\Sigma X^2 - (\Sigma X)^2}\ \sqrt{N\Sigma Y^2 - (\Sigma Y)^2}}$$

$$= \frac{10(1{,}302) - (106)(116)}{\sqrt{10(1{,}308) - 11{,}236}\ \sqrt{10(1{,}434) - 13{,}456}}$$

$$= \frac{13{,}020 - 12{,}296}{\sqrt{13{,}080 - 11{,}236}\ \sqrt{14{,}340 - 13{,}456}}$$

$$= \frac{724}{\sqrt{1{,}844}\ \sqrt{884}}$$

$$= \frac{724}{1{,}276.61}$$

$$= .567$$

obtained r (from Table B.10) of .567 is less than the critical value, we do not reject the null hypothesis.

Notice that we do not reject the null hypothesis in this case, even though the magnitude of r is fairly large. Recall the discussion of nonsignificant results from Chapter 14. It is possible that a significant correlation would be obtained if you used a larger sample size or more sensitive and reliable measures of the variables.

Statistical Tables

RANDOM NUMBER TABLE

The random number table can be used to select data when an arbitrary sequence of numbers is needed. To obtain a series of random numbers, enter the table at any arbitrary point and read in sequence either across or down.

Subject Order	Random Number	Group Assignment
1	10	1
2	37	2
3	08	1
4	99	3
5	12	1
6	66	2
7	31	1
8	85	3
9	63	2
10	73	2
11	98	3
12	11	1
13	83	2
14	88	3
15	99	3

To use the random number table, first order your subjects in some way. This could be by name or by assigning a number to each subject. Suppose that you have three groups and want 5 subjects per group, for a total of 15 subjects. Above is a list of 15 subjects ordered from first to fifteenth. Enter the random number table and assign a number to each subject (if there is a duplicate number, ignore it and use the next number in the sequence). In the example here, the table was entered in the upper left-hand corner and was read downward. Now assign the subjects to groups: The 5 subjects who receive the lowest random numbers are assigned to group 1, the next 5 subjects are assigned to group 2, and the 5 subjects with the highest numbers are assigned to group 3. These general procedures can be followed with any number of groups in an experiment.

To use the random number table for random sampling, first make a list of all members of your population. Enter the random number table and assign a number to each member of the population. Determine your desired sample size (N). Your sample, then, will be composed of the first N individuals. For example, if you want to take a random sample of 15 faculty members at your school, use the random number table to give each faculty member a number. The 15 faculty with the lowest numbers would be selected for the sample.

TABLE C.1   Random Number Table

10 09 73 25 33	76 52 01 35 86	34 67 35 48 76	80 95 90 91 17	39 29 27 49 45
37 54 20 48 05	64 89 47 42 96	24 80 52 40 37	20 63 61 04 02	00 82 29 16 65
08 42 26 89 53	19 64 50 93 03	23 20 90 25 60	15 95 33 47 64	35 08 03 36 06
99 01 90 25 29	09 37 67 07 15	38 31 13 11 65	88 67 67 43 97	04 43 62 76 59
12 80 79 99 70	80 15 73 61 47	64 03 23 66 53	98 95 11 68 77	12 17 17 68 33
66 06 57 47 17	34 07 27 68 50	36 69 73 61 70	65 81 33 98 85	11 19 92 91 70
31 06 01 08 05	45 57 18 24 06	35 30 34 26 14	86 79 90 74 39	23 40 30 97 32
85 26 97 76 02	02 05 16 56 92	68 66 57 48 18	73 05 38 52 47	18 62 38 85 79
63 57 33 21 35	05 32 54 70 48	90 55 35 75 48	28 46 82 87 09	83 49 12 56 24
73 79 64 57 53	03 52 96 47 78	35 80 83 42 82	60 93 52 03 44	35 27 38 84 35
98 52 01 77 67	14 90 56 86 07	22 10 94 05 58	60 97 09 34 33	50 50 07 39 98
11 80 50 54 31	39 80 82 77 32	50 72 56 82 48	29 40 52 42 01	52 77 56 78 51
83 45 29 96 34	06 28 89 80 83	13 74 67 00 78	18 47 54 06 10	68 71 17 78 17
88 68 54 02 00	86 50 75 84 01	36 76 66 79 51	90 36 47 64 93	29 60 91 10 62
99 59 46 73 48	87 51 76 49 69	91 82 60 89 28	93 78 56 13 68	23 47 83 41 13
65 48 11 76 74	17 46 85 09 50	58 04 77 69 74	73 03 95 71 86	40 21 81 65 44
80 12 43 56 35	17 72 70 80 15	45 31 82 23 74	21 11 57 82 53	14 38 55 37 63
74 35 09 98 17	77 40 27 72 14	43 23 60 02 10	45 52 16 42 37	96 28 60 26 55
69 91 62 68 03	66 25 22 91 48	36 93 68 72 03	76 62 11 39 90	94 40 05 64 18
09 89 32 05 05	14 22 56 85 14	46 42 75 67 88	96 29 77 88 22	54 38 21 45 98
91 49 91 45 23	68 47 92 76 86	46 16 28 35 54	94 75 08 99 23	37 08 92 00 48
80 33 69 45 98	26 94 03 68 58	70 29 73 41 35	53 14 03 33 40	42 05 08 23 41
44 10 48 19 49	85 15 74 79 54	32 97 92 65 75	57 60 04 08 81	22 22 20 64 13
12 55 07 37 42	11 10 00 20 40	12 86 07 46 97	96 64 48 94 39	28 70 72 58 15
63 60 64 93 29	16 50 53 44 84	40 21 95 23 63	43 65 17 70 82	07 20 73 17 90
61 19 69 04 45	26 45 74 77 74	51 92 43 37 29	65 39 45 95 93	42 58 26 05 27
15 47 44 52 66	95 27 07 99 53	59 36 78 38 48	82 39 61 01 18	33 21 15 94 66
94 55 72 83 73	67 89 75 43 87	54 62 24 44 31	91 19 04 23 92	92 92 74 59 73

TABLE C.1 *(continued)*

42 48 11 62 13	97 34 40 87 21	16 86 84 87 67	03 07 11 20 59	25 70 14 66 70
23 52 37 83 17	73 20 88 98 37	68 93 59 14 16	26 25 22 96 63	05 52 28 25 62
04 49 35 24 94	75 24 63 38 24	43 86 25 10 25	61 96 27 93 35	65 33 71 24 72
00 54 99 76 54	64 05 18 81 39	96 11 96 38 96	54 89 28 23 91	23 28 72 95 29
35 96 31 53 07	26 89 80 93 54	33 35 13 54 62	77 97 45 00 24	90 10 33 93 33
59 80 80 83 91	45 42 72 68 42	83 60 94 97 00	13 02 12 48 92	78 56 52 01 06
46 05 88 32 36	01 39 00 22 86	77 28 14 40 77	93 91 08 36 47	70 61 74 29 41
32 17 90 05 97	87 37 92 52 41	05 56 70 70 07	86 74 31 71 57	85 39 41 18 38
69 23 46 14 06	20 11 74 52 04	15 95 66 00 00	18 74 39 24 23	97 11 89 63 38
19 56 54 14 30	01 75 87 53 79	40 41 92 15 85	66 67 43 68 06	84 96 28 52 07
45 15 51 49 38	19 47 60 72 46	43 66 79 45 43	59 04 79 00 33	20 82 66 95 41
94 86 43 19 94	36 18 81 08 51	34 88 88 15 53	01 54 03 54 56	05 01 45 11 76
09 18 82 00 97	32 82 53 95 27	04 22 08 63 04	83 38 98 73 74	64 27 85 80 44
90 04 58 54 97	51 98 15 06 54	94 93 88 19 97	91 87 07 61 50	68 47 68 46 59
73 18 95 02 07	47 67 72 62 69	62 29 06 44 64	27 12 46 70 18	41 36 18 27 60
75 76 87 64 90	20 97 18 17 49	90 42 91 22 72	95 37 50 58 71	93 82 34 31 78
54 01 64 40 56	66 28 13 10 03	00 68 22 73 98	20 71 45 32 95	07 70 61 78 13
08 35 86 99 10	78 54 24 27 85	13 66 15 88 73	04 61 89 75 53	31 22 30 84 20
28 30 60 32 64	81 33 31 05 91	40 51 00 78 93	32 60 46 04 75	94 11 90 18 40
53 84 08 62 33	81 59 41 36 28	51 21 59 02 90	28 46 66 87 93	77 76 22 07 91
91 75 75 37 41	61 61 36 22 69	50 26 39 02 12	55 78 17 65 14	83 48 34 70 55
89 41 59 26 94	00 39 75 83 91	12 60 71 76 46	48 94 27 23 06	94 54 13 74 08
77 51 30 38 20	86 83 42 99 01	68 41 48 27 74	51 90 81 39 80	72 89 35 55 07
19 50 23 71 74	69 97 92 02 88	55 21 02 97 73	74 28 77 52 51	65 34 46 74 15
21 81 85 93 13	93 27 88 17 57	05 68 67 31 56	07 08 28 50 46	31 85 33 84 52
51 47 46 64 99	68 10 72 38 21	94 04 99 13 45	42 83 60 91 91	08 00 74 54 49
99 55 96 83 31	62 53 52 41 70	69 77 71 28 30	74 81 97 81 42	43 86 07 28 34
33 71 34 80 07	93 58 47 28 69	51 92 66 47 21	58 30 32 98 22	93 17 49 39 72
85 27 48 68 93	11 30 32 92 70	28 83 43 41 37	73 51 59 04 00	71 14 84 36 43
84 13 38 96 40	44 03 55 21 66	73 85 27 00 91	61 22 26 05 61	62 32 71 84 23
56 73 21 62 34	17 39 59 61 31	10 12 39 16 22	85 49 65 75 60	81 60 41 88 80
65 13 85 66 06	87 64 88 52 61	34 31 36 58 61	45 87 52 10 69	85 64 44 72 77
38 00 10 21 78	81 71 91 17 11	71 60 29 29 37	74 21 96 40 49	65 58 44 96 98
37 40 29 63 97	01 30 47 75 86	56 27 11 00 65	47 32 46 26 05	40 03 03 74 38
97 12 54 03 48	87 08 33 14 17	21 81 53 92 50	75 23 76 20 47	15 50 12 95 78
21 82 64 11 34	47 14 33 40 72	64 63 88 59 02	49 13 90 64 41	03 85 65 45 52
73 13 54 27 42	95 71 90 90 35	85 79 47 42 96	08 78 98 81 56	64 69 11 92 02
07 63 87 79 29	03 06 11 80 72	96 20 74 41 56	23 82 19 95 38	04 71 36 69 94
60 52 88 34 41	07 95 41 98 14	59 17 52 06 95	05 53 35 21 39	61 21 20 64 55
83 59 63 56 55	06 95 89 29 83	05 12 80 97 19	77 43 35 37 83	92 30 15 04 98
10 85 06 27 46	99 59 91 05 07	13 49 90 63 19	53 07 57 18 39	06 41 01 93 62
39 82 09 89 52	43 62 26 31 47	64 42 18 08 14	43 80 00 93 51	31 02 47 31 67

SOURCE: From tables of the Rand Corporation from *A Million Random Digits With 100,000 Normal Deviates* (New York: Free Press, 1955). © 1955, 1983 by Rand Corporation. Reprinted by permission.

TABLE C.2   Critical Values of Chi-Square

Degrees of Freedom	Probability Level		
	.10	*.05*	*.01*
1	2.706	3.841	6.635
2	4.605	5.991	9.210
3	6.251	7.815	11.345
4	7.779	9.488	13.277
5	9.236	11.070	15.086
6	10.645	12.592	16.812
7	12.017	14.067	18.475
8	13.362	15.507	20.090
9	14.684	16.919	21.666
10	15.987	18.307	23.209
11	17.275	19.675	24.725
12	18.549	21.026	26.217
13	19.812	22.362	27.688
14	21.064	23.685	29.141
15	22.307	24.996	30.578
16	23.542	26.296	32.000
17	24.769	27.587	33.409
18	25.989	28.869	34.805
19	27.204	30.144	36.191
20	28.412	31.410	37.566

SOURCE: Table adapted from Fisher and Yates (1974), *Statistical Tables for Biological, Agricultural, and Medical Research,* 6th ed. London: Longman. Reprinted by permission of Addison Wesley Longman Ltd.

TABLE C.3   Critical Values of *t*

df	.05 .10	.025 .05	.01 .02	.005 .01

Significance Level*

df	.05 / .10	.025 / .05	.01 / .02	.005 / .01
1	6.314	12.706	31.821	63.657
2	2.920	4.303	6.965	9.925
3	2.353	3.182	4.541	5.841
4	2.132	2.776	3.747	4.604
5	2.015	2.571	3.365	4.032
6	1.943	2.447	3.143	3.707
7	1.895	2.365	2.998	3.499
8	1.860	2.306	2.896	3.355
9	1.833	2.262	2.821	3.250
10	1.812	2.228	2.764	3.169
11	1.796	2.201	2.718	3.106
12	1.782	2.179	2.681	3.055
13	1.771	2.160	2.650	3.012
14	1.761	2.145	2.624	2.977
15	1.753	2.131	2.602	2.947
16	1.746	2.120	2.583	2.921
17	1.740	2.110	2.567	2.898
18	1.734	2.101	2.552	2.878
19	1.729	2.093	2.539	2.861
20	1.725	2.086	2.528	2.845
21	1.721	2.080	2.518	2.831
22	1.717	2.074	2.508	2.819
23	1.714	2.069	2.500	2.807
24	1.711	2.064	2.492	2.797
25	1.708	2.060	2.485	2.787
26	1.706	2.056	2.479	2.779
27	1.703	2.052	2.473	2.771
28	1.701	2.048	2.467	2.763
29	1.699	2.045	2.462	2.756
30	1.697	2.042	2.457	2.750
40	1.684	2.021	2.423	2.704
60	1.671	2.000	2.390	2.660
120	1.658	1.980	2.358	2.617
∞	1.645	1.960	2.326	2.576

*Use the top significance level when you have predicted a specific directional difference (a one-tailed test; e.g., group 1 will be greater than group 2). Use the bottom significance level when you have only predicted that group 1 will differ from group 2 without specifying the direction of the difference (a two-tailed test).

TABLE C.4   Critical Values of _F_

df for Denominator (Error)	α	df for Numerator (Systematic)											
		_1_	_2_	_3_	_4_	_5_	_6_	_7_	_8_	_9_	_10_	_11_	_12_
1	.10	39.9	49.5	53.6	55.8	57.2	58.2	58.9	59.4	59.9	60.2	60.5	60.7
	.05	161	200	216	225	230	234	237	239	241	242	243	244
2	.10	8.53	9.00	9.16	9.24	9.29	9.33	9.35	9.37	9.38	9.39	9.40	9.41
	.05	18.5	19.0	19.2	19.2	19.3	19.3	19.4	19.4	19.4	19.4	19.4	19.4
	.01	98.5	99.0	99.2	99.2	99.3	99.3	99.4	99.4	99.4	99.4	99.4	99.4
3	.10	5.54	5.46	5.39	5.34	5.31	5.28	5.27	5.25	5.24	5.23	5.22	5.22
	.05	10.1	9.55	9.28	9.12	9.01	8.94	8.89	8.85	8.81	8.79	8.76	8.74
	.01	34.1	30.8	29.5	28.7	28.2	27.9	27.7	27.5	27.3	27.2	27.1	27.1
4	.10	4.54	4.32	4.19	4.11	4.05	4.01	3.98	3.95	3.94	3.92	3.91	3.90
	.05	7.71	6.94	6.59	6.39	6.26	6.16	6.09	6.04	6.00	5.96	5.94	5.91
	.01	21.2	18.0	16.7	16.0	15.5	15.2	15.0	14.8	14.7	14.5	14.4	14.4
5	.10	4.06	3.78	3.62	3.52	3.45	3.40	3.37	3.34	3.32	3.30	3.28	3.27
	.05	6.61	5.79	5.41	5.19	5.05	4.95	4.88	4.82	4.77	4.74	4.71	4.68
	.01	16.3	13.3	12.1	11.4	11.0	10.7	10.5	10.3	10.2	10.1	9.96	9.89
6	.10	3.78	3.46	3.29	3.18	3.11	3.05	3.01	2.98	2.96	2.94	2.92	2.90
	.05	5.99	5.14	4.76	4.53	4.39	4.28	4.21	4.15	4.10	4.06	4.03	4.00
	.01	13.7	10.9	9.78	9.15	8.75	8.47	8.26	8.10	7.98	7.87	7.79	7.72
7	.10	3.59	3.26	3.07	2.96	2.88	2.83	2.78	2.75	2.72	2.70	2.68	2.67
	.05	5.59	4.74	4.35	4.12	3.97	3.87	3.79	3.73	3.68	3.64	3.60	3.57
	.01	12.2	9.55	8.45	7.85	7.46	7.19	6.99	6.84	6.72	6.62	6.54	6.47
8	.10	3.46	3.11	2.92	2.81	2.73	2.67	2.62	2.59	2.56	2.54	2.52	2.50
	.05	5.32	4.46	4.07	3.84	3.69	3.58	3.50	3.44	3.39	3.35	3.31	3.28
	.01	11.3	8.65	7.59	7.01	6.63	6.37	6.18	6.03	5.91	5.81	5.73	5.67
9	.10	3.36	3.01	2.81	2.69	2.61	2.55	2.51	2.47	2.44	2.42	2.40	2.38
	.05	5.12	4.26	3.86	3.63	3.48	3.37	3.29	3.23	3.18	3.14	3.10	3.07
	.01	10.6	8.02	6.99	6.42	6.06	5.80	5.61	5.47	5.35	5.26	5.18	5.11
10	.10	3.29	2.92	2.73	2.61	2.52	2.46	2.41	2.38	2.35	2.32	2.30	2.28
	.05	4.96	4.10	3.71	3.48	3.33	3.22	3.14	3.07	3.02	2.98	2.94	2.91
	.01	10.0	7.56	6.55	5.99	5.64	5.39	5.20	5.06	4.94	4.85	4.77	4.71
11	.10	3.23	2.86	2.66	2.54	2.45	2.39	2.34	2.30	2.27	2.25	2.23	2.21
	.05	4.84	3.98	3.59	3.36	3.20	3.09	3.01	2.95	2.90	2.85	2.82	2.79
	.01	9.65	7.21	6.22	5.67	5.32	5.07	4.89	4.74	4.63	4.54	4.46	4.40
12	.10	3.18	2.81	2.61	2.48	2.39	2.33	2.28	2.24	2.21	2.19	2.17	2.15
	.05	4.75	3.89	3.49	3.26	3.11	3.00	2.91	2.85	2.80	2.75	2.72	2.69
	.01	9.33	6.93	5.95	5.41	5.06	4.82	4.64	4.50	4.39	4.30	4.22	4.16

TABLE C.4   *(continued)*

df for Denominator (Error)	α	1	2	3	4	5	6	7	8	9	10	11	12
						df for Numerator (Systematic)							
13	.10	3.14	2.76	2.56	2.43	2.35	2.28	2.23	2.20	2.16	2.14	2.12	2.10
	.05	4.67	3.81	3.41	3.18	3.03	2.92	2.83	2.77	2.71	2.67	2.63	2.60
	.01	9.07	6.70	5.74	5.21	4.86	4.62	4.44	4.30	4.19	4.10	4.02	3.96
14	.10	3.10	2.73	2.52	2.39	2.31	2.24	2.19	2.15	2.12	2.10	2.08	2.05
	.05	4.60	3.74	3.34	3.11	2.96	2.85	2.76	2.70	2.65	2.60	2.57	2.53
	.01	8.86	6.51	5.56	5.04	4.69	4.46	4.28	4.14	4.03	3.94	3.86	3.80
15	.10	3.07	2.70	2.49	2.36	2.27	2.21	2.16	2.12	2.09	2.06	2.04	2.02
	.05	4.54	3.68	3.29	3.06	2.90	2.79	2.71	2.64	2.59	2.54	2.51	2.48
	.01	8.68	6.36	5.42	4.89	4.56	4.32	4.14	4.00	3.89	3.80	3.73	3.67
16	.10	3.05	2.67	2.46	2.33	2.24	2.18	2.13	2.09	2.06	2.03	2.01	1.99
	.05	4.49	3.63	3.24	3.01	2.85	2.74	2.66	2.59	2.54	2.49	2.46	2.42
	.01	8.53	6.23	5.29	4.77	4.44	4.20	4.03	3.89	3.78	3.69	3.62	3.55
17	.10	3.03	2.64	2.44	2.31	2.22	2.15	2.10	2.06	2.03	2.00	1.98	1.96
	.05	4.45	3.59	3.20	2.96	2.81	2.70	2.61	2.55	2.49	2.45	2.41	2.38
	.01	8.40	6.11	5.18	4.67	4.34	4.10	3.93	3.79	3.68	3.59	3.52	3.46
18	.10	3.01	2.62	2.42	2.29	2.20	2.13	2.08	2.04	2.00	1.98	1.96	1.93
	.05	4.41	3.55	3.16	2.93	2.77	2.66	2.58	2.51	2.46	2.41	2.37	2.34
	.01	8.29	6.01	5.09	4.58	4.25	4.01	3.84	3.71	3.60	3.51	3.43	3.37
19	.10	2.99	2.61	2.40	2.27	2.18	2.11	2.06	2.02	1.98	1.96	1.94	1.91
	.05	4.38	3.52	3.13	2.90	2.74	2.63	2.54	2.48	2.42	2.38	2.34	2.31
	.01	8.18	5.93	5.01	4.50	4.17	3.94	3.77	3.63	3.52	3.43	3.36	3.30
20	.10	2.97	2.59	2.38	2.25	2.16	2.09	2.04	2.00	1.96	1.94	1.92	1.89
	.05	4.35	3.49	3.10	2.87	2.71	2.60	2.51	2.45	2.39	2.35	2.31	2.28
	.01	8.10	5.85	4.94	4.43	4.10	3.87	3.70	3.56	3.46	3.37	3.29	3.23
22	.10	2.95	2.56	2.35	2.22	2.13	2.06	2.01	1.97	1.93	1.90	1.88	1.86
	.05	4.30	3.44	3.05	2.82	2.66	2.55	2.46	2.40	2.34	2.30	2.26	2.23
	.01	7.95	5.72	4.82	4.31	3.99	3.76	3.59	3.45	3.35	3.26	3.18	3.12
24	.10	2.93	2.54	2.33	2.19	2.10	2.04	1.98	1.94	1.91	1.88	1.85	1.83
	.05	4.26	3.40	3.01	2.78	2.62	2.51	2.42	2.36	2.30	2.25	2.21	2.18
	.01	7.82	5.61	4.72	4.22	3.90	3.67	3.50	3.36	3.26	3.17	3.09	3.03
26	.10	2.91	2.52	2.31	2.17	2.08	2.01	1.96	1.92	1.88	1.86	1.84	1.81
	.05	4.23	3.37	2.98	2.74	2.59	2.47	2.39	2.32	2.27	2.22	2.18	2.15
	.01	7.72	5.53	4.64	4.14	3.82	3.59	3.42	3.29	3.18	3.09	3.02	2.96
28	.10	2.89	2.50	2.29	2.16	2.06	2.00	1.94	1.90	1.87	1.84	1.81	1.79
	.05	4.20	3.34	2.95	2.71	2.56	2.45	2.36	2.29	2.24	2.19	2.15	2.12
	.01	7.64	5.45	4.57	4.07	3.75	3.53	3.36	3.23	3.12	3.03	2.96	2.90

TABLE C.4   *(continued)*

df for Denominator (Error)	α	\multicolumn{12}{c}{df for Numerator (Systematic)}											
		1	*2*	*3*	*4*	*5*	*6*	*7*	*8*	*9*	*10*	*11*	*12*
30	.10	2.88	2.49	2.28	2.14	2.05	1.98	1.93	1.88	1.85	1.82	1.79	1.77
	.05	4.17	3.32	2.92	2.69	2.53	2.42	2.33	2.27	2.21	2.16	2.13	2.09
	.01	7.56	5.39	4.51	4.02	3.70	3.47	3.30	3.17	3.07	2.98	2.91	2.84
40	.10	2.84	2.44	2.23	2.09	2.00	1.93	1.87	1.83	1.79	1.76	1.73	1.71
	.05	4.08	3.23	2.84	2.61	2.45	2.34	2.25	2.18	2.12	2.08	2.04	2.00
	.01	7.31	5.18	4.31	3.83	3.51	3.29	3.12	2.99	2.89	2.80	2.73	2.66
60	.10	2.79	2.39	2.18	2.04	1.95	1.87	1.82	1.77	1.74	1.71	1.68	1.66
	.05	4.00	3.15	2.76	2.53	2.37	2.25	2.17	2.10	2.04	1.99	1.95	1.92
	.01	7.08	4.98	4.13	3.65	3.34	3.12	2.95	2.82	2.72	2.63	2.56	2.50
120	.10	2.75	2.35	2.13	1.99	1.90	1.82	1.77	1.72	1.68	1.65	1.62	1.60
	.05	3.92	3.07	2.68	2.45	2.29	2.17	2.09	2.02	1.96	1.91	1.87	1.83
	.01	6.85	4.79	3.95	3.48	3.17	2.96	2.79	2.66	2.56	2.47	2.40	2.34
200	.10	2.73	2.33	2.11	1.97	1.88	1.80	1.75	1.70	1.66	1.63	1.60	1.57
	.05	3.89	3.04	2.65	2.42	2.26	2.14	2.06	1.98	1.93	1.88	1.84	1.80
	.01	6.76	4.71	3.88	3.41	3.11	2.89	2.73	2.60	2.50	2.41	2.34	2.27
∞	.10	2.71	2.30	2.08	1.94	1.85	1.77	1.72	1.67	1.63	1.60	1.57	1.55
	.05	3.84	3.00	2.60	2.37	2.21	2.10	2.01	1.94	1.88	1.83	1.79	1.75
	.01	6.63	4.61	3.78	3.32	3.02	2.80	2.64	2.51	2.41	2.32	2.25	2.18

TABLE C.5   Critical Values of r (Pearson Product-Moment Correlation Coefficient)

df	Level of Significance for Two-Tailed Test		
	.10	.05	.01
1	.988	.997	.9999
2	.900	.950	.990
3	.805	.878	.959
4	.729	.811	.917
5	.669	.754	.874
6	.622	.707	.834
7	.582	.666	.798
8	.549	.632	.765
9	.521	.602	.735
10	.497	.576	.708
11	.476	.553	.684
12	.458	.532	.661
13	.441	.514	.641
14	.426	.497	.623
15	.412	.482	.606
16	.400	.468	.590
17	.389	.456	.575
18	.378	.444	.561
19	.369	.433	.549
20	.360	.423	.537
25	.323	.381	.487
30	.296	.349	.449
35	.275	.325	.418
40	.257	.304	.393
45	.243	.288	.372
50	.231	.273	.354
60	.211	.250	.325
70	.195	.232	.303
80	.183	.217	.283
90	.173	.205	.267
100	.164	.195	.254

NOTE: The significance level is halved for a one-tailed test.

◆ *Glossary*

ABA design *See* reversal design.

abstract A brief summary of the research report.

ageism Bias toward older adults that may be expressed in written test materials and experimental procedures.

alpha level A specific probability level, stated in advance, that indicates what the researcher considers significant; typically set at .05 (*See also* significance level.)

analysis of variance (*F* test) A statistical significance test for determining whether two or more means are significantly different. *F* is the ratio of systematic variance to error variance.

applied research Research conducted to address a practical problem to suggest solutions.

archival research The use of existing sources of information for research. Sources include statistical records, survey archives, and written records.

attention control group A control group that receives an equal amount of attention as the group receiving the manipulation but that does not receive the independent variable treatment.

authority An approach to knowledge that accepts information based on faith from a trusted source.

bar graph *See* histogram.

baseline In a single-subject design, the subject's behavior during a control period before introduction of the experimental manipulation.

basic research Research designed to uncover evidence about fundamental behavioral processes.

behavioral measure A dependent measure in which the researcher directly observes the participant's behavior.

between subjects design *See* independent groups design.

carry-over effect A problem that may occur in repeated measures designs if the effects of one treatment are still present when the next treatment is given. (*See also* contrast effect.)

case study A descriptive account of the behavior, past history, and other relevant factors concerning a specific individual.

ceiling effect Failure of a dependent measure to detect a difference because it was too easy. (*See also* floor effect.)

central tendency A single number or value that describes the typical or central score among a set of scores.

chronological age Definition of age based on year of birth; using a chronological age approach, older adults are defined as 65 and over.

closed-ended question In questionnaires and interviews, a question that presents the respondent with a limited number of alternatives to select.

cluster sampling A method of sampling in which clusters of individuals are identified. Clusters are sampled, and then all individuals in each cluster are included in the sample.

coding system In systematic observation and content analysis, a set of rules used to categorize observations.

cohort A group of people born at about the same time and exposed to the same societal events; cohort effects are confounded with age in a cross-sectional study.

comparative rating scale Rating scale that provides a standard of comparison so the respondent makes ratings against some standard frame of reference.

conceptual replication Replication of research using different procedures for manipulating or measuring the variables.

confederate A person posing as a participant in an experiment who is actually part of the experiment.

confidentiality In research ethics, the researcher protects the identity of research participants to ensure that personal information is not revealed to unauthorized sources.

confounding Failure to control for the effects of a third variable in an experimental design.

construct validity The degree to which a measurement device accurately measures the theoretical construct it is designed to measure.

content analysis Systematic analysis of the content of documents such as written records.

contrast effect In repeated measures design, a response in one condition is affected by comparison to other conditions an individual has completed already. (*See also* carry-over effect.)

convergent validity Assessment of the validity of a measure by demonstrating that the measure is related to other variables in predicted ways.

correlation coefficient (Pearson *r* correlation coefficient) An index of how strongly two variables are related to each other in a group of participants.

correlational method A method of determining whether two variables are related by measurement or observation of the variables.

counterbalancing A method of controlling for order effects in a repeated measures design by either including all orders of treatment presentation or randomly determining the order for each participant.

criterion validity The degree to which a measurement device accurately predicts behavior on a criterion measure.

criterion variable A behavior that a researcher wishes to predict using a predictor variable.

cross-sectional method A developmental research method in which persons of different ages are studied at only one point in time; conceptually similar to an independent groups design.

cultural research Research that studies the relationship between variables across different cultures.

curvilinear relationship A relationship in which increases in the values of the first variable are accompanied by both increases and decreases in the value of the second variable.

debriefing Explanation of the purposes of the research that is given to participants following their participation in the research.

deception A research situation in which participants are deliberately not told about all aspects of the research.

degrees of freedom (df) A concept used in tests of statistical significance; the number of observations that are free to vary to produce a known outcome.

demand characteristics Cues that inform the participant of how he or she is expected to behave.

demographic measures Variables that assess personal characteristics such as gender, age, socioeconomic status, race, and ethnicity.

dependent variable (response variable) The variable that is the participant's response to, and is dependent on, the independent variable.

descriptive statistics Statistical measures that describe the results of a study; descriptive statistics include measures of central tendency (e.g., mean), variability (e.g., standard deviation), and correlation (e.g., Pearson *r*).

developmental research Research that examines changes in human development and the process of development, including age-related changes in individuals, families, or sociocultural contexts.

discriminant validity Assessment of the validity of a measure by demonstrating that the measure is not related to other variables that it theoretically should not be related to.

discussion section Part of a research report that evaluates the research findings, comparing the results to the hypotheses and to previous research.

double-blind procedure A procedure in which both the participant and the investigator are unaware of the treatment or group to which the participant has been assigned. (*See also* single-blind procedure.)

ecological validity Extent to which a research situation accurately represents behavior as it would occur in real-world settings.

effect size The extent to which two variables are associated. In experimental research, the magnitude of the impact of the independent variable on the dependent variable.

empirical approach Essential feature of the scientific method that knowledge relies on observation of actual behavior.

error variance Random variability in a set of scores that is not the result of the independent variable. Statistically, the variability of each score from its group mean.

ethical concerns Ethical issues for research including informed consent, confidentiality, and psychological risk.

ethics code   Set of ethical principles and standards for research, teaching, and therapy with adults and children; a set of ethics also exists for working with animals.

ethnography   Field observation in which the researcher spends an extended period of time in the natural setting of a social group to document their customs, habits, and actions.

evaluation research (program evaluation)   Research designed to evaluate programs (e.g., social reforms, innovations) that are designed to produce certain changes or outcomes in a target population.

event manipulation   *See* staged manipulation.

event sampling   In systematic observation, observer records behavior only when particular events or behaviors occur.

exact replication   Replication of research using the same procedures for manipulating and measuring the variables that were used in the original research.

expectancy effects   *See* experimenter bias.

experimental control   In an experiment, keeping all extraneous variables constant so that only the independent variable can affect the dependent variable.

experimental method   A method of determining whether variables are related in which the researcher manipulates the independent variable and controls all other variables either by randomization or by direct experimental control.

experimental realism   The extent to which the experiment has an impact on the participants, making them take the experiment seriously.

experimenter bias (expectancy effects)   Any intentional or unintentional influence that the experimenter exerts on subjects to confirm the hypothesis under investigation.

external validity (generalizability)   The degree to which the results of an experiment may be extended to other populations, experimenters, and settings.

***F* test**   *See* analysis of variance.

face validity   The degree to which a measurement device appears to measure a variable accurately.

factorial design   A design in which all levels of each independent variable are combined with all levels of the other independent variables. A factorial design allows investigation of the separate main effects and interactions of two or more independent variables.

factorial notation   A format for describing the number of independent variables and the number of levels for each independent variable in a factorial design.

fatigue effect   In repeated measures design, a decline in performance as the participant becomes tired, bored, or distracted. (*See also* order effect.)

field experiment   An experiment that is conducted in the field rather than in a laboratory setting.

field observation   *See* naturalistic observation.

financial capital   A component of socioeconomic status that determines family income derived from all sources of income such as investments, rent, unemployment, and food stamps.

floor effect   Failure of a measure to detect a difference because it was too difficult. (*See also* ceiling effect.)

frequency distribution   An arrangement of a set of scores from lowest to highest that indicates the number of times each score was obtained.

frequency polygon   A graphic display of a frequency distribution in which the frequency of each score is plotted on the vertical axis, with the plotted points connected by straight lines.

functional age   Definition of age based on ability to live independently and engage in work and intellectual activity.

functional design   An experiment that contains many levels of the independent variable to determine the exact functional relationship between the independent and dependent variables.

generalizability   *See* external validity.

goals of science   Primary purposes of science are description, prediction, and explanation of behavior.

graphic rating scale   Rating scale that asks the survey respondent to place a check mark along a continuous line anchored by descriptive adjectives.

haphazard sampling   Selecting participants in a haphazard manner, usually on the basis of availability, and not with regard to having a representative sample of the population; a type of nonprobability sampling.

Hawthorne effect   A change in performance (usually improvement) related to knowledge that research is being conducted. (*See also* reactivity.)

histogram   Graphic display of the scores in a frequency distribution; vertical or horizontal bars represent the frequencies of each score.

history confound   As a threat to the internal validity of an experiment, refers to any outside event that is not part of the manipulation but that could be responsible for the results.

human capital   A component of socioeconomic status that assesses maternal education.

hypothesis   A statement that makes an assertion about what is true in a specific situation; often a statement asserting that two or more variables are related to one another.

illusory correlation   A cognitive bias that occurs when two events occur together, creating an incorrect perception of cause and effect.

independent groups design (between subjects design)   An experiment in which different participants are assigned to each group.

independent variable (situational variable)   The variable that is manipulated to observe its effect on the dependent variable.

individual difference variable   *See* subject variable.

inferential statistics   Statistics designed to determine whether results based on sample data are generalizable to a population.

informed consent   In research ethics, the principle that participants in a study be informed in advance of all aspects of the research that may influence their decision to participate.

Institutional Review Board (IRB)   An ethics review committee established to review research proposals. The IRB is composed of scientists, nonscientists, and legal experts.

instructional manipulation   *See* straightforward manipulation.

instrument decay   *See* instrumentation confound.

instrumentation confound   As a threat to internal validity, the possibility that a change in the characteristics of the measurement instrument is responsible for the results.

interaction effect   The differing effect of one independent variable on the dependent variable, depending on the level of another independent variable.

internal validity   The certainty with which results

of an experiment can be attributed to the manipulation of the independent variable rather than to some other, confounding variable.

interobserver reliability (interrater reliability)   A reliability coefficient determined by the correlation between scores on a measure coded by one observer (or rater) and scores on the same measure coded by a second observer (or rater).

interrater reliability   *See* interobserver reliability.

interval scale   A scale of measurement in which the intervals between numbers on the scale are all equal in size.

interviewer bias   Intentional or unintentional influence exerted by an interviewer in such a way that the actual or interpreted behavior of respondents is consistent with the interviewer's expectations.

introduction section   Part of a research report that describes the problem being investigated, including past research and theories in the area under investigation.

intuition   An approach to gathering knowledge based on acceptance of one's personal judgment about events.

IV × SV design   A factorial design that includes both an experimental independent variable (IV) and a correlational subject variable (SV).

Likert scale   Rating scale consisting of a set of statements on a topic; typically uses five categories ranging from strongly agree to strongly disagree.

literature review   A description of past research and theory. Brief literature reviews are included in the introduction section of a research report; major literature reviews may appear as journal articles.

longitudinal method   A developmental research method in which the same persons are observed repeatedly as they grow older; conceptually similar to a repeated measures design.

main effect   The direct effect of an independent variable on a dependent variable.

manipulated variable   The variable that is manipulated by the researcher to observe its effect on the dependent variable; also known as the independent variable.

manipulation check   A measure used to determine whether the manipulation of the independent variable had its intended effect on a participant.

marginal means In a factorial design, the average of cell means calculated across the levels of each independent variable.

matched random assignment A method of assigning participants to groups in which pairs of participants are first matched on some characteristic and then individually assigned randomly to groups.

maturation control group A control group that receives no treatment but is tested at the end of the study to see whether any changes were produced by the physical or mental maturation of the participants.

maturation effect As a threat to internal validity, the possibility that any naturally occurring change within the individual is responsible for the results.

mean A measure of central tendency, obtained by summing scores and then dividing the sum by the number of scores.

measurement error The degree to which a measurement deviates from the true score value.

median A measure of central tendency; the middle score in a distribution of scores that divides the distribution in half.

Mental Measurements Yearbook (MMY) A book that indexes standardized tests in psychology, education, vocational aptitude, and related areas.

meta-analysis A set of statistical procedures for combining the results of a number of studies to provide a general assessment of the relationship between variables.

method section Part of a research report that describes the participants, design, apparatus, and procedure used in a study.

minimal risk Research in which potential risk to participants is no greater than normally encountered in daily life or routine physical or psychological tests.

mixed factorial design A design that includes both independent groups (between subjects) and repeated measures (within subjects) variables.

mode A measure of central tendency; the most frequent score in a distribution of scores.

mortality The loss of participants who decide to leave an experiment. Mortality is a threat to internal validity when the mortality rate is related to the nature of the experimental manipulation.

multiple baseline design Observing behavior before and after a manipulation under multiple circumstances (across different individuals, different behaviors, or different settings).

multiple correlation A correlation between one variable and a combined set of predictor variables.

mundane realism The extent to which the independent variable manipulation is similar to events that occur in the real world.

naturalistic observation (field observation) Descriptive method in which observations are made in a natural social setting.

negative linear relationship A relationship in which increases in the values of the first variable are accompanied by decreases in the values of the second variable.

nominal scale A scale of measurement with two or more categories that have numeric properties.

nonequivalent control group design A poor experimental design in which nonequivalent groups of individuals participate in the different experimental groups, and there is no pretest.

nonequivalent control group pretest-posttest design A quasi-experimental design in which nonequivalent groups are used, but a pretest allows assessment of equivalency and pretest-posttest changes.

nonprobability sampling Type of sampling procedure in which one cannot specify the probability that any member of the population will be included in the sample.

nonsignificant results Results that are probably due to error factors and indicate a decision not to reject the null hypothesis.

nontreated controls A control group in an experiment that does not receive a potentially beneficial treatment. Ethical principles hold that such participants deserve to receive the treatment if it is found to be of benefit.

null hypothesis The hypothesis, used for statistical purposes, that the variables under investigation are not related in the population, that any observed effect based on sample results is due to random error.

numerical scales Rating scales that use a sequence of numbers such as a 5-point scale for the response categories; the numbers may be stated or implied.

observational research   Descriptive research in which data are obtained by observing activities in naturalistic or laboratory settings.

one-group pretest-posttest design   A poor experimental design in which the effect of an independent variable is inferred from the pretest-posttest difference in a single group.

one-shot case study   A poor experimental design in which a single group of participants is assessed only once after an experimental manipulation.

open-ended question   A question that permits the respondent to generate a reply; no response options are provided.

operational definition   Definition of a concept that specifies the operation used to measure or manipulate the concept.

order effect   In a repeated measures design, the effect that the order of introducing treatment has on the dependent variable. (*See also* fatigue effect and practice effect.)

ordinal scale   A scale of measurement in which the measurement categories form a rank order along a continuum.

panel study   In survey research, questioning the same people at two or more points in time.

partial correlation   The correlation between two variables with the influence of a third variable statistically controlled.

participant observer   In field observation, an observer who is an active participant in the social setting being studied.

Pearson r correlation coefficient   *See* correlation coefficient.

physiological measure   A dependent measure that records physiological responses of the body such as heart rate, skin temperature, or galvanic skin response (GSR).

pilot study   A small-scale study conducted prior to conducting an actual experiment; designed to test and refine procedures.

placebo control group   In drug research, a group given an inert substance to assess the psychological effect of receiving a treatment.

placebo effect   Change in behavior caused by psychological expectations about a treatment, not by the treatment itself.

population   The defined group of individuals from which a sample is drawn.

positive linear relationship   A relationship in which increases in the values of the first variable are accompanied by increases in the values of the second variable.

posttest only control group design   A true experimental design in which the dependent variable is measured only once (posttest) after manipulation of the independent variable.

practice effect   In a repeated measures design, an improvement in performance as a result of repeated practice with a task. (*See also* order effect.)

predictor variable   A measure that is used to predict behavior on another measure (a criterion variable).

pretest-posttest control group design   A true experimental design in which the dependent variable is measured both before (pretest) and after (posttest) manipulation of the independent variable.

prevention science   Branch of research that studies the prevention of human dysfunction.

probability   The likelihood that a given event (among a specific set of events) will occur.

probability sampling   Type of sampling procedure in which one is able to specify the probability that any member of the population will be included in the sample.

program evaluation research   *See* evaluation research.

Psychological Abstracts   Contains nonevaluative summaries of research in psychology and related disciplines.

psychological risk   Ethical principle that researchers must use experimental procedures that do not create psychological distress.

qualitative data   Verbal, descriptive data that is typically presented in everyday language without numbers or statistics.

quantitative data   Numerical data that is typically reported in tables, figures, and statistics.

quasi-experimental design   A type of design that approximates the control features of true experiments to infer that a given treatment had its intended effect.

quota sampling   A sampling procedure in which the sample is chosen to reflect the numerical composition of various subgroups in the population. A haphazard sampling technique is used to obtain the sample.

random assignment Assigning participants to groups in a random manner such that assignment is determined entirely by chance.

randomization Controlling for the effects of extraneous variables by ensuring that the variables operate in a manner determined entirely by chance.

range A measure of the variability of scores around the mean; the difference between the highest and lowest score.

ratio scale A scale of measurement in which there is an absolute zero point, indicating an absence of the variable being measured. An implication is that ratios of numbers on the scale can be formed. Generally these are physical measures such as weight or timed measures such as duration or reaction time.

reactivity A problem of measurement in which the measure changes the behavior being observed. (*See also* Hawthorne effect.)

regression equation A mathematical equation that allows prediction of one behavior when the score on another variable is known.

reliability The degree to which a measure is consistent.

repeated measures design (within subjects design) An experiment in which the same participants are assigned to each group.

replication Repeating a research study to determine whether the results can be duplicated.

research hypothesis The hypothesis that the variables under investigation are related in the population, that the observed effect based on sample data is true in the population.

research proposal A written report summarizing an investigator's plans and research procedures that is frequently required to obtain funding.

response rate In survey research, the percentage of people who complete the survey.

response set A pattern of individual responses to questions on a self-report measure that is not related to the content of the questions.

response variable *See* dependent variable.

restriction of the range A problem for interpreting correlations when all possible values of a dependent variable are not sampled, leading to inaccurate conclusions.

results section Part of a research report that presents the findings in narrative and statistical form, often including tables and figures of major results.

retrospective memory Memory for past events or behaviors; inaccurate recall leads to problems for self-report measures.

reversal design (ABA design) A single-subject design in which the treatment is introduced after a baseline period and then withdrawn during a second baseline period. It may be extended by adding a second introduction of the treatment.

sample size Refers to the number of participants included in a study; important for generalizability.

sampling The process of choosing members of a population to be included in a sample.

sampling bias A problem when sampling procedures overlook certain categories of people in the population, creating a nonrepresentative sample.

sampling distribution A probability distribution for the values of an inferential statistic, given the assumption that the null hypothesis is true.

scatterplot A diagram depicting the pairs of scores in a correlation coefficient.

scientific method An approach to gathering knowledge that relies on an objective set of rules for gathering, evaluating, and reporting information.

selection differences Differences in the type of participants who make up each group in an experimental design.

self-report measure A dependent measure in which participants provide information about themselves, for example, by filling out a questionnaire or responding to interview questions.

semantic differential scale Rating scale on which respondents evaluate a concept by using 7-point scales anchored by bipolar adjectives such as good-bad, strong-weak.

sensitivity The ability of a dependent measure to detect differences between groups.

sequential design A combination of cross-sectional and longitudinal designs to study developmental research questions.

significance level The probability of rejecting the

null hypothesis when it is true. (*See also* alpha level.)

significant result   *See* statistical significance.

simple random assignment   Assigning participants to groups in a random manner such that assignment is determined entirely by chance.

simple random sampling   A sampling procedure in which each member of the population has an equal probability of being included in the sample.

single-blind procedure   A procedure in which the participant does not know which group he or she has been assigned to; for example, in medical research when the patient does not know whether a pill is actual medication or a placebo. (*See also* double-blind procedure.)

single-subject experiment   An experiment in which the effect of the independent variable is assessed using data from a single participant.

situational variable   *See* independent variable.

social capital   A component of socioeconomic status that assesses the number of adults in a child's home.

social desirability   A response set in which respondents attempt to answer questions in a socially desirable or approved manner.

split-half reliability   A reliability coefficient determined by the correlation between scores on the first half of the items on a measure with scores on the second half of the measure.

staged manipulation (event manipulation)   A manipulation of the independent variable in an experiment involving a staged event, usually with one or more confederates.

standard deviation   The average deviation of scores from the mean; the square root of the variance.

statistical phrase   In statistics, the statistical symbol, degrees of freedom, obtained value, and probability level.

statistical records   A type of archival data consisting of extensive records collected by public and private organizations.

statistical regression   The tendency of extreme scores on a measure to become less extreme (regress or move toward the mean) when the measurement is made a second time.

statistical significance (significant result)   Rejection of the null hypothesis when an outcome has a low probability (usually .05 or less) of occurrence if the null hypothesis is correct.

straightforward manipulation (instructional manipulation)   A manipulation of the independent variable in an experiment accomplished by giving different sets of instructions to different experimental groups.

stratified random sampling   A sampling procedure in which the population is divided into strata followed by random sampling from each stratum.

structural model   A model of an expected pattern of relationships among a set of variables. The proposed pattern is based on a theory of how the variables are causally related to one another.

subject variable   A variable that is a characteristic of a person such as marital status, birth order, or intelligence; subject variables cannot be manipulated.

survey archives   A type of archival data consisting of data obtained from surveys that are stored on computers and available to other researchers for analysis.

survey research   A research method that uses self-report techniques such as questionnaires or interviews to question people about themselves.

systematic observation   Careful observation of one or more behaviors in a specific setting.

systematic variance   Variability in a set of scores that is the result of the independent variable; statistically, the variability of each group mean from the grand mean of all participants.

***t* test**   A statistical test used to evaluate whether two groups are significantly different.

testing confound   A threat to internal validity in which taking a pretest changes behavior without any effect by the independent variable.

test-retest reliability   A reliability coefficient determined by the correlation between scores on a measure given at one time with scores on the same measure given at a later time.

theory   A set of explanatory statements about behavior that can be tested through empirical research.

third variable problem   The possibility that a relationship between two variables is caused by some other variable.

time sampling   In systematic observation, observer records behavior at predetermined time intervals.

treatment period   In single-subject designs, refers to the portion of the design when the experimental treatment or independent variable is introduced.

true score   An individual's actual score on a variable being measured, as opposed to the score the individual obtained on the measure itself.

Type I error   An incorrect decision to reject the null hypothesis when it is true.

Type II error   An incorrect decision to accept the null hypothesis when it is false.

unobtrusive measure   A measure of behavior that is made without the participant's awareness.

validity   The degree to which a measurement instrument measures what it is intended to measure.

variability   The amount of dispersion of scores around some central value.

variable   A general class or category of objects, events, or situations within which specific instances are found to vary.

variance   A measure of the variability of scores around a mean; the mean of the sum of squared deviations of scores from the group means.

within subjects design   *See* repeated measures design.

written records   A type of archival data consisting of documents preserved by historical societies, public documents, and media records.

young-old versus old-old   Definition of age based on age brackets such as 65 to 74 for young-old and 75+ for old-old.

◆ References

Aber, J. L., Brooks-Gunn, J., & Maynard, R. A. (1995). Effects of welfare reform on teenage parents and their children. *The Future of Children, 5*(2), 53–71.

Abernathy, T. J., Massad, L., & Romano-Dwyer, L. (1995). The relationship between smoking and self-esteem. *Adolescence, 30,* 900–907.

Abidin, R. R. (1990). *Parenting Stress Index manual.* Charlottesville, VA: Pediatric Psychology Press.

Abramovitch, R., Freedman, J. L., Thoden, K., & Nikolich, C. (1991). Children's capacity to consent to participation in psychological research: Empirical findings. *Child Development, 6,* 1100–1109.

Adams, C. A., & Drabman, R. S. (1995). Improving morning interactions: Beat-the-Buzzer with a boy having multiple handicaps. *Child and Family Behavior Therapy, 17,* 13–26.

Ainsworth, M. D. S., Blehar, M. C., Waters, E., & Wall, S. (1978). *Patterns of attachment: A psychological study of the strange situation.* Hillsdale, NJ: Erlbaum.

American Psychological Association. (1992). Ethical principles of psychologists and code of conduct. *American Psychologist, 47,* 1597–1611.

American Psychological Association. (1994). *Publication manual of the American Psychological Association* (4th ed.). Washington, DC: Author.

Anderson, C. A., & Anderson, D. C. (1984). Ambient temperature and violent crime: Test of the linear and curvilinear hypothesis. *Journal of Personality and Social Psychology, 46,* 91–97.

Anderson, D. R., Lorch, E. P., Field, D. E., Collins, P. A., & Nathan, J. G. (1986). Television viewing at home: Age trends in visual attention and time with TV. *Child Development, 57,* 1024–1033.

Andersson, H. W. (1996). The Fagan Test of Infant Intelligence: Predictive validity in a random sample. *Psychological Reports, 78,* 1015–1026.

Angelou, M. (1969). *I know why the caged bird sings.* New York: Random House.

Aquilino, W. (1990). The likelihood of parent-child coresidence: Effects of family structure and parental characteristics. *Journal of Marriage and the Family, 52,* 405–419.

Aristotle. (1984). Rhetoric. (W. Rhys Roberts, Trans.). In J. Barnes (Ed.), *The complete works of Aristotle: The revised Oxford translation* (Vol. 2). Princeton, NJ: Princeton University Press.

Aronson, E., Brewer, M., & Carlsmith, J. M. (1985). Experimentation in social psychology. In G. Lindzey & E. Aronson (Eds.), *Handbook of social psychology* (3rd ed., Vol. 1, pp. 441–486). New York: Random House.

Aronson, E., Stephan, C., Sikes, J., Blaney, N., & Snapp, M. (1978). *The jigsaw classroom.* Newbury Park, CA: Sage.

Attie, I., & Brooks-Gunn, J. (1989). Development of eating problems in adolescent girls: A longitudinal study. *Developmental Psychology, 25,* 70–79.

Azar, B. (1997, April). Psychologists are watching debate over 2000 census. *APA Monitor,* 28.

Babbie, E. (1995). The practice of social research (7th ed.). Belmont, CA: Wadsworth.

Bahrick, H. P. (1984). Semantic memory content in permastore: Fifty years of memory for Spanish learned in school. *Journal of Experimental Psychology: General, 113,* 1–26.

Bahrick, H. P., Bahrick, P. O., & Wittlinger, R. P. (1975). Fifty years of memory for names and faces: A cross-generational approach. *Journal of Experimental Psychology: General, 104,* 54–75.

Bahrick, H. P., Hall, L. K., & Berger, S. A. (1996). Accuracy and distortion in memory for high school grades. *Psychological Science, 7,* 265–271.

Bakeman, R., & Brownlee, J. R. (1980). The strategic use of parallel play: A sequential analysis. *Child Development, 51,* 873–878.

Bakeman, R., & Gottman, J. M. (1986). *Observing interaction.* Cambridge, England: Cambridge University Press.

Ballmer, H. B., & Cozby, P. C. (1981). Family environments of women who return to college. *Sex Roles, 7,* 1019–1026.

Baltes, P. B. (1987). Theoretical propositions of life-span developmental psychology: On the dynamics between growth and decline. *Developmental Psychology, 23,* 611–626.

Baltes, P. B. (1993). The aging mind: Potential and limits. *Gerontologist, 33,* 580–594.

Baltes, P. B. (1997). On the incomplete architecture of

human ontogeny: Selection, optimization, and compensation as foundation of developmental theory. *American Psychologist, 52,* 366–380.

Bandura, A., Ross, D., & Ross, S. A. (1961). Transmission of aggression through imitation of aggressive models. *Journal of Abnormal and Social Psychology, 63,* 375–382.

Bandura, A., Ross, D., & Ross, S. A. (1963). Imitation of film-mediated aggressive models. *Journal of Abnormal and Social Psychology, 66,* 3–11.

Barlow, D. H., & Hersen, M. (1984). *Single case experimental designs.* New York: Pergamon Press.

Barnett, W. S. (1995). Long-term effects of early childhood programs on cognitive and school outcomes. *The Future of Children, 5*(3), 25–50.

Barratt, M. S., Roach, M. A., Morgan, K. M., & Colbert, K. K. (1996). Adjustment to motherhood by single adolescents. *Family Relations, 45,* 209–215.

Bauer, P. J. (1996). What do infants recall of their lives? Memory for specific events by one- to two-year-olds. *American Psychologist, 51,* 29–41.

Baumeister, R. F., & Newman, L. S. (1994). How stories make sense of personal experiences: Motives that shape autobiographical narratives. *Personality and Social Psychology Bulletin, 20,* 676–690.

Bayley, N. (1969). *The Bayley Scales of Infant Development.* New York: The Psychological Corporation.

Beaman, A. (1991). An empirical comparison of meta-analytic and traditional reviews. *Personality and Social Psychology Bulletin, 17,* 252–257.

Becker, H. S. (1963). *Outsiders: Studies in the sociology of deviance.* New York: Free Press.

Belmont, L., & Marolla, F. A. (1973). Birth order, family size, and intelligence. *Science, 182,* 1096–1101.

Bem, D. J. (1981). Writing the research report. In L. H. Kidder (Ed.), *Research methods in social relations* (pp. 342–364). New York: Holt, Rinehart & Winston.

Bem, S. L. (1974). The measurement of psychological androgyny. *Journal of Consulting and Clinical Psychology, 42,* 155–162.

Benasich, A. A., & Bejar, I. I. (1992). The Fagan Test of Infant Intelligence: A critical review. *Journal of Applied Developmental Psychology, 13,* 153–171.

Benson, J., & Hocevar, D. (1985). The impact of item phrasing on the validity of attitude scales for elementary school children. *Journal of Educational Measurement, 22,* 231–240.

Berk, R. A., Boruch, R. F., Chambers, D. L., Rossi, P. H., & Witte, A. D. (1986). Social policy experimentation: A position paper. In D. S. Cordray & M. W.

Lipsey (Eds.), *Evaluation studies review annual: Vol. 11* (pp. 630–672). Newbury Park, CA: Sage.

Bernard, H. R. (1994). *Research methods in anthropology: Qualitative and quantitative approaches.* Thousand Oaks, CA: Sage.

Bickman, L. (1996). A continuum of care: More is not always better. *American Psychologist, 51,* 689–701.

Biddle, B. J., & Marlin, M. M. (1987). Causality, confirmation, credulity, and structural equation modeling. *Child Development, 58,* 4–17.

Bjorklund, D. F. (1997). In search of a metatheory for cognitive development (or, Piaget is dead and I don't feel so good myself). *Child Development, 68,* 144–148.

Bjorklund, D. F., Miller, P. H., Coyle, T. R., & Slawinski, J. L. (1997). Instructing children to use memory strategies: Evidence of utilization deficiencies in memory training studies. *Developmental Review, 17,* 411–441.

Black, M. M., Hutchinson, J. J., Dubowitz, H., Starr, R. H., Jr., & Berenson-Howard, J. (1996). The roots of competence: Mother-child interaction among low income, urban, African-American families. *Journal of Applied Developmental Psychology, 17,* 367–391.

Bolger, K. E., Patterson, C. J., & Thompson, W. W. (1995). Psychosocial adjustment among children experiencing persistent and intermittent family economic hardship. *Child Development, 66,* 1107–1129.

Bordens, K. S., & Abbott, B. B. (1991). *Research designs and methods: A process approach* (2nd ed.). Mountain View, CA: Mayfield.

Bouchard, T. J., Jr., & McGue, M. (1981). Familial studies of intelligence: A review. *Science, 212,* 1055–1059.

Bowman, C., & Okada, M. (1997, April). *The impact of the O.J. Simpson trial.* Poster session presented at the annual meeting of the Western Psychological Association, Seattle, WA.

Boyatzis, C. J., Matillo, G. M., & Nesbitt, K. M. (1995). Effects of the "Mighty Morphin Power Rangers" on children's aggression with peers. *Child Study Journal, 25,* 45–55.

Bradley, R., Caldwell, B. M., Rock, S. L., Ramey, C. T., Barnard, K. E., Gray, C., Hammond, M. A., Mitchell, S., Gottfried, W., Siegel, L., & Johnson, D. L. (1989). Home environment and cognitive development in the first 3 years of life: A collaborative study involving six sites and three ethnic groups in North America. *Developmental Psychology, 25,* 217–235.

Brazelton, T. B. (1973). *Neonatal Behavioral Assessment Scale.* London: Spastics International Medical Publications.

Broberg, A. G., Wessels, H., Lamb, M. E., & Hwang, C. P. (1997). Effects of day care on the development of cognitive abilities in 8-year-olds: A longitudinal study. *Developmental Psychology, 33,* 62–69.

Brody, G. H., Stoneman, Z., & Flor, D. (1996). Parental religiosity, family processes, and youth competence in rural, two-parent African American families. *Developmental Psychology, 32,* 696–706.

Bronfenbrenner, U. (1977). Toward an experimental ecology of human development. *American Psychologist, 32,* 513–531.

Bruck, M., Ceci, S. J., Francoeur, E., & Barr, R. (1995). "I hardly cried when I got my shot!" Influencing children's reports about a visit to their pediatrician. *Child Development, 66,* 163–208.

Bryant, B. K. (1982). An index of empathy for children and adolescents. *Child Development, 53,* 412–425.

Bureau of Labor Statistics. (1992, September). *BLS handbook of methods* (Bulletin 2414). Washington, DC: U.S. Government Printing Office.

Bushman, B. J., & Stack, A. D. (1996). Forbidden fruit versus tainted fruit: Effects of warning labels on attraction to television violence. *Journal of Experimental Psychology: Applied, 2,* 207–226.

Butler, S., Gross, J., & Hayne, H. (1995). The effect of drawing on memory performance in young children. *Developmental Psychology, 31,* 597–608.

Cacioppo, J. T., & Tassinary, L. G. (1990). Inferring psychological significance from physiological signals. *American Psychologist, 45,* 16–28.

Cairns, R. B., Cairns, B. D., & Neckerman, H. J. (1989). Early school dropout: Configurations and determinants. *Child Development, 60,* 1437–1452.

Caldwell, B., & Bradley, R. (1984). *Manual for the Home Observation for Measurement of the Environment.* Little Rock, AR: University of Arkansas Press.

Campbell, A. J., Borrie, M. J., & Spears, G. F. (1989). Risk factors for falls in a community-based prospective study of people 70 years and older. *Journal of Gerontology: Medical Sciences, 44,* M112–117.

Campbell, D., & Fiske, D. (1959). Convergent and discriminant validation by the multitrait-multimethod matrix. *Psychological Bulletin, 54,* 81–105.

Campbell, D., & Stanley, J. C. (1966). *Experimental and quasi-experimental designs for research.* Boston: Houghton Mifflin.

Campbell, D. T. (1968). Experimental design: Quasi-experimental design. In D. L. Gillis (Ed.), *International encyclopedia of the social sciences* (Vol. 5, pp. 259–262). New York: Macmillan and Free Press.

Campbell, D. T. (1969). Reforms as experiments. *American Psychologist, 24,* 409–429.

Cavan, S. (1966). *Liquor license: An ethnography of bar behavior.* Chicago: Aldine.

Ceci, S. J., & Bruck, M. (1993). The suggestibility of the child witness. *Psychological Bulletin, 113,* 403–439.

Ceci, S. J., Ross, D. F., & Toglia, M. P. (1987). Suggestibility of children's memory: Psycholegal implications. *Journal of Experimental Psychology: General, 116,* 38–49.

Chen, C., & Stevenson, H. W. (1995). Motivation and mathematics achievement: A comparative study of Asian-American, Caucasian American and East Asian high school students. *Child Development, 66,* 1215–1234.

Chesterfield, R. A. (1986). Qualitative methodology in the evaluation of early childhood bilingual curriculum models. In D. M. Fetterman & M. A. Pitman (Eds.), *Education evaluation: Ethnography in theory, practice, and politics* (pp. 145–168). Beverly Hills, CA: Sage.

Children whose mothers drink to excess get injured more. (1992, June 17). *Orange County Register,* p. A8.

Children's Defense Fund. (1994). *Wasting America's future: The Children's Defense Fund report on the costs of child poverty.* Boston: Beacon Press.

Chisholm, K. (1997, April). Attachment and indiscriminant friendliness in Romanian adoptees three years post-adoption. In M. Dozier (Chair), *The effects of early deprivation: Investigations of a continuum of caregiving experiences.* Symposium conducted at the meeting of the Society for Research in Child Development, Washington, DC.

Chisholm, K., Carter, M. C., Ames, E. W., & Morison, S. J. (1995). Attachment security and indiscriminately friendly behavior in children adopted from Romanian orphanages. *Development and Psychopathology, 7,* 283–294.

Chiu, L. H. (1987). Development of the Self-Esteem Rating Scale for Children (revised). *Measurement and Evaluation in Counseling and Development, 20,* 36–41.

Christianson, S.-Å. (1992). Emotional stress and eyewitness memory: A critical review. *Psychological Bulletin, 112,* 284–309.

Cialdini, R. B. (1988). *Influence: Science and practice* (2nd ed.). Glenview, IL: Scott, Foresman.

Clark, R. M. (1983). *Family life and school achievement: Why poor Black children succeed or fail.* Chicago: University of Chicago Press.

Cognition and Technology Group at Vanderbilt. (1997).

The Jasper Project: Lessons in curriculum, instruction, assessment, and professional development. Mahwah, NJ: Erlbaum.

Cohen, J. (1960). A coefficient of agreement for nominal scales. *Educational and Psychological Measurement, 20,* 37–46.

Coie, J. D., & Dodge, K. A. (1988). Multiple sources of data on social behavior and social status in the school: A cross-age comparison. *Child Development, 59,* 815–829.

Coie, J. D., Watt, N. F., West, S. G., Hawkins, J. D., Asarnow, J. R., Markman, H. J., Ramey, S. J., Shure, M. B., & Long, B. (1993). The science of prevention: A conceptual framework and some directions for a national research program. *American Psychologist, 48,* 1013–1022.

Conger, R. D., Ge, X., Elder, G. H., Jr., Lorenz, F. O., & Simons, R. L. (1994). Economic stress, coercive family process, and developmental problems of adolescents. *Child Development, 65,* 541–561.

Converse, J. M., & Presser, S. (1986). *Survey questions: Handcrafting the standardized questionnaire.* Beverly Hills, CA: Sage.

Cook, T. D., & Campbell, D. T. (1979). *Quasi-experimentation: Design and analysis issues for field settings.* Chicago: Rand McNally.

Coopersmith, S. (1967). *The antecedents of self-esteem.* San Francisco: W. H. Freeman.

Corsaro, W. A. (1985). *Friendship and peer culture in the early years.* Norwood, NJ: Ablex.

Crabb, P. B., & Bielawski, D. (1994). The social representation of material culture and gender in children's books. *Sex Roles, 30*(1/2), 69–79.

Craig, W. M., & Pepler, D. J. (1995). A peek behind the fence: Naturalistic observations of aggressive children with remote audiovisual recording. *Developmental Psychology, 31,* 548–553.

Crockenberg, S., & Litman, C. (1991). Effects of maternal employment on maternal and two-year-old behavior. *Child Development, 62,* 930–953.

Crook, T. H., & West, R. L. (1990). Name recall performance across the adult life-span. *British Journal of Psychology, 81,* 335–349.

Csikszentmihalyi, M., & Larson, R. (1987). The experience sampling method. *Journal of Nervous and Mental Disease, 175,* 526–536.

Curtiss, S. R. (1977). *Genie: A psycholinguistic study of a modern-day "wild child."* New York: Academic Press.

Darley, J. M., & Latané, B. (1968). Bystander intervention in emergencies: Diffusion of responsibility. *Journal of Personality and Social Psychology, 8,* 377–383.

de Haan, M., & Nelson, C. A. (1997). Recognition of the mother's face by six-month-old infants: A neurobehavioral study. *Child Development, 68,* 187–210.

Deater-Deckard, K., Dodge, K. A., Bates, J. E., & Pettit, G. S. (1996). Physical discipline among African American and European American mothers: Links to children's externalizing behaviors. *Developmental Psychology, 32,* 1065–1072.

Deffenbacher, K. A. (1983). The influence of arousal on reliability of testimony. In S. M. A. Lloyd-Bostock & B. R. Clifford (Eds.), *Evaluating witness evidence* (pp. 235–251). New York: Wiley.

Denmark, F., Russo, N. P., Frieze, I. H., & Sechzer, J. A. (1988). Guidelines for avoiding sexism in psychological research: A report of the Ad Hoc Committee on Nonsexist Research. *American Psychologist, 43,* 582–585.

DiLalla, L. F., Thompson, L. A., Plomin, R., Phillips, K., Fagan, J. F., III, Haith, M. H., Cyphers, L. H., & Fulker, D. W. (1990). Infant predictors of preschool and adult IQ: A study of infant twins and their parents. *Developmental Psychology, 26,* 759–769.

Dishion, T. J., Patterson, G. R., Stoolmiller, M., & Skinner, M. L. (1991). Family, school, and behavioral antecedents to early adolescent involvement with antisocial peers. *Developmental Psychology, 27,* 172–180.

Douglass, F. (1968). *Narrative of Frederick Douglass: An American slave written by himself.* New York: Signet. (Original work published 1845)

Dozier, M., & Stovall, C. (1997, April). Coping with disruptions in early caregiving: Factors affecting attachment strategies among foster infants. In M. Dozier (Chair), *The effects of early deprivation: Investigations of a continuum of caregiving experiences.* Symposium conducted at the meeting of the Society for Research in Child Development, Washington, DC.

Dretzke, B. J., & Levin, J. R. (1996). Assessing students' application and transfer of a mnemonic strategy: The struggle for independence. *Contemporary Educational Psychology, 21,* 83–93.

Dumka, L. E., Roosa, M. W., Michaels, M. L., & Suh, K. W. (1995). Using research and theory to develop prevention programs for high risk families. *Family Relations, 44,* 78–86.

Duncan, G. J., Brooks-Gunn, J., & Klebanov, P. K. (1994). Economic deprivation and early childhood development. *Child Development, 65,* 296–318.

Durlak, J. A., & Lipsey, M. W. (1991). A practitioner's guide to meta-analysis. *American Journal of Community Psychology, 19,* 291–332.

Elder, G. H., Jr. (1974). *Children of the Great Depression: Social change in life experience.* Chicago: University of Chicago Press.

Elder, G. H., Jr. (1979). Historical change in life patterns and personality. In P. B. Baltes & O. G. Brim, Jr. (Eds.), *Life span development and behavior* (Vol. 2, pp. 117–159). New York: Academic Press.

Elder, G. H., Jr., Liker, J. K., & Cross, C. E. (1984). Parent-child behavior in the Great Depression: Life course and intergenerational influences. In P. Baltes & O. G. Brim, Jr. (Eds.), *Life span development and behavior* (Vol. 6, pp. 109–158). New York: Academic Press.

Elder, G. H., Jr., Nguyen, T. V., & Caspi, A. (1985). Linking family hardship to children's lives. *Child Development, 56,* 361–375.

Entwisle, D. R., & Astone, N. M. (1994). Some practical guidelines for measuring youth's race/ethnicity and socioeconomic status. *Child Development, 65,* 1521–1540.

Espinosa, M. P., Sigman, M. P., Neumann, C. G., Bwibo, N. O., & McDonald, M. A. (1992). Playground behaviors of school-age children in relation to nutrition, schooling, and family characteristics. *Developmental Psychology, 28,* 1188–1195.

Fagan, J. F., & Detterman, D. K. (1992). The Fagan Test of Infant Intelligence: A technical summary. *Journal of Applied Developmental Psychology, 13,* 173–193.

Fagan, J. F., & Shepherd, P. A. (1987). *The Fagan Test of Infant Intelligence: Training manual.* Cleveland, OH: Infantest Corporation.

Fantuzzo, J. W., McDermott, P. A., Manz, P. H., Hampton, V. R., & Burdick, N. A. (1996). The Pictorial Scale of Perceived Competence and Social Acceptance: Does it work with low-income urban children? *Child Development, 67,* 1071–1084.

Farver, J. M., & Frosch, D. L. (1996). L.A. stories: Aggression in preschoolers' spontaneous narratives after the riots of 1992. *Child Development, 67,* 19–32.

Farver, J. M., Kim, Y. K., & Lee, Y. (1995). Cultural differences in Korean- and Anglo-American preschoolers' social interaction and play behaviors. *Child Development, 66,* 1088–1099.

Feshbach, N. D., & Roe, K. (1968). Empathy in six- and seven-year-olds. *Child Development, 39,* 133–145.

Fetterman, D. M. (1989). *Ethnography step by step.* Newbury Park, CA: Sage.

Fielding, N. G., & Lee, R. M. (Eds.). (1991). *Using computers in qualitative research.* London: Sage.

Fiske, S. T., & Taylor, S. E. (1984). *Social cognition.* New York: Random House.

Flaks, D. K., Ficher, I., Masterpasqua, F., & Joseph, G. (1995). Lesbians choosing motherhood: A comparative study of lesbian and heterosexual parents and their children. *Developmental Psychology, 31,* 105–114.

Flanagan, C. A., & Eccles, J. S. (1993). Changes in parents' work status and adolescents' adjustment at school. *Child Development, 64,* 246–257.

Flavell, J. H., Green, F. L., Flavell, E. R., & Grossman, J. B. (1997). The development of children's knowledge about inner speech. *Child Development, 68,* 39–47.

Flavell, J. H., Speer, J. R., Green, F. L., & August, D. L. (1981). The development of comprehension monitoring and knowledge about communication. *Monographs of the Society for Research in Child Development, 46* (Whole No. 192).

Ford, D. Y., & Harris, J. J., III (1996). Perceptions and attitudes of Black students toward school, achievement, and other educational variables. *Child Development, 67,* 1141–1152.

Friedman, A., Tzukerman, Y., Wienberg, H., & Todd, J. (1992). The shift in power with age: Changes in perception of the power of women and men over the life cycle. *Psychology of Women Quarterly, 16,* 513–525.

Friedman, H. S., Tucker, J. S., Tomlinson-Keasey, C., Schwartz, J. E., Wingard, D. L., & Criqui, M. H. (1993). Does childhood personality predict longevity? *Journal of Personality and Social Psychology, 65,* 176–185.

Fuligni, A. J., & Stevenson, H. W. (1995). Time use and mathematics achievement among American, Chinese, and Japanese high school students. *Child Development, 66,* 830–842.

Galton, F. (1909). *Memories of my life.* London: Methuen.

Garbarino, J., & Kostelny, K. (1996). The effects of political violence on Palestinian children's behavior problems: A risk accumulation model. *Child Development, 67,* 33–45.

García-Coll, C., Crnic, K., Lamberty, G., Wasik, B. H., Jenkins, R., García, H. V., & McAdoo, H. P. (1996). An integrative model for the study of developmental competencies in minority children. *Child Development, 67,* 1891–1914.

Gardner, H. (1983). *Frames of mind: The theory of multiple intelligences.* New York: Basic Books.

Gardner, L. E. (1988). A relatively painless method of introduction to the psychological literature search. In M. E. Ware & C. L. Brewer (Eds.), *Handbook for teaching statistics and research methods.* Hillsdale, NJ: Erlbaum.

Gelfand, H., & Walker, C. J. (1990). Mastering APA

style. Washington, DC: American Psychological Association.

Gibbs, J. C., Widaman, K. F., & Colby, A. (1982). Construction and validation of a simplified, group-administered equivalent to the moral judgment interview. *Child Development, 53,* 895–910.

Gilger, J. W. (1991). Differential assortative mating found for academic and demographic variables as a function of time of assessment. *Behavior Genetics, 21,* 131–150.

Gilgun, J. F., Daly, K., & Handel, G. (Eds.). (1992). *Qualitative methods in family research.* Thousand Oaks, CA: Sage.

Gilmore, G. C., Wenk, H. E., Naylor, L. A., & Stuve, T. A. (1992). Motion perception and aging. *Psychology and Aging, 7,* 654–660.

Gilovich, T. (1991). *How we know what isn't so: The fallibility of human reason in everyday life.* New York: Free Press.

Gottfried, A. W. (1985). Environment of newborn infants in special care units. In A. W. Gottfried & J. L. Gaiter (Eds.), *Infant stress under intensive care* (pp. 23–54). Baltimore: University Park Press.

Graham, S. (1992). "Most of the subjects were White and middle class": Trends in published research on African Americans in selected APA journals. *American Psychologist, 47,* 629–639.

Greenfield, T. A. (1995). Sex differences in science museum exhibit attraction. *Journal of Research in Science Teaching, 32,* 925–938.

Greenwald, A. G. (1976). Within-subjects designs: To use or not to use? *Psychological Bulletin, 83,* 314–320.

Grigorenko, E. L., Wood, F. B., Meyer, M. S., Hart, L. A., Speed, W. C., Shuster, A., & Pauls, D. L. (1997). Susceptibility loci for distinct components of developmental dyslexia on chromosomes 6 and 15. *American Journal of Human Genetics, 60,* 27–39.

Gubrium, J. F., & Sankar, A. (Eds.). (1993). *Qualitative methods in aging research.* Thousand Oaks, CA: Sage.

Gwaltney-Gibbs, P. A. (1986). The institutionalization of premarital cohabitation: Estimates from marriage license applications, 1970 and 1980. *Journal of Marriage and the Family, 48,* 423–434.

Hall, J. A., & Halberstadt, A. G. (1980). Masculinity and femininity in children: Development of the Children's Personal Attributes Questionnaire. *Developmental Psychology, 16,* 270–280.

Hammersley, M. (1992). *What's wrong with ethnography? Methodological explorations.* NY: Routledge.

Harold, G. T., & Conger, R. D. (1997). Marital conflict and adolescent distress: The role of adolescent awareness. *Child Development, 68,* 333–350.

Harris, K. M., & Marmer, J. K. (1996). Poverty, paternal involvement, and adolescent well-being. *Journal of Family Issues, 17,* 614–640.

Harter, S. (1982). The Perceived Competence Scale for Children. *Child Development, 53,* 87–97.

Harter, S., & Pike, R. (1984). The Pictorial Scale of Perceived Competence and Social Acceptance for Young Children. *Child Development, 55,* 1969–1982.

Harwood, R. L. (1992). The influence of culturally derived values in Anglo and Puerto Rican mothers' perceptions of attachment behavior. *Child Development, 63,* 822–839.

Hatcher, P. J., Hulme, C., & Ellis, A. W. (1994). Ameliorating early reading failure by integrating the teaching of reading and phonological skills: The phonological linkage hypothesis. *Child Development, 65,* 41–57.

Hauser, R. M. (1994). Measuring socioeconomic status in studies of child development. *Child Development, 65,* 1541–1545.

Heatherton, T. F., Mahamedi, F., Striepe, M., Field, A. E., & Keel, P. (1997). A 10-year longitudinal study of body weight, dieting, and eating disorder symptoms. *Journal of Abnormal Psychology, 106,* 117–125.

Henle, M., & Hubbell, M. B. (1938). "Egocentricity" in adult conversation. *Journal of Social Psychology, 9,* 227–234.

Henry, B., Caspi, A., Moffitt, T. E., & Silva, P. A. (1996). Temperamental and familial predictors of violent and nonviolent criminal convictions: Age 3 to age 18. *Developmental Psychology, 32,* 614–623.

Hernandez, D. J. (1997). Child development and the social demography of childhood. *Child Development, 68,* 149–169.

Herrmann, D., & Guadagno, M. A. (1997). Memory performance and socioeconomic status. *Applied Cognitive Psychology, 11,* 113–120.

Herrnstein, R. J., & Murray, C. (1994). *The bell curve: Intelligence and class structure in American life.* New York: Free Press.

Hill-Lubin, M. A. (1991). The African-American grandmother in autobiographical works by Frederick Douglass, Langston Hughes, and Maya Angelou. *International Journal of Aging and Human Development, 33,* 173–185.

Hinde, R. A. (1992). Developmental psychology in the context of other behavioral sciences. *Developmental Psychology, 28,* 1018–1029.

Holmes, T. H., & Rahe, R. H. (1967). The Social Readjustment Rating Scale. *Journal of Psychosomatic Research, 11,* 213–218.

Holsti, O. R. (1969). *Content analysis for the social sciences and humanities.* Reading, MA: Addison-Wesley.

Hudley, C., & Graham, S. (1993). An attributional intervention to reduce peer-directed aggression among African American boys. *Child Development, 64,* 124–138.

Hughes, L. (1940). *The big sea.* New York: Alfred Knopf.

Iverson, A. M., Barton, E. A., & Iverson, G. L. (1997). Analysis of risk to children participating in a sociometric task. *Developmental Psychology, 33,* 104–112.

Jacobs, J. (1974). *Fun city: An ethnographic study of a retirement community.* New York: Holt, Rinehart & Winston. (Reissued by Waveland Press.)

Jacobson, J. L., & Jacobson, S. W. (1996). Methodological considerations in behavioral toxicology in infants and children. *Developmental Psychology, 32,* 390–403.

Jewett, J. J., Hibbard, J. H., & Weeks, E. C. (1992). Predictors of health care utilization for the young-old and the old-old: A structural modeling approach. *Behavior, Health & Aging, 2,* 29–41.

Johnson, T. C., Stoner, G., & Green, S. K. (1996). Demonstrating the experimenting society model with classwide behavior management interventions. *School Psychology Review, 25,* 199–214.

Jones, M. S., Yokoi, L., Johnson, D. J., Lum, S., Cafaro, T., & Kee, D. W. (1996). Effectiveness of elaborative strategy use: Knowledge access comparisons. *Journal of Experimental Child Psychology, 62,* 401–409.

Josselson, R., & Lieblich, A. (1993). *The narrative study of lives.* Newbury Park, CA: Sage.

Jourard, S. M. (1969). The effects of experimenters' self-disclosure on subjects' behavior. In C. Spielberger (Ed.), *Current topics in community and clinical psychology* (Vol. 1, pp. 109–150). New York: Academic Press.

Joy, L. A., Kimball, M. M., & Zabrack, M. L. (1986). Television and children's aggressive behavior. In T. M. Williams (Ed.), *The impact of television: A natural experiment in three communities* (pp. 303–339). Orlando, FL: Academic Press.

Judd, C. M., Smith, E. R., & Kidder, L. H. (1991). *Research methods in social relations* (6th ed.). Fort Worth, TX: Holt, Rinehart & Winston.

Kagan, J., Rosman, B. L., Day, D., Albert, J., & Phillips, W. (1964). Information processing in the child: Significance of analytic and reflective attitudes. *Psychological Monographs, 78* (Whole No. 578).

Kazdin, A. E. (1995). Preparing and evaluating research reports. *Psychological Assessment, 7,* 228–237.

Kee, D. W., & Rohwer, W. D., Jr. (1973). Noun-pair learning in four ethnic groups: Conditions of presentation and response. *Journal of Educational Psychology, 65,* 226–232.

Kehn, D. J. (1995). Predictors of elderly happiness. *Activities, Adaptation, & Aging, 19,* 11–30.

Kenny, D. A. (1979). *Correlation and causality.* New York: Wiley.

Kerlinger, F. N. (1986). *Foundations of behavioral research* (3rd ed.). New York: Holt, Rinehart & Winston.

Keyser, D. J., & Sweetland, R. C. (Eds.). (1991). *Test critiques.* Kansas City, MO: Test Corporation of America.

Kochanska, G. (1997). Mutually responsive orientation between mothers and their young children: Implications for early socialization. *Child Development, 68,* 94–112.

Kopp, C. B., Baker, B. L., & Brown, K. W. (1992). Social skills and their correlates: Preschoolers with developmental delays. *American Journal on Mental Retardation, 96,* 357–366.

Kramer, J. J., & Conoley, J. C. (1991). *The eleventh mental measurements yearbook.* Lincoln, NE: Buros Institute of Mental Measurements.

Kratochwill, T. R., & Levin, J. R. (Eds.). (1992). *Single-case research design and analysis: New directions for psychology and education.* Hillsdale, NJ: Erlbaum.

Krause, N. (1996). Welfare participation and self-esteem in later life. *Gerontologist, 36,* 665–673.

Kubar, W. L., Rodrigue, J. R., & Hoffmann, R. G., III. (1995). Children and exposure to the sun: Relationships among attitudes, knowledge, intentions, and behavior. *Psychological Reports, 77,* 1136–1138.

La Greca, A. M. (1990). *Through the eyes of the child: Obtaining self-reports from children and adolescents.* Boston: Allyn & Bacon.

Ladd, G. W., & Profilet, S. M. (1996). The Child Behavior Scale: A teacher-report measure of young children's aggressive, withdrawn, and prosocial behaviors. *Developmental Psychology, 32,* 1008–1024.

Lancy, D. F. (1996). *Playing on the mother-ground: Cultural routines for children's development.* New York: Guilford.

Landau, S., Lorch, E. P., & Milich, R. (1992). Visual attention to and comprehension of television in attention-deficit hyperactivity disordered and normal boys. *Child Development, 63,* 928–937.

Larson, R. W. (1989). Beeping children and adolescents: A method for studying time use and daily experience. *Journal of Youth and Adolescence, 18,* 511–530.

Larson, R. W., Richards, M. H., Moneta, G., Holmbeck, G., & Duckett, E. (1996). Changes in adolescents' daily interactions with their families from ages 10 to 18: Disengagement and transformation. *Developmental Psychology, 32,* 744–754.

Leichtman, M. D., & Ceci, S. J. (1995). The effects of stereotypes and suggestions on preschoolers' reports. *Developmental Psychology, 31,* 568–578.

Lempers, J. D., Clark-Lempers, D., & Simons, R. L. (1989). Economic hardship, parenting, and distress in adolescence. *Child Development, 60,* 25–39.

Lerner, R. M. (1995). *America's youth in crisis: Challenges and options for programs and policies.* Thousand Oaks, CA: Sage.

Levine, F. J. (1993, May). ASA files amicus brief protecting confidential research information. *Footnotes, 21*(5), 2.

Levine, R. V. (1990). The pace of life. *American Scientist, 78,* 450–459.

Liebert, R. M., & Sprafkin, J. (1988). *The early window: Effects of television on children and youth* (3rd ed.). New York: Pergamon Press.

Likert, R. (1932). A technique for the measurement of attitudes. *Archives of Psychology, 140,* 1–55.

Lindley, C. J. (1989). Who is the older person? In T. Hunt & C. J. Lindley (Eds.), *Testing adults: A reference guide for geropsychological assessments* (pp. 2–23). Austin, TX: Pro-Ed.

Lindsay, D. S., Jack, P. C., Jr., & Christian, M. A. (1991). Other-race face perception. *Journal of Applied Psychology, 76,* 587–589.

Locke, C. J., Southwick, K., McCloskey, L. A., & Fernandez-Esquer, M. E. (1996). The psychological and medical sequelae of war in Central American refugee mothers and children. *Archives of Pediatrics and Adolescent Medicine, 150,* 822–828.

Locke, H. J., & Wallace, K. M. (1959). Short marital adjustment and prediction tests: Their reliability and validity. *Marriage and Family Living, 21,* 251–255.

Lofland, J., & Lofland, L. H. (1995). *Analyzing social settings: A guide to qualitative observation and analysis* (3rd ed.). Belmont, CA: Wadsworth.

Loftus, E. F. (1979). *Eyewitness testimony.* London: Harvard University Press.

Loftus, E. F., Levidow, B., & Duensing, S. (1992). Who remembers best?: Individual differences in memory for events that occurred in a science museum. *Applied Cognitive Psychology, 6,* 93–107.

Loftus, E. F., & Palmer, J. C. (1974). Reconstruction of automobile destruction: An example of the interaction between language and memory. *Journal of Verbal Learning and Verbal Behavior, 13,* 585–589.

Luscre, D. M., & Center, D. B. (1996). Procedures for reducing dental fear in children with autism. *Journal of Autism and Developmental Disorders, 26,* 547–556.

Luus, C. A. E., Wells, G. L., & Turtle, J. W. (1995). Child eyewitnesses: Seeing is believing. *Journal of Applied Psychology, 80,* 317–326.

MacPhee, D., Fritz, J., & Miller-Heyl, J. (1996). Ethnic variations in personal social networks and parenting. *Child Development, 67,* 3278–3295.

MacPhee, D., Kreutzer, J. C., & Fritz, J. J. (1994). Infusing a diversity perspective into human development courses. *Child Development, 65,* 699–715.

Mahoney, J. L., & Cairns, R. B. (1997). Do extracurricular activities protect against early school dropout? *Developmental Psychology, 33,* 241–253.

Mangen, D. J., & Peterson, W. A. (1982a). *Research instruments in social gerontology, Vol 1: Clinical and social gerontology.* Minneapolis, MN: University of Minnesota Press.

Mangen, D. J., & Peterson, W. A. (1982b). *Research instruments in social gerontology, Vol 2: Social roles and social participation.* Minneapolis, MN: University of Minnesota Press.

Markman, E. M. (1977). Realizing you don't understand: A preliminary investigation. *Child Development, 46,* 986–992.

Markman, H. J. (1991). Constructive marital conflict is NOT an oxymoron. *Behavioral Assessment, 13,* 83–96.

Marsh, H. W. (1986). Negative item bias in ratings scales for preadolescent children: A cognitive-developmental phenomenon. *Developmental Psychology, 22,* 37–49.

Maxwell, J. A. (1996). *Qualitative research design: An interactive approach. Applied social research methods series: Vol. 41.* Thousand Oaks, CA: Sage.

Maxwell, J. A., Bashook, P. G., & Sandlow, L. J. (1986). Combining ethnographic and experimental methods in educational evaluation: A case study. In D. M. Fetterman & M. A. Pitman (Eds.), *Educational evaluation: Ethnography in theory, practice and politics* (pp. 121–143). Beverly Hills, CA: Sage.

McGuigan, F. J. (1963). The experimenter: A neglected stimulus. *Psychological Bulletin, 60,* 421–428.

McKenna, M. C., Kear, D. J., & Ellsworth, R. A. (1995). Children's attitudes toward reading: A national survey. *Reading Research Quarterly, 30,* 934–956.

McLeod, J. D., & Shanahan, M. J. (1993). Poverty, parenting, and children's mental health. *American Sociological Review, 58,* 351–366.

McLoyd, V. C. (1990). The impact of economic hardship on Black families and children: Psychological distress, parenting, and socioemotional development. *Child Development, 61,* 311–346.

McLoyd, V. C., Jayaratne, T. E., Ceballo, R., & Borquez, J. (1994). Unemployment and work interruption among African American single mothers: Effects on parenting and adolescent socioemotional functioning. *Child Development, 65,* 562–589.

McLoyd, V. C., & Randolph, S. M. (1985). Secular trends in the study of Afro-American children: A review of child development, 1936–1980. In A. B. Smuts & J. W. Hagen (Eds.), History and research in child development (pp. 78–93). *Monographs of the Society for Research in Child Development, 50* (4–5, Serial No. 211).

McLoyd, V. C., & Wilson, L. (1992). Telling them like it is: The role of economic and environmental factors in single mothers' discussions with their children. *American Journal of Community Psychology, 20,* 419–444.

McNamee-McGrory, V., & Cipani, E. (1995). *Reduction of inappropriate "clinging" behaviors in a preschooler through social skills training and utilization of the "Premack" principle.* (ERIC Document Reproduction Service No. ED 401 001)

Mead, L. M. (1992). *The new politics of poverty: The nonworking poor in America.* New York: Basic Books.

Miles, M. B., & Huberman, A. M. (1994). *Qualitative data analysis: An expanded sourcebook* (2nd ed.). Thousand Oaks, CA: Sage.

Milgram, S. (1963). Behavioral study of obedience. *Journal of Abnormal and Social Psychology, 67,* 371–378.

Milgram, S. (1964). Group pressure and action against a person. *Journal of Abnormal and Social Psychology, 69,* 137–143.

Milgram, S. (1965). Some conditions of obedience and disobedience to authority. *Human Relations, 18,* 57–76.

Miller, D. C. (1991). *Handbook of research design and social measurement.* Newbury Park, CA: Sage.

Mischel, W., & Ebbesen, E. B. (1970). Attention in delay of gratification. *Journal of Personality and Social Psychology, 16,* 329–337.

Mischel, W., Ebbesen, E. B., & Zeiss, A. (1972). Cognitive and attentional mechanisms in delay of gratification. *Journal of Personality and Social Psychology, 21,* 204–218.

Montee, B. B., Miltenberger, R. G., & Wittrock, D. (1995). An experimental analysis of facilitated communication. *Journal of Applied Behavior Analysis, 28,* 189–200.

Moos, R. H., & Moos, B. S. (1981). *Family Environment Scale manual.* Palo Alto, CA: Consulting Psychologists Press.

Munson, L. J. (1996). Review of rating scales that measure parent-child interaction. *Topics in Early Childhood Special Education, 16,* 1–25.

Nederhof, A. J. (1985). A comparison of European and North American response patterns in mail surveys. *Journal of the Market Research Society, 27,* 55–63.

Neugarten, B. L., Havighurst, R. J., & Tobin, S. S. (1961). The measurement of life satisfaction. *Journal of Gerontology, 16,* 134–143.

Nisbett, R. E., & Ross, L. (1980). *Human inference: Strategies and shortcomings of social judgment.* Englewood Cliffs, NJ: Prentice-Hall.

Nisbett, R. E., & Wilson, T. D. (1977). Telling more than we can know: Verbal reports on mental processes. *Psychological Review, 84,* 231–259.

Noll, R. B., Zucker, R. A., Fitzgerald, H. E., & Curtis, W. J. (1992). Cognitive and motoric functioning of sons of alcoholic fathers and controls: The early childhood years. *Developmental Psychology, 28,* 665–675.

Oliker, S. J. (1994). Does workfare work? Evaluation research and workfare policy. *Social Problems, 41,* 195–213.

Ono, H., Phillips, K. A., & Leneman, M. (1996). Content of an abstract: De jure and de facto. *American Psychologist, 51,* 1338–1339.

Osgood, C. E., Suci, G. J., & Tannenbaum, P. H. (1957). *The measurement of meaning.* Urbana, IL: Univerity of Illinois Press.

Palumbo, D. J., & Ferguson, J. L. (1995). Evaluating Gang Resistance Education and Training (GREAT): Is the impact the same as that of Drug Abuse Resistance Education (DARE)? *Evaluation Review, 19,* 597–619.

Parke, R. D. (1977). Some effects of punishment on children's behavior—revisited. In E. M. Hetherington & R. D. Parke (Eds.), *Contemporary readings in child psychology* (pp. 208–220). New York: McGraw-Hill.

Parten, M. (1932). Social participation among preschool children. *Journal of Abnormal and Social Psychology, 27,* 243–269.

Patterson, G. R., & Moore, D. (1979). Interactive patterns as units of behavior. In M. E. Lamb, S. J. Suomi,

& G. L. Stephenson (Eds.), *Social interaction analysis: Methodological issues* (pp. 77–96). Madison, WI: University of Wisconsin Press.

Patton, M. Q. (1980). *Qualitative evaluation and research methods.* Newbury Park, CA: Sage.

Pentz, M. A., Dwyer, J. H., MacKinnon, D. P., Flay, B. R., Hansen, W. B., Wang, E. Y. I., & Johnson, C. A. (1989). A multicommunity trial for primary prevention of adolescent drug abuse: Effects of drug use prevalence. *Journal of the American Medical Association, 261,* 3259–3266.

Peterson, J. L., & Zill, N. (1986). Marital disruption, parent-child relationships, and behavior problems in children. *Journal of Marriage and the Family, 48,* 295–307.

Piaget, J. (1952). *The origins of intelligence in children.* New York: International Universities Press.

Piers, E., & Harris, D. (1969). *The Piers-Harris Children's Self-Concept Scale.* Nashville, TN: Counselor Recordings and Tests.

Pillemer, D. B., Picariello, M. L., & Pruett, J. C. (1994). Very long-term memories of a salient preschool event. *Applied Cognitive Psychology, 8,* 95–106.

Potts, R., Runyan, D., Zerger, A., & Marchetti, K. (1996). A content analysis of safety behaviors of television characters: Implications for children's safety and injury. *Journal of Pediatric Psychology, 21,* 517–528.

Pressley, M., & Brewster, M. E. (1990). Imaginal elaboration of illustrations to facilitate fact learning: Creating memories of Prince Edward Island. *Applied Cognitive Psychology, 4,* 359–369.

Quittner, A. L., & Opipari, L. C. (1994). Differential treatment of siblings: Interview and diary analyses comparing two family contexts. *Child Development, 65,* 800–814.

Ramasamy, R., Taylor, R. L., & Ziegler, E. W. (1996). Eliminating inappropriate classroom behavior using a DRO schedule: A preliminary study. *Psychological Reports, 78,* 753–754.

Rauscher, F. H., Shaw, G. L., & Ky, K. N. (1993). Music and spatial performance. *Nature, 365,* 611.

Rauscher, F. H., Shaw, G. L., Levine, L. J., Wright, E. L., Dennis, W. R., & Newcomb, R. L. (1997). Music training causes long-term enhancement of preschool children's spatial-temporal reasoning. *Neurological Research, 19,* 2–8.

Reed, J. G., & Baxter, P. M. (1992). *Library use: A handbook for psychology.* Washington, DC: American Psychological Association.

Rest, J. R. (1979). *Development in judging moral issues.* Minneapolis, MN: University of Minnesota Press.

Rest, J. R. (1986). Moral research methodology. In S. Modgil & C. Modgil (Eds.), *Lawrence Kohlberg: Consensus and controversy* (pp. 455–469). Philadephia, PA: Taylor & Francis.

Richardson, V. E., & Kilty, K. M. (1995). Gender differences in mental health before and after retirement: A longitudinal analysis. *Journal of Women & Aging, 7*(1/2), 19–35.

Riessman, C. K. (Ed.). (1993). *Qualitative studies in social work research.* Thousand Oaks, CA: Sage.

Riley, D. (1997). Using local research to change 100 communities for children and families. *American Psychologist, 52,* 424–433.

Riley, D., Meinhardt, G., Nelson, C., Salisbury, M. J., & Winnett, T. (1991). How effective are age-paced newsletters for new parents? A replication and extension of earlier studies. *Family Relations, 40,* 247–253.

Ring, K., Wallston, K., & Corey, M. (1970). Mode of debriefing as a factor affecting subjective reaction to a Milgram-type obedience experiment: An ethical inquiry. *Representative Research in Social Psychology, 1,* 67–68.

Roberson, M. T., & Sundstrom, E. (1990). Questionnaire design, return rates, and response favorableness in an employee attitude questionnaire. *Journal of Applied Psychology, 75,* 354–357.

Robinson, J. P., Shaver, P. R., & Wrightsman, L. S. (Eds.). (1991). *Measures of personality and social psychological attitudes.* San Diego, CA: Academic Press.

Roethlisberger, F. J., & Dickson, W. J. (1939). *Management and the worker.* Cambridge, MA: Harvard University Press.

Rollins, B. C. (1989). Marital quality at midlife. In S. Hunter & M. Sundel (Eds.), *Midlife myths.* Newbury Park, CA: Sage.

Rose, D. (1987). *Black American street life: South Philadelphia, 1969–1971.* Philadelphia: University of Pennsylvania Press.

Rosenhan, D. (1973). On being sane in insane places. *Science, 179,* 250–258.

Rosenthal, R. (1966). *Experimenter effects in behavior research.* New York: Appleton-Century-Crofts.

Rosenthal, R. (1967). Covert communication in the psychological experiment. *Psychological Bulletin, 67,* 356–367.

Rosenthal, R. (1969). Interpersonal expectations: Effects of the experimenter's hypothesis. In R. Rosenthal & R. L. Rosnow (Eds.), *Artifact in behavioral research* (pp. 181–277). New York: Academic Press.

Rosenthal, R. (1991). *Meta-analytic procedures for social research* (Rev. ed.). Newbury Park, CA: Sage.

Rosenthal, R., & Jacobson, L. (1968). *Pygmalion in the classroom.* New York: Holt, Rinehart & Winston.

Rosenthal, R., & Rosnow, R. L. (1975). *The volunteer subject.* New York: Wiley.

Rosnow, R. L., & Rosnow, M. (1995). *Writing papers in psychology* (3rd ed.). Belmont, CA: Wadsworth.

Rothbaum, F., & Weisz, J. R. (1994). Parental caregiving and child externalizing behavior in nonclinical samples: A meta-analysis. *Psychological Bulletin, 116,* 55–74.

Rubin, Z. (1975). Disclosing oneself to a stranger: Reciprocity and its limits. *Journal of Experimental Social Psychology, 11,* 233–260.

Russell, C. H., & Megaard, I. (1988). *The general social survey, 1972–1986: The state of the American people.* New York: Springer-Verlag.

Russell, D., Peplau, L. A., & Cutrona, C. E. (1980). The revised UCLA Loneliness Scale: Concurrent and discriminant validity evidence. *Journal of Personality and Social Psychology, 39,* 472–480.

Russell, D., Peplau, L. A., & Ferguson, M. L. (1978). Developing a measure of loneliness. *Journal of Personality Assessment, 42,* 290–294.

Sacuzzo, D. P., Johnson, N. E., & Guertin, T. L. (1994). Information processing in gifted versus nongifted African American, Latino, Filipino, and White children: Speeded versus nonspeeded paradigms. *Intelligence, 19,* 219–243.

Scarce released from jail. (1993, November). *Footnotes, 21*(8), 1.

Scarce remains jailed; ASA Council advocates for researcher's privilege. (1993, October). *Footnotes, 21*(7), 1, 12.

Schaie, K. W. (1986). Beyond calendar definitions of age, time, and cohort: The general developmental model revisited. *Developmental Review, 6,* 252–277.

Schaie, K. W. (1993). Ageist language in psychological research. *American Psychologist, 48,* 49–51.

Schaie, K. W. (1994). The course of adult intellectual development. *American Psychologist, 49,* 304–313.

Schaie, K. W. (1996). *Adult intellectual development: The Seattle Longitudinal Study.* New York: Cambridge University Press.

Schaie, K. W., & Willis, S. L. (1986). Can intellectual decline in the elderly be reversed? *Developmental Psychology, 22,* 223–232.

Schaie, K. W., & Willis, S. L. (1993). Age difference patterns of psychometric intelligence in adulthood: Generalizability within and across ability domains. *Psychology and Aging, 8,* 44–55.

Schreiber, F. R. (1973). *Sybil.* Chicago: Regnery.

Schuman, H., & Scott, J. (1987). Problems in the use of survey questions to measure public opinion. *Science, 236,* 957–959.

Sears, D. O. (1986). College sophomores in the laboratory. Influences of a narrow data base on social psychology's view of human nature. *Journal of Personality and Social Psychology, 51,* 515–530.

Sechrest, L., & Walsh, M. (1997). Dogma or data: Bragging rights. *American Psychologist, 52,* 536–540.

Seidel, J. V., & Clark, J. A. (1984). The Ethnograph: A computer program for the analysis of qualitative data. *Qualitative Sociology, 7*(1/2), 110–125.

Senate action. (1991, September). *Footnotes, 19*(7), 1, 12.

Senturai, Y. D., Christoffel, K. K., & Donovan, M. (1996). Gun storage patterns in US homes with children: A pediatric practice-based survey. *Archives of Pediatrics and Adolescent Medicine, 150,* 265–269.

Shaw, M. E., & Wright, J. M. (1967). *Scales for the measurement of attitudes.* New York: McGraw-Hill.

Sheingold, K., & Tenney, Y. J. (1982). Memory for a salient childhood event. In U. Neisser (Ed.), *Memory observed: Remembering in natural contexts* (pp. 201–212). San Francisco: W. H. Freeman.

Sieber, J. E. (1992). *Planning ethically responsible research: A guide for students and internal review boards.* Newbury Park, CA: Sage.

Simeonsson, R. J. (1986). *Psychological and developmental assessment of special children.* Boston: Allyn & Bacon.

Skinner, B. F. (1953). *Science and human behavior.* New York: Macmillan.

Slavin, R. E. (1986). Cooperative learning: Engineering social psychology in the classroom. In R. S. Feldman (Ed.), *The social psychology of education: Current research and theory* (pp. 153–231). Cambridge, England: Cambridge University Press.

Slavin, R. E. (1991). Cooperative learning and group contingencies. *Journal of Behavioral Education, 1,* 105–115.

Snowdon, D. A., Kemper, S. J., Mortimer, J. A., Greiner, L. H., Wekstein, D. R., & Markesbery, W. R. (1996). Linguistic ability in early life and cognitive function and Alzheimer's disease in late life. Findings from the Nun Study. *Journal of the American Medical Association, 275,* 528–532.

Society for Research in Child Development (1996).

Ethical standards for research with children. *SRCD Directory of Members*, 337–339.

Spanier, G. B. (1976). Measuring dyadic adjustment: New scales for assessing the quality of marriage and similar dyads. *Journal of Marriage and the Family, 38*, 15–28.

Spence, J. T., & Helmreich, R. L. (1978). *Masculinity and femininity: Their psychological dimensions, correlates, and antecedents.* Austin, TX: University of Texas Press.

Squire, L. R. (1989). On the course of forgetting in very long-term memory. *Journal of Experimental Psychology: Learning, Memory and Cognition, 15*, 241–245.

Stanovich, K. E. (1990). Concepts in developmental theories of reading skill: Cognitive resources, automaticity, and modularity. *Developmental Review, 10*, 72–100.

Stanovich, K. E., West, R. F., & Harrison, M. R. (1995). Knowledge growth and maintenance across the life span: The role of print exposure. *Developmental Psychology, 31*, 811–826.

Steinberg, L., & Dornbusch, S. M. (1991). Negative correlates of part-time employment during adolescence: Replication and elaboration. *Developmental Psychology, 27*, 304–313.

Steinberg, L., Dornbusch, S. M., & Brown, B. B. (1992). Ethnic differences in adolescent achievement. *American Psychologist, 47*, 723–729.

Sternberg, R. J. (1993). *The psychologist's companion: A guide to scientific writing for students and researchers.* Cambridge: Cambridge University Press.

Stevenson, H. W., Chen, C., & Lee, S. Y. (1993). Mathematics achievement of Chinese, Japanese & American children: Ten years later. *Science, 259*, 53–58.

Stevenson, H. W., Lee, S., Chen, C., & Lummis, M. (1990). Mathematics achievement of children in China and the United States. *Child Development, 61*, 1053–1066.

Stevenson, H. W., Lee, S., Chen, C., Stigler, J. W., Hsu, C., & Kitamura, S. (1990). Contexts of achievement: A study of American, Chinese, and Japanese children. *Monographs of the Society for Research in Child Development, 55* (1–2, Serial No. 221).

Stigler, J. W., Lee, S., & Stevenson, H. W. (1987). Mathematics classrooms in Japan, Taiwan, and the United States. *Child Development, 58*, 1272–1285.

Stone, W. L., & Lemanek, K. L. (1990). Developmental issues in children's self-reports. In A. M. La Greca (Ed.), *Through the eyes of a child: Obtaining self-reports from children and adolescents* (pp. 18–56). Boston: Allyn & Bacon.

Stough, C., Kerkin, B., Bates, T., & Mangan, G. (1994). Music and spatial IQ. *Personality and Individual Differences, 17*, 695.

Strough, J., Berg, C. A., & Sansone, C. (1996). Goals for solving everyday problems across the life span: Age and gender differences in the salience of interpersonal concerns. *Developmental Psychology, 32*, 1106–1115.

Sugar, J. A., & McDowd, J. M. (1992). Memory, learning, and attention. In J. E. Birren, R. B. Sloane, & G. D. Cohen (Eds.), *Handbook of mental health and aging* (2nd ed., pp. 307–339). San Diego, CA: Academic Press.

Sugland, B. W., Zaslow, M., Blumenthal, C., Moore, K. A., Smith, J. R., Brooks-Gunn, J., Griffin, T., Coates, D., & Bradley, R. (1995). The Early Childhood HOME Inventory and the HOME-Short Form in differing racial/ethnic groups. *Journal of Family Issues, 16*, 632–663.

Swarr, A. E., & Richards, M. H. (1996). Longitudinal effects of adolescent girls' pubertal development, perceptions of pubertal timing, and parental relations on eating problems. *Developmental Psychology, 32*, 636–646.

Taylor, K. M., & Shepperd, J. A. (1996). Probing suspicion among participants in deception research. *American Psychologist, 51*, 886–887.

Terman, L. M. (1925). *Genetic studies of genius: Vol. 1. Mental and physical traits of a thousand gifted children.* Stanford, CA: Stanford University Press.

Terman, L. M., & Oden, M. H. (1947). *Genetic studies of genius: Vol. 4. The gifted child grows up: Twenty-five years' follow-up of a superior group.* Stanford, CA: Stanford University Press.

Terman, L. M., & Oden, M. H. (1959). *Genetic studies of genius: Vol. 5. The gifted group in mid-life: Thirty-five years' follow-up of the superior child.* Stanford, CA: Stanford University Press.

Thapar, A., & McGuffin, P. (1995). Are anxiety symptoms in childhood heritable? *Journal of Child Psychology and Psychiatry, 36*, 439–447.

Thoman, E. B., & Graham, S. E. (1986). Self-regulation of stimulation by premature infants. *Pediatrics, 78*, 855–860.

Thoman, E. B., Hammond, K., Affleck, G., & DeSilva, H. N. (1995). The breathing bear with preterm infants: Effects on sleep, respiration, and affect. *Infant Mental Health Journal, 16*, 160–168.

Thorndike, R. L., Hagen, E. P., & Sattler, J. M. (1985). *Stanford-Binet* (4th ed.). Chicago, IL: Riverside.

Thrasher, S. P., & Mowbray, C. T. (1995). A strengths perspective: An ethnographic study of homeless women with children. *Health and Social Work, 20*(2), 93–101.

Timmer, S. G., Veroff, J., & Hatchett, S. (1996). Family ties and marital happiness: The different marital experiences of Black and White newlywed couples. *Journal of Social and Personal Relationships, 13,* 335–359.

Toner, I. J., Holstein, R. B., & Hetherington, E. M. (1977). Reflection-impulsivity and self-control in preschool children. *Child Development, 48,* 239–245.

Touba, J. R. (1987). Cultural effects on sex role images in elementary school books in Iran: A content analysis after the revolution. *International Journal of Sociology of the Family, 17,* 143–158.

Toufexis, A. (1991, February 4). Delays that can cause death: Debate grows over when to publicize life-saving research findings. *Time,* 69.

Touliatos, J., Perlmutter, B. F., & Straus, M. A. (Eds.). (1990). *Handbook of family measurement techniques.* Newbury Park, CA: Sage.

Tufte, E. R. (1983). *The visual display of quantitative information.* Cheshire, CT: Graphics Press.

Tufte, E. R. (1990). *Envisioning information.* Cheshire, CT: Graphics Press.

U.S. Department of Health and Human Services. (1981, January 26). Final regulations amending basic HHS policy for the protection of human research subjects. *Federal Register, 46*(16), 8366–8392.

Usher, J. A., & Neisser, U. (1993). Childhood amnesia and the beginning of memory for four early life events. *Journal of Experimental Psychology: General, 122,* 155–165.

Vasta, R., Rosenberg, D., Knott, J. A., & Gaze, C. E. (1997). Experience and the water-level task revisited: Does expertise exact a price? *Psychological Science, 8,* 336–339.

Viney, L. L. (1983). The assessment of psychological states through content analysis of verbal communications. *Psychological Bulletin, 94,* 542–563.

Wakschlag, L. S., Chase-Lansdale, P. L., & Brooks-Gunn, J. (1996). Not just "ghosts in the nursery": Contemporaneous intergenerational relationships and parenting in young African-American families. *Child Development, 67,* 2131–2147.

Webb, E. J., Campbell, D. T., Schwartz, R. D., Sechrest, R., & Grove, J. B. (1981). *Nonreactive measures in the social sciences* (2nd ed.). Boston: Houghton Mifflin.

Wechsler, D. (1981). *Wechsler Adult Intelligence Scale: Revised.* New York: Psychological Corporation.

Wechsler, D. (1989). *Manual for the Wechsler Preschool and Primary Scales of Intelligence: Revised.* New York: Psychological Corporation.

Wechsler, D. (1991). *Manual for the Wechsler Intelligence Test for Children–III.* New York: Psychological Corporation.

Weiderman, M. W., & Sensibaugh, C. C. (1995). The acceptance of legalized abortion. *Journal of Social Psychology, 135,* 785–787.

Weiss, M. (1994). Nonperson and nonhome: Territorial seclusion of appearance-impaired children. *Journal of Contemporary Ethnography, 22,* 463–487.

Weiss, R. S. (1994). *Learning from strangers: The art and method of qualitative interviewing.* New York: Free Press.

Weissert, W. G. (1986). Hard choices: Targeting long-term care to the "at risk" aged. *Journal of Health, Politics, Policy, and Law, 11,* 463–481.

Weisz, J. R., Chaiyasit, W., Weiss, B., Eastman, K. L., & Jackson, E. W. (1995). A multimethod study of problem behavior among Thai and American children in school: Teacher reports versus direct observations. *Child Development, 66,* 402–415.

Weisz, J. R., Suwanlert, S., Chaiyasit, W., Weiss, B., Achenbach, T. M., & Trevathan, D. (1988). Epidemiology of behavioral and emotional problems among Thai and American children: Teacher reports for ages 6–11. *Journal of Child Psychology and Psychiatry, 30,* 471–484.

Weitzman, E. A., & Miles, M. B. (1995). *Computer programs for qualitative data analysis: A software sourcebook.* Thousand Oaks, CA: Sage.

Wells, L. E., & Rankin, J. H. (1991). Families and delinquency: A meta-analysis of the impact of broken homes. *Social Problems, 38,* 71–93.

Werner, O., & Schoepfle, G. M. (1987a). *Systematic fieldwork, Vol. 1: Foundations of ethnography and interviewing.* Beverly Hills, CA: Sage.

Werner, O., & Schoepfle, G. M. (1987b). *Systematic fieldwork, Vol. 2: Ethnographic analysis and data management.* Beverly Hills, CA: Sage.

Whalen, C. K., Henker, B., Hinshaw, S. P., Heller, T., & Huber-Dressler, A. (1991). Messages of medication: Effects of actual versus informed medication status on hyperactive boys' expectancies and self-evaluations. *Journal of Consulting and Clinical Psychology, 59,* 602–606.

Whitbourne, S. K., Zuschlag, M. K., Elliot, L. B., & Waterman, A. S. (1992). Psychosocial development in adulthood: A 22-year sequential study. *Journal of Personality and Social Psychology, 63,* 260–271.

Whitehurst, G. J., Arnold, D. S., Epstein, J. N., Angell,

A. L., Smith, M., & Fischel, J. E. (1994). A picture book reading intervention in day care and home for children from low-income families. *Developmental Psychology, 30,* 679–689.

Williams, J. D., & Klug, M. G. (1996). Aging and cognition: Methodological differences in outcome. *Experimental Aging Research, 22,* 219–244.

Willis, S. L. (1990). Contributions of cognitive training research to understanding late life potential. In M. Perlmutter (Ed.), *Late life potential* (pp. 25–42). Washington, DC: Gerontological Society of America.

Yin, R. K. (1994). *Case study research: Design and methods* (2nd ed.). Newbury Park, CA: Sage.

Yoshikawa, H. (1995). Long-term effects of early childhood programs on social outcomes and delinquency. *The Future of Children, 5*(3), 51–75.

Zajonc, R. B. (1976). Family configuration and intelligence. *Science, 192,* 227–236.

Zajonc, R. B., & Mullally, P. R. (1997). Birth order: Reconciling conflicting effects. *American Psychologist, 52,* 685–699.

◆ *Index*